Africa

healthy travel

Isabelle Young
revised by Tony Gherardin

AFRICA

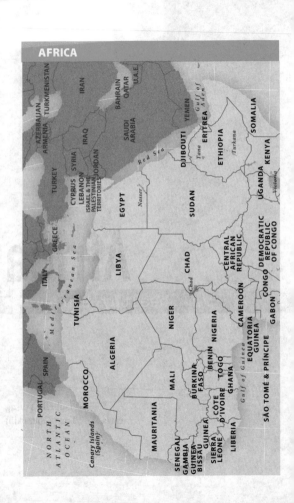

AFRICA

Map labels:

INDIAN OCEAN

SEYCHELLES

COMOROS

MAYOTTE

MADAGASCAR

MAURITIUS

RÉUNION

Pemba
Zanzibar
Mafia

RWANDA
BURUNDI

(ZAÏRE)

TANZANIA

Malawi

ZAMBIA MALAWI

Tanganyika

MOZAMBIQUE

Mozambique Channel

ANGOLA

ZIMBABWE

SWAZILAND

NAMIBIA

BOTSWANA

LESOTHO

SOUTH
AFRICA

SOUTH
ATLANTIC
OCEAN

2000 km

1000 mi

Healthy Travel – Africa
2nd edition, July 2008

Published by
Lonely Planet Publications Pty Ltd ABN 36 005 607 983

Lonely Planet Offices
Australia Locked Bag 1, Footscray, Victoria 3011
USA 150 Linden St, Oakland, CA 94607
UK 2nd Floor, 186 City Road, London EC1V 2NT

ISBN 978 1 74059 143 0

Printed through The Bookmaker International Ltd.
Printed in China.

Illustrations: Martin Harris & Kate Nolan
Production: Recapture

Contents...

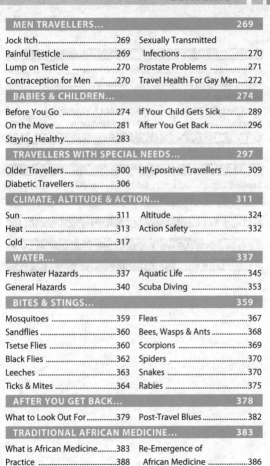

The Authors...

ISABELLE YOUNG

Dr Isabelle Young qualified as a doctor in Britain before deciding there must be more to life than bleeps and hospital coffee. Her travels through various parts of the world have provided her with plenty of opportunity for putting her training into practice.

TONY GHERARDIN

Dr Tony Gherardin is currently National Medical Adviser of the Travel Doctor-TMVC Group in Australia. He is a keen traveller and has spent several years living and working as a doctor overseas. When not travelling with his family, he spends most of his time providing travel health advice to travellers heading in all directions around the globe.

Medical Advisers...

To ensure that the information included in this guide is the best available and in line with current practice, a team of expert medical advisers was on hand every step of the way.

CORINNE ELSE

Help..., Coughs, Rashes & Other Common Problems, Ears, Eyes & Teeth (Ears), Mental Wellbeing, Women Travellers, First Aid (Wound Care), Buying & Using Medicines

Dr Corinne Else spends most of her time working as a general practitioner in the UK. Every now and again she manages to take time off to travel in Africa with her husband, helping him to research and write Lonely Planet guidebooks.

CHRISTOPHER VAN TILBERG

Climate & Altitude, Water Safety, First Aid

Dr Christopher Van Tilberg specialises in wilderness and emergency medicine. He is adventure sports editor for *Wilderness Medicine Letter* and active in mountain rescue and wilderness safety education in the US. He is the author of *Backcountry Snowboarding* and *Canyoneering*, both published by The Mountaineers Books.

JOHN MASON
Babies & Children, Buying & Using Medicines

Dr John Mason was a family physician for 13 years before becoming Clinical Director of the UK-based Preventative Healthcare Company. Part of his responsibility is to provide international travel care and advice to client company employees and their families, as well as managing their healthcare while abroad.

BRIAN MULHALL
HIV/AIDS & Sexual Health

Dr Brian Mulhall is a Clinical Senior Lecturer in the Department of Public Health and Community Medicine at the University of Sydney, Australia. He has travelled extensively and has written several texts on sex and travel. His contribution was sponsored by the New South Wales Health Department and the Commonwealth Department of Health as part of a sexual health promotion program for travellers.

LARRY & PAUL GOODYER
Medical Kit (Before You Go), Safe Drinking Water, Insect Bites (Staying Healthy)

Dr Larry Goodyer is Chief Pharmacist for Nomad Travel Stores & Travel Clinics, London, UK. He is also a senior lecturer in clinical pharmacy at King's College, London. His travels in India and Australia give him the first-hand experience to produce medical kits for both tropical and developing world travel. Paul Goodyer is the CEO of Nomad Travel Stores & Travel Clinics. His travels over the last 20 years include trips to Africa, Asia, South America and the Middle East. Getting ill on the road due to lack of knowledge led to the concept of a travellers' medical centre.

SPECIAL THANKS
Special thanks go to the World Health Organization for permission to reproduce the data for the maps between the first two chapters.

From the Authors...

First, a big thank you to all the medical advisers, without whom this book would not have come into existence. Thank you also to Fred Peterson MD for his helpful comments on the text of *Healthy Travel Central & South America,* many of which are incorporated in the text of this guide.

Thanks go to the following experts who contributed text to the guide: Graeme Johnson for the section on Eyes; Iain Corran for the section on Teeth; Michelle Sobel for the Diabetic Travellers section in Travellers with Special Needs; Chris Wheeler for the text on foot care and blisters (in Staying Healthy and Wilderness Health & Safety); Bernadette Saulenier for the boxed text 'Alternative First Aid for Travellers'; and Elissa Coffman for the section on Alternative Therapies.

Some of the information in this guide was drawn from Lonely Planet guides, which are researched and written by a global team of staff and authors.

Many other people helped make this guide what it is through generously providing information, constructive comments and helpful suggestions. In no particular order, thanks go to Chris Banks and Patrick Honan of Melbourne Zoo for helpful information on snakes, spiders and scorpions; Moya Tomlinson of Women's Health (London) for suggestions for the Women Travellers chapter; Dr Michael Thomas of the Blood Care Foundation and Professor Neil Boyce of the Australian Red Cross for pointers for information on blood transfusions; Dr John Putland of the Qantas Aviation Health Services Department and the British Airways Medical Service in Heathrow for providing heaps of background information on air travel for the On the Move chapter; the National Sports Information Centre (Australia) for great reference material on climatic extremes; John Nathan for helpful insights on older travellers; Roslyn Bullas of Lonely Planet's Diving & Snorkelling series and Susannah Farfor for suggestions for the scuba diving section; the staff at IAMAT for generously providing us with information on their organisation; Darren Elder of Lonely Planet's Cycling series for finding the time to come up with the safety tips for cyclists that appear in the Wilderness Health & Safety chapter; and Jenny Thorpe and Suzanne Harrison, travelling mothers extraordinaire, for invaluable insights into the rigours of travelling with children. Thanks also go to Leonie Mugavin for her helpful suggestions, book-acquiring abilities and moral support.

Finally, in time-honoured tradition, Isabelle would like to thank her partner, David Petherbridge, for his help and unfailing support throughout this project – next time we'll climb mountains instead.

From the Publisher...

This book was commissioned from Lonely Planet's Melbourne office by commissioning editor Bridget Blair and associate publisher Chris Rennie. Production was coordinated by Recapture under director Ivan Levacic, including editing by Julian Lange and design by Katrina Tan. The cover was designed by Mik Ruff, Wayne Murphy created the maps, and Martin Harris is responsible for all the illustrations except for the cone shell illustration by Kate Nolan.

Introduction...

Lonely Planet's aim has always been to enable adventurous travellers to get out there, to explore and better understand the world. Falling ill or getting injured on your travels prevents you from getting the most out of your travelling experience, which is why we've decided to produce this *Healthy Travel* series.

Travelling can expose you to health risks you most probably would not have encountered had you stayed at home, but many of these risks are avoidable with good preparation before you go and some common-sense measures while you are away. Concern about how to cope if you do become ill far from home is natural; this guide aims to alleviate those fears by giving you the background information to make informed decisions about what action to take in a given situation. *We should point out that this guide is not intended as a substitute for seeking medical help.*

Some chapters in this guide are designed to be read through in their entirety; the rest are there for you to dip into if the need arises. Before you leave, we suggest you take a look at the Overview chapter, which summarises the potential health risks of travel in the region, and read through the Before You Go chapter, which gives you the complete low-down on preparations for the trip. Because travel medicine is an ever-changing topic, we've given you plenty of guidance on where to get up-to-the-minute advice and information.

The Staying Healthy chapter gives you detailed advice on avoiding illness and injury while you are away, and is essential reading for everyone. It's a good idea to have a quick read through the When You Get Back chapter on your return as it gives guidance on when you need a check-up and what to look out for.

The rest of the chapters are there in case you need them – and most travellers won't need them. If you do get ill, turn to the Help ... chapter. This gives guidelines on how to go about finding medical help (and can be used in conjunction with the Medical Services appendix if necessary), as well as some basic measures for looking after yourself. This chapter also summarises the possible causes of various symptoms you may have. You can use this as a guide to working out what you may have or, if you think you know what the problem is, you can turn to the relevant chapter later in the book. Alternatively, you could look up your symptom in the index.

We've tried to group diseases and other medical problems into easily identifiable categories, which are reflected in the chapter names. However, it's difficult to please everyone – if something is not where you think it should be, it's always worth looking it up in the index.

To cater for the differing needs of a wide range of travellers, we've included four chapters tailored to the needs of women, men, young and special needs travellers.

Because accidents do happen, and help may not be as rapidly available as at home, we've included advice on basic first aid measures, including what to do in an emergency, although bear in mind that you shouldn't rely solely on a book to be able to do resuscitation techniques effectively. If you are going to be travelling in remote areas, it's definitely worth doing a first aid course before you go.

We hope that having this guide will ensure you have a healthy trip, and that if you do encounter problems, it gives you the confidence to deal with them.

Overview...

Travel in Africa can expose you to plenty of health hazards but you'd have to be pretty unlucky or just plain careless to succumb to most of these – so long as you are up to date with your immunisations and you take some basic preventive measures. If you expect to get at least a few sick days, you probably won't be disappointed, but don't bank on not needing that return ticket.

True, Africa does offer a wide selection of tropical diseases but you're much more likely to get a bout of diarrhoea, a cold or an infected mosquito bite than something more exotic like river blindness or sleeping sickness. Malaria, however, is a real threat to travellers in sub-Saharan Africa, although there's much you can do to prevent this serious disease, which we discuss at length in the Before You Go and Staying Healthy chapters.

WHAT TRAVELLERS ACTUALLY GET

You'll have to try very hard to get anything more interesting than diarrhoea or an infected mosquito bite on your travels in Africa. Here are some frequently quoted and reassuring figures on the health problems travellers get, compiled by leading travel medicine experts Steffen & Lobel and published in the highly respected reference book *Manson's Tropical Diseases*.

Most common complaint:
• travellers diarrhoea (about 50% of travellers)

Less than 10% of travellers:
• malaria (in travellers to West Africa)
• coughs and colds

Less than 1% of travellers:
• hepatitis A
• gonorrhoea
• animal bites
• hospitalised abroad or had to be evacuated

In many developing or war-ravaged nations in Africa, lack of clean drinking water and adequate sewage disposal systems mean that diseases transmitted by contaminated food and water (diarrhoea, dysentery, hepatitis and typhoid) are common. You can do a lot to reduce your risk of getting these diseases by being immunised before you go, and by taking some basic precautions with food, water and general cleanliness while you are away. We discuss these measures fully in the Staying Healthy chapter.

HIV/AIDS occurs worldwide but it's currently a public health problem of alarming proportions in sub-Saharan Africa. It's an issue you need to take very seriously, but don't get too paranoid about it. You can do a lot to avoid risk situations. If you need medical treatment, most hospitals and doctors in major centres in the region will be well aware of the risks and will have adequately sterilised needles and other equipment. Clinics in rural areas may be less reliable because they have fewer resources, so it's a good idea to carry a few sterile needles and possibly other equipment on you in case you need it. You're very unlikely to need a blood transfusion while you are away, but in case you do it's best to make sure the blood you receive is from a safe source. In the Staying Healthy chapter we give guidelines on what you can do.

Attacks from wild animals are another great topic for campfire tales among travellers, but you're much more likely to be injured by a marauding bush taxi than a wild animal. In fact, accidents and injury, especially road traffic accidents, are the leading cause of death in travellers, along with complications from preexisting illnesses like heart disease. If you're aware of the risks, there's plenty you can do to minimise them – as we discuss in detail in the Accidents & Injury section of the Staying Healthy chapter.

Lots of factors can affect your individual risks. If you're planning on overlanding or travelling rough in remote areas, your health risks are obviously going to be different than they would be if you were planning on a two week stay in a five star tourist resort. The length of your trip is

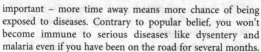

important – more time away means more chance of being exposed to diseases. Contrary to popular belief, you won't become immune to serious diseases like dysentery and malaria even if you have been on the road for several months.

Activity holidays anywhere carry special risks of injury, and it goes without saying that you should take all possible safety precautions. In most parts of Africa emergency services are generally nonexistent, especially in remote areas.

Your geographic destination is also important, as certain insect-borne diseases (like yellow fever) are limited to particular regions in Africa (see the maps at the end of this chapter). Some diseases (like sleeping sickness) occur mainly in rural areas, so they are less of a risk if you are going to be spending most of your time in urban areas.

It's true that medical facilities in most parts of Africa are extremely limited outside major cities and tourist resorts. Even where they are available, they are not usually of a standard you may be used to in your own country. (There are exceptions of course, the obvious one being South Africa – see the Medical Services appendix for more details.) You'll be able to get reasonable care for any minor injuries or illnesses, but for anything more serious, you'll need to consider going to a regional centre or coming home. You'll need to take this into account when planning your trip, especially if have any ongoing medical problems or special health needs.

Here's a brief summary of what health risks you might be up against and what you can do about them; for more details on all these issues, see the Before You Go and Staying Healthy chapters.

IMMUNISATIONS (p33)
These can help protect you from some infections that are generally less common now in the West (through immunisation programs) but are still significant health risks in many parts of Africa. Ideally, you should get these organised at least six weeks before you go, although it's always worth seeking advice up to the last minute if necessary.

- You'll need to be up to date with routine immunisations like tetanus, polio and other childhood illnesses including measles, mumps and rubella.
- Hepatitis A is strongly recommended for all travellers to Africa, as is influenza.
- Depending on your travel plans, you may need immunisation against hepatitis B, meningococcal meningitis, rabies, typhoid and yellow fever.
- You may need an immunisation certificate for yellow fever (and sometimes cholera) before you will be allowed to enter some countries.

MALARIA PILLS (p44)

Malaria is a serious, but preventable, risk in sub-Saharan Africa. Africa has lots of malaria and some of the highest rates of the disease in the world. Most travellers who get malaria acquire it in sub-Saharan Africa, so it is vital that you get the best possible and current advice on avoiding this disease, including which malaria prevention medication to take, before you go.

DISEASES CARRIED IN FOOD & WATER (p78)

Risk

Illnesses carried in this way include diarrhoea, dysentery and hepatitis A. These are the most common causes of illness in travellers in Africa, although you're at much less risk of these in countries with good infrastructure, like South Africa.

Other diseases carried in food and water include intestinal worms and cholera, typhoid and polio. Apart from intestinal parasites which are common and not particularly harmful in general, travellers are at very low risk of cholera, typhoid and polio. Note that all of these diseases are more of a risk in the wet season.

Prevention

Avoid getting sick with a few basic precautions:

- take care over what you eat
- drink safe water
- wash your hands frequently, especially after you use the toilet and before you eat

DISEASES CARRIED BY INSECTS (p88)

Risk

Malaria (carried by infected mosquitoes) is a major risk to travellers in most parts of sub-Saharan Africa (see map p23) and a few parts of North Africa, including Egypt.

Other diseases carried by insects that are prevalent in parts of Africa include yellow fever (see map p24), dengue fever and filariasis (all spread by mosquitoes); onchocerciasis (also called river blindness and spread by blackflies); leishmaniasis and sandfly fever (spread by sandflies); sleeping sickness (also called trypanosomiasis and spread by tsetse flies); typhus and other tick fevers (spread by lice and ticks). Although these diseases are major public health problems in the local population, they are a low risk to travellers.

Rare but frightening diseases like plague (spread by fleas), Ebola and Lassa fever occur but are extremely unlikely to affect travellers.

Prevention

It makes sense to take measures to prevent insect bites wherever you go in Africa. Currently, yellow fever is the only disease you may be at risk for in this way that can be prevented by immunisation.

SCHISTOSOMIASIS (BILHARZIA) (p337)

Risk

This disease (see map p25) is caused by tiny worms that live in freshwater snails. You can get it by swimming, bathing or paddling in fresh water. Several cases are reported each year in travellers returning from Africa, even among those who did not consider themselves particularly at risk.

Prevention

Avoid swimming, bathing or paddling in any body of fresh water, including the Nile River and Lake Malawi.

OTHER DISEASES

Risk

Although tuberculosis (TB) (p40) is a major and growing problem in Africa, the risk to short-term travellers is very low unless you will be living in close contact with locals.

Outbreaks of meningococcal meningitis (p38) occur periodically in the Sahel belt of Africa, particularly during the dry season. Although the risk to travellers is small, immunisation is usually recommended.

Rabies (p39) exists throughout Africa, and pretravel immunisation may be recommended in some circumstances.

Going barefoot can put you at risk of hookworm (an intestinal parasite) (p165) or jiggers (a skin parasite) (p207).

Avian influenza occurs in birds in different parts of Africa, but the risk to travellers is very low.

Prevention

You can avoid all these risks with some basic precautions:

- if necessary, get immunised against rabies, TB and meningitis
- avoid contact with animals to prevent potentially rabid bites
- don't walk barefoot or in sandals, especially in rural areas

HIV/AIDS & SEXUALLY-TRANSMITTED INFECTIONS (p209)

Risk

Any traveller is at risk if you don't take measures to protect yourself. HIV/AIDS is mainly transmitted through heterosexual sex in Africa, and it's a major public health problem in the region, especially sub-Saharan Africa. Hepatitis B is common throughout the region but generally poses a small risk for the majority of travellers, although expatriates are much more at risk. The classical STIs, including gonorrhoea and syphilis, are common.

Prevention

Sensible precautions to take wherever you go include the following:

- always use a latex condom if you have sex with a new partner
- avoid all injections and any procedure that involves skin-piercing
- avoid any unnecessary medical or dental procedures
- minimise your chance of injury in accidents
- carry an emergency kit containing sterile needles and syringes

BLOOD TRANSFUSION (p102)

Risk

In Africa, blood supplies available for general use are not thought to be as safe from diseases like HIV/AIDS, hepatitis B and malaria as they are in Australia, New Zealand, North America and Western Europe.

Prevention

Minimise the chances of needing a blood transfusion by taking steps to avoid injury and by not travelling if you have a condition that makes blood transfusion a possibility. If blood transfusion is unavoidable for medical reasons, try to find a source of safe blood.

ACCIDENTS & INJURY (p93)

Risk

Accidents *do* happen, and they're a common cause of injury (and sometimes death) in travellers. Road traffic accidents, especially involving motorbikes, are a major risk to travellers.

Prevention

Using your common sense and being aware of potential risks can help you avoid accidents and injury.

ENVIRONMENTAL HAZARDS (p311)

Risk

Sunburn is a major risk in most parts of Africa. Never underestimate the potential dangers of travelling in a hot climate, especially if you are planning on an activity-packed holiday. Hot, humid conditions, as well as poor environmental cleanliness, make infection of cuts and scratches common.

Cold and unpredictable weather are significant risks in many highland areas. You need to be aware of the effects of altitude on your health if you are planning to climb mountains like Mt Kenya or Kilimanjaro or trek in highland areas.

Prevention

It's a good idea to minimise the impact of environmental challenges with a few basic precautions:

- protect your skin from the effects of the sun
- remember to allow yourself time to acclimatise to the heat and take steps to avoid dehydration
- look after cuts and scratches to prevent them getting infected
- always be prepared for climatic extremes, especially if you are trekking or walking in highland areas
- inform yourself about the effects of altitude and follow the rules for safe ascent

OTHER HAZARDS

Risk

Fleas (p367), lice (p206) and scabies (p204) are potential hazards in most places, especially if you are staying in budget accommodation, but don't generally cause serious illness. Ticks (p364) and mites (p364) are a hazard if you are planning on trekking in rural areas, and can transmit diseases like typhus. Leeches (p363) are common in damp, forested areas throughout Africa, but they don't carry any diseases.

Crocodiles, wild animals, snakes, scorpions (p369) and marine creatures (p348) are all hazards to be aware of, but generally pose very little risk to you.

Prevention

Take steps to avoid these hazards where necessary:

- cover up and use insect repellents
- sleep under a treated net
- treat any wild animal with due respect

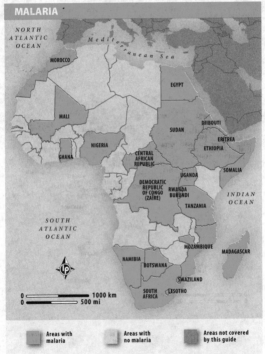

Map data supplied by World Health Organization

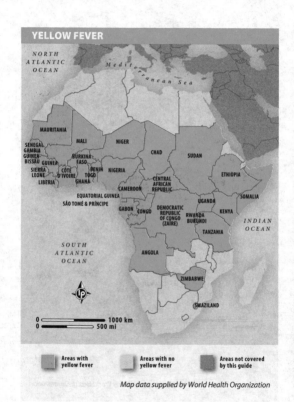

YELLOW FEVER

NORTH
ATLANTIC
OCEAN

Mediterranean Sea

MAURITANIA

MALI   NIGER   CHAD   SUDAN

SENEGAL
GAMBIA
GUINEA-   BURKINA
BISSAU   GUINEA   FASO
SIERRA   CÔTE   BENIN   ETHIOPIA
LEONE   D'IVOIRE TOGO NIGERIA
LIBERIA   GHANA   CAMEROON   CENTRAL
AFRICAN   SOMALIA
REPUBLIC

EQUATORIAL GUINEA   UGANDA   KENYA
SÃO TOMÉ & PRÍNCIPE   GABON   CONGO   DEMOCRATIC
REPUBLIC   INDIAN
OF CONGO   RWANDA   OCEAN
(ZAÏRE)   BURUNDI

SOUTH   TANZANIA
ATLANTIC
OCEAN   ANGOLA

ZIMBABWE

SWAZILAND

0 ———————— 1000 km
0 ———————— 500 mi

Areas with   Areas with no   Areas not covered
yellow fever   yellow fever   by this guide

Map data supplied by World Health Organization

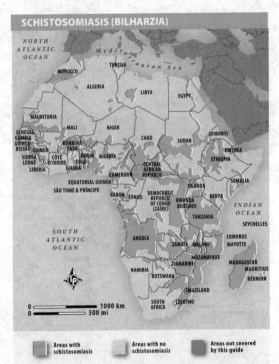

SCHISTOSOMIASIS (BILHARZIA)

NORTH ATLANTIC OCEAN

Mediterranean Sea

MOROCCO
TUNISIA
ALGERIA
LIBYA
EGYPT
MAURITANIA
MALI
NIGER
CHAD
SUDAN
DJIBOUTI
SENEGAL
GAMBIA
GUINEA-BISSAU
GUINEA
BURKINA FASO
BENIN
NIGERIA
ERITREA
ETHIOPIA
SIERRA LEONE
CÔTE D'IVOIRE
TOGO
GHANA
CAMEROON
CENTRAL AFRICAN REPUBLIC
LIBERIA
EQUATORIAL GUINEA
SÃO TOMÉ & PRÍNCIPE
GABON
CONGO
DEMOCRATIC REPUBLIC OF CONGO (ZAIRE)
RWANDA
BURUNDI
UGANDA
KENYA
SOMALIA
TANZANIA
SEYCHELLES

SOUTH ATLANTIC OCEAN

INDIAN OCEAN

ANGOLA
ZAMBIA
MALAWI
COMOROS
MAYOTTE
MOZAMBIQUE
ZIMBABWE
MADAGASCAR
MAURITIUS
RÉUNION
NAMIBIA
BOTSWANA
SWAZILAND
SOUTH AFRICA
LESOTHO

0 —— 1000 km
0 —— 500 mi

Areas with schistosomiasis

Areas with no schistosomiasis

Areas not covered by this guide

Map data supplied by World Health Organization

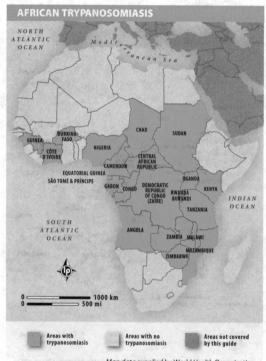

AFRICAN TRYPANOSOMIASIS

NORTH
ATLANTIC
OCEAN

Mediterranean Sea

GUINEA
BURKINA
FASO
CÔTE
D'IVOIRE
NIGERIA
CHAD
SUDAN
CAMEROON
CENTRAL
AFRICAN
REPUBLIC
EQUATORIAL GUINEA
SÃO TOMÉ & PRÍNCIPE
GABON
CONGO
DEMOCRATIC
REPUBLIC
OF CONGO
(ZAÏRE)
UGANDA
RWANDA
BURUNDI
KENYA

INDIAN
OCEAN

SOUTH
ATLANTIC
OCEAN

ANGOLA
TANZANIA
ZAMBIA
MALAWI
MOZAMBIQUE
ZIMBABWE

0 ⎯⎯⎯⎯ 1000 km
0 ⎯⎯⎯⎯ 500 mi

Areas with
trypanosomiasis

Areas with no
trypanosomiasis

Areas not covered
by this guide

Map data supplied by World Health Organization

Before You Go...

Staying healthy on your travels in Africa (except perhaps if you're just going to South Africa) requires a bit of pretravel effort. It may seem like a chore now, but it could save you much hassle later – it's not worth worrying about scary diseases you could have been protected against if you'd made time to see your doctor before you left.

It's tempting to leave all this preparatory stuff to the last minute – don't! You'll have a hundred and one other things to do just before you go, and you don't want to have to do them with a sore arm. It's best to start thinking about travel-related health issues as early as possible, and certainly at least six weeks in advance.

Even if things don't work out as planned, it's always worth visiting your doctor or travel health clinic for advice and immunisations, however late you've left it.

SOURCES OF INFORMATION & ADVICE

Part of your pretravel preparations should be to find out about the health risks of your destination, and this has never been easier. You can get up to date information and advice on your travel health risks from your family doctor, travel health clinics, and national and state health departments. Even handier, you've got a great information source at your fingertips – the internet.

Specialist travel health clinics are probably the best places for immunisations and travel health advice. If you have an ongoing medical condition or any general health concerns, you may prefer to go to your usual doctor as well. Some travel health clinics provide specific travel health briefs (usually for a fee) by mail, phone or fax, which you can then take to your doctor.

Most clinics sell health-related traveller essentials like insect repellent, mosquito nets, and needle and syringe kits; you can also get these from travel equipment suppliers (many via mail order) or your doctor.

For more general information on a variety of travel health issues, you could try some of the many publications available – we've listed a selection under Books at the end of this chapter. There are also authoritative websites providing information on more specialist areas like diving medicine and altitude listed in the relevant sections in this book.

UK

You can get pretravel health advice and immunisations from your GP, university or college health centre, travel medicine clinic or a specialist centre. To get you started, you could try any of the following:

Department of Health (www.doh.gov.uk) – government travel health advice is on the Policy and Guidance page. The booklet *Health Advice for Travellers* (available on the website or phone ☎ 0870-155 54 55 to order a copy) has basic advice and details of reciprocal health care agreements – of limited use, as this doesn't include any countries in Africa.

Hospital for Tropical Diseases Travel Clinic (☎ 020-7388 9600, www.thehtd.org/content/travel.asp, Mortimer Market Building, Capper Street, Tottenham Court Rd, London WC1E 6AU) – it has a Healthline on ☎ 020-7950 7799 and advice by country on the Destinations page of its website.

Liverpool School of Tropical Medicine Travel Clinic (☎ 0151-708 9393, www.liv.ac.uk, travel health advice line ☎ 0906-110 0210), Pembroke Place, Liverpool L3 5QA) – ring the health line for advice from a qualified travel health nurse.

MASTA (Medical Advisory Services for Travellers, www.masta-travel-health.com, enquiries@masta.org) – provides a network of travel clinics as well as information and travel health products.

Nomad Travel Stores & Travel Clinics (☎ 020-8889 7014, Healthline ☎ 090-6863 3414, www.nomadtravel.co.uk) – has travel clinics in London, Bristol, Manchester and Southampton (immunisations, travel health advice etc) and sells a wide range of travel equipment, as well as health-related products.

USA

To find a travel health clinic in your area, you could call your state health department, or you could try one of the following:

Centers for Disease Control & Prevention (CDC, **wwwn.cdc.gov/travel**) in Atlanta, Georgia – this is the central source of travel health information in North America. The CDC has phone (☎ 877-FYI-TRIP, 877-394-8747) and fax (☎ 888-CDC-FAXX, 888-232-3299) travel health information lines; it can also advise you on travel medicine providers in your area. It publishes an excellent booklet, *Health Information for International Travel*, also known as *The Yellow Book*, which is available on the website.

American Society of Tropical Medicine & Hygiene (☎ 847-480-9592, fax 847-480-9282, **www.astmh.org**, 60 Revere Drive, Suite 500, Northbrook, IL 60062) can also provide you with a comprehensive list of travel health providers in your area.

International Society of Travel Medicine (☎ 770-736-7060, **www.istm.org**, 2386 Clower Street, Suite A-102, Snellville, GA 30078) – contact the ISTM for a list of ISTM member clinics.

The US Department of State Overseas Citizens Services website **http://travel.state.gov** has regularly updated travel advisories and health information. Remember to take the phone number (☎ 202-647-5225) with you, as staff can provide you with access to medical advice and assistance over the phone if you are in an emergency situation overseas.

CANADA

You can get information and advice from your physician, a travel medicine clinic, Health Canada or the Canadian Society for International Health. The latter two resources can provide you with a list of travel medicine clinics in your area.

Health Canada (**http://hc-sc.gc.ca/hl-vs/travel-voyage/index_e.html**) – the Travel Health section of this government department provides information on disease outbreaks, immunisations and general health advice for travellers, and more detailed information on tropical diseases, as well as information on travel medicine clinics. You can access this information via the web or through a fax service (613-941-3900).

Canadian Society for International Health (☎ 613-241-5785, fax 241-3845, **www.csih.org**, 1 Nicholas St, Suite 1105, Ottawa, ON K1N 7B7 Canada) – this is a source of basic health information for Canadian travellers, as well as a comprehensive list of travel medicine clinics in Canada.

AUSTRALIA & NEW ZEALAND

To find clinics or advice, try:

Smartraveller – the Australian Department of Foreign Affairs & Trade's travel advisory website (**www.smartraveller.gov.au**) includes a good section on general travel health advice.

The Travel Doctor-TMVC (Travellers Medical & Vaccination Centre) group has a network of clinics in most major cities – use the phone book to find your nearest clinic or check out their website (**www.traveldoctor.com.au**). They can provide an online personalised travel health report (for a fee) via their website.

GENERAL INTERNET RESOURCES

There's heaps of good, reliable information on travel health issues on the internet, and the best thing is that it's accessible while you are on the road (so long as you can find a cybercafe) as well as before you go. Two authoritative websites are the first point of call for the latest on travel health issues:

WHO (**www.who.int**) – the official site of the World Health Organization has all the information you'll ever need on the state of the world's health, including disease distribution maps and all the latest health recommendations for risks and vaccination certificates required worldwide. The section that's probably going to be most useful to you (**www.who.int/csr**) has disease outbreak news and health advice for travellers. WHO publishes a superb book called *International Travel and Health*, which is revised annually and is available online at no cost.

CDC (**wwwn.cdc.gov/travel**) – the official site of the US Centers for Disease Control & Prevention has loads of useful information for all travellers, including disease outbreak news and disease risks according to destination.

Other sites worth checking out include:

African Medical & Research Foundation (www.amref.org) –
AMREF is primarily a medical aid organisation based in eastern Africa
and maintains an excellent website, which includes a section on health
advice for travellers to Africa. It has a hardcopy leaflet, *Health Code for
Travellers to Africa*, available by contacting the organisation. See the
boxed text 'African Medical & Research Foundation (AMREF)' in this
chapter for more details.

MASTA (www.masta-travel-health.com) – this highly recommended
site of the Medical Advisory Services for Travellers (see earlier under
UK) is easy to use and provides concise, readable information on all the
important issues. It provides online, individualised briefs.

MD Travel Health (www.mdtravelhealth.com) – provides complete
travel health recommendations for every country, updated daily.

**Medical College of Wisconsin Healthlink (http://health
link.mcw.edu)** – this site has useful information on all the usual travel
health issues, and an impressively comprehensive list of links to a variety
of other travel health information sites. Browse till you drop.

Shorelands (www.tripprep.com) – this well organised site is easy
to navigate and has lots of good travel health information, as well as a
comprehensive directory of travel medicine providers around the world
(including South Africa and Tanzania) and handy country profiles that
contain US State Department travel advisory information.

Travel Doctor-TMVC (www.traveldoctor.com.au) – this Australian-
based site has lots of useful information, including disease outbreak
news and good sections on travelling while pregnant and with children.

USEFUL ORGANISATIONS

**The International Association for Medical Assistance to
Travelers** (IAMAT) is a nonprofit foundation that can provide
you with a list of English-speaking doctors worldwide, as well as
travel health information. Doctors affiliated to IAMAT charge
a fixed fee. Membership is free, but the foundation welcomes
a donation. For more details or to join up, check out IAMAT's
website **www.iamat.org.**

MedicAlert Foundation International is a nonprofit organisation providing (for a membership fee) medical identification bracelets or tags with details of any drug allergies or important medical conditions you have, plus a call collect number for MedicAlert's 24 hour Emergency Response Center. You might want to consider this if you have asthma, diabetes or severe allergy, or if you're taking steroids or blood-thinning medicine. US residents can enrol at **www.medicalert.org**, by calling

AFRICAN MEDICAL & RESEARCH FOUNDATION (AMREF)

This nonprofit health charity is based in eastern Africa and works with local communities in this region and southern Africa to help them tackle problems like malaria and HIV/AIDS, as well as issues like safe water supplies and sanitation. AMREF also incorporates the Flying Doctors' Service, which airlifts patients, including travellers, to medical facilities.

You might want to consider taking out a temporary membership of the Flying Doctors' Service (for a fee). It operates in Kenya, Tanzania and Uganda, and membership entitles you to a free evacuation to Nairobi (from within a certain radius) in the event of an emergency. Check if your insurance covers this. You might end up using the service anyway, as it contracts out work to insurance companies. It welcomes donations to support the valuable work it does.

In Britain, AMREF can be contacted on ☎ 020-7269 5520 or fax 020-7269 5521. Its mailing address is Clifford's Inn, Fetter Lane, London EC4A 1BZ, UK (there's also a head office in Nairobi); or find it on the web at **www.amref.org**.

☎ 1-800-ID-ALERT (1-800-432-5378) or by email customer_
service@medicalert.org. Non-US residents can contact affiliate
offices locally, see **www.medicalert.com.au/international.html**
for a complete list.

International SOS (**www.internationalsos.com**) is an international medical assistance and travel insurance provider who
offers 24-hour telephone advice to travellers and may be able to
recommend English-speaking doctors in Africa.

IMMUNISATIONS

Immunisations help protect you from some of the diseases you
may be at risk of getting on your travels. Unfortunately, there
are many more diseases you may encounter while travelling in
Africa that can't be prevented by vaccination (for example
diarrhoea, malaria and dengue fever).

Many countries in Africa require you to have a certificate
showing you've been vaccinated against yellow fever (and
sometimes cholera, although this is contrary to international law)
before they will let you into the country – read the sections on
Cholera and Yellow Fever later in this chapter for more details.

Wherever you're going, it's a good idea to make sure your
immunisations are recorded on an official certificate – your
doctor or travel health centre will usually issue you with a
record. This is useful for your own information so you know
what you're protected against and when you're due for a top-
up; you will also be able to show it to any doctor treating you,
if necessary.

Be wary of advice on immunisations and other health issues
given to you by travel agents or embassies, especially if they say
that 'no immunisations are needed'. What they mean is that
you won't be asked for any vaccination certificates when you
roll up at the border, not that you don't need the jabs for your
own protection.

A HOMOEOPATHIC ALTERNATIVE?

Yes, there are homoeopathic alternatives to 'conventional' immunisations. But be aware that their effectiveness has not been fully explored, especially under travelling conditions.

In its leaflet *Homoeopathy and Foreign Travel*, the UK-based Society of Homoeopaths (☎ 0845-450 6611, **www.homeopathy-soh.org**, email info @homeopathy-soh.org) states, 'Whilst the value of homoeopathic remedies in the treatment of disease is well established, their value in the prevention of specific disease is not well documented'.

There are practical issues to consider, too: homoeopathic immunisations need to be taken regularly, as their action is short-lived, and it's easy to forget doses and perhaps put yourself at unnecessary risk. Also, because you take these remedies orally (rather than by injection), their effectiveness may be reduced if you get a bout of diarrhoea and vomiting.

Discuss these remedies with your homoeopath as well as with your doctor or a travel medicine specialist before you go, but you might want to consider them if have left your immunisations to the last minute. You could boost protection with a homoeopathic remedy for a week or so until the protective effect of the injection kicks in. Homoeopathic immunisations may be useful if you can't have the injections.

To find out more about homoeopathic immunisations, contact a registered homoeopathic practitioner or your national organisation of homoeopaths. Some of the publications on homoeo-pathic medicine listed under Books at the end of this chapter cover this topic.

SPECIAL CONSIDERATIONS

Just bear in mind that immunisations are not suitable for everyone. If you're pregnant, for example, there are some immunisations that are best avoided – see p267 for more details. Babies and children are also a special case – we discuss this in more detail in the section on Immunisations (p277) in the Babies & Children chapter.

Other considerations include any serious reactions you may have had to immunisations in the past, or if your immunity is lowered for some reason (eg you're taking steroids or you're HIV-positive). In this situation, some immunisations are best avoided – you should discuss this with your doctor well in advance of travelling. For more details, see the Travellers with Special Needs chapter.

TIMING

Ideally, you'll need to make the first appointment for travel health advice, including immunisations, about six to eight weeks before you travel. This is because you usually need to wait one to two weeks after a booster or the last dose of a course before you're fully protected, and some courses may need to be given over a period of several weeks. Although there's no medical reason why you can't have all your injections together, it's a bit masochistic and may make side effects like fever or sore arm worse. Generally, if you've had a full course of an immunisation before, you should only need a booster injection now.

Don't panic if you have left it to the last minute. Immunisation schedules can be rushed if necessary and most vaccinations you'll need for Africa can be given together two weeks, or even one week, before you go. Just bear in mind that you won't be as well protected for the first week or two of your trip as you would be if you'd had them earlier.

Note that a full course of rabies vaccine takes a month.

Vaccine	Full course	Booster	Comments
cholera	2 doses of oral vaccine	after 2 years	rarely used for travellers
hepatitis A vaccine	single dose	booster at 6 to 12 months	gives good protection for at least 12 months; with booster, it probably protects you for life
hepatitis B	two doses 1 month apart plus a third dose 6 months later	not routinely required	more rapid courses are available if necessary imunity probably lifelong
meningococcal meningitis	one dose	3 years	protection lasts 3 years
polio	3 doses given at 4 weekly intervals	10 years after primary course, single booster in adult life confers lifelong immunity	full course is usually given in childhood
rabies (pre-exposure)	3 doses over 1 month	2 years	Pre-immunisation safer than post-exposure treatment only
tetanus, usually given with diphtheria	3 doses given at 4 -week intervals	every 10 years	full course is usually given in childhood
tuberculosis	single dose	limited protection for life	often given in childhood, so you may already be immune
typhoid	single injection OR 3 or 4 oral doses	injection: every 3 years oral: 1 to f5 years	oral typhoid vaccine needs to be completed one week before you start malaria prevention medication
yellow fever	one dose	10 years	generally only given at designated yellow fever vaccination centres; certificate is valid 10 days after the injection

WHICH ONES?

Working out which immunisations you're going to need doesn't just depend on your destination in Africa. Your doctor will also take the following into account: the length of your trip, whether you're going to be travelling in rural areas or sticking to the resorts, which vaccinations you've had in the past, any medications you're on and any allergies you have. So while we can give you an idea of the immunisations you're *likely* to need, for a definitive list you'll need to discuss your requirements with your doctor.

Immunisations can be categorised into those given routinely, irrespective of whether you are travelling or not, and travel-related ones.

Routine Immunisations

Whatever your travel plans, you'll need to be up to date with these:

- tetanus (often given together with diphtheria)
- polio
- 'childhood illnesses': measles, mumps and rubella, possibly also *Haemophilus influenzae* (Hib) and chicken pox (varicella)
- influenza

In addition, you'll need some travel-related immunisations, depending on your destination and style of trip.

Travel-Related Immunisations

We've listed these in alphabetical order.

Cholera

Note that immunisation against cholera is no longer generally recommended (except in special circumstances). As a traveller you're very unlikely to be at risk of this diarrhoeal disease. A problem historically is that at some borders (eg entering Zanzibar) officials may demand to see a certificate of immunisation before allowing you across the border, even though this is contrary to international law. They may even force you to be immunised on the spot, which you obviously want to avoid at all costs.

Your best bet is to discuss this issue with your travel health clinic or doctor before you go. You may be able to get a certificate of exemption or some other form of relevant documentation to carry with you just in case.

Hepatitis A

All travellers to Africa should be protected against this common disease. You should have the hepatitis A vaccine, which gives good protection for several years (probably forever if you have a booster). Hepatitis A immunoglobulin, which protects you for a limited time and carries a theoretical possibility of blood-borne diseases like HIV, is no longer recommended. A combined hepatitis A and typhoid vaccine has recently become available, which will help cut down on the number of injections you need to put up with.

Hepatitis B

Protection against this is recommended for all long-term travellers to Africa, where the disease is common. You might also need it if you're going to be working as a medic or nurse in Africa or if needle sharing or sexual contact is a possibility at your destination. This immunisation is given routinely to children in some countries, including Australia and the USA. If you need both hepatitis A and B immunisations, a combined vaccine is available.

Meningococcal Meningitis

Epidemics of this occur periodically, mainly in the Sahel area in the hot dry season, although the so-called 'meningitis belt' extends as far south as Zambia and Malawi. Epidemics tend to be widely reported and immunisation is usually recommended if you are travelling in risk areas in the dry season. Be aware that there have been reports of travellers being required to be immunised at borders into Burkina Faso and possibly other countries in the region.

Rabies

With rabies, you have the choice of either having the injections before you go (called preexposure) or only if you are bitten (postexposure) by a potentially rabid animal.

Preexposure vaccination involves receiving three injections over the course of a month before you leave. This primes your system against rabies, giving you some, but not complete, protection against the disease. If you then get bitten by a suspect animal, you will need to have two boosters to prevent rabies developing.

If you are bitten by a suspect animal and didn't have the preexposure vaccination, you will need the full course of rabies vaccination (five injections over a month) as well as an immediate injection of rabies antibodies (also called human rabies immunoglobulin, or RIG). RIG can be made from horse or human blood. Human-derived RIG can be difficult to obtain in many countries in Africa and, even if it is available, it's probably best to avoid locally produced human blood products. RIG is very expensive, and both types are often in short supply and may be difficult to obtain. That is why pre-exposure vaccination is recommended.

To save yourself hassle, worry and a huge medical bill, take all possible precautions to avoid getting bitten. Consider having preexposure rabies vaccination if you will be travelling through Africa for more than three months or if you will be handling animals. Children are at particular risk of being bitten, so they may need to be vaccinated even if you're going for a short time; discuss this with your doctor or a travel health clinic.

Finally, if you've heard of the old rabies injections which were given into the stomach and were extremely uncomfortable, be reassured. The modern rabies vaccine is usually given in your arm and has few side effects. However, the older vaccine is still used in many less developed areas. For more advice on postexposure rabies treatment, see p377.

Tuberculosis

You may already have been immunised against this as a child. But if you weren't, you probably won't need it unless you're going to be living with local people (eg if you're going back to visit relatives) for three months or longer.

Typhoid

You'll need vaccination against typhoid if you're travelling in Africa for longer than a couple of weeks. The oral typhoid vaccine (if available) can sometimes upset your tummy. The new injectable vaccine causes few side effects.

Yellow Fever

There are two things you need to be aware of with this immunisation. First, proof of immunisation against yellow fever is a statutory requirement for entry into all African countries if you are coming from a yellow-fever infected country in Africa or South America. Second, regardless of whether you need a certificate, you should protect yourself against the disease if you are planning to visit rural areas of infected countries (see map p24).

Yellow fever does not exist in all parts of Africa but mosquitoes capable of transmitting it do. Theoretically, this means that it could exist if travellers from infected areas bring the disease with them. Yellow fever-free countries protect themselves from this risk by requiring you to be immunised if you are coming from an infected area. Countries differ in how they define 'infected' – discuss this with your doctor before you go, or check any of the information sources listed earlier in this chapter.

The yellow fever vaccine occasionally causes low-grade fever and a sore arm. It's not recommended if you have severe hypersensitivity to eggs or are immunocompromised for some reason.

SIDE EFFECTS

Immunisations are like any other medication: they can have unwanted effects. These are generally unpleasant rather than dangerous, although occasionally serious allergic reactions can occur. There's no evidence that immunisations damage your immune system in any way.

If you tend to faint after injections, plan to sit quietly for 10 minutes or so afterwards. The most common reactions are soreness around the injection site, sometimes with redness and swelling, and maybe a slight fever or a general feeling of being unwell. Tetanus, for example, commonly gives you a sore arm, while the hepatitis A vaccine can occasionally give you a fever in the evening. These reactions generally settle quickly with painkillers and rest, while an ice pack on your arm can help soothe any soreness.

> If you get more serious reactions that don't settle overnight, you should contact the doctor or clinic where you got your injections.

Very occasionally immunisations can provoke allergic reactions because of substances they may contain, like albumin from eggs, which is why you sometimes have to stay at the clinic for half an hour after the injection. Allergic reactions are a possibility with any immunisation, but some (for example yellow fever) are more likely to cause this than others. These reactions are more likely if you know you are allergic to eggs or if you have multiple allergies, especially to bee stings – something else to discuss with your doctor.

MALARIA PREVENTION

If you're going to sub-Saharan Africa (see map p23), malaria is probably the most serious health risk you will face. Of the approximately 500 million cases of malaria worldwide and one million deaths due to malaria every year, 90% are in Africa.

Your risk of getting malaria in most parts of tropical Africa is high, much higher than the risk in most Asian countries, for example. Every year a couple of thousand travellers returning to Australia, Britain or North America develop malaria, usually acquired in sub-Saharan Africa. Every year a few returning travellers die from malaria.

! If you're going to a malarial area in Africa, you must take precautions against this potentially fatal disease.

To protect yourself, don't rely on just one measure (eg malaria prevention medication). Your best approach is to attack on all fronts:

- **A**wareness of the risk: find out from a reliable source the most up to date information on the risks for the areas you are going to; there have been stories of travellers being told they will be at risk when they are not and, conversely, of travellers not taking precautions when it was appropriate.

- **B**ite avoidance: if you don't get bitten, you won't get malaria. This is even more important now that resistance to antimalarials is increasing. For the low-down on giving mozzies the slip, see p90.

- **C**hemoprophylaxis (ie antimalarial drugs) can significantly reduce your risk of malaria, but they won't prevent you from getting it altogether.

- **D**iagnosis: if you suspect you have malaria, don't delay getting medical help or, if you are far from any medical assistance, carry emergency stand-by treatment and a diagnostic kit with you (and be sure you know when to use it). Most deaths due to malaria in returning travellers are because the diagnosis was missed. For more details on the diagnosis and treatment of malaria, see p127.

For some low-risk malarial areas (eg some parts of North Africa), you may not need to take malaria prevention medication; instead you may be advised to carry emergency malaria treatment to use if necessary. If you do, your doctor will need to give you clear guidelines on when to take it and what to do – for more details, see the section on Emergency Standby Treatment later in this chapter.

MALARIA FACTS

- Malaria is spread by mosquitoes.
- Malaria is a potentially fatal disease.
- Malaria is becoming more common and more difficult to treat because of drug resistance.
- Most cases of malaria in travellers occur in people who didn't take malaria prevention medication or who didn't take them properly.
- Most malaria deaths in travellers occur because the diagnosis is delayed or missed.
- Malaria is particularly dangerous in children and pregnant women.
- Malaria can be transmitted by transfusion of blood and other blood products, by needle sharing among intravenous drug users and from mother to foetus.

MALARIA INFORMATION SOURCES

Preventing illness and death from malaria has become more complicated in recent years with the rise in resistance of the malarial parasite to drugs like chloroquine that were commonly used to prevent and treat the disease. Because it's such a complex and rapidly changing issue, it's not a good idea to rely on advice from friends or other travellers, however well intentioned or knowledgeable they are.

Up to date and accurate information about all aspects of malaria, including risks and prevention, is readily available from travel health clinics, travel healthlines and via the web (see Information Sources earlier in this chapter).

For more general information on all aspects of the disease, you could try the Malaria Foundation website (**www.malaria.org**).

MALARIA RISK

Malarial mosquitoes bite at night and tend to like rural areas: if you are in rural areas during the hours of darkness in a malaria zone, you're generally at higher risk of the disease than if you spend all your time in urban areas.

Mosquitoes breed in stagnant water, so the risk of malaria is seasonal to a certain extent, with a higher risk just after the rainy season. You're generally safe from malarial mosquitoes above altitudes of 2500m.

Areas within the same country can have different risks of malaria (eg in South Africa, only the northeastern provinces have malaria) and different areas may have different levels of resistance to drugs used to treat malaria.

The following commonly visited areas in Africa currently have a low malarial risk and no malaria prevention medication is recommended – but these may change, so make sure you get the latest information before you leave:

- Egypt (except Al-Faiyoum area from June to October)
- Morocco
- Cape Verde islands
- Nairobi and highland areas of Kenya
- the southern provinces in South Africa (except the northeastern corner, including Kruger National Park)

WHICH PILLS?

Preventive pills against malaria work by killing off the malarial parasites before they can cause the disease. Currently mefloquine, doxycycline and atovaquone-proguanil are the most effective malaria preventives for sub-Saharan Africa. A less effective alternative is chloroquine plus proguanil. In Zimbabwe and some neighbouring countries, local residents often take Maloprim (pyrimethamine with dapsone) as a preventive, although this has been discontinued in Western countries due to safety concerns.

Because of recent concerns and publicity over the potential side effects of mefloquine, authorities in Britain recommend chloroquine plus proguanil instead of the more effective mefloquine if you're going for two weeks or less to tourist resorts of Gambia (between January and May), coastal Kenya or coastal Tanzania. Other international authorities do not recommend this change.

You need to start taking malaria pills before you leave, so that they have a chance to reach maximum protective levels in your body before you arrive at your destination. It also gives any side effects a chance to show themselves so you can change medication before you go if necessary.

- Chloroquine (with or without proguanil) needs to be started at least one week in advance.
- It's best to start mefloquine two to three weeks before you go – see the boxed text on mefloquine (p48) for more details.
- Doxycycline needs to be started two days before you enter a malaria area.
- Atovoquone-proguanil (Malarone) needs only to be started one day before the risk area.

Don't be tempted to stop taking your malaria pills as soon as you leave, or you may get malaria from parasites you picked up in the last few days of your trip.

Most malaria prevention medication needs to be continued for four weeks after returning home, except Malarone which can be stopped after seven days.

It's best to take your malaria pills after food, as this makes side effects like nausea and stomach upset less likely. For the best protection, you need to take antimalarials regularly.

Minor side effects are common with all the drugs, but if you get major side effects (see the following section) that make you unsure about continuing the drug, seek advice about changing to a medication that suits you better.

As far as possible, it's best to take with you all the malaria prevention medication you think you will need, as some antimalarials may not be available where you're going and you may not be able to get exactly what you want. Discuss the alternatives with your doctor or travel health clinic before you go. If you do end up needing to buy malaria pills when you are away, make sure you get expert advice on this.

LONG-HAUL TRAVELLERS

If you're planning on travelling in a malarial area for six months or more, you may be wondering what to do about malaria prevention medication. You've got two main options: you can either continue to take the usual malaria preventive pills or you can decide not to take them. If you do decide to stop them (discuss this with your doctor before you go), you need to be extremely vigilant about avoiding mosquito bites, and you need to be very clear about where your nearest doctor is and when to take emergency standby treatment. Taking malaria pills for more than six months can work out to be quite expensive, and, unless you're really conscientious, it can be easy to forget to take your pills. Note that you don't build up immunity to malaria with time, so you're still at risk of getting it, even if you've been in a risk area for a long time.

Side Effects

All drugs have side effects and malaria prevention medication is no exception (see Doses & Side Effects later in this section). However, if you don't take your recommended malaria pills because you experience unpleasant side effects or you are sufficiently concerned about them, they are clearly not an effective preventive.

Ideally, for any medication the benefits of taking it (ie in this case preventing you from being ill with malaria) should

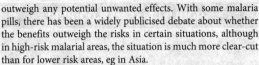

outweigh any potential unwanted effects. With some malaria pills, there has been a widely publicised debate about whether the benefits outweigh the risks in certain situations, although in high-risk malarial areas, the situation is much more clear-cut than for lower risk areas, eg in Asia.

You'll need to decide for yourself on this one, but bear in mind that if you can't, or would prefer not to, take a particular antimalarial, there are other possibilities that may be better than taking nothing at all.

What's the Point?

You can get malaria even if you're taking malaria prevention medication, so what's the point in taking them? It's true, you can still get malaria even if you take malaria pills religiously, and there are several reasons for this. Drug resistance varies immensely from area to area, and some drug recommendations may not be appropriate for a particular area. Other reasons include not taking your tablets regularly; and if you have diarrhoea or vomiting, the pills may not be absorbed properly. But bear in mind that if you take malaria pills, the disease is likely to be less severe if you do get it.

Increases Malarial Resistance?

There's no doubt that widespread use of chloroquine has resulted in resistance of the parasite to the drug, which has made treatment of malaria in travellers, as well as the local population, more difficult. However, on an individual basis, it's difficult to see how not using malaria pills and putting yourself at risk of illness and death will help change this, especially as resistance has arisen in parasites not exposed to drugs such as mefloquine.

The answer to the problem of malarial resistance currently vexes whole departments of experts, but it's generally believed to lie in controlling the mosquitoes that spread the disease. There are hopes of a malarial vaccine, but there's still a long way to go before this becomes a reality.

SHOULD I TAKE MEFLOQUINE?

Here's a brief rundown of the issues surrounding this controversial malaria drug.

No one doubts that mefloquine (Lariam) is currently one of the most effective drugs at preventing malaria; the issue is side effects. Mefloquine commonly causes 'minor' side effects like nausea and diarrhoea, as do the other malaria prevention medications, but it can also have more disturbing side effects. These range from weird dreams, dizziness and anxiety to panic attacks, depression and even fits (seizures). Some travellers claim to be permanently affected by mefloquine. Equally, a large proportion of travellers take mefloquine and have no problems.

Experts disagree on how common the disabling side effects are. Figures from studies range from one in 10,000 (about the same number as for travellers taking chloroquine and proguanil) to much higher rates (one in 140 in a recent study by the London School of Hygiene & Tropical Medicine).

While serious side-effects are probably rare, the nuisance common side-effects appear to occur more frequently than with other malaria prevention medications and this may affect whether a traveller takes the tablets properly, or at all. As a result of the controversy, the British guidelines for the use of mefloquine were thoroughly reviewed in 1997, and it was agreed that because of the risk of side effects, mefloquine should only be used when the risk of resistant malaria is high.It is, however, widely prescribed by other countries, especially in the US.

We suggest you find out for yourself what different people have to say about mefloquine and then make up your own mind.

You can get information on mefloquine from any travel health clinic, your doctor, a pharmacist or any of the web sites listed earlier in this chapter. For more specific information about the mefloquine issue, you could check out the Lariam Action USA web site (**www.lariaminfo.org**), which has good links to other resources on mefloquine, or the excellent 'Lariam or not to Lariam' (**www.geocities.com/The Tropics/6913/lariam.htm**), which has an incredibly comprehensive list of links, including one to the manufacturer of Lariam, Hoffman LaRoche. Alternatively, contact Lariam Action USA (info@lariaminfo.org), # 64 El Pavo Real Circle, San Rafael, CA 94903-3521.

Whatever you decide, remember that malaria is a potentially fatal disease and it's vital you take precautions against it.

DOSES & SIDE EFFECTS

Mefloquine (Lariam)

This drug is taken weekly. It was developed as an alternative to chloroquine when it became clear that chloroquine resistance was becoming widespread. It is currently the most effective malaria prevention medication for sub-Saharan Africa.

See the boxed text 'Should I Take Mefloquine?' for a discussion of possible side effects. If they do occur, it's usually after the first two to three doses. Starting mefloquine two to three weeks before you leave gives you time to change to an alternative.

Mefloquine is not suitable for everyone: you should not take it if you have epilepsy (fits) or if you have had severe depression or other major mind problems in the past, or if you are on medicines (for example beta blockers) for a heart condition – check with your doctor.

Mefloquine is best avoided in the first three months of pregnancy, and is not licenced for babies below 5kg.

! Note that because of the risk of dizziness and fits, mefloquine is best avoided if you're going to be doing precision tasks like scuba diving or flying a plane, or if you are going to high altitude (it could mask signs of altitude sickness).

Chloroquine plus Proguanil

This regimen involves taking a weekly chloroquine tablet plus daily proguanil. Proguanil is not available in the USA, but if you wanted to take it, it is widely available in Europe, Canada and Africa. Advantages are that both agents are relatively safe, and there's long experience of use. The disadvantage is that this combination is not as protective in many parts of the world. Resistance is now widespread to both agents world-wide, including Africa. It may be useful if you aren't able to take mefloquine.

Minor side effects are quite common and include headaches, nausea, diarrhoea and indigestion. You can get itching, especially if you're dark-skinned, and temporarily blurred vision. Prolonged use of chloroquine (usually more than five years) can cause more serious eye problems but this tends to be of more concern for expatriates than travellers. Proguanil is safe but can cause mouth ulcers.

This combination is safe in pregnancy (you may need to take a folate supplement with proguanil) and for children. Chloroquine isn't suitable for everyone: you shouldn't take it if you have epilepsy or are taking medication for epilepsy.

Doxycycline

This tetracycline antibiotic is an effective option for malaria, and it's been used for treatment of other infections for some time. It needs to be taken daily. Drug resistance hasn't been reported yet, but it's probably only a matter of time. It's useful where mefloquine-resistant malaria is present (see under Mefloquine earlier) or if you can't or would prefer not to take mefloquine.

Side effects include diarrhoea, sensitivity to sunlight and vaginal thrush, and it may make the oral contraceptive pill less effective, so you should seek advice on this if necessary. It can cause irritation in your gullet, so you should always swallow it with plenty of water.

Doxycycline is best avoided in pregnancy and is not suitable for children under eight years.

Atovaquone-proguanil (Malarone)

This is a relatively new combination drug with good effect at both prevention and treatment of malaria. It is taken daily, can be started only one day before entering the malaria area, and needs to be taken for only one week after leaving a risk area.

It is suitable for children down to 5-10 kg in weight, and has no specific general contraindications, although is not recommended for pregnant women.

It is remarkably free from side-effects, though it occasionally causes nausea or loose motions. The big catch is cost; it is very expensive, and so is often not suitable for long travel as the cost is too high.

Pyrimethamine with Dapsone (Maloprim)

Dropped from use generally because of the risk of side effects, this is very much a last-resort antimalarial, but it's better than nothing if you have no other options. It's usually taken weekly with chloroquine. It is known to cause blood problems, especially if you overdose.

EMERGENCY STANDBY TREATMENT

+ For detailed guidelines on emergency treatment of malaria, see the section on p128.

If you are going to a high-risk malarial area without access to medical care, you need to take treatment doses of malaria prevention medication with you for use in an emergency. Discuss this issue with your doctor or travel health clinic before you go. It's not just a question of popping the pills; you also need to be clear about when to use it and what to do if problems arise. For treatment you need to use a different medication from the one you used for prevention.

If you can get hold of one, it's a good idea to take a malaria diagnostic test kit (eg MalaQuick) with you too. These kits are fairly accurate, although not so easy to use in the field. You can get them from selected travel health clinics (including Travel Doctor-TMVC in Australia and New Zealand, and Nomad Travel Stores & Travel Clinics in the UK). You can use the kits to confirm the diagnosis if you suspect you have malaria, even if you were taking antimalarials. They usually contain two tests and you'll need to try to keep them as cool as possible, as this prolongs their lifespan.

TRAVEL HEALTH INSURANCE

However lucky (or poor) you're feeling, it's vital you have adequate travel health insurance to cover your whole trip, usually as part of a general travel insurance covering loss of belongings, flight cancellations etc. Even if the costs of medical care in some countries are low, the costs of medical evacuation are always phenomenal. If you have medical insurance in your home country, remember that it may not cover you for travel in Africa.

Travel insurance policies are available from a variety of sources related to the travel industry, including credit or charge card companies, travel agents and travel health clinics, as well as from insurance brokers. Insurance policies vary in the details of the services they provide, so shop around to find exactly what you want. Always check the small print so you're clear on exactly what the policy covers.

Many insurance providers have a 24 hour hotline you can ring for assistance in an emergency, and they can usually provide you with names of English-speaking doctors, arrange referral to a hospital and guarantee payment if you need to pay upfront (as is usual in most African countries).

Most insurance policies should cover you for medical evacuation if necessary, but it's worth checking this. Some companies provide their own air transport and emergency services, while others contract it out.

You will need to inform the insurance providers of any medical condition you have, as this may increase the premium you have to pay. Once you're over a certain age, usually 65 years, your premium automatically increases. Note that routine health problems and preexisting conditions (which sometimes include pregnancy) are not usually covered by travel health insurance policies.

Check if your policy covers the following:

- the total cost of any medical or surgical treatment you might need
- any additional costs you might incur if you were delayed by illness or injury or had to travel when injured
- emergency evacuation – without insurance this can cost thousands of dollars, which you would need to provide upfront
- provision of safe blood supplies
- dental treatment
- travel while pregnant
- adventure sports, eg altitude, trekking or scuba diving – consider getting special insurance to cover these activities if necessary (for details about insurance for diving see p353)

Note that you will generally have to pay cash upfront for medical treatment and be reimbursed later, so it's a good idea to have an emergency stash just in case (your insurance provider may be able to provide a guarantee of payment which may be accepted instead, but don't count on it). Always keep any receipts in case you need to present them later to be reimbursed.

If you're going somewhere remote, you may want to consider registering with a local air ambulance service in case you need to be evacuated for medical reasons. Recommended local air ambulance services include AMREF's Flying Doctors Service in East Africa (see the boxed text 'African Medical & Research Foundation (AMREF)' earlier in this chapter) and Medical Air Rescue Service (☎ 4-734513, fax 4-734517, http://int.mars.co.zw) in Zimbabwe. Air rescue may be already be covered by your insurance policy, so check this before you go.

PRETRAVEL CHECK–UPS & OTHER PREPARATIONS

MEDICAL CHECK–UP

Not everyone needs a medical check-up before going on a trip, but in some situations it's a good idea.

If you're going to be away for more than about six months or you're going to remote areas, a medical check-up is a good idea to make sure there are no problems waiting to happen. If you've had any niggling problems, now is the time to get them checked out.

If you're going to be doing something strenuous like trekking at altitude and you're on the good side of 40, it's probably a good idea to have a fitness check before you go.

You'll need to get any prescription medicines from your doctor before you go. If you take any medicines regularly, you'll need to take sufficient supplies with you, as well as a record of your prescription. If you are going to be travelling to remote areas, you might want to discuss taking emergency treatment for diarrhoea or chest infections with you, which you will need to get on prescription.

Women Travellers

There are some 'women only' issues that it might be a good idea to talk about with your doctor before you go. Travel can pose problems with certain forms of contraception, or you might want to discuss your options if you think you may need to start contraception. You might want to consider the possibility of stopping your periods temporarily (eg if you're going to be trekking in a remote area).

Another issue you might want to discuss is taking pre-scription treatment for cystitis or thrush with you.

If you're planning on travelling while you're pregnant, you'll definitely want to discuss this with your doctor as early as possible – see the Travel & Pregnancy section in the Women Travellers chapter for more on this.

HEALTH-RELATED DOCUMENTS

When you're travelling, try to keep the following health-related information on your person at all times, in case of emergency:

- travel insurance hotline number
- serial number of your travel insurance policy
- contact details of your nearest embassy
- US State Department's Citizen's Emergency Center number (US citizens only)
- summary of any important medical conditions you have
- contact details of your doctor back home if necessary
- copy of prescription for any medication you take regularly
- any serious allergies
- blood group
- prescription for glasses or contact lenses
- if you are a diabetic, a letter from your doctor explaining why you need syringes etc

Babies & Children

If you're travelling with babies or young children, it might be reassuring to discuss tactics for dealing with any problems you might come up against while you are away. For a more detailed discussion of the special health issues surrounding travel with little ones, see the Babies & Children chapter later in this book.

DENTAL CHECK-UP

You know it makes sense...You don't want to find you need a filling when you're travelling in a remote area far from the nearest painkilling injection. It's definitely worth making time for this before you go, especially if you haven't been for a while. Your teeth can get quite a battering when you're travelling, as you often end up drinking large quantities of sweet drinks, and inadequate water supplies mean you have to take a break from your usual dental health routine. For guidelines on keeping your teeth healthy while you are away, see the section on Teeth in the Ears, Eyes & Teeth chapter.

EYES

If you wear contact lenses, it's probably a good idea to talk to your optometrist about hygiene and other issues on the road. It's a good idea to take a plentiful supply of any cleaning solutions you use. If you wear glasses, consider taking a replacement pair, and take a copy of your prescription with you. It will be understood in any language, in case you need to have a pair made up while you are away. See the Eyes section of the Ears, Eyes & Teeth chapter for more details.

ACTIVITIES & EXPEDITIONS

If you're going to be spending time in remote areas more than a day or so away from medical help (eg if you're trekking), you might want to consider doing a first aid course before you leave. Contact your local first aid organisation for details of courses available. You may want to consider a more specialist survival skills course, especially if you're going trekking in remote or isolated areas in harsh environmental conditions.

If you're planning an expedition, the Geography Outdoors centre at the Royal Geographical Society (☎ 020-7591 3000, **www.rgs.org/eac**, 1 Kensington Gore, London SW7 2AR, UK) has good information aimed at serious expeditioners.

If you're planning on driving round Africa, check out the classic manual, *Sahara Handbook* by Simon Glen or the new book by desert specialist Chris Scott, *Sahara Overland*. Chris Scott is also author of *Adventure Motorcyclists Handbook,* which contains a heap of good information. Another classic book that may be worth checking out is *Africa by Road*, by Bob Swain & Paula Snyder. Alternatively, check out the excellent website put together by Chris Scott (**www.sahara-overland.com**).

If you're planning on doing some diving in Africa, remember to get a diving medical check before you leave as, in theory at least, you'll need a certificate of fitness before any dive centre will let you dive. You might also want to do a diving course before you leave.

WHAT TO TAKE

You don't need to weigh yourself down with a heap of obscure remedies you may never need, but it's handy to have a good stock of reliable and familiar basics with you. Apart from the very real problem of limited supplies and possibly dubious quality of medications that are available in many countries, it saves you the hassle of having to find a supply and then decipher instructions written in another language.

Be Prepared

Before you go, make sure you are clear about when and how to use any medication you have with you – side effects are more likely if medicines are taken inappropriately or in the wrong dose. Many medicines come with an information leaflet from the manufacturers giving safety information and guidance for use, so keep this for reference.

If you take any medicine regularly (eg for a heart condition or the contraceptive pill), remember to take a written record, as well as a prescription of the generic name and dose in case you need to replace it for any reason.

If you're allergic to any drugs (eg penicillin), you should carry this information with you at all times. You can get engraved bracelets or tags with this information from specialist companies like MedicAlert (see Useful Organisations earlier in this chapter).

Customs

Customs officials can sometimes be suspicious of medications you may be carrying (there have been a few horror stories along the lines of 'Innocent Traveller Arrested for Carrying Painkillers') so it's best to keep medicines in their original packaging or container where possible, ideally with a pre-scription or doctor's letter showing what it is and why you need to take it. If you keep all your medications in an official-looking medical kit, you're less likely to have problems.

The Kit

You can make up your own kit, or pre-packed kits are widely available from travel health clinics and other travel equipment suppliers, saving you the trouble of having to think about what you might need. Better still, you can take a pre-packed kit and add your own extras to it, perhaps using a combination of 'conventional' and 'natural' supplies.

Zip-lock plastic bags are handy for keeping medical supplies, and it's probably best to keep the whole kit together in a waterproof container, such as a clear plastic box.

'Sterile kits' containing needles and syringes are usually easily recognised as such and shouldn't cause you problems at customs, but carrying loose syringes and needles is not a good idea, unless you are a diabetic, for example, and you have a doctor's letter to say you need them.

What To Take

What you take depends on where you're going and what you're planning to do. If you're travelling with children, turn to the Babies & Children chapter for more guidance on what to take. What products you actually take will also depend on what your favourite brands are and what's available in your country – check with your pharmacist.

Try to keep medicines as cool as possible (ie in the middle of your pack) and out of direct sunlight. Remember to keep all medicines out of reach of babies and children.

DRUG NAMES

This is a confusing issue for everyone, medics included. All drugs have two names: a generic (official medical) name and the brand name (chosen by the manufacturer). Because brand names vary from country to country, we've used the official medical name for all drugs mentioned in this book. This may seem a bit frustrating to you if you're reading this at home, but it means that any doctor or pharmacist anywhere in the world will be able to recognise the generic name (or at least can look it up) and should be able to suggest brands available locally.

If you want to find out the generic name of a drug, look on the packet or leaflet accompanying the drug – the generic name should be there, usually in smaller type just below the brand name – or ask a pharmacist.

You'll find more information on all aspects of buying and using medicines while you are away in the appendix at the back of this book.

Lotions, Potions & Pills

Consider including these for travel to most destinations in Africa:

- any prescription medicines, including malaria prevention medication if necessary
- paracetamol (acetaminophen) or aspirin for pain and fever; consider also taking a stronger painkiller like co-codamol or an anti-inflammatory like ibuprofen
- antidiarrhoeals – loperamide (probably the most useful and effective) or bismuth subsalicylate (Pepto-Bismol)
- 'indigestion' remedies such as antacid tablets or liquids
- oral rehydration sachets and measuring spoon for making up your own solution
- antihistamine tablets for hay fever and other allergies, and for itching

- sting relief spray or hydrocortisone cream for insect bites
- emergency bee sting kit containing adrenaline (epinephrine) if you are allergic to stings
- sunscreen and lip salve with sun block
- insect repellent (DEET or plant-based) and permethrin (for treating mosquito nets and clothes)
- anti-motion sickness remedies (eg promethazine or natural remedies)
- water-purifying tablets or water filter/purifier
- over-the-counter cystitis treatment
- antifungal cream for athlete's foot, crotch rot and thrush
- calamine cream or aloe vera for sunburn and other skin rashes

In addition, you could consider taking:
- sugar-free chewing gum to keep your mouth moist in hot dry climates
- cough and cold remedies, and sore throat lozenges
- eye drops for tired or dusty eyes
- multivitamins

First Aid Equipment

We don't want to weigh you down, but you'll probably be glad to have at least some of these with you:
- thermometer
- scissors
- tweezers – to remove splinters and ticks
- sticking plasters (such as Band-Aids) of various sizes
- gauze swabs and adhesive tape
- bandages and safety pins to fasten them
- nonadhesive dressings
- antiseptic powder or solution (eg povidone-iodine), antiseptic wipes
- sterile kit, including needles, syringes, suture kit, cannula for giving a drip
- wound closure strips or butterfly closures (can sometimes be used instead of stitches)

Prescription Medicines

Discuss with your doctor, if you need to take the following with you:

- emergency treatment for malaria plus malaria diagnosis kit (see p128)
- antibiotics for treating diarrhoea
- a course of antibiotics for chest, ear, skin etc infections, if you're going to be travelling off the beaten track
- antibiotics to treat cystitis
- treatment for vaginal thrush (may be available without prescription in some countries)

Remote Areas

Items you probably should consider taking with you if you are planning on trekking or travelling in remote or highland areas include:

- sterile kit with an intravenous-fluid giving set, blood substitute solution and other intravenous fluids
- medicines to treat altitude sickness
- antibiotic eye and ear drops
- antibiotic cream or powder
- emergency inflatable splints
- blister kit
- elasticated support bandage
- triangular bandage for making an arm sling
- dental first aid kit

And Finally...

If you have any medicines left over at the end of your trip, dispose of them carefully. You could perhaps consider giving them to a hospital or clinic, but don't be tempted to just leave them in your hotel room for the cleaner because medicines are only effective if used appropriately and can actually be harmful otherwise.

TRAVEL FIRST AID – ALTERNATIVE SUGGESTIONS

Bernadette Saulenier is a naturopath and Reiki practitioner who travels regularly between Australia and Europe. She has the following tips for travellers on homoeopathic/naturopathic first aid. The remedies mentioned here are not likely to be available where you're going, so you will need to bring what you need with you. Remember that as a general rule, these remedies are best used for non-serious conditions and are not intended to replace medical diagnosis and treatment in serious cases.

Diarrhoea can ruin the best planned holiday and, as with anything else, prevention is better than cure. Treat water with tea tree oil, a natural antiseptic: use two drops of tea tree oil in 1L of water and let it stand overnight. Another preventive is to take slippery elm capsules orally before each meal – the powder coats and protects the delicate lining of the bowels against inflammation. If you get diarrhoea, homoeopathic remedies include arsenicum album, carbo vegetalis, podophyllum, ipecac or nux vomica – what to take depends on the characteristics of your illness. Ask your practitioner for guidance on this before you leave.

Constipation is also common when you're travelling: try pear or prune juice, or a tablespoon of linseeds /psyllium husks sprinkled on your food. Remember to drink plenty of water. If you are really desperate, you could try taking a mixture of cascara, senna and chelidonium herbs.

If you're hopping in and out of buses carrying heavy luggage, you're quite likely to get a few bruises. Arnica cream is a great remedy, applied on the bruise immediately (but avoid using it on open wounds and cuts). For bleeding wounds, take arnica 30c under your tongue.

Cocculus drops or ginger tablets are good remedies for preventing motion sickness, and homoeopathic melatonin drops are excellent for jetlag. Gelsemium drops or tablets will alleviate the aches and pains of sore muscles, and taking any form of antioxidant such as grapeseed extract or vitamin A, C or E will help your body to cope with fatigue, stress and lack of fresh air – all common on a long journey.

Mosquitoes hate the smell of geranium, so avoid getting bitten by putting a few drops of geranium oil on your skin. If you get bitten in spite of all your precautions, a drop of lavender oil will soothe the itch. For other bites and stings (spiders, bees, wasps or fleas) a few drops of Ledum 30c under your tongue is beneficial.

For sunburn, try a few drops of soothing hypericum oil, which also promotes healing, or comfrey cream. If you're feeling the heat, take the tissue salt of calcium sulphate (Calc. Sulph 6x) every 15 minutes until you feel refreshed, or try Dr Bach's Rescue Remedy.

For irritant skin rashes and minor burns, try soothing calendula or comfrey cream. Lycopodium in a homeopathic form will help fungal infections at the constitutional level, but topically you may find tea-tree oil, thuja and comfrey creams helpful.

Colds and flu seem to be common wherever you go. Echinacea tablets or vitamin C will boost your immune system and help you avoid illness. If you are stricken, combination 'Q' of tissue salts will help with sinus and throat infections, and herbal tea of thyme or sage will alleviate sore throat and feverish symptoms. Gelsemium will get rid of muscular aches and pains, and allium cepa will help with a runny nose and watery eyes.

For stress or panic attacks, Dr Bach's Rescue Remedy is invaluable. A few drops under the tongue every 15 minutes works wonders. If sleep eludes you, a tincture or tablet of combined valerian, scullcap and passionflower (or any of these herbs alone) is the best cure. Hops is another herb with soothing effect. If you cannot find herbs, a good alternative is to take tissue salts of magnesium phosphate (Mag. Phos. 6x) before bed.

ALTERNATIVE TRAVEL KITS

You can make up your own travel kit with your favourite natural remedies, or you can buy a ready-made kit. Unless you're planning to take just a few familiar remedies, you should get advice from your practitioner or local homoeopathic or naturopathic pharmacy. Alternatively, we give some guidance on homoeopathic and naturopathic remedies in the boxed text 'Travel First Aid – Alternative Suggestions' (p62). Some of the texts listed under Books have suggestions for alternative travel kits.

From England, Neal's Yard Remedies (**www.nealsyard remedies.com** or **www.nyrusa.com**, mailorder@nealsyard remedies.com, advice@nealsyardremedies.com) is a long-established supplier of natural remedies. It has a variety of mini-kits pre-packed with first aid remedies.

Also in the UK, Helios Homoeopathic Pharmacy (☎ 01892-537254, fax 01892-546850, **www.helios.co.uk**, email pharmacy@helios.co.uk) has a compact and incredibly comprehensive homoeopathic travel kit containing 36 remedies for travel-related problems (everything from drowning to fear of flying), with a helpful leaflet giving guidance on what to use when. It's probably suitable for someone with prior experience of homoeopathy.

You can order plant-based remedies like Echinacea and Sweet Annie (good for digestive upsets) from Joanne Alexander at Snow Mountain Botanicals (smb@pacific.net, fax 707-743-2037); check out the website at **www.snowmountainbotanicals.com.**

BOOKS

If you're looking for more information or perhaps just some bedtime reading before you go, here's a small selection of some of the many books available on travel health and related issues. Books are published in different editions by different publishers in different countries, but a bookshop or library should be able to track down the following recommendations from the author or title.

GENERAL REFERENCE

For an authoritative, comprehensive and earnest reference source, try *Travellers' Health* by Dr Richard Dawood. *Where There is No Doctor* by David Werner is an excellent 'how-to-do-it' manual for the medically naive, aimed at people going to live in remote areas of developing countries. There's a companion text (only for sadists, surely), *Where There Is No Dentist*.

For a chatty, entertaining and comprehensive guide aimed at travellers and expatriates, try Dr Jane Wilson-Howarth's wonderfully titled *Bugs, Bites & Bowels*. A similar, very detailed guide for travelling parents is *Your Child's Health Abroad* by Dr Jane Howarth and Dr Matthew Ellis. *Staying Healthy in Asia, Africa & Latin America* by Dirk Schroeder is a good, well-organised, no-nonsense health guide for travellers. The *International Travel Health Guide* by Stuart R Rose is updated annually, and is a good source of general information.

If you're looking for a first aid manual, get hold of the authorised manual of your national primary care organisation such as the Red Cross or St John Ambulance Society.

ALTERNATIVE THERAPIES

For something a bit different, try *The Traveller's Guide to Homoeopathy* by Phyllis Speight *or The World Travellers' Manual of Homoeopathy* by Dr Colin Lessel, which is incredibly comprehensive, full of fascinating detail – a work of love. *Homoeopathic Alternatives to Immunisation* by Susan Curtis makes interesting reading and is available by mail order from Neal's Yard Remedies (for contact details, see the Alternative Travel Kits section earlier in this chapter).

CLIMATE, ALTITUDE & ACTION

If you're planning on trekking or doing other adventure activities in Africa, you may want to read up on some health and safety issues before you go. For a comprehensive overview of health, safety and general outdoor survival issues, Tim Macartney-Snape's *Being Outside*, is hard to beat. *Hiking & Backpacking, A Complete Guide* is an excellent, comprehensive, easy to read and practical guide to all aspects of walking in the wilderness, with a North American slant.

Medicine for Mountaineering (edited by J Wilkerson) is a classic reference for travellers likely to be more than 24 hours from medical care or try the very readable *The High Altitude Medicine Handbook* by Andrew J Pollard and David R Murdoch (although it's aimed primarily at medical practitioners). There are a couple of good pocket guides for trekkers, including *Altitude Illness – Prevention & Treatment* by Stephen Bezruchka and *Mountain Sickness – Prevention, Recognition & Treatment* by Peter H Hackett.

If you want to make yourself really paranoid, try the surprisingly readable *Bites & Stings, The World of Venomous Animals* by John Nichol, and you'll never want to venture into the water again after you've read *Dangerous Marine Creatures* by Dr Carl Edmonds.

If you've ever wondered what to do if a volcano erupts at your feet, or how to improvise a cooking pot from a length of bamboo, you'll find all the answers and much, much more in the *SAS Survival Guide*.

On the Move...

Getting there is half the fun they say... If you don't enjoy the moving experience (and many travellers don't), you'll want to read this chapter before you leave terra firma. Or bounce over it.

FIT TO FLY?

If you're normally fit and healthy, flying shouldn't be any particular problem for you beyond the stresses involved in any form of travelling. However, there are certain situations in which you should check with your doctor before flying:

- if you've got preexisting heart or lung problems, although as a general rule you shouldn't need extra oxygen if you can climb a flight of stairs

- if you've had an operation within 10 days of flying, check with the airline if you are able to fly

- if you've had blood clots in your blood vessels in the past, as sitting immobile for long periods of time during the flight may make further clots likely

- if you're more than 36 weeks pregnant (most airlines will not let you fly after 35 weeks)

- if you have a bad cold, sinus infection or a middle ear infection, it's best to avoid flying until you're better, as you're at risk of severe ear pain and possibly a burst eardrum – see p181 for more details

- if you've been scuba diving, you shouldn't fly for 12 hours after any dive and for 24 hours after a dive requiring decompression stops; note that you will need medical clearance before you fly if you required recompression treatment

TRAVELLING WELL

If you're flying, the low cabin-air humidity is great for minimising the odoriferous effects of squashing 300 or so stressed people into a closed space for eight or more hours, but it does dry you out. You'll feel better if you drink lots of nonalcoholic fluids – avoid tea, coffee and alcohol, as they can all increase fluid loss. Mineral-water aerosol sprays and skin moisturisers can also be helpful.

FEAR OF FLYING?

If even the thought of flying reduces you to a quivering wreck, you may not be reading this book. If you are, you might like to know that help is at hand and that courses are available to cure you of your trembles. These usually involve behavioural therapy – you're exposed to various flying situations under controlled conditions, eg in a flight simulator, and in this way learn to combat your fears. Some psychologists specialise in this area.

Considerable success is reported, and improvement can last up to five years after the course. Ask your airline or travel health provider for details of courses available to you. Or you could try a virtual reality clinic – check out **www.virtuallybetter.com** for details of one US-based clinic.

At cruising altitude, the volume of enclosed gases (for example in your ears) expands by about a third, but this shouldn't cause a problem if you can pop your ears (try swallowing or holding your nose and puffing out your cheeks). You may find your abdomen swells up, though, so you might want to avoid bubbly drinks.

Aromatherapy is great for when you're on the move – try a few drops of rosemary or lavender in a tissue or handkerchief, and waft it under your nose every so often.

Sitting inactive for long periods of time on any form of transport, especially in hot climates, can give you swollen feet and ankles, and may make blood clotting in your leg veins more likely, especially if you are prone to these, or are pregnant. Known perhaps unfairly as 'economy-class syndrome', clots forming in the legs is properly called 'deep-venous thrombosis', or DVT. This is a potentially dangerous syndrome, as clots can leave the leg and go to the lungs causing severe illness. Immobility is the key factor, and the overall risk for long-haul travellers is that DVT occurs at about 1 in 6000 people. People at higher risk of DVT include those with underlying clotting disorders, obesity, certain medications, and chronic illness.

Prevention is relatively simple. Wriggle your toes and flex your calves while you're sitting and, as often as you can, get out of your seat, stretch and walk around. All the modern carriers provide instructions for in-flight exercises. Drink plenty of water or fruit juice during the flight to avoid dehydration, and avoid putting bulky luggage at your feet so you can move your feet and legs with relative freedom. Compression socks and stockings are helpful where swelling of legs and feet is likely. If you are known to be prone to blood clotting, you may want to discuss this with your doctor before you leave, as you may need to take low-dose aspirin or an injection of a blood thinner.

Obviously, you'll need to keep any as-needed medications (for example for asthma or angina) readily at hand during any journey, especially a long one.

FLYANA

For an incredibly comprehensive discussion of all the worries you may ever have had about flying and health, check out the web site at **www.flyana.com.** If you can fight your way through the ads and glowing testimonials from grateful users, you can find out all about dehydration, use of insecticide sprays, fear of flying and much, much more. Just bear in mind that the woman behind it all, Diana Fairechild, has something of an axe to grind with the airline industry.

JET LAG

If you're going to be flying across three or more time zones, you may experience jet lag. This term describes a syndrome that long-haul travellers will be all too familiar with: tiredness (but you can't sleep at the new night-time), headache, irritability, difficulty concentrating, loss of appetite and other gut disturbances (such as diarrhoea or constipation). Some of these effects are due to the physical stresses of the flight, like dehydration and immobility, but others are the result of having to reset your body clock to the new time.

Over a 24 hour period, your body shows rhythmical changes in various functions (including body temperature, levels of hormones and blood pressure), which are designed to prime you to be active during the daylight hours and to sleep during night-time. The trouble is that your internal clock takes time to adjust to a new routine. When you fly directly to a new time, there's a temporary mismatch between the time your internal clock thinks it is and the new time at your destination, which results in the set of symptoms we recognise as jet lag.

If you've crossed a few time zones on your flight, jet lag can make you feel below par for up to a week after you arrive. It tends to be more of a problem if you're flying west to east. If you're crossing many time zones, you might want to consider having a stopover, as this can help your body adjust more quickly.

Unfortunately, there's no wonder pill for jet lag and, considering how many different factors are involved in setting and maintaining body rhythms, there's unlikely to be one in the future. However, you can speed up the adjustment process by helping out the *zeitgebers* (don't you love it? It's German for 'timegivers'). These are external influences that impact on your internal rhythms, the most important ones being meal times, sleep times and exposure to bright light. Try the following strategies for reducing the impact of jet lag:

- recognise that jet lag may be a problem in the first few days and adjust your itinerary accordingly. Stopovers, if possible, can be helpful

- on the plane, set your watch to the new destination time and adjust your schedule to this time

- if it's daytime on arrival, get active and don't give yourself the chance to doze off

- eating is a potent time-setter, so try to take all your meals at the appropriate new destination time

- it can be torture, but try to stay awake until at least a reasonable bed time
- if you just can't keep your eyelids open, take a short nap, but beware – set your alarm or get someone to wake you
- the first night's sleep may be a bit fragile, but after that things should improve

Drug remedies you could consider to help your body clock to adjust include sleeping tablets or melatonin. Sleeping tablets can help by enabling you to sleep at the appropriate time, but they can make you feel 'hungover' the next day and are not suitable for everyone.

There's been much excitement about melatonin, a naturally occurring hormone which influences body rhythms. Although melatonin is widely available from naturopathic suppliers, you should be aware that it's not as yet officially sanctioned (which means that it hasn't been fully studied for safety and possible side effects, and the optimum dose hasn't been determined), so it's not available on a medical prescription. If you decide to try it, follow the dosing instructions on the packaging. Melatonin needs to be taken at an appropriate time before sleep (usually about 8 pm at the new time).

Other less practical options (for the desperate only, surely) include mind-bogglingly complicated fasting/food regimens (check out the regimes in *Overcoming Jetlag* by Dr Charles F Ehret & Lynne Waller Scanlon – said to be used by the US Army Rapid Deployment Forces) and bright light exposure via special light bulbs (but try carrying those in your pack).

MOTION SICKNESS

There are plenty of winding roads, diesel fumes, crowded public transport and various less than sweet odours to get you chundering when you're on the move in this part of the world, so take a good supply of motion sickness remedies if you know you're susceptible to this. Children and pregnant women are most likely to get motion sickness, but it can strike anyone.

In case you're fortunate enough not to know, early signs of an impending puke include headaches, dizziness and clammy skin. This is the time to take action. Put this book down...

If you can, fix your eyes firmly on the horizon and keep your head still (for example, brace it against a headrest). If you're below deck on a ship, lie down and close your eyes. If you can, try eating something bland, like a dry biscuit – tasting and smelling a lemon may help. Cigarette smoke is guaranteed to make you feel worse, so avoid it if you can – not always easy in non-Western countries. Place yourself in the most stable part of the vehicle if you can: between the wings on a plane, in the middle of a boat or in the front seat of a car.

You'll find a variety of anti-sickness remedies on the market. Preparations containing ginger or mint (including mint sweets) are helpful, and don't need to be taken in advance. Other remedies need to be taken before you travel. Eating lightly before the journey may also help.

Hyoscine (as tablets or skin patches) is effective for short journeys, but has side effects like dry mouth and blurred vision, and is not suitable for everyone. It's best avoided by children, older people and pregnant women. Hyoscine skin patches are known as Scopoderm in the UK and Transderm-Scop in the US.

Antihistamines (for example cinnarizine, cyclizine, dimen-hydrinate or promethazine, with various brand names; see p401) are longer-lasting and have fewer side effects. They're generally available without prescription. Some antihistamines may make you drowsy, which can be an advantage on a long journey, but you should avoid driving and alcohol if you take them.

Alternatively, you could try something a bit different: special elasticated wristbands are available that work by applying pressure to acupuncture points, or there's a considerably more expensive battery-operated version.

Staying Healthy...

If you thought that staying healthy on your travels is only about getting the right immunisations and a supply of malaria pills, you'll need to think again. Only a few travel-related illnesses, and none of the common problems like sunburn, diarrhoea and infected cuts, are preventable by immunisation. The good news is that you don't need a degree in medical science to stay healthy, just an awareness of the likely problems and some common sense.

- Worried about close encounters with wildlife? Turn to p373 in the Bites & Stings chapter for reassurance.
- Healthy mind, healthy body – for tips on cutting down on the mental stresses of travelling, see the Mental Wellbeing chapter.
- Planning to let your hair down? For some safety tips on alcohol and drugs, see p241.

ACCLIMATISATION

Don't plan on hitting the ground running, especially at the start of a long trip. It's worth taking some time to allow yourself to adjust physically and mentally to your new environment and lifestyle. Factor in some time to take a breather, recover from jet lag and catch up on sleep and perhaps missed meals.

HEAT

If you've gone from a cool, temperate climate back home to a hot tropical one (much of Africa!), give yourself a chance to get used to the heat. Your body has an amazing capacity to adjust to temperature changes, but it doesn't happen overnight. You're probably going to feel hot and easily exhausted for about a week. After this, your body will have made adjustments to cope with the heat, and you'll find your capacity for activity is about back to normal. Never underestimate the dangers of the heat – for a full discussion of the effects of the heat, see the section on Heat in the Climate, Altitude & Action chapter.

GOLDEN OLDIES

We found that much of the following advice, from the Medical Hints section of *Cook's Traveller's Handbook Egypt and the Sudan*, dated 1929, still holds true.

'...With ordinary care the traveller who is not an invalid or already under medical care should need neither physician nor medicine. In summer those who have experience of the country are careful not to drink wine or spirits in any great quantity until after sundown. Headache and sunstroke are common in Egypt. Effectual remedies are cold compresses, warm baths, and rest in a shaded, cool place. Great care should be taken to protect the head and back of the neck with a good broad-brimmed hat or cork or pith helmet...the nape of the neck should always be covered when walking or riding in the sun, even comparatively early in the day, for the sun's rays are powerful, and may cause severe headaches...

Each individual will of course have a good idea of the medicines he most needs, but the following will be generally useful: ginger, bismuth for stomachic [sic] troubles...ammonia for treating the bites of gnats, mosquitoes and scorpions...eau de Cologne, and an emergency flask of liqueur brandy...'

Many people find that they sweat heavily in the heat. You'll need to drink plenty of fluids to replace the amount you're sweating out – cool bottled, boiled or purified water is best, but any not-too-sweet soft drinks, fruit juice or green coconut milk are OK.

- Always have a supply of safe drinking water with you and remind yourself to sip from it regularly while you're out, or stop at lots of drinks stalls.
- Remember that tea, coffee and alcohol all have a diuretic effect (ie they make you lose fluid inappropriately), so go easy on them.

■ Avoid overexerting yourself (and this includes eating a big meal) during the hottest part of the day – it's the perfect time for a siesta or for reading that airport novel.

Physical activity generates heat, which means that your body has to work even harder to stay cool. If you're going on an activity-packed holiday, plan to take it easy during the first week, building up to maximal activity as you acclimatise.

It's probably best to leave those body-hugging Lycra outfits at home for this trip; loose, light-coloured clothing (dark colours absorb the heat more) made of natural fibres like cotton will help protect your skin from the sun without preventing heat loss.

Prickly heat and fungal skin infections are common in the heat, and can be a nuisance. You can help prevent them by washing regularly with water (but not at the expense of the local water supply – shortages are common in desert regions) and carefully drying all those nooks and crannies, especially between your toes.

You'll probably find that your feet and ankles swell in the heat, especially at first, so it's a good idea to take footwear that will accommodate this. For more guidelines on looking after this vital part of your travel equipment, see the section on Feet starting on p97.

SAFE SUN

If you've come to Africa to escape from the gloom of a temperate climate, it can be hard to resist the temptation to stretch out in the sun and make that crawled-out-from-under-a-stone pallor just a distant memory. Unless you've been in a media blackout zone for the last decade or so, you'll know that there's no such thing as a safe suntan. Before you settle in for some serious sun worshipping, take a few steps to limit the potential damage. Remember that the bronzed Adonis of today is the wizened *biltong* of tomorrow...

! Remember to protect yourself during any outdoor activity (especially if you're near water or at altitude), including sightseeing, riding in the backs of open pick-ups or lorries or on top of buses.

So what makes sunlight so deadly? Sunlight or solar energy is made up of radiation of many different wavelengths. The rays in the ultraviolet (UV) part of the spectrum are the bad guys. In the short term, they can cause sunburn (and snow blindness if you're somewhere snowy). This is bad news, but the long-term effects are even scarier:

- skin ageing: wrinkles, crow's feet, liver spots, warty rough areas (solar keratoses), broken veins
- skin cancer, including malignant melanoma (the nastiest type)
- eye problems: cataracts and malignant melanoma of the back of the eye

Sun intensity is affected by many factors, including obvious things like latitude (greater around the equator), time of the year and time of the day (greater at midday). Sun intensity is also increased at altitude and by reflection off sea, snow and buildings. And we're doing our best to destroy the one thing that protects us from the harmful rays: the ozone layer.

Stay pale and interesting by covering up with clothes and wearing a hat. These provide by far the best protection from harmful rays (much better than any sunscreen). A wide-brimmed hat (or a Legionnaire's cap with a neck protector – oh so flattering, but effective) keeps damaging rays off all those easily forgotten bits: nose, ears, back of the neck, bald patch... Protect your eyes with sunglasses that block out UV rays. You could consider wearing a 'sunsuit' on the beach. These are popular in places like Australia, where skin cancer rates are among the highest in the world, and are ideal for kiddies.

The sun is generally at its fiercest between 11 am and 3 pm, so it makes sense to spend this time resting in the shade or indoors. Only mad dogs and Englishmen...

Note the following traps for the unwary:

- sunscreens need to be applied 20 to 30 minutes before going into the sun and reapplied frequently after that, especially after swimming

- you can get sunburnt through water (for example if you're snorkelling), so take care to cover up with a T-shirt and use plenty of water-resistant sunscreen
- how hot it is doesn't make any difference to whether you'll burn – you can still get burnt on a cold day if the sun is shining
- you can burn on a cloudy day because clouds still let through some UV radiation; and you can burn in the shade from reflected light, especially off water

SUNSCREEN

These products increase the length of time you can stay in the sun before you burn by reducing the amount of harmful radiation that penetrates the skin. The SPF (sun protection factor) rating is a rough guide to how long you can last without burning, but don't rely too much on it. Laboratory conditions are no match for the realities of beach life. It's probably best to start with the highest SPF you can find (ideally 30+). Check that it blocks out both UVA and UVB (usually labelled as 'broad spectrum').

A suntan is a layer of skin pigment called melanin formed in response to sunlight on your skin. It can protect against sunburn, but not against the ageing effects of the sun. It takes two to three weeks before a suntan can provide good protection against sunburn, although there is evidence that having a suntan doesn't protect you from the harmful effects of the sun's rays.

If you do decide you want to tan, make sure you allow your skin to tan slowly without burning, starting with 15 or 20 minutes exposure a day, increasing this gradually. As soon as your skin starts to feel sore or look red, head for the shade.

Remember that while freckles may be cute, they're also a sign that you've had too much sun.

COLD

Although you probably associate Africa more with heat than the opposite extreme, be aware that cold and unpredictable weather are significant hazards in many highland areas, including the Atlas Mountains in North Africa, the Simien Mountains in Ethiopia, the Rwenzoris, highland areas of Malawi and the Drakensbergs in South Africa, as well as obvious risk areas like Kilimanjaro and Mt Kenya. Protect yourself from this hazard by making sure you're always prepared for the worst possible weather, even if you're on a day trip or just planning to cross the mountains on your way somewhere. For more details on the effects of excess cold and how to prevent them, see the section on Cold in the Climate, Altitude & Action chapter.

ALTITUDE

This is an environmental challenge you need to take into account if you are planning on trekking in any of Africa's admittedly few high places (by 'high' we mean over about 2500m). Kilimanjaro and Mt Kenya are popular treks that take you to altitudes at which you are at risk of altitude sickness. Be aware that a few travellers a year die from the effects of altitude in Africa – make sure it's not you. For a more detailed discussion of this issue see the section on Altitude in the Climate, Altitude & Action chapter later in this book.

FOOD & WATER PRECAUTIONS

SAFE FOOD

+ As well as eating safely, staying healthy is also about eating properly – for more details, see the Diet & Nutrition section at the end of this chapter.

It's generally agreed that food, not water, is the most common source of gut troubles in travellers. The impressive list of diseases you can get in this way includes most forms of diarrhoea, including dysentery, hepatitis A and E and typhoid (not common in travellers generally but relatively more common if you're travelling in North Africa).

The fact is that you can get sick from food anywhere, but it's more likely when you're travelling. Inadequate or nonexistent sewage systems in many of the less developed nations in Africa, coupled with high levels of disease in the population, makes it much more likely that food, utensils and hands are going to be contaminated with disease-causing microorganisms, mainly from faeces. For example, if a fly lands on your food in many Western countries, it probably hasn't had a chance to wipe its feet on a pile of faeces beforehand, but this isn't true in many African countries.

Travelling usually means you're eating out three meals a day for perhaps weeks on end, relying on other people to prepare your food safely. Most countries in Africa don't have enforceable food safety standards (although even in countries with supposedly high food safety standards, like Australia, outbreaks of food poisoning occur with alarming regularity).

Microorganisms love hot, humid climates, and will multiply gleefully in food left sitting around in these conditions, especially if power shortages (common in most less developed parts of Africa) mean refrigeration is inadequate.

You can build up immunity to some diarrhoeal diseases, but you can't build up immunity to many of the more serious diseases (like dysentery or food poisoning) or to parasites (like hookworm), so it's worth taking a few precautions to minimise your risks. However, advice on safe food can seem unrealistic at best and ludicrous at worst. Examine the cook's fingernails before wolfing down your *matoke* and beans? Throw away your *brochette* because a fly landed on it? Get real...

STREET FOOD

Whether or not to eat 'street food' is one of those classic travellers conundrums. By street food we mean all those tasty-looking (and sometimes not-so-tasty-looking) morsels that assail you on all sides when you walk down the main drag in just about any African town – brochettes, roast yam, fried dough balls, chapattis and so on. Your common sense may be telling you that most street vendors probably don't have access to adequate (if any) washing facilities or toilets, and they certainly can't afford the best ingredients. And you can't really expect your average street vendor in Africa to be up with the latest food hygiene practices. On the other hand...street food is ubiquitous in much of Africa, and arguably very much part of the travel experience. It's definitely your call, but you can minimise the undoubted risks by careful selection, following the guidelines we give in the Safe Food section.

We can't tell you exactly what to avoid in every situation in every country because there are so many variables, but we can give you some guidelines to help you decide what's likely to be less safe. It's down to common sense, plus a little background knowledge.

- Heating kills germs, so food that's served piping hot is likely to be safer than lukewarm or cold food, especially if it's been sitting around; note that freezing doesn't kill germs.

- Fruit and vegetables are difficult to clean (and may be contaminated where they are grown), but they should be safe if they're peeled or cooked.

- Well cooked meat and seafood should be OK; raw or lightly cooked meat and seafood can be a source of parasites in many areas.

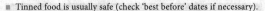

- Tinned food is usually safe (check 'best before' dates if necessary).

- You'll be delighted to know that all forms of bread and cakes are usually safe, although it's best to avoid cream-filled goodies if you can, as bugs like salmonella love cream.

- Popular eating places have an incentive to provide safe food to keep the customers coming.

- Your stomach's natural defences (mainly acid) can cope with small amounts of contaminated foods – if you're not sure about something, don't pig out on it!

And a few cautions:

- the more food has been handled (eg peeled, sliced or arranged), the more likely it is to have been contaminated by unwashed hands

- good food can be contaminated by dirty dishes, cutlery or utensils; blenders or pulpers used for fruit juices are often suspect

- food that looks and smells delicious can still be seething with disease-causing microorganisms

- hot spices don't make food safe, just more palatable

- salads are best avoided because they are hard to clean adequately and they are often contaminated with dirt, which can contain disease-causing microorganisms

- unpasteurised milk and dairy products should be avoided, as they can transmit lots of diseases including TB, brucellosis and salmonella. Pasteurised milk is available throughout South Africa and in major cities in other countries but milk is likely to be unpasteurised in rural areas. If necessary, boiling unpasteurised milk makes it safe to drink

- fruit juices and other drinks may be diluted with unsafe water

- be wary of food, including ice cream, that has been kept frozen; if power cuts are a feature, the food may have thawed and then been refrozen

- avoid raw meat and seafood – find out why by turning to the section on p164

DRUGS TO PREVENT DIARRHOEA?

Before you get your hopes up too high, you should know this isn't an option for most travellers and is just not practical for long-term travellers. However, in some situations, it may be advisable, for example if you have a preexisting condition (eg HIV infection or inflammatory bowel disease) that makes it particularly important for you to avoid illness, or if you're a businessperson on a short trip.

The two main possibilities are antibiotics or bismuth subsalicylate (trade name Pepto Bismol), which is not an antibiotic. Although some antibiotics have been shown to be effective in preventing diarrhoea in travellers, there are concerns that this may make antibiotic resistance more likely; there's also a risk of side effects. Bismuth subsalicylate works by reducing the amount of fluid your gut produces in response to toxins from bugs. It comes in liquid form (60ml four times daily) but tablets are more practical for most travellers (take two tablets four times daily). It's a possibility to consider (and preferably to discuss with your doctor first) if you are on a short trip, although it's not suitable for everyone – see the section on p402 for more details. The current cholera vaccine also has a limited effect on preventing travellers diarrhoea, an effect that lasts for two months or so.

 Alternative remedies that have been recommended for prevention of travellers diarrhoea include lacto-bacillus (the bacteria in live natural yoghurt) and slippery elm capsules, or you could try taking a general 'immune-booster' like echinacea.

CLEAN HANDS

Before you skip over this uninspiringly titled but surprisingly important section, we're talking about washing your hands before you eat. Obvious perhaps, but in Western countries we've been able to become complacent or perhaps just lazy about this because we have efficient waste disposal systems and (usually) safe, plentiful water supplies.

Many of the diseases you associate with tropical countries (eg dysentery, typhoid and hepatitis) are actually diseases of poor hygiene rather than 'tropical' diseases. So it's worth reminding yourself to wash your hands before you eat and always after using the toilet. This is particularly important if you're eating with your hands. Short fingernails are easier to keep clean than long ones. It's a good idea to take your own utensils (plastic cup, bowl, spoon) with you so you can use them for street food or eating meals on trains.

Try to remember to keep your hands away from your mouth and eyes, especially on public transport, as you can introduce infection in this way.

It's tempting to assume that because environmental hygiene is poor due to lack of infrastructure and resources, personal cleanliness will also be poor. But it's worth observing local customs and perhaps adopting them yourself if they make sense to you, eg not letting your mouth touch a shared drinking vessel (pour the water into your mouth). The widespread custom in Africa of using one hand (usually the left) for toilet duty and the other for eating is a sensible habit to adopt, and you might want to practise both of these at home first.

SAFE DRINKING WATER

The problem with water is that not only can *you* not live without it, neither can all sorts of disease-causing bugs. Although contaminated food is probably the most important source of gut infections when you're travelling in Africa, contaminated water is also a major source of illness, including diarrhoea, dysentery, hepatitis and typhoid.

In countries with good infrastructure and resources, communal water supplies are generally safe from contamination, but you can't rely on this in most countries in Africa; exceptions include Namibia, South Africa and Tunisia. Water mains supplies in Egypt are chlorinated but can be fairly unpalatable.

Elsewhere, it's best to assume the worst. There's often contamination of the water supply at some point, usually by human or animal sewage. Never assume that water from rivers, streams or lakes is safe, as even in relatively unpopulated areas it can be contaminated by animals – or trekkers.

For most countries in Africa, this means not drinking tap water and not brushing your teeth in it. Ice is obviously only as safe as the water it's made from, so it's best to avoid this too. If you're desperate for a cool drink, seal the ice in a plastic bag before putting it in your drink – but make sure the bag is clean first. Alcohol has some disinfectant properties, but at drinking strength it won't make water safe to drink. Consider carrying your own cup if the available cups look suspect.

How you deal with the water issue depends on where you are and what sort of travelling you're doing. Drinking bottled water is one obvious option, and it's generally widely available in Africa. But remember that the quality of some local brands is little better than tap water, and plastic bottles can be refilled with any old water and sold to unsuspecting travellers. As a general rule, it's best to stick to major brands of bottled water, preferably with serrated tops; always check the seal carefully.

However, the cost of bottled water can add up over a long trip, especially if you're travelling in hot climates, and there's a very real concern over the environmental – and aesthetic – effect of millions of discarded and unrecycled plastic bottles. If you're trekking or travelling off the beaten track, bottled water is a less practical option anyway.

You have three main alternatives: boiling water, chemical disinfectants and water purifiers.

CLEAN WATER

As you sip your clean, bottled water, spare a thought for the many Africans for whom clean and safe water is an unimaginable luxury. This basic and enormously important need is being addressed by aid organisations and governments but there's still a long way to go. For example, Medecins Sans Frontieres has recently set up a water and sanitation program in Amukoko, a suburb of Lagos, Nigeria, where 300,000 people live in rudimentary shelters with no running water or toilets and no waste collection system. Drinking water is mostly supplied by water sellers who obtain water, usually contaminated from leaked pipes, by illegally tapping the mains supply. MSF is tackling this problem by raising awareness among the people of Amukoko of the importance of clean drinking water and good hygiene practices.

Boiling

The simplest and most effective way of making water safe to drink is to boil it, which kills all disease-causing bugs. You just need to bring it to a rolling boil for a minute or two and then let it cool – prolonged boiling is not necessary. Water boils at lower temperatures at high altitude; this is not likely to be a problem at the altitudes you're going to be reaching, but to be absolutely sure you could let it boil for about five minutes in these circumstances.

Chemical Disinfectants

If boiling doesn't sound like a practical option, it's easy to disinfect clear water with chemicals. Chlorine and iodine are the chemicals most widely used. Both are available in tablet form, and iodine is also available as a liquid (add five drops of 2L tincture of iodine to every litre of water) or as crystals you can make up into a liquid. If you're dealing with *Giardia*, a higher concentration is required.

Follow the manufacturer's instructions and remember that you need to leave the water for about 20 minutes before it's safe to drink, or longer (an hour or two) if the water is really cold. Chlorine is generally less reliable than iodine, as it is more likely to be affected by factors such as water alkalinity. Note that iodine can cause thyroid problems if used continuously over a long time (more than six weeks), and you'll need to avoid it if you're pregnant or have thyroid problems. It's not suitable for children under 12 years of age. Silver tablets are also available, but they are not effective against parasite cysts so they shouldn't be used without filtration.

The taste of chemically treated water can be a major turn-off, but there are ways of neutralising this. Charcoal resins or a carbon filter can remove the taste and smell of chemicals, or you can add ascorbic acid (vitamin C) to the iodine-treated water. Remember only to add these after the treated water has been allowed to stand for the required length of time.

Remember: if the water is cloudy, chemicals won't be effective because organic matter tends to neutralise the chemical – you'll need to filter the water first.

Water Filters & Purifiers

No, you don't need to be a rocket scientist to understand what these devices do – it's actually pretty straightforward. Any travel equipment suppliers worth their salt will be able to tell you all you need to know about the products they supply, but it's worth having an idea beforehand of what you're looking for.

Not sure about the terminology? Simple filters are just sieves or strainers and their effectiveness depends on how fine they are. Generally they don't make water safe to drink without further treatment (boiling or disinfectant chemicals), as they don't remove the smallest disease-causing bugs (viruses and some bacteria), although fine-pore ceramic filters are exceptions.

Purifiers are dual action: they filter water and disinfect it (eg with an iodine resin).

Filters and purifiers can be gravity or pump action. Pump action is probably the more realistic option unless you have plenty of time on your hands, but can be hard work. Water purifiers often contain a carbon filter to remove traces of chemicals used to disinfect the water, but note that using carbon on its own does not make water safe to drink.

Things you might want to consider before buying any device include:

- what does it claim to remove? Does it make water totally safe to drink?

- what do you want to use it for? Some devices are suitable for occasional or emergency use, whereas others are good for continuous use over a long period of time

- what's the flow rate like? You don't want to pump for two hours for a sip of water

- how portable/breakable is it? Ceramic filters are very effective, but need a bit of care as they crack

- how often does the filter need to be replaced? Filters can get clogged and there's a risk of bacterial growth occurring in them, so they usually need to be cleaned or replaced after a while

- how easy is it to take apart and clean if it becomes clogged?

- is it endorsed by an independent organisation?

There are some interesting variations available, such as a filter that fits onto a tap and a straw (for reaching those inaccessible puddles...), so it's worth shopping around to find what you want. Water filters and purifiers are available from most major travel health clinics and from outdoor equipment suppliers, often by mail order. Alternatively, a search on the internet brings up a heap of possibilities.

Make sure you have more than one means of purifying water in case one method fails (eg take some iodine as well as a pump action purifier).

! Even if you're using a water purifier, try to choose the cleanest water source possible, and never drink water from rivers, lakes or wells without purifying it first.

INSECTS & PARASITES

✚ For the complete low-down on little – and large – critters that bite and sting, see the Bites & Stings chapter later in this book.

INSECT BITES

Small bloodsuckers tend to rate highly in the travellers 'most hated' list. The itch and discomfort from their bites is enough

HEALTH BOOSTERS

Travel can involve many stresses healthwise, leaving you vulnerable to illness at a time you could really do without it. One way to help avoid problems is by making sure you are as fit and healthy as possible before you go. Many travellers, however, take the additional precaution of boosting their body's powers to fight off infection with natural remedies. You'll probably find it helpful to consult a practitioner to get individually tailored advice, but here's a rundown of some of the options available. Follow the dosing instructions on the packaging or your practitioner's advice, and remember to take basic food and water precautions as well.

• Acidophilus – one of a number of 'probiotics', this bacteria is present in live natural yoghurt and is claimed to have a beneficial effect on the balance of bacteria in the intestine; it's popularly used by travellers to prevent diarrhoea, although some experts question whether the bacteria would survive the acid conditions in the stomach.

to drive anyone up the wall, but to add insult to injury, a handful of insects are responsible for transmitting a variety of serious and not so serious diseases. In Africa, these include:

- mosquitoes – malaria, dengue fever, filariasis, yellow fever
- ticks – typhus, relapsing fever and other fevers
- lice – typhus
- flea – plague
- sandfly – leishmaniasis, sandfly fever
- tsetse fly – trypanosomiasis (sleeping sickness)
- blackfly – onchocerciasis (river blindness)

- **Aloe vera** – an immune enhancer when taken by mouth, this widely available plant also has antiseptic properties when applied topically.
- **Cat's claw** – originally from the Latin American rainforest, this herb is said to have antiinflammatory and antioxidant properties.
- **Echinacea** – the top-selling herb in the US, this is a good, readily available (back home at least) general immune-booster.
- **Garlic** – popular immune booster; often comes in combination with horseradish.
- **Glutamine** – this amino acid is needed for the immune system to function properly.
- **Grapefruit seed extract** – said to have anti-bacterial, antifungal and antiviral activity, this is recommended for intestinal and other infections.
- **L-arginine** – an amino acid involved in immune function, and promotes wound healing.
- **Vitamin C** – cheap and readily available in many different forms.

The risks of meeting a disease-carrying insect vary to a certain extent depending on where you're headed, but it obviously makes sense wherever you go to make sure you don't get bitten by any of these bloodsuckers. Immunisations are currently not available against any of the diseases listed. Don't let yourself get bitten, and you won't get any of these diseases.

Use chemical repellents and physical barriers (clothes, nets, screening) to minimise your chances of getting bitten. Biting insects are attracted by the most surprising things, including body heat, chemicals in your sweat, perfumes, soap and types of clothing. Most mosquitoes are night-biters, but some (such as the mosquito that transmits dengue) bite mainly during the day.

Beat the little vampires with the following measures:

- cover up with long-sleeved tops and long trousers or skirt; light-coloured clothing is thought to be less attractive to mosquitoes than dark colours

- use insect repellents on any exposed areas; if you're using sunscreen or other lotions, apply insect repellent last, and reapply after swimming if necessary; note that insect repellent may reduce the protection of a sunscreen

- sleep in a screened room or, if this is not possible (quite likely), sleep under a treated mosquito net. Always cover children's beds or cots with treated mosquito nets; air-conditioned rooms are usually insect-free zones

- remember day-biting mosquitoes, and avoid shady conditions in the late afternoon or taking an afternoon siesta without the protection of a mosquito net

- spray your room or tent with an insect spray before you retire for the night to get rid of any lurking insects

- consider using electric insecticide vaporisers or mosquito coils which you burn – both are widely available in Africa, but you need a power socket for a vaporiser, and both are less effective if you have a fan going

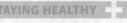

There are many insect repellent products on the market, but the most effective are those containing the compound DEET (diethyltoluamide) – check the label or ask your pharmacist to tell you which brands contain DEET. These include Rid, Doom, Jungle Formula and Repel.

DEET is very effective against mosquitoes, midges, ticks, bedbugs and leeches, and slightly less effective against flies. One application should last up to four hours, although if it's very humid or you're very sweaty, it may not last as long. Basically, the higher the concentration, the longer it will last, with around 50% being optimal, although there are some longer acting formulations with lower strengths of DEET. Remember to try a test dose before you leave to check for allergy or skin irritation.

If you're worried about the safety of DEET, be reassured: it's generally agreed that safety concerns over DEET are largely unfounded. However, for children, it's probably best to err on the cautious side. Choose a lower strength long-acting cream.

 You may prefer to use one of the new lemon eucalyptus-based natural products, which have been shown to be an effective alternative to DEET, with similar action times (although DEET is probably still your best bet in high-risk areas). Other natural repellents include citronella and pyrethrum, but these tend to be less effective and to have a short action (up to an hour), making them less practical to use.

Cotton bands soaked in insect repellent can be useful to wear on your wrists and ankles (especially ankles, as these are a prime target for mosquitoes), and the repellent won't rub off as easily.

Taking vitamin B1 (thiamine), garlic or brewer's yeast have all been advocated as making you less attractive to insects (but be aware that they haven't been shown to work in trials). They may be worth a try, in conjunction with insect repellents on exposed areas. Electronic buzzing devices have not been shown to be effective.

Permethrin is an effective insecticide that can be applied to clothes and mosquito nets. It repels and kills mosquitoes, fleas, ticks, mites, bedbugs, cockroaches and flies. If you're planning on trekking through tick-infested areas (rainforests, scrubland, pastures), consider treating your clothes, particularly trousers and socks, with permethrin before you go.

! Permethrin-treated clothes plus DEET application to the skin is considered to give the best level of protection against mosquitoes.

The quality of screening and nets provided by accommodation in Africa varies from nonexistent to positively airtight, but beware – there always seems to be at least one mosquito-sized hole in any net or screen. For most of tropical Africa, it's worth taking your own net with you, especially one that has been soaked in permethrin. Most travel-equipment suppliers have a wide variety of mosquito nets to suit your individual needs, and most nets are very light and don't take up much room in a pack. If you don't want to bother with finding ways to put your net up, consider taking a stand-alone version (Long Road is one supplier; contact it on ☎ 800-359-6040 in the USA or web site **www.longroad.com**).

SCHISTOSOMIASIS (BILHARZIA)

This parasitic disease is a significant risk to you in most parts of Africa (see map p25). It's caused by a tiny worm that lives in freshwater snails for part of its life cycle and in humans for the second part. For a full description of the disease, including the symptoms and diagnosis, see the section on p337.

Schistosomiasis can be treated but it's best not to get infected in the first place. In risk areas, you should take precautions to avoid it. You can get schistosomiasis if you swim, wade, paddle, wash or do water sports in fresh water, so you it's sensible to:

■ avoid swimming in fresh water in risk areas, whatever locals tell you – local hotel operators have their livelihoods to consider, not your health

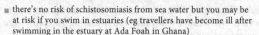

- there's no risk of schistosomiasis from sea water but you may be at risk if you swim in estuaries (eg travellers have become ill after swimming in the estuary at Ada Foah in Ghana)

- you don't just have to swim in the water to be at risk – paddling, crossing streams and water sports that involve immersion in water are risky

- wear waterproof footwear to cross waterways if necessary

- although infection is less likely, you are still at risk further offshore, eg if you swim from a boat

- if you do get wet, dry off quickly, as the disease-causing worms can't survive long out of water

- snail-free, chlorinated swimming pools are safe, but stagnant water is especially dangerous (eg a lake behind a dam)

- resist the temptation to dive into an oasis after a hot desert safari – you may not be the first visitor

- if you're using water to wash in, either boil and chlorinate it or keep it in a snail-free container for at least two days (the infective worms die off in 48 hours if they don't reach a human)

- boil or chlorinate all drinking water as you can get schistosomiasis by drinking affected water

ACCIDENTS & INJURY

It's time to mention the 'D' word. It might come as a surprise to you, but the commonest cause of death in younger travellers is accidents, not nasty tropical illnesses (for older people it's preexisting illnesses like heart disease). Accidents are the main reason for needing a blood transfusion or other medical treatment, with all the potential for problems that this entails, including HIV and hepatitis B infection.

When you're on holiday, you tend to take all sorts of risks you probably would not dream of taking at home – it's part of what makes travelling so exciting. But remember that you're not immune from danger just because you're on holiday in a tropical paradise. Accidents are, well, just that, and they can and do happen. If they depend on your actions, they're preventable to a certain extent, especially if you're aware of the risks.

While we don't want to rain on your beach party, just be aware that alcohol and other mind-altering substances are major factors in accidents of all types in travellers, from dignity-challenging falls to life-threatening road traffic accidents.

So now that we've thoroughly depressed you, what steps can you take to ensure you come back in one piece? Accidents are preventable to a great extent, especially if you're aware of the potential risks. A little common sense goes a long way towards preventing accidents.

ROAD SAFETY

Much has been written in travel guidebooks and elsewhere about the alarmingly low road safety standards in Africa, from the unbelievably congested traffic chaos of Cairo, the suicidal maniacs who appear to drive most of West Africa's bush taxis to the dangerously competitive *matatu* wars of East Africa. Pedestrians, vehicle passengers and, especially, motorcycle riders are all at risk.

They may be obvious, but the following safety measures may help:

- avoid alcohol when driving, even if there are no laws to break
- use a seat belt if possible and resist the temptation to go as fast as the other lunatics
- wear a helmet and protective clothing if you're riding a bicycle, motorcycle or moped – shorts and T-shirt don't provide much protection against road rash if you come off
- check that your hire car has the minimum safety features – like brakes
- avoid travelling at night, which can be tricky in the best of conditions and entails all sorts of unexpected hazards

Public transport can be risky in most parts of Africa, as a lack of resources and the need to make a living have to take precedence over basic safety considerations. But while it's all very well for us to advise you to choose the safest vehicle you can, often you have little choice in the matter.

BEACH SAFETY

Africa's magnificent coastline is a major drawcard for tourists, but beaches pose many hazards for the unwary. Drowning is a common cause of death in travellers, especially children and young adults. Even strong swimmers get taken by unexpectedly strong currents, for example on West Africa's Atlantic coast. Lifeguards and safety notices aren't generally part of the scene on most African beaches, except in South Africa, so don't rely on them to keep you safe. In most places you'll be on your own if you get into trouble. It's obvious but:

- check locally for advice on currents and safe swimming hazards– just because there are no warning signs doesn't necessarily mean it's safe
- play safe and avoid going in if you're unused to surf or you're unsure of your swimming capabilities
- never run and dive in the water, even if you've checked the depth before, in case it's unexpectedly shallow
- don't swim straight after a meal, as you are more likely to get cramps
- don't swim if you've had alcohol or other mind-altering substances
- wear shoes to protect your feet from injury
- check the beach for sharp objects and soft objects before you sit down – many beaches double as public toilets and general dumping grounds
- some marine creatures can sting or bite – check locally but don't touch anything you don't recognise

FIRE & FIXTURES

Fire is another obvious hazard, particularly in countries where smoking is a national pastime. Never smoke in bed. Any self-respecting phobic will work out well in advance potential escape routes from a hotel room.

Balconies are a notable hazard for the unwary and the inebriated – stay well away from the edge.

HAZARDS OF WAR

It's hard not to associate Africa with war – the civil war in Rwanda and ongoing conflicts in Sudan, Guinea-Bissau and the Democratic Republic of Congo are just some of the problems to have hit the headlines in recent years. It obviously makes sense for you to avoid problem areas, but in some parts of the continent you may be at risk from the legacy of past conflicts: undetonated mines, mortars and bombs.

Egypt has the highest numbers of undetonated mines, mostly as a result of WWII, but because mines are mostly in remote border areas, they have not caused the sort of devastation they might have in more populated areas. Angola tops the league table of countries worst affected by mines, with an estimated 20 million of them. Other affected countries include Eritrea, Mozambique, Sudan, Ethiopia and Namibia. This isn't a complete list, so you should check your guidebook, and US State Department or UK Foreign Office Travel Advisories, as well as locally, for more information about risk areas in your destination. You're unlikely to wander through minefields if you stick to usual tourist routes, but take extreme care if you are going off the beaten track in affected countries, especially near border areas. Bear in mind some basic guidelines:

- never stray from well marked paths and stick to the main tourist attractions in badly affected countries like Angola
- if you accidentally wander into a mined area, retrace your steps if you can clearly see them; otherwise, stay where you are and call for help

- never touch any war relics you may come across, especially one that looks even remotely like a mine
- don't rush in to help a mine victim, as there may be other mines nearby; find someone who knows how to safely enter a mined area

You may be aware of several high-profile campaigns aimed at tackling this important humanitarian issue. Mines have far-reaching effects, long after the original conflict is past. They not only kill many thousands of innocent people each month, but also have a huge social and medical cost. For more information on how you may be able to help, contact the International Committee of the Red Cross (☎ 22 734 6001), 19 avenue de la Paix, CH-1202 Geneva, Switzerland; or your national Red Cross Crescent Branch; or check out its web site at **www.icrc.org**. There are also national organisations working locally to cope with the effects of landmine injuries.

FEET

Chris Wheeler, Melbourne-based podiatrist (when he's not off road-testing his own advice), has the following to say about that most vital piece of travel equipment – your feet.

To paraphrase the sage: 'while travel makes the heart grow fonder, it is true that the smile comes from the feet'. Your feet come in for a lot of wear and tear when you're travelling, and even relatively minor afflictions can make your life a misery. The good news is that with just a bit of care you can avoid most problems.

FOOTWEAR
If you're not going too far off the beaten track, your best bet is likely to be light-weight walking shoes (the next step up from

running shoes). These are supportive where they need to be (around the heel), cushioned where they should be (under the base of the heel and under the ball of the foot) and allow the foot to bend where it's happiest to. Most importantly, you have a wide range of brands to choose from so you can find one that suits the shape of your foot best. Unless you're planning on trekking, it's probably best to avoid serious hiking boots because they're heavy and stiff. Open footwear such as sandals or thongs are tempting in a hot climate, but they leave your feet open to injury (and subsequent infection), and over a long period of time they can cause your skin to dry out, giving you cracked and painful heels.

FOOT HYGIENE

Try to make sure you wash your feet once a day, and dry them carefully, especially between the toes. If you're a sweaty foot person, consider wiping between the toes with methylated spirits (pre-injection swabs are available from pharmacists and won't take up much space in your medical kit).

If you wear open footwear, you can help prevent cracked heels by using a skin-softening agent (any simple moisturiser will do) and a pumice stone to remove dry skin.

Deliciously soothing foot sprays, moisturisers and balms are available for tired feet – well worth the extra weight in your pack.

BLISTERS

The scourge of hikers, blisters occur when there is repeated friction to the skin. Prevention is all-important. Make sure your footwear is well worn in before you set off sightseeing or on a hike. At the very least, wear them on a few short walks before you leave – don't plan to wear them in for the first time while you are away. Your boots should fit comfortably with enough room to move your toes, and be sure your socks fit properly. If you're going to be doing lots of walking, it's worth investing in socks specifically made for walkers. Socks made from a synthetic fibre called orlon have been shown to decrease the size and frequency of blisters. Wet and muddy socks can also cause blisters, so slip a spare pair of socks in your daypack and change your socks when necessary. Keep your toenails clipped, but not too short.

If you do feel a blister coming on, take immediate action. Apply a simple sticking plaster or preferably one of the special blister plasters which act as a second skin, and follow the instructions on the packaging for replacement. 'Second skin' products reduce the shearing forces that cause blisters. You could try stretching the offending part of the shoes or wearing a different pair of socks.

If you're planning on going on a hike and you haven't time to toughen the skin of your feet up by graduated walking, you could consider soaking your feet in a weak solution of potassium permanganate for 20 minutes daily (add a teaspoon of crystals to 4L of warm water) to toughen the skin. In the army, new recruits were once told to urinate on their feet to toughen the skin, but this won't endear you to your travelling companions.

A blister won't get infected as long as it is intact. If the blister looks as if it is about to burst or is already broken, apply an antiseptic ointment such as chlorhexidine to reduce the risk of infection and cover it with a thick pad of sterile gauze (preferably over a nonadherent dressing like melolin). If you've got hydrodermic dressings such as Duoderm with you, apply it and leave it in place for seven days or so.

OTHER PROBLEMS

Prevent ingrowing toenails by proper toenail cutting techniques ie use nail clippers to trim the nail straight across (not curved). Gently trim the corners if they are sharp. Corns and calluses can arise from repeated irritation. A callus is where repeated irritation causes the top layer of skin to thicken. If this irritation continues, usually over a bony prominence, the callus will thicken to form a corn. Much like a blister, these are best treated by avoiding the irritation that leads to their formation. Use of a pumice stone will slow the rate of return of a callus, but corns need to be removed by a foot specialist.

SEX & TRAVEL

It seems that not even the runs, rickety beds, paper thin walls, sunburn and sand can dampen the ardour of many travellers. Maybe it's the aphrodisiac properties of the heat, or the feeling of freedom travelling can give. Or is it just the cheap beer? Maybe sex is the reason you're going travelling. Whatever the reason, it makes sense to arm yourself with the facts about your risks of getting a sexually transmitted infection (STI), as well as a pack of condoms. STIs are a worldwide problem.

A sexual encounter with a new partner anywhere carries a risk of HIV or one of the other STIs, but it can be even riskier when you're travelling. This is partly because the countries you're travelling in may have higher infection rates for HIV and STIs than your own, but also because when you're travelling you're more likely to be in contact with people who are at greater risk of being infected. More worrying still, surveys have shown that, in spite of the risks, many travellers don't take precautions to protect themselves.

It's easy to think 'it could never happen to me', but it can and does (sex *and* STIs). Anyone who's having sex can get an STI, 'nice' girls and college boys included. You may think you're safe, for example, because you're not going to have sex with someone in a high-risk group or you're only going to have sex with fellow travellers. Think again. Who has your fellow traveller had sex with before you? Can you trust them to have been as careful or as aware of the risks as you?

Traditionally, high-risk groups are men who have sex with men, people who inject drugs, sex workers, anybody who's had multiple partners and anybody who's had sex with people in these groups. You'll know if you're in the first group, and perhaps you'll recognise and be able to avoid the second and third groups, but are you sure you'd know if someone was in one of the last two groups? It's difficult to be sure of your new partner's sexual history and you may just be getting the edited highlights. 'Sex worker' is a pretty vague category anyway, and starts to look even vaguer when you've included the guy who has sex with women travellers in return for free meals, drinks or status, or an unmarried woman in a country where most women are married or don't go out. You can be fairly sure that you're not going to be the first traveller they've had sex with.

In theory at least, STIs are simple to prevent – don't have sex. But...for many people, risk reduction is a more realistic option. Remember:

- consider safer ways of having casual sex that don't involve intercourse
- always use condoms with any new partner; if you have a regular partner, play fair by making sure you don't transmit an STI to them
- many STIs are passed in an alcoholic haze – try to avoid getting into situations where this might happen
- you never know when you might need a condom, so be prepared – it doesn't mean you have to have sex

We're not suggesting you become a celibate saint, but keep your head out of the clouds – avoid obviously risky situations (use your common sense and don't believe everything your new partner may tell you) and always practise safer sex by using condoms (spermicide is not necessary) with any new sexual partner. If you do slip up while you're away, don't just pretend it never happened and perhaps put yourself and other partners at risk – arrange for a check-up when you get home.

INJECTIONS & BLOOD TRANSFUSIONS

INJECTIONS

If you need an injection or other medical treatment, it'll usually be in hospitals or clinics where staff will be well aware of the importance of adequate sterilisation of equipment. However, in clinics in rural areas, resources may be more limited, and you may be at risk of HIV/AIDS or hepatitis B from inadequately sterilised needles and other medical or dental equipment. As a general rule, it's a good idea to avoid injections and any other procedures that involve breaking the skin.

Carry a few sterile needles and syringes in your medical kit (with an official note to say why you are carrying them) – but this is only useful if you always carry them and are prepared to insist on them being used, if necessary. Pre-packed 'AIDS packs' are available from most travel health clinics and travel equipment suppliers. If you do need an injection, make sure you see the sterile wrapping opened in front of you.

A few points to remember:

- you can minimise your risks of needing medical or dental procedures while you are away by having medical and dental check-ups before you go, and taking good care of yourself while away

- any equipment used for a medical or dental procedure can be contaminated if it is not properly sterilised

- injections tend to be a popular method of administering medicines in Africa – ask if there is a tablet you can take instead

- boiling needles for 20 minutes will inactivate HIV

- never share needles

- acupuncture needles, tattooing and ear, nose or body piercing all carry risks of infection

BLOOD TRANSFUSIONS

The AIDS epidemic has brought this issue into the limelight for travellers, especially in Africa where the levels of HIV/AIDS in some populations are alarmingly high (for more details see the section on HIV/AIDS in Africa on p209) Although transfusion can be lifesaving in certain situations, it's worth remembering that it's a risky procedure wherever you are and this risk rises in Africa, where resources for screening blood are generally extremely limited. Problems associated with blood transfusions include:

- transmission of HIV, malaria, hepatitis B, C and D, and syphilis
- serious reactions if the blood is not matched properly

Reliable sources of blood are only available in some 40 to 50 countries in the world, which is obviously a hugely unsatisfactory – and unfair – situation. Efforts are being made to increase the provision of safe blood throughout the world, but there's a long way to go. Even when blood is screened for all the endemic diseases there's still a risk that early infections will have been missed. In Africa, it's best to assume that no locally screened blood is safe.

Before you get too paranoid, remember that the chances that you will need a blood transfusion while you are away are pretty small. One study estimated that in a two week trip, about one in 10,000 travellers would need a blood transfusion. Your risk obviously increases the longer you are away, and if you are doing 'risky' activities like rock climbing or trekking. It's vital to have adequate medical insurance, covering emergency evacuation if necessary.

Although it's probably down to fate in the end, there's a lot you can do to minimise your risks of needing a blood transfusion:

- take steps to avoid injury, especially road traffic accidents (the most likely reason for needing a blood transfusion if you're otherwise healthy) – see the earlier Accidents & Injury section for details

- try to avoid diseases like malaria and dengue which carry a risk of needing a blood transfusion

- think twice about travelling in less developed countries in Africa if you are pregnant or have a condition that might mean that you need a blood transfusion, eg stomach ulcer

- remember that blood should be transfused only when absolutely necessary, and in many cases non-blood fluids can be used safely instead in the short term – in practice, however, you'll have to rely on someone else's opinion on this

- consider carrying sterile fluids for use in an emergency, although this is not likely to be a practical option unless you are in a very remote area away from medical help

If a blood transfusion is unavoidable, try to make sure it's from as reliable a source as possible – check with your embassy, your travel insurance company, clinics dealing with international travellers, the local Red Cross or Red Crescent Society, or the local expatriate community for safe local sources. You should be able to find a source of adequately screened blood in most major cities.

Check what arrangements your travel insurance company has for providing safe blood and other fluids in an emergency. Alternatively, you might want to consider joining the Blood Care Foundation. This charitable organisation has a global network of blood banks that claim to supply travellers with safe blood and sterile transfusion equipment within 12 hours anywhere in the world, for a membership fee. The Blood Care Foundation (☎ 01732 742 427, fax 451 199) can be contacted at 16 Lonsdale Gardens, Tunbridge Wells, Kent TN1 1NU, UK.

It's a good idea to make a note of your blood type and to keep it with you on your travels.

Your blood group	Blood types you can receive
A	A, O
B	B, O
AB	A, B, AB, O
O	O
rhesus positive	rhesus positive, rhesus negative
rhesus negative	rhesus negative

O rhesus negative blood can be given to anyone, and is known as the universal donor.

There's a useful online summary of the currently accepted guidelines on blood transfusion for international travellers at **www.armchair.com/info/bloodtrf.html**.

DIET & NUTRITION

Eating well is all about making sure you get enough of the right nutrients for you to function at your best, mentally and physically. It also makes you less vulnerable to illness. When you're on the road, your diet may be very different to normal, while a different lifestyle and new activities may mean your nutritional requirements are increased. Activity (eg sightseeing or trekking) and stress can increase your nutritional requirements. If you get sick or injured, you need a good diet to give your body the best chance to combat the illness and for damaged tissues to repair themselves.

Being unfamiliar with local foods may make you less likely to vary your diet and you may be uncertain about their nutritional value. You may skip good things like fresh fruit and vegetables if you're worried about possible effects on your health. If you're on the move all the time, it may be difficult not to miss meals. It can all add up to you feeling below par and being more vulnerable to infection and other illnesses.

In general, with a little bit of effort, it shouldn't be too difficult to make sure you eat a balanced diet in most parts of Africa. However, in some places and in some situations, this might not be so easy. You may find the food unpalatable, and alternatives may be limited. And you can get the budgeting bug so badly that your diet suffers.

EATING THE RIGHT STUFF

Reminds me of my safari in Africa. Somebody forgot the corkscrew and for several days we had to live on nothing but food and water. (WC Fields)

Everybody needs six basics for life: water, carbohydrates, protein, fat, vitamins and minerals. Foods aren't a pure source of just of one type of nutrient – they contain various elements in different quantities, so the best way to make sure you get enough of the right things is to eat a varied diet.

In Africa, the local diet tends to consist of a carbohydrate staple (maize meal, plantains, cassava, rice, potatoes, bread) which you eat with a protein source (meat, fish, beans and pulses) and vegetables. Fresh fruit is widely available, and you'll find bananas everywhere.

If you do find yourself relying on tinned foods (eg if you're trekking), these are generally a poor nutritional substitute for fresh food. You may want to consider taking vitamin and mineral supplements.

You need to eat a variety of foods from each of five core groups:

- bread, other cereals (couscous, rice, maize meal etc), potatoes, yams – eat lots of these, as they provide carbohydrate, fibre, some calcium and iron, and B vitamins

- fruit and vegetables – eat lots of these, they give you vitamin C, carotenes (vitamin A), folates, fibre and some carbohydrate
- milk & dairy products – eat moderate amounts for calcium, zinc, protein, vitamin B12, vitamin B2, vitamin A and vitamin D
- meat, fish; nuts, beans and pulses (lentils) – these provide iron, protein, B vitamins (especially B12; meat only), zinc and magnesium; eat from this group in moderation
- fat and sugar-containing foods (butter, oil, margarine, cakes, biscuits, sweets, soft drinks etc) – eat sparingly from this group, which mainly provides fat, including essential fatty acids, some vitamins, salt

If you're sick, your requirements change, and you may need to increase the amounts of some food groups, eg to build up your intake of protein, vitamins and minerals.

CASSAVA POISONING

Cassava (also called manioc) is a staple food in many parts of Africa. Although this root vegetable naturally contains cyanide, traditional methods of processing it, like drying or fermenting, usually ensure that it is harmless. In hard times, however, people may take shortcuts in the processing, with disastrous results – over a couple of years, 30,000 people in Mozambique are thought to have been affected. Cyanide poisoning results in paralysis of the limbs, which may be permanent, and sometimes blindness.

Vitamins & Minerals

These nutrients are needed in small amounts for many of the processes carried out in your body and are essential for health. Unlike in most African countries, in many developed countries, common foods like bread and breakfast cereals are fortified with vitamins. Vegetables in African main dishes tend to be stewed to death, which leaches out most of the useful vitamins.

Although most nutritionists would agree that it's best to get what you need by varying your diet, when you're travelling there are some situations when it may be a good idea to take multivitamin and mineral supplements. Many vitamins and minerals come from fresh fruit and vegetables, so supplements are a good idea if you think you'll be missing out on them for any reason (eg you're on a long trek or you're travelling somewhere where they are likely to be in short supply).

If you have heavy menstrual periods, especially if you've cut out animal products from your diet, you may need to take multivitamin supplements containing iron to prevent anaemia. If you don't eat any foods of animal origin, you will need to take a vitamin B12 supplement.

Finally, if you're recovering from illness, you might want to give your body a helping hand by taking multivitamin supplements.

Energy & Protein

Complex carbohydrates in the form of starchy staples are the main source of food energy, and they're a big feature of most African diets. Simple sugars are good as instant energy suppliers, but complex carbohydrates are better for providing more sustained energy, as they are broken down more slowly in the body.

Sources of simple sugars include fruit, jam, honey and milk. If you don't have enough carbs in your diet, more protein is used instead, making less available for growth and repair. If your blood sugar gets low, you may start to feel weak, wobbly and headachey, signalling that it's time for that chocolate fix.

Protein is an important component of your diet, but healthy adults only need a small amount of protein daily. Protein is important for growth and repair, so it's vital that growing children get sufficient quantities. Protein can also help with wound healing, so try to increase the amount you are eating if you have been sick.

BUSHMEAT

If you're travelling through rural, forested parts of West and Central Africa, you may see – and be offered – a variety of local wildlife to eat. Bushmeat, as it is called, can include different types of monkeys, deer, elephants and snakes, and is the traditional food of forest dwellers. It's up to you whether or not you decide to try these species, but be aware of some recently highlighted concerns over this source of food. Apart from any aesthetic considerations, many of these species are making an appearance on the endangered list. When they were just hunted locally for the needs of the village population, this was not an issue, but urbanisation and the presence of logging companies has rapidly put the situation out of control. There is a very real danger that many of these animals will be extinct within decades because of deforestation and hunting.

Before tucking into a close relative like the chimpanzee, you might want to reflect on the fact that the AIDS epidemic is thought to have begun when an HIV-like virus made the jump from apes to humans, probably through bushmeat preparation and eating. Outbreaks of Ebola, the most scary of the haemorrhagic fevers, have also been linked to bushmeat preparation.

Good sources of animal protein include meat, fish, poultry, eggs and dairy foods (milk, cheese etc). Non-animal sources include cereals (bread, rice, oats etc), nuts, seeds and pulses (beans, lentils etc).

Fat is the most concentrated source of energy, providing, weight for weight, just over twice as much as carbohydrate or protein. Foods rich in fat include all the obvious things like oil, butter, ghee and any foods cooked in these; meat; egg yolks; many processed and fast foods; and less obvious foods of plant origin like coconut milk, avocado and nuts. Dare we tell you that alcohol provides nearly as much energy as fat?

FADING AWAY?

You may find that you lose weight while you're travelling in Africa, especially if you're on a long trip. There are lots of reasons for this, including getting sick, having a change in diet and perhaps being more active.

You may have a bit of padding to spare, but keep an eye on how much weight you're losing and don't allow yourself to lose too much, as this may put you at risk of illness as well as draining you of energy. If you find you're losing weight and you're eating a vegetarian diet, remember that you generally have to eat larger quantities of plant foods to get the same amount of energy. Increase your quota of energy-giving foods, including fats, and consider taking multivitamin supplements. If you're ill, get medical advice on this. If you have ongoing diarrhoea, you may not be absorbing nutrients properly.

We should point out that probably an equal number of travellers find they put on weight, so don't rely on shedding those extra pounds.

VEGGING OUT

If you've somehow managed to close your eyes to the realities of meat production back home, you may find that wandering through a few African markets brings it up close and personal. Disease-causing bugs love meat, so you may decide to avoid the risk and go veg.

Meat and fish are an integral part of the African diet for those who can afford it but, depending on how strict a vegetarian you are and where you're travelling, it's not too hard to have a reasonably healthy vegetarian diet in Africa – although beans and rice can get a bit monotonous.

FEED ME BUGS

Looking for a protein supplement? Something to provide a crunch to your meal? Try a deep-fried beetle, or if that sounds too crunchy, a juicy mopane worm. Various creepy crawlies you'd probably be happier to examine in a glass case than on your plate are served up as snack food in some parts of Africa. And why not? Insects are a good and readily available source of protein. Bugs you may see in the frying pan include – in ascending order of crunch – midges (handfuls are pressed together to form 'cakes'), ants, stink bugs, grasshoppers and locusts. If you're travelling on public transport, as well as piles of snake-like 'ropes' of prepared cassava (manioc), you may find yourself sitting next to baskets of preciously guarded, silently writhing, fat grubs or mopane worms. These grubs live in the roots of mopane trees and are quite a delicacy. They're usually eaten when still alive – bite off the head and let the juicy body slide down your throat.

If you've just turned vegetarian, be aware that your body takes a bit of time to adjust to getting some nutrients from plant sources, so take a bit of care with your diet. Getting enough protein isn't generally a problem, especially if you eat eggs (eg omelettes are available everywhere), although dairy products like cheese can be difficult to find outside major towns. Peanuts are used widely in West African cooking in particular, and you'll see piles of ground peanuts in markets everywhere.

Note that proteins from plant sources are often deficient in one or more amino acids (the building blocks of protein). Most traditionally vegetarian diets have dealt with this by basing meals around a combination of protein sources so that deficiencies are complemented. Examples of combinations include pulses and rice (beans or lentils and rice), pulses and cereal (chickpeas and couscous) and nuts and cereal (nut butter on bread).

Because iron from plant sources is less well absorbed than iron from meat, iron deficiency anaemia is a risk if you aren't careful, especially if you're menstruating. You might not get enough vitamin B12, as it's only derived from animal sources. If you cut out all animal foods from your diet, you'll need to take a supplement to make up for this.

Good plant sources of nutrients include:

- protein – pulses, bread, grains, seeds (eg sesame), potatoes
- calcium (for healthy bones) – seeds, green leafy vegetables, nuts, bread, dried fruit (eg apricots)
- iron – pulses, green vegetables, dried fruits, nuts, plain chocolate; you can improve absorption of iron by having a source of vitamin C (eg fruit, fruit juice or vegetables) at the same time; conversely tea, coffee, and phytate and oxalates from plants will reduce the absorption of iron

FOOD FOR ACTION

Food is fuel, and if you're active you need lots of it. For example, you can use up to 4000KCal a day if you're active in a temperate climate. You need more energy to keep warm in a cold climate, when you might need up to 5000KCal a day. There's nothing worse than trying to keep going on an empty stomach. If you are going trekking and you have to carry all your food with you, you will need to balance up the weight, bulk and energy-giving properties of what's available. Keep in mind that if you're going on a long-ish hike, you'll want to have some variety in what you eat. Tinned food and fresh fruit tend to be out for all but short trips. Take enough for three main meals a day plus lots of between-meal snacks. On top of this, it's a good idea to have an emergency stash with you just in case.

What you take depends on what's available locally and whether you are taking stuff from home. Dehydrated meals are a camping stalwart, if not exactly a favourite, but may not be available in many areas. Good snack foods that you shouldn't have trouble getting hold of include dried fruit (eg apricots and dates, which are good sources of vitamins and iron too), nuts, chocolate and biscuits. Good protein sources are nuts, dried chickpeas and other pulses, lentils, tinned meats and fish. Make sure you include plenty of starchy foods for energy.

BANANARAMA

Bananas are big in Africa. You'll see them everywhere, in many different shapes and sizes. Not only are bananas an integral part of the diet – and landscape – every part of the banana tree is put to good use. You'll see banana leaves used to shield heads from the rain, to eat from, as containers, to make huts and the fibre is used as rope. You won't forget your first glimpse of the astonishingly voluptuous banana flower. Different varieties include standard yellow bananas, intriguingly apple-scented red ones, tiny finger-like sweet yellow ones, and the ubiquitous green ones, plantains. The yellower they are, the sweeter they taste as the starch is converted to sugar. Plantains need to be cooked before they are edible; they can be boiled, mashed or fried in deep orange palm oil, and are widely used as a starchy staple around which meals are based. You'll see plantain or banana chips everywhere and these make a delicious and nutritious snack. You may even be tempted to try plantain wine. Nutritionally, bananas are mainly starch: an average-sized banana provides about 500kJ of energy. They've also got a moderate amount of fibre, and are rich in potassium. As for other fruits, they're a reasonable source of vitamin C. Bananas make a great energy-giving snack food when you are on the move, as the carbohydrate is broken down more slowly than simple sugars.

Help...

✚ Remember that it's always best to seek help as soon as possible if a child is ill – see the Babies & Children chapter for more advice.

✚ First aid is covered in the appendix starting on p419.

Being ill far from home is miserable, but it's even worse when you don't speak the language and the medical system is unfamiliar and possibly less reliable than you are used to. Scarier still is the thought of all those nasty tropical diseases that everyone's been talking about and that you now think you must have.

Take heart: you're generally at pretty low risk of most 'tropical' diseases – you're much more likely to get diarrhoea, an infected insect bite or a cold. Don't forget that your body has an enormous potential to fight off infection, and most minor illnesses respond to simple, nondrug treatments.

Travel medicine clinics have medical kits containing various prescription and non-prescription medications for common travel illnesses. As a general rule, you should only self-medicate if there is no alternative (usually because you're in a remote area far from medical help) and you are confident you know what you are doing. The treatment guidelines we give in this book are to help you make decisions about what to do in a given situation; they are not intended as a substitute for getting medical advice.

❗ You must see a doctor if you're seriously ill or you've tried all the simple measures without any effect or there's no improvement in your condition after a day or two.

If you're concerned about getting medical help while travelling, remember that doctors in touristed areas will be used to treating common travellers ailments. Also, doctors who work in tropical countries will have substantial experience in diagnosing and treating tropical diseases (such as malaria) – much more than your doctor back home is likely to have.

> ! It's best to avoid treating fellow travellers unless you know what you're doing, as you probably won't be doing them any favours.

HOW TO GET MEDICAL HELP

If you need medical assistance, your embassy should be able to provide you with a list of local doctors. Otherwise, you could try some of the following options.

- Ring your travel insurance hotline – they should be able to recommend a local doctor. Make sure you always carry the number on you while you are away.

- If you are a member of IAMAT (see Useful Organisations in the Before You Go chapter for details), they will supply you with the names of local doctors – again, make sure you carry this information on you at all times.

- Upmarket hotels can often recommend a doctor and usually have a doctor attached to the staff.

- In an emergency, US citizens could try contacting the State Department's Citizen's Emergency Center (see p29) for advice.

- You could try asking other travellers, members of the expat community or members of international aid organisations for the names of reliable doctors.

- Some key hospitals are listed at the end of this book in the Medical Services appendix, or you could try the telephone book or check your guidebook.

- Remember, you could always try contacting your doctor back home for advice, especially for exacerbations or complications arising from preexisting conditions.

See the Medical Services appendix for more details about the availability of medical services at your destination. You should have no trouble finding doctors and hospitals in all major towns. If you are in more remote areas, missionary hospitals or hospitals run by international organisations are a good bet. In rural areas, healthworkers can usually provide basic medical advice.

Pharmacists and drugstore owners are a source of basic health advice for a large section of the local population. Bear in mind, though, that they are generally not medically qualified and their advice is no substitute for a proper medical consultation. They may recommend dangerously inappropriate treatment (for example tuberculosis treatment for a simple cough), with potentially disastrous effects.

BASICS

WORKING OUT WHAT'S WRONG

Try to decide what your main problem is: do you feel feverish, have you got a headache, diarrhoea, a skin rash or a cough? If you think you know what's wrong, turn to the appropriate chapter later in this book (look up your symptom in the index); otherwise, ask yourself some simple questions.

- What diseases am I at risk for? See the summary at the beginning of this book and the maps; if you're outside the danger zone, then these diseases are very unlikely.

- Am I in a malarious area? (See map p23 and check locally.) If the answer is yes, read the section on malaria and seek medical advice as soon as possible (within 8 hours). Remember you can get malaria even if you are taking malaria prevention medication but that it's unlikely less than a week after you first arrive in a malarial area.

- Did I complete my vaccination courses properly before leaving? If yes, then these diseases are very unlikely.

- Have I been in any specific risk situations recently? Have I been bitten by insects (malaria, dengue fever etc), ticks (typhus, relapsing fever), had contact with animals (rabies), had any injections or transfusions (HIV, hepatitis B) or swum in rivers or lakes (schistosomiasis)?

- Have any of my travelling companions been ill? If yes, you may be suffering from the same illness.

- Is a sexually transmitted infection a possibility?

BASIC MEASURES

If you're ill, there are some simple things you can do to give your body the best chance to get better.

- Stop travelling and rest up for a while.

- Make sure you're as comfortable as the circumstances allow: get a room with a fan if it's hot or extra blankets if it's cold. It's probably worth spending a bit more on a decent room, as you'll be surprised at the difference cheerful surroundings can make.

- Drink plenty of fluids (safe water, weak tea or herbal teas), especially if it's hot or you have a temperature.

- If necessary, give yourself a break from alcohol, tobacco and strong tea or coffee.

If you are ill, it is always a good idea to take your temperature (see following section) and possibly get someone to take your pulse.

! Seek medical help if you don't improve after 48 hours (or before then if you get a lot worse).

TEMPERATURE

Take your temperature at regular intervals (for example four times a day) while you're ill, as this can give you an idea of how quickly you are improving or whether you need to try something different – see the section on Fever later in this chapter for more guidelines.

There are three main types of thermometer: mercury, digital and liquid crystal ('fever strip'). Mercury ones are the most accurate, but they're also the most delicate and you can't take them with you in the cabin on a plane. Liquid crystal thermometers are the least accurate, but they're very convenient – follow the instructions on the packaging. The following instructions are for mercury and digital thermometers:

WHAT'S NORMAL?

Temperature

Normal temperature is 37°C or 98.6°F and up to 0.2°C above or 0.4°C below.

Fever is any temperature above this.

Dangerously high fever is 40°C (104°F) and over – take measures immediately to bring the temperature down (see Fever later in this chapter).

Pulse & Breathing Rate

	pulse (beats/min)	breathing rate (breaths/min)
adults	60 to 80	12 to 20
children	80 to 100	up to 30
babies	100 to 140	40

- wipe the thermometer with a small amount of antiseptic solution to make sure it's clean

- shake the thermometer so that the mercury is down in the bulb

- place the thermometer under the tongue; if there is a chance it may be bitten (for example a young child or if the person is very sick) place it in the armpit or (for young babies) grease it slightly and slip it in the rectum

- leave the thermometer in place for two to three minutes (or follow the instructions on the packet), then remove it

- read and make a note of the temperature; temperatures are usually read in degrees Celsius, but may also be read in degrees Fahrenheit

PULSE & BREATHING RATE

Feeling the pulse and measuring the breathing rate is an important part of any medical assessment. Both can provide a great deal of useful information, but only if you know what to look for and how these clues fit in with the rest of the picture. They're probably not going to be that useful in most common situations when you feel ill, although they are important to note in an emergency situation. For more guidance on how to deal with an emergency, see the inside back cover.

Pulse

To take your pulse, put two fingers on the inside of the wrist at the base of the thumb, and count how many beats there are to the minute; don't use your thumb because this has a pulse of its own that may confuse things. In an emergency situation, if you can't feel a pulse in the wrist, try feeling the side of the neck beside the Adam's apple in men – see the illustrations on p431 for more guidance.

As well as counting the pulse, think about what it feels like: is it strong or weak? Is it regular or irregular? Some abnormalities you may notice, and what they may mean if you are ill, are as follows. You need to seek medical advice urgently in all these situations:

- regular fast pulse (eg up to 120 or 140 beats/min, or bpm) – associated with high fever and serious illness
- weak, rapid pulse – shock (severe illness, major trauma etc); see inside back cover for guidelines on emergency resuscitation
- irregular, very slow or very rapid pulse – heart problems
- slow pulse in spite of fever – could be typhoid (see p137)

Breathing Rate

Count the number of breaths per minute (get someone else to do this, as it's impossible to get an accurate count on yourself). The breathing rate can be increased in many different situations, including lung problems (such as a chest infection) and fever.

OTHER SIGNS

Other things you should check for and note include:

- any rashes, wounds, lumps or bumps
- yellow colour of the skin and whites of the eyes – jaundice

- pale lips and nails, pale inside of eye – anaemia
- blueness of the lips – may indicate a serious lung or heart problem
- unequal or otherwise abnormal pupils of the eyes
- abnormal drowsiness and/or confusion – this always indicates serious illness

SIGNS OF SERIOUS ILLNESS

You must seek medical attention if you experience any of the following problems.

- any severe blood loss
- any severe continuous pain
- more than a day without passing any urine

Blood anywhere it shouldn't be:
- blood in urine
- blood in vomit – this may look like 'coffee grounds'; it won't always look bright red
- blood in faeces – may be bright red, more likely to be browny red and mixed in, or faeces may be black like tar (but remember that taking iron tablets can turn your faeces black)
- blood coughed up in spit
- any vaginal bleeding during pregnancy

Fever:
- high fever (more than 40°C or 104°F) that can't be brought down by the measures outlined on p121
- any fever without obvious cause that lasts more than two to three days

Problems with your digestive system:
- severe diarrhoea and vomiting lasting more than a day (see p152 for more guidance)
- abdominal pain and vomiting without being able to defecate
- severe vomiting that means you can't take any fluids for more than a day
- severe weight loss (usually more than a tenth of your normal body weight)

'Head' problems:

- convulsions
- severe headache with neck stiffness and sensitivity to light
- dizziness or extreme weakness, especially on standing

Lumps, bumps etc:

- any sores that won't go away
- any lumps that appear and grow
- any mole that bleeds or changes shape

COMMON SIGNS & SYMPTOMS

FEVER

Note that children can get very high temperatures very quickly and this can be dangerous if it causes fits (convulsions). See the section on p291 for more details.

The term 'fever' means having a temperature higher than normal (see p117). It always means that there is a disease process going on, and in travellers it's most likely to be a sign of infection. Producing a fever is thought to help the body's natural defences to fight infection.

Having a fever usually makes you feel pretty rough. You may feel intermittently hot and cold, with 'goose bumps' or shivering, and you usually feel completely drained of energy. The fever process itself causes aches and pains (often backache) in your muscles and joints and headache.

You can feel hot without having a temperature above normal and sometimes you can feel cold even though your temperature is raised, so it's always worth taking your temperature with a thermometer to be sure. (Trying to decide if you have a temperature by touching your forehead with the back of your hand is notoriously unreliable.) Take your temperature at regular intervals – four times a day – and note what it is so that you can keep track of any improvement or changes, and also to give you an idea of the pattern of the fever.

> ! Although the pattern of the fever can sometimes be helpful in determining the cause, in practice many diseases don't show the textbook fever patterns, especially in travellers, so it's best not to rely on this.

If you have a really high temperature, you may experience rigors – unpleasant episodes of violent shivering and drenching sweating. They are always a sign of very serious illness, and you should seek medical advice as soon as possible, and immediately try simple measures to lower your temperature.

If you have a fever:

- take paracetamol (acetaminophen) to lower your temperature and relieve any aches and pains
- dehydration is a risk with any fever, especially in hot climates, so drink plenty of fluids
- help your body to cool down – take cool showers or use wet cloths or sponges and a fan
- make sure you don't get cold (although piling the blankets on to 'sweat it out' is not helpful)

Having a fever increases your metabolic rate and can make you lose weight – this is just the fever part of the illness, if you have diarrhoea and vomiting as well, this will exacerbate the problem. Because of this, it's important to try to maintain a basic intake of food while you are ill and to make up for this as you start feeling better and your appetite increases. See the Diet & Nutrition section at the end of the Staying Healthy chapter for more guidelines.

These measures all treat the symptoms of the fever, not the underlying cause. You'll also need to work out what's causing the fever.

Causes

Many fevers, as at home, are caused by viral illnesses, such as colds and flu (see the Respiratory System chapter) which can start suddenly and rarely last more than about three to five days. With any fever, always check for any obvious causes:

- runny nose – cold (p172)
- cough – bronchitis, pneumonia (p178)

- sore throat – tonsillitis, glandular fever (p175)
- earache – ear infection (p182)
- facial or sinus pain – acute sinusitis (p172)
- abdominal pain – see following section
- bladder symptoms (p250)
- pelvic infection (p248)
- skin infection (p202)
- toothache – dental abscess (p194)

If you've ruled out all these, then you can start thinking about some other causes of fever, which we've summarised in the table.

ABDOMINAL PAIN

It can be notoriously difficult to work out what's causing this – if the pain is severe, it's safer to seek medical advice as soon as possible. To give you some guidance, we've listed a few of the more common scenarios:

- often occurs with diarrhoea, when it's usually crampy; comes in waves and may be relieved by passing wind or faeces; you may have a fever
- constipation is often associated with spasms of pain in the lower abdomen
- central lower abdomen – bladder infection, period pains, pelvic infection
- upper abdomen, just under rib cage, burning, worse after meals – heart burn, indigestion
- upper right abdomen, just under ribs – hepatitis (sometimes), liver abscess, gall stones
- appendicitis – see p170
- severe, colicky (comes and goes) pain that makes you writhe around and may go down into your pelvis (or testicles in men); could be a kidney stone – see p171

NAUSEA AND VOMITING

When you're travelling you often get short episodes of nausea, sometimes with vomiting. They usually settle within a day without any specific treatment. They're usually due to viral infections, but there are many other causes:

Disease	Page	Associated symptoms/other clues
flu	p174	may cause generalised aches and pains without any other symptoms
diarrhoea (various causes)	p147	see the Digestive System chapter later in the book for guidelines on diagnosing and treating diarrhoea
heatstroke	p316	headache, weakness, muscle cramps; more likely if you've been very active in unaccustomed heat
malaria	p125	fever often intermittent, joint aches, chills, headache; also possibly cough, abdominal pain, diarrhoea and jaundice*
dengue fever	p132	fever may seem to go, but comes back after a few days; headache, severe aches and pains, rash (possibly)
glandular fever-like illnesses	p172	sore throat, swollen neck glands, no energy
hepatitis	p141	nausea, vomiting, jaundice, dark urine, light faeces
meningitis	p135	fever, headache followed by neck stiffness, vomiting, sensitivity to light
schistosomiasis (bilharzia)	p337	itching, wheezy cough and diarrhoea, but often no symptoms
amoebic liver abscess	p162	pain in right upper part of abdomen
typhoid (and related illnesses)	p137	often causes a persistent fever; diarrhoea may be a late symptom
tuberculosis	p138	recurrent evening or night fever, usually with cough
typhus	p366	red rash, distinctive sore at site of tick bite, more likely if you've been trekking in rural areas
sleeping sickness	p361	small risk if you've visited rural areas or wildlife parks in East or West Africa

*jaundice = yellowing of the skin and whites of the eyes

- medicines, eg malaria pills, antibiotics
- motion sickness (p71)
- food poisoning (p149)
- diarrhoeal illnesses (p147)
- dehydration or heatstroke (p316)
- meningitis (p135)
- migraine headache (p191)
- pregnancy (p265)

HEADACHE

Most fevers cause headache. Other possibilities are:

- dehydration, heatstroke (p316)
- migraine (p191)
- stress headache
- trapped nerve (sharp stabbing pains, intermittent)
- neck problems (eg arthritis)
- malaria (p125)
- dengue fever (p132)
- meningococcal meningitis (p135)
- altitude illness (p324)
- typhoid fever (p137)
- sleeping sickness (p361)

RASH

There are many causes of rashes. See the Skin chapter on p198 for a more detailed discussion of skin problems, but causes include:

- viral illnesses
- measles & other childhood illnesses (p229)
- fungal infections (p202)
- allergic reactions, dermatitis (p200)
- dengue fever (p132)
- typhus (p366)
- haemorrhagic fevers (p223)
- cutaneous leishmaniasis (p224)
- schistosomiasis (p366)
- sleeping sickness (p361)

Fever & Hepatitis...

In this chapter we've grouped some infections that usually have fever as their main symptom – for a summary of the causes of fever, see p121.

➕ For guidance on how to take a temperature see p116.

MALARIA

➕ Note: this section gives you guidelines on diagnosing and treating malaria; for the complete low-down on preventing malaria, including malaria prevention drugs, see the sections on Malaria Pills (p44) and Insect Bites (p88) earlier in this book.

Malaria (see map p23) is caused by a parasite called *Plasmodium* which is carried by a type of night-biting mosquito present in most tropical and subtropical areas below about 2000m.

When an infected female mosquito bites you, malarial parasites are injected into your bloodstream and get carried to your liver, where they multiply. During this phase you don't get any symptoms.

Symptoms appear when the malarial parasites enter your bloodstream again, which occurs after a variable length of time depending on the type of malaria (usually about one to three weeks, but sometimes up to a year). The malarial parasites enter and multiply in red blood cells, eventually destroying them. This can have effects on many organs in your body, including your guts (causing vomiting and diarrhoea), kidneys (causing kidney failure) and brain (cerebral malaria).

There are four types of *Plasmodium* parasites, but the one of most concern is *P. falciparum*, which causes the most severe disease and is responsible for most malaria deaths worldwide. In Africa, 95% of malaria is falciparum.

The other types, *P. vivax* (common worldwide but less common in Africa), *P. ovale* (uncommon, found mostly in West Africa) and *P. malariae* (uncommon), are less likely to cause severe complications so rapidly, but infection with any of them still needs to be treated promptly. *P. vivax* and *P. ovale* can remain inactive in the liver for some time and can cause disease several weeks or months after you've left a risk area.

You can't tell the different forms of malaria apart on the basis of the early symptoms, so you have to assume that any malaria is due to *P. falciparum* unless proved otherwise (by a blood test).

Malaria can be effectively treated with drugs and the symptoms quickly disappear as the parasites are cleared from the blood. If malaria is treated appropriately, it won't recur. The picture you may have of recurring attacks of malaria is only true when the disease is not treated.

> **!** The most important point to remember about malaria is that it can progress rapidly to severe complications (sometimes within 24 hours), so it's extremely important to seek medical help urgently if you get a fever in a malarial area.

SYMPTOMS

Unfortunately, the symptoms of malaria are very variable and rather nonspecific, making it notoriously difficult to diagnose. The most important sign of malaria is having a fever (38°C or higher).

In theory at least, you should notice three stages: a cold stage when you shiver and your temperature rockets up; followed by a hot stage when you feel hot, flushed and have a high temperature (this lasts for several hours); finally you get a wet stage when you become drenched in sweat, and your temperature falls. This is the textbook scenario – in reality the picture is likely to be much more vague, especially if you were taking malaria prevention medication.

Suspect malaria if you have a fever – it may just feel like an attack of flu – with or without any of the following symptoms:

- headache and aching muscles and joints
- nausea and vomiting, or diarrhoea (especially in children)
- cough
- abdominal discomfort and jaundice (yellowing of the skin and whites of the eyes)
- confusion, leading to coma (cerebral malaria)

Remember that you can still get malaria even if you are taking malaria prevention pills.

> ! Note that it takes at least a week for the disease to appear after an infective bite, so a fever within the first week of your arrival in a malarial area is very unlikely to be malaria (unless you've come from a malarial area).

DIAGNOSIS & TREATMENT

Malaria can be quickly and simply diagnosed from a sample of your blood, usually taken by pricking your finger. The test may need to be repeated if it's initially negative and you know malaria is likely. Most doctors and clinics in malarial areas will have facilities for doing a malaria blood test, or you can do a test yourself if you have a kit with you. You may be able to buy kits locally in some countries.

If you think you may have malaria:

- rest and take steps to bring down the fever –
  see p396 for guidelines on general measures
- drink plenty of fluids
- seek medical help as soon as possible for a blood test
  to confirm the diagnosis
- once the diagnosis is confirmed, take the doctor's advice on
  treatment, as they are likely to be experienced in treating
  malaria and will know what the most appropriate treatment
  is for the area you are in

If your symptoms recur or continue despite treatment, seek medical advice, as you will need further treatment or you may have another illness that needs treating.

Don't forget that you will still need to take malaria pills after you recover – get medical advice on what would be most appropriate in your situation.

> ! Malaria can appear after you've left the malaria risk zone – if you get a fever in the weeks or months after you were in a malarial risk area, seek medical help urgently and be sure to tell your doctor where you've been and which malaria pills (if any) you were taking.

In certain situations, it may be necessary for you to treat yourself with antimalarial drugs while you seek medical help.

EMERGENCY SELF-TREATMENT

Self-treatment of any serious disease isn't something to be undertaken lightly, and with malaria there are some special issues you need to be aware of.

First of all, it can be difficult to know when you have malaria, as the symptoms are so nonspecific, and there's a worry that you might miss treating another potentially serious disease (although if you are carrying one of the new diagnosis kits, this is less of a problem – see p127 for more details).

Secondly, because of drug resistance, you need to be sure you are taking the appropriate treatment for the area you are in, especially as inadequately treated malaria can recur later. Thirdly, most antimalarial treatments have a risk of significant side effects, and you are more likely to experience side effects at the doses used for treatment; in addition, they can interact with other drugs you may be taking.

For these reasons:

- you should only consider self-treatment in an emergency, ie if you do not have access to medical care within 24 hours of the start of symptoms
- emergency self-treatment is a first aid measure only – you still need to get yourself to medical help as soon as possible

When? If you are in a risk area, you must suspect malaria if you have an otherwise unexplained fever (over 38°C) that lasts more than eight hours without responding to simple fever-reducing measures (see p396).

Which Drugs? Although we give currently accepted guidelines here, recommendations change as resistance patterns vary and new facts come to light, so it's best to get the most up to date advice from your doctor or travel health clinic before you go, or to seek reliable local advice if necessary.

Treatment depends on what, if any, malaria prevention medication you were taking, as well as the presence of any malarial drug resistance. You need to take an antimalarial that is different from the one that you were taking as prevention. This is because the strain of malaria you have may be resistant to the antimalarial you were taking, and also because you are more likely to experience side effects if you take the same antimalarial for treatment.

Chloroquine resistance is widespread in Africa, with pockets of multidrug resistance, especially in eastern Africa. Resistance to sulphadoxine/pyrimethamine (Fansidar) is variable. Treatment options in Africa include:

- atovaquone-proguanil (Malarone) – this is good if you were taking mefloquine or doxycycline for prevention
- sulphadoxine/pyrimethamine (Fansidar) –this is good if you weren't taking any preventive malaria pills or you were taking chloroquine plus proguanil
- quinine sulphate – with this you will need to take another agent, usually one of the following: sulphadoxine/pyrimethamine (Fansidar) OR doxycycline OR tetracycline
- mefloquine – can be used if you were taking doxycycline as prevention
- artemether-lumefantrine (Riamet) Highly effective combination treatment

In the small pockets of chloroquine-sensitive malaria in parts of North Africa, options are:

- chloroquine – if you were not taking any prevention
- sulphadoxine/pyrimethamine (Fansidar) – if you were taking chloroquine plus proguanil for prophylaxis

SIDE EFFECTS & CAUTIONS

➕ For more details about mefloquine and chloroquine, see the section on Malaria Pills in the Before You Go chapter.

MALARIA STANDBY TREATMENT: DOSES & SCHEDULES

Although we have done our best to ensure that these doses are correct at the time of going to print, there are many variables to take into account, so you should check these with your doctor before you leave, most notably the resistance in various parts of the world. Note that although we give doses for children here, we do not recommend that you take children to high risk malarial areas.

Treatment	Adult	Child (by weight)
atovaquone-proguanil (Malarone)	four tablets once daily for three days	11 to 20kg one tablet once daily; 21 to 30kg two tablets once daily; 31 to 40kg three tablets once daily; over 40kg, as for adult
sulphadoxine/ pyrimethamine (Fansidar)	single dose of three tablets	5 to 10kg half tablet; 11 to 20kg one tablet; 21 to 30kg 1.5 tablets; 31 to 45kg 2 tablets; over 45kg 3 tablets
quinine sulphate PLUS sulphadoxine/ pyrimethamine (Fansidar)	two 300mg tablets three times daily for 7 days	10mg/kg three times daily for seven days
	dose above	dose above
OR PLUS doxycycline	100mg once daily	over 8 years: 2mg/kg twice daily for seven days
OR PLUS tetracycline	250mg four times daily for 7 days	over 8 years: 5mg/kg four times daily for seven days
mefloquine	two 250mg tablets and a further two six hours later	child 15kg or over: 15mg/kg single dose
chloroquine	4 tablets (150mg base) each on days 1 & 2, & 2 on day 3 (ie total of 10 tablets)	25mg base/kg over three days
artemether-lumefantrine (Riamet)	4 tabs together at 0, 8, 24, 36, 48 and 60 hrs	12 years and older as for adult, not used for children under12

Atovaquone plus proguanil (Malarone) is highly effective against multidrug resistant strains of malaria. It's also safe and unlikely to cause you any adverse effects.

Sulphadoxine/pyrimethamine (Fansidar) has been widely used to treat malaria. Resistance has emerged in parts of Africa, especially eastern Africa. It's generally safe and effective at the doses used for treatment. However, it is no longer recommended as a prevention treatment because serious skin reactions have occurred when it has been used in this way weekly. You shouldn't take Fansidar if you are allergic to sulpha drugs.

Side effects with **mefloquine** are common at the doses used for treatment, and include lightheadedness, nausea, dizziness and vertigo; more serious side effects occur in about one in 100 people at this dose.

Quinine is the most effective drug against chloroquine-resistant malaria, but side effects are common. These include ringing in the ears, muffled hearing and sometimes dizziness, usually on the second or third day of treatment. These side effects usually go away once you stop taking it. Quinine can cause heart problems, so you need medical supervision if you are on any heart medications, and these problems are more likely if you have been taking mefloquine for prevention. It can also cause your blood sugar to drop. Be aware that quinine is very toxic if taken at more than the recommended dose, and you should always keep it well out of reach of children. Because of these problems, it's not usually recommended as emergency standby treatment.

Artemether-lumefantrine (Riamet) combination is a highly effective treatment, is fast-acting and has few side-effects. It is suitable for those of 12 years and above.

OTHER TREATMENTS

You may hear talk of **artesunate** or **artemether** in connection with the treatment of malaria. Riamet is an example of one of these drugs that has been brought to commercial reality. These compounds are related to artemisinin, or qinghaosu, which has been used for over two millennia in traditional medical practice in China. They appear to be safe and effective in the treatment (but not prevention) of severe malaria. However, they are not generally available for use in Africa because of fears of the emergence of resistance.

> ❗ Note that halofantrine, which was commonly used in the treatment of malaria, is known to cause heart rhythm problems in susceptible people; these effects are more likely if you have been taking chloroquine, mefloquine or quinine, so it is no longer recommended for standby treatment. It may still be available in some areas and is better than nothing in an emergency.

DENGUE & DENGUE HAEMORRHAGIC FEVER

This disease is caused by a virus transmitted to humans via the bite of an infected mosquito. Dengue has spread rapidly in the last decade and is now one of the top public health problems in the tropical world. At the latest count, there were 50 million new cases annually – and this is probably a conservative figure.

Dengue has the potential to occur in all tropical regions, including Africa, although it's less of a problem here than in the current hotspot, South-East Asia. Large outbreaks occur periodically, so check before you go with a travel health clinic or the other information sources listed on p27.

There is no vaccine against dengue, with none likely in the near future. You can avoid dengue by taking steps to prevent mosquito bites, bearing in mind that the dengue mosquito bites mainly during the day.

✚ See p90 for guidelines on how to prevent mosquito bites.

SYMPTOMS

The illness usually starts quite suddenly with fever, nausea and vomiting, headache and joint and muscle pains. The aches and pains can be severe, hence the old name 'breakbone fever'.

The fever sometimes appears to settle after a few days, only to reappear a few days later (known as 'saddleback fever'). Typically, you get a fine red rash, often around the third to fifth day, which signals the second phase of the disease, and recovery usually follows soon after.

The illness can last anything from three to about 10 days, settling spontaneously without any specific treatment. However, many travellers report experiencing extreme tiredness with muscle wasting and lack of energy for several weeks or months after, which can be debilitating and may be a good reason to cut your trip short. On the other hand, the symptoms can be mild and you may not realise that you've had it.

Rarely, you can get a more severe, potentially fatal form of dengue called dengue haemorrhagic fever (DHF), which is associated with uncontrolled bleeding and shock from loss of blood. Although DHF receives a lot of publicity and is frightening, it is rare in travellers and extremely rare in Africa. You can get minor bleeding – nose bleeds, bleeding gums, bruising – with simple dengue, so it doesn't necessarily mean that you've got the most serious form of DHF. DHF is thought to be due to infection with a second strain of the dengue virus within a certain period of time. A blood test can help to diagnose dengue fever.

DENGUE AGAIN?

There are four different strains of the dengue virus. If you get dengue, you develop immunity against the infecting strain, but you'll still be vulnerable to the three remaining strains, so you could get it again. You're more likely to get a severe form of the disease second time around so if you've had dengue in the past, you should discuss the risks with your doctor before you go, and be very careful to avoid mosquito bites at all times.

DIAGNOSIS & TREATMENT

There's no specific treatment, but if you think you have dengue fever:

- seek medical advice as soon as possible so that the diagnosis can be confirmed and other diagnoses, including malaria, can be ruled out
- rest and drink plenty of fluids
- take simple painkillers if necessary but avoid aspirin, as this can increase the likelihood of bleeding problems

You need to keep a look out for signs of DHF. Seek medical help urgently if you have any of the following (if they do occur, it's usually around the third day of illness):

- any worsening of your condition, especially if associated with any of the following symptoms
- spontaneous bruising of the skin, nose bleeds, bleeding from the gums, vomiting blood or abdominal pain
- signs of blood loss – thin, rapid pulse, restlessness, pale face and cold fingers and toes; see the first aid section p419 for dealing with shock

DENGUE-LIKE FEVERS

The virus that causes dengue is a member of a large family of viruses called arboviruses which are responsible for many different diseases worldwide. Some are carried by mosquitoes (eg dengue and yellow fever), others by sandflies (eg sandfly fever) and ticks (eg Crimea-Congo haemorrhagic fever), and some by direct contact between people. They often occur in quite specific geographical areas (eg Rift Valley Fever, West Nile Fever), so doctors in those areas will know what to look for.

A recent resurgence of one of these, Chikungunya fever, spread from East Africa across the Indian Ocean to India, with hundreds of thousands of cases. Arthritis and fever are the main symptoms and a blood test has been developed.

We've covered a few of these diseases in the Rarities chapter on p221. None of them poses a significant risk to you as a traveller, but it is important to take measures wherever you go to prevent insect bites (see p90). There's no specific treatment for any of these diseases and no vaccine.

YELLOW FEVER

You're at pretty low risk of this viral disease (see map p24), a relative of dengue fever and mainly a disease of monkeys in forested areas. It's transmitted through the bite of an infected mosquito. Humans can get infected when they stray into risk areas (eg forest workers). Infected humans can take the disease back to urban areas, where lots of mosquitoes are hanging around with nothing better to do – this is how epidemics periodically arise.

There is an effective vaccine against yellow fever, so if you have been immunised, you can basically rule this disease out. If you're just going to be travelling in urban areas, you're at very low risk of the disease, unless an epidemic is occurring. There is more of a risk of acquiring yellow fever if you travel in rural areas.

Symptoms of yellow fever range from a mild fever which resolves over a few days to more serious forms with fever, headache, muscle pains, abdominal pain and vomiting. This can progress to bleeding, shock and liver and kidney failure. The liver failure causes jaundice, or yellowing of your skin and the whites of your eyes – hence the name.

There's no specific treatment but you should seek medical help urgently if you think you have yellow fever.

MENINGOCOCCAL MENINGITIS

! Not every headache is likely to be meningitis – see p124 for a list of common causes of headache.

Recurring epidemics of meningococcal meningitis occur in savannah areas (mainly the Sahel countries) of sub-Saharan Africa during the dry season (December to June). There was a big outbreak in 1996, when more than 10,000 people died. Check with your doctor or travel health clinic for the most up to date information on outbreaks. There is an effective vaccine available which is often recommended for travel to these areas – for details see p36.

MENINGITIS

Meningitis is any infection of the lining of the brain and spinal cord. Lots of different infectious agents can cause meningitis, including bacteria and viruses. Viral meningitis usually settles without any treatment, whereas bacterial meningitis can rapidly cause death and is the one you're most likely to have heard of.

Generally, you're at pretty low risk of getting meningococcal meningitis, unless an epidemic is ongoing, but the disease is important because it can be very serious and rapidly fatal. You get infected by breathing in droplets coughed or sneezed into the air by sufferers or, more likely, by healthy carriers of the bacteria. You're more at risk in crowded, poorly ventilated places, including public transport and eating places.

SYMPTOMS

The symptoms of meningitis are fever, severe headache, neck stiffness that prevents you from bending your head forward, nausea, vomiting and sensitivity to light, making you prefer to stay in darkness. With meningococcal meningitis, you may get a widespread, blotchy purple rash before any other symptoms appear.

TREATMENT

Meningococcal meningitis is an extremely serious disease that can cause death within a few hours of you first feeling unwell. Seek medical help without delay if you have any of the symptoms listed earlier, especially if you are in a risk area.

Treatment is with large doses of penicillin (eg 1.2g of benzylpenicillin in adults, 600mg for children up to 10 years) given directly into the bloodstream or, if that's not possible, intramuscularly. If you're allergic to penicillin, an intramuscular injection of cefotaxime OR chloramphenicol are suitable alternatives.

If you've been in close contact with a sufferer, you can protect yourself from infection by taking antibiotics, usually rifampicin 500mg twice daily for two days (child 10mg/kg, child under one year 5mg/kg) OR ciprofloxacin 500mg single dose (not suitable for children), but it's best to seek medical advice on this.

TYPHOID (ENTERIC) FEVER

Also known as enteric fever, typhoid occurs throughout most of Africa and is most common where standards of personal and environmental hygiene are low. Occasional large outbreaks occur. It's rare in travellers (although it's slightly more common in travellers in North Africa), but it's worth taking general precautions to avoid even this low risk.

Typhoid is transmitted via food and water, and symptomless carriers, especially when they're working as foodhandlers, are an important source of infection.

Typhoid is caused by a type of salmonella bacteria, *Salmonella typhi*. Paratyphoid is a similar but milder disease.

SYMPTOMS

These are variable, but you almost always get a fever and headache to start with, initially very similar to flu, with aches and pains, loss of appetite and generally feeling unwell. Typhoid may be confused with malaria.

The fever gradually rises during a week. Characteristically your pulse is relatively slow compared with the fever (eg 80 beats/min for an adult instead of perhaps 100) – but this is something a medic will pick up better than you, so don't agonise over it too much. Other symptoms you may have are constipation or diarrhoea and stomach pains.

You may feel worse in the second week, with a constant fever and sometimes a red skin rash. Serious complications occur in about one in 10 cases, including, most commonly, damage to the gut wall with subsequent leakage of the gut contents into the abdominal cavity. Sometimes this is the first indication of an infection. Other symptoms you may have are severe headache, sore throat and jaundice.

DIAGNOSIS & TREATMENT

Diagnosis is by blood test, and the earlier it is diagnosed the better. Seek medical help for any fever (38°C and higher) that does not improve after 48 hours. Typhoid is a serious disease and is not something you should consider self-treating.

Rehydration therapy is important if diarrhoea has been a feature of the illness, but antibiotics are the mainstay of treatment. Chloramphenicol is generally the first line treatment in Africa, but resistance is spreading. An alternative is ciprofloxacin 500mg twice daily.

TUBERCULOSIS (TB)

Called consumption in the old days because people just wasted away with it, TB is making a comeback globally. It's a huge public health problem in sub-Saharan Africa, killing more people here than malaria. It is closely linked to HIV infection and is responsible for about 40% of AIDS-related deaths here.

In spite of these alarming statistics, it is rarely seen in short-term travellers, as you need close contact with a sufferer with active disease to catch it. TB is transmitted by breathing in droplets expelled by TB-infected people through coughing, talking or sneezing. Your risk of being infected increases the closer you are to the person and the longer you are exposed to them. You can also get a form of TB through drinking unpasteurised milk.

TB is therefore a risk if you are planning to live or work closely with locals (eg most cases of TB in travellers returning to the UK are of young people who visited family in high-risk areas) or you are planning to stay for more than a few months in sub-Saharan Africa. It doesn't cause an immediate life-threatening illness like, say, malaria or dengue, but problems can appear later.

Discuss this with your doctor, but it might be useful for long-term travellers to have a skin or blood test for TB before you go and when you come back.

There is a vaccination against TB which has a useful level of effectiveness, especially for children. You may already have had a routine TB vaccination as a teenager (but not in North America).

TB – A GROWING PROBLEM

If you thought TB was on the way out, you were wrong. It looks set to be one of the biggest health threats of the 21st century. The World Health Organization (WHO) is so alarmed at the re-emergence of this age-old killer that in 1993 it declared TB a global health emergency. It estimates that one-third of the world's population is infected with TB, with sub-Saharan Africa one of the worst affected regions.

The rise of TB worldwide is thought to be related to the explosion of HIV/AIDS as well as to the increase in air travel, which helps infection to spread. HIV/AIDS is a major public health problem in Africa, and it has a special relationship with TB. HIV infection lowers your body's defences against TB, making recurrence of infection more likely.

The biggest worry currently is the emergence of treatment-resistant TB. Until 50 years ago, TB was incurable but drugs were discovered in the middle of the 20th century that were effective in treating the infection. It takes several months of drug treatment to get rid of TB, even though people start to feel better after a few weeks. People stop taking their treatment too early, either because they feel better or they can't afford to pay for treatment, and this has resulted in the rise of drug-resistant TB. So once again we are faced with the prospect of untreatable TB.

If you want to find out all about this global threat, WHO maintains a TB homepage (**www.who.int/gtb**).

SYMPTOMS

TB is caused by a bacterium, with only about 15% of people who become infected going on to develop the disease or become infectious. The TB bacteria may lie dormant for years until your resistance is lowered for some other reason eg poor nutrition or another disease like HIV.

TB classically affects the lungs but it can affect almost any other part of the body, including your joints, bones, brain and gut. Pulmonary TB is the commonest way in which TB shows itself in adults. Symptoms develop slowly, often over the course of several months, and include weight loss, fever, night sweats and a cough with blood-stained spit. Diagnosis is by a laboratory test of your spit. Sometimes the disease can be much more severe, especially in children, presenting symptoms of meningitis (headache, neck stiffness, sensitivity to light) and leading to coma.

DIAGNOSIS & TREATMENT

TB is not something you're going to be self-treating, so seek specialist advice if you think you may be infected. Treatment is with a combination of antibiotics over a prolonged period of time (six to eight months, but sometimes up to a year). Multidrug-resistant TB is common in Africa and is obviously a major headache to treat but it is possible, although treatment is expensive.

PREVENTION

Avoid prolonged exposure to circumstances that make transmission more likely, eg sleeping in crowded communal dormitories or travelling on crowded public transport.

You're more likely to get infected if your resistance is low, eg through ill health or bad diet, so it makes sense to look after yourself while you are on the road. Never drink unpasteurised milk or milk products – if you're in any doubt, boil it first.

SOMETHING IN THE AIR?

Because TB is transmitted by droplets, and the air in plane cabins is recycled throughout the flight, there's been much concern in recent years about the possibility of transmission of TB during flights. A recent case illustrates the dangers: when a Ukrainian emigre with TB coughed his way through an eight hour flight to New York, 13 of 40 passengers sitting near him were infected. This case was made worse by the fact that the Ukrainian had drug-resistant TB (the former Soviet states are a major source of this).

While you can't do much about who boards your flight, it's worth being aware of the risks. It's generally agreed that your risk is directly related to how close you are to the person, and it's only significant if you're close to them for a long time.

VIRAL HEPATITIS (JAUNDICE)

This infection of the liver can be caused by at least five different viruses: hepatitis A, B, C, D and E. All five viruses cause a similar short-term disease but three (B, C and D) can cause persistent infection in a proportion of sufferers, resulting in long-term liver problems. The different viruses are transmitted in different ways: A and E are spread by faecal contamination of food and water, and B, C and D are spread via blood or sexual contact. A blood test can diagnose which type you have, but you'll probably have a good idea anyway.

! Note that hepatitis is a much more serious disease in pregnancy, so you must seek medical help urgently in this situation.

SYMPTOMS

You may not realise you've got hepatitis at first, as the illness starts with vague flu-like symptoms, including fever, chills, headache, and joint aches and pains. You feel listless and washed out, with no appetite. Smokers often report being turned off cigarettes.

The flu-like symptoms can go on for two to three days before you get gut symptoms. These include nausea, vomiting, diarrhoea (possibly) and pain in the upper right-hand side of your abdomen. A little later you may notice that you're passing dark urine and your faeces are a lighter colour than normal. The whites of your eyes turn yellow, and later your skin starts to look yellow. This yellowing is called jaundice, which occurs because your liver isn't able to work properly.

Although these are the classic symptoms, hepatitis can be a mild illness without jaundice in many people, especially children, although older people tend to get quite severe jaundice.

You usually find that you start to feel better as the jaundice appears. It can leave you feeling very washed out and weak for some time after – about six weeks on average but sometimes up to three months. It might be one reason to come home early if you're on a long trip.

Rarely, instead of getting better as the jaundice appears, the illness can progress to overwhelming liver failure, which is a very serious condition. Seek medical help urgently if you get suddenly worse or if you have any of the following:

- severe vomiting and dehydration
- bruising for no reason
- bleeding from your gums or nosebleeds
- blood in your urine or faeces
- confusion and drowsiness

TREATMENT

There's no specific treatment for hepatitis A and E apart from rest and tender loving care. You probably won't feel like doing much for a while, so make sure you've got somewhere comfortable to stay. There's no particular need to stay in bed; just do as much or as little as you feel up to.

Drink plenty of fluids, especially if you don't feel like eating because of the nausea. Once you do feel like eating again, try to stick to a low-fat (the liver has to work harder to deal with fatty foods), high carbohydrate diet – eat lots of starchy foods like bread, potatoes and rice.

Be nice to your liver while it's indisposed and avoid things that might damage it further, like alcohol and medications, including aspirin and paracetamol (acetaminophen). In fact, it's a good idea to avoid any medications if possible while you are ill, because drugs won't be disposed of as efficiently as normal and can have unpredictable effects. If you're using the oral contraceptive pill, you'll need to stop taking it until the illness settles.

! If you think you have hepatitis, seek medical advice as soon as possible to have the diagnosis confirmed, so that people you have been in contact with while you have been infectious can be protected (by having the vaccination).

If you've got hepatitis, you need to take care not to spread it around. With hepatitis A and E, you're most infectious for about two weeks or so before symptoms appear until a few days after the jaundice develops. Pay particular attention to your personal hygiene, don't prepare food for other people, don't share cutlery and avoid sharing drinks or cigarettes. Once you've had hepatitis A or E, you're immune for life.

! Anybody you have been in close contact with needs to receive the hepatitis A vaccine (or immunoglobulin) if they haven't been vaccinated, unless they have already developed symptoms.

With hepatitis B, you're infectious for the course of the illness, usually about three to six months, and for about a month before symptoms appear. Take care not to spread the disease by practising safer sex using condoms, by letting doctors and dentists know of your infection before they carry out any treatment, by not donating blood and by not sharing needles.

New drug combinations have been developed to help treat acute hepatitis B and C.

CAUSES OF JAUNDICE

- viral hepatitis
- glandular fever (p177)
- typhoid (p137)
- malaria (p125)
- amoebic liver abscess (p162)
- schistosomiasis (p337)
- liver flukes (p380)
- medications
- gall bladder disease (may be associated with sudden, gripping pain)

PREVENTION

Hepatitis A & E

Hepatitis A is extremely common in all parts of Africa and a real risk to travellers. Although hepatitis E occurs in Africa, it's less common than in parts of Asia. It's particularly likely to affect pregnant women. You're quite likely to get hepatitis A unless you take steps to avoid it.

The hepatitis A vaccine is very effective but there's no vaccine against hepatitis E. Prevention of hepatitis E is by taking basic precautions with food and water, and making sure your personal hygiene standards are high. Note that shellfish are a source of hepatitis A and E if they have been obtained from sewage-contaminated water, so as a rule it's best to avoid these, especially when they are served raw or you can't be sure they are well cooked (steaming won't make them safe). It's also possible to get hepatitis A or E by swimming in water contaminated by faeces.

Hepatitis B

In many countries (including Australia and the USA), hepatitis B vaccination is becoming routine and you may have been immunised at school. Unlike hepatitis A and E, infection with hepatitis B can persist in about 5 to 10% of people, and these carriers are important sources of infection. Hepatitis B is less common than hepatitis A and occurs worldwide. There are high levels of carriers throughout Africa. Hepatitis C is a major cause of blood transfusion-related hepatitis in the West and appears to be a growing problem worldwide, but is not going to be a major worry for you as a traveller. Hepatitis D only occurs in conjunction with hepatitis B infection.

You're at risk of hepatitis B if you have sexual contact with a carrier, especially when this is between men, so practise safer sex by using condoms. Other risk situations to avoid are blood transfusions or inadequately sterilised medical (or dental) equipment, including acupuncture needles. Other obvious hazards are needle sharing, getting your ears or other body parts pierced with inadequately sterilised equipment, having a tattoo or being shaved with a re-used cut-throat razor. In children, hepatitis B can be transmitted by prolonged contact with a carrier.

Infection with hepatitis B causes a similar illness to type A, but the symptoms can be more severe and there's a higher risk of liver failure. Note that the illness can take up to six months to appear after infection. Persistent infection carries the risk of long-term liver damage, and liver cancer in a minority of cases.

! If you think you may have been exposed to hepatitis B, a protective
shot of antibody can help protect against it, although it can be hard
to find, or you can start a course of the usual hepatitis B vaccination
– discuss this with your doctor.

Prevention involves avoiding risk situations and having the
vaccination (if you have not already been immunised), if you
think you might be at high risk of hepatitis B through sexual
contact or needle sharing, or if you're planning on living in a
highly endemic area, or working as a medic or dentist.

Digestive System...

We've devoted quite a bit of space to this topic, in recognition of its high ranking in the league table of ailments afflicting travellers.

DIARRHOEA

➕ See also treatment of diarrhoea in babies and children (p292) and preventing diarrhoea (p82).

No matter how careful you are, you're likely to get at least one episode of diarrhoea while you're away. Diarrhoea (usually with vomiting) is the commonest travel-related illness. About half of all travellers going to Africa will get diarrhoea, so be prepared. It's more common in younger travellers, especially if you're roughing it, and you have more chance of succumbing if you're on a long trip. If you're going to get it, diarrhoea usually strikes about the third day after you arrive.

CAUSES OF TRAVELLERS DIARRHOEA

About one third of cases, usually mild, are due to non-specific causes including:

- stress
- jet lag
- new foods and a change in eating habits

The rest are divided up as follows:

- bacteria, the commonest cause
- viruses ('gastric flu')
- parasites (including *Giardia* and amoeba)
- food poisoning (eg from a toxin, often bacterial, in the food)

There are many possible causes, but in travellers diarrhoea is usually caused by bacteria.

If you understand how diarrhoea is passed from person to person, it will help you avoid it. It sounds gross, but basically you get diarrhoea by eating other people's faeces – in food (mainly), water and other drinks, and from dirty utensils (plates, spoons, cups etc). Hands used to prepare food may not have been washed thoroughly after toilet duty, flies can transfer bugs via their feet, and a lack of environmental cleanliness means that dust and dirt is more likely to be contaminated with faeces.

You can also get diarrhoea from contact with an infected person (if you touch hands etc that haven't been washed adequately) or, more rarely, from swimming in contaminated water (by swallowing small amounts). Some infective agents such as *Giardia* can survive even in chlorinated water, and both fresh and sea water may be contaminated with sewage. For the low-down on avoiding diarrhoea and other illnesses transmitted in the same way, turn to the Staying Healthy chapter.

Diarrhoea is a hot topic of conversation among travellers, and it can be hard to separate fact from fiction at times. It's worth keeping the following in mind:

- travellers diarrhoea is generally a short, mild illness lasting on average about three to five days
- because of this, you don't usually need to get medical advice or have a test to find out what's causing your diarrhoea
- replacing lost fluids and salts is the most important part of treating any watery diarrhoea, whatever the cause
- you don't usually need antibiotic treatment for mild to moderate diarrhoea (although there is some controversy among doctors over this)
- there are certain situations when antibiotics need to be used – in these situations it's best to get medical advice

TYPES OF DIARRHOEAL ILLNESS

You'll probably find your illness fits into one of three main patterns, as follows.

Vomiting & Diarrhoea

➕ Remember that there are many causes of nausea and vomiting – for a summary of these, see p124.

If you suddenly get an attack of nausea and profuse vomiting soon after eating something dodgy, it's probably due to food poisoning. This is a worldwide problem that is more likely when you're eating food not prepared by yourself, especially where food preparation and storage procedures may be suspect. Vomiting is the main symptom, although you may get quite bad stomach cramps with it and some watery diarrhoea later. The whole episode should be over in about 24 to 48 hours. You may have a suspicion that you've eaten something that wasn't fresh (such as seafood); another clue is if everyone who ate the same thing comes down with the same illness.

No specific treatment is needed as a rule. You should rest, sip fluids if possible, and wait for it to settle down, which it should start doing in about 12 to 24 hours. It's best to avoid anti-vomiting medication, as vomiting is your body's way of getting rid of the bad stuff.

❗ Note that if the illness doesn't settle down within 24 hours, if it gets much worse, if there's any blood in the vomit or diarrhoea, if you have a high fever, if you have very severe stomach pains or a severe headache, you should seek medical help urgently.

Watery Diarrhoea

This is the type of diarrhoea you're most likely to get when you are away. The cause varies with your destination, but it's usually bacterial, often a strain of a bacteria called *Escherichia coli*. This bug normally lives in your gut, but this strain has turned nasty.

You're usually not that ill (up to six visits to the toilet a day) and the episode generally resolves itself in a few days (on average three to five). It rarely causes severe dehydration (although the potential is always there and this is a greater risk in children and older travellers).

If you get a fever with it, it's usually low (less than 38°C). You often get nausea and vomiting with it, at least to start with, but it's not a major feature of the illness – unlike food poisoning (see Vomiting & Diarrhoea earlier). You commonly get stomach cramps, bloating and frequent gas. Sometimes the illness can progress to a bloody diarrhoea (dysentery).

The mainstay of treatment is replacing lost fluids and salts, which you should start doing straight away. You don't usually need antibiotics for this type of diarrhoea.

Dysentery

Dysentery is any diarrhoea with blood in it. It can be more severe and protracted than the more common watery diarrhoea described earlier. Out of every 10 travellers stricken with diarrhoea, only about one will have dysentery. It's usually caused by bacteria, including various shigella and salmonella species, but it may be caused by a parasite, *Entamoeba histolytica* ('amoeba').

Dysentery usually begins with nonspecific flu-like symptoms, including headache, high fever, muscle aches and pains, and feeling washed out, which can be quite severe. The diarrhoea may start watery and in large quantities, but it usually gets smaller in quantity, and you'll notice blood and mucus (slime) in it. You often get painful stomach cramps, which usually herald a dash to the little room.

As for any diarrhoeal illness, fluid and salt replacement is important. Because it's usually a more severe illness and complications can occur, specific antibiotic treatment is indicated, especially for shigella and amoeba infections, so you should find a doctor and get a laboratory test done. While you're waiting for the diagnosis, you should start a course of norfloxacin 400mg twice daily for three days or ciprofloxacin 500mg twice daily for five days.

- Avoid antidiarrhoeal medications like loperamide or diphenoxylate in dysentery because there is a risk of serious complications, including dilation and bursting of the colon.

DIARRHOEA AT A GLANCE

Some characteristics of various diarrhoeal illnesses are summarised here, with their treatments, but remember that diarrhoeal illnesses are notoriously difficult to diagnose on the basis of symptoms alone. The only way to be sure of the diagnosis is through a a laboratory test.

Illness	Incubation period	Characteristics
food poisoning	usually comes on soon after eating	symptoms come on rapidly after eating the bad food; tends to cause vomiting predominantly; usually over in 24 to 48 hours
bacterial watery diarrhoea	usually strikes about the third day after you arrive	diarrhoea tends to be watery, less bloating and less flatulence than with giardiasis
shigella	two to three days	high temperature, blood in diarrhoea, abdominal cramps can be severe
giardiasis	two to six weeks	symptoms are variable but usually sudden onset explosive diarrhoea, associated typically with abdominal distension, cramps and flatulence
amoeba	minimum one week, may be as long as several weeks	bloody diarrhoea (not profuse like bacterial diarrhoea causes), cramps, tends to be prolonged
Cyclospora	2 days to 2 weeks	prolonged diarrhoea with weight loss
irritable bowel syndrome	may start for the first time after an acute attack	may have alternating diarrhoea and constipation, abdominal pains, but no weight loss
tropical sprue	usually develops after an acute attack of diarrhoea	prolonged watery diarrhoea, usually associated with profound weight loss

DEALING WITH DIARRHOEA

If diarrhoea strikes, you don't necessarily need to raid your medical kit for 'stoppers' and antibiotics; there are some simple measures you can take:

- rest – this gives your body the best chance to fight whatever is making you ill; in any case, being on the move with diarrhoea presents a few logistical problems
- drink plenty of fluids – see What to Drink in this section for more guidance on what and how much
- take your temperature and note what it is; repeat this to see how the illness is progressing
- examine what's coming out of your guts to check for blood or mucus (slime) – see Dysentery earlier in this section for what to do if these are present
- be aware of how often you're passing urine and what colour it is, so you can check you're not getting dehydrated
- note any other symptoms you may have – diarrhoea can occur in many other illnesses, including malaria and hepatitis
- remember that diarrhoea is contagious so be scrupulous about washing your hands after you use the toilet

When to See a Doctor

Avoid using antidiarrhoeal remedies (apart from oral re-hydration salts) and get medical help if you experience any of the following:

- you can't keep any fluids down because of vomiting for more than 24 hours (less for a child, eg a couple of hours if they really can't take any fluids)
- the diarrhoea is coming out of you in a watery torrent
- your temperature is 38°C or over
- there's blood or slime in your faeces
- the diarrhoea doesn't clear up after four or five days, or more than a day in a child with moderate to severe diarrhoea
- you think you may have malaria (see p125)
- if you're jaundiced (your skin and the whites of your eyes are yellow)

IF YOU GET DIARRHOEA

Take basic measures: rest, drink plenty of fluids (ORS essential for children and older travellers) and avoid antidiarrhoeals

↓

More than six times in 24 hours?

NO

— YES → See a doctor OR take a single dose of ciprofloxacin 500mg

↓

No better after 24 to 48 hours?

↓

Temperature 38°C or more?

NO

— YES → See a doctor OR if no doctor, take ciprofloxacin 500mg twice daily for five days OR norfloxacin 400mg twice daily for three days

↓

Passing blood in the diarrhoea?

NO

— YES →

↓

No improvement after taking antibiotics?

↓

Can't keep any fluids down because of vomiting?

NO

↓

See a doctor OR if no doctor consider taking metronidazole 250mg three times daily for five to 10 days OR tinidazole 2g single dose (will treat giardiasis and amoebiasis)

↓

Drink lots of fluids; wait for diarrhoea to settle

↓

Persistent diarrhoea (ie more than about seven days)

Remember that children very quickly become dehydrated with diarrhoea or vomiting, so you need to seek help more readily for them. See the section on diarrhoea (p292) in the Babies & Children chapter for more details.

What to Drink

You need to replace what's being lost through the diarrhoea and any vomiting: mainly salts (sodium, potassium and chloride) and water.

You can either use pre-packaged oral rehydration salts (essential in children and older travellers) or you can do it yourself (usually OK for adults with mild or moderate diarrhoea).

Sachets of oral rehydration salts (ORS) are readily available throughout Africa and contain optimum amounts of glucose and salts. Glucose (sugar) is necessary because it encourages the absorption of sodium and water, and it makes you feel better by boosting your energy levels. Read the instructions and make up the ORS in the specified quantity of purified or bottled water. There's no magic ingredient in these, but the relative quantities of salt and sugar are important.

You can easily make up your own solution if necessary by adding six teaspoons of sugar (or honey) and half a teaspoon of table salt to 1L of boiled water. Make it more palatable by adding any flavour you like, eg lemon, ginger or the juice of two oranges.

Although ORS is essential in children and elderly travellers, if you're a normally fit and healthy adult, and the diarrhoea is mild to moderate (up to six bursts a day), you can make do without ORS. Instead, make sure you drink plenty of fluids, including soup (contains salt) and fruit juices (contain glucose and potassium).

You should also try to eat small regular amounts of starchy foods like bread, rice, potato, plain noodles or salty crackers (or local variations on these). Starchy foods are recommended in addition to fluids because they encourage more absorption of sodium and glucose.

Other liquids you can drink include weak black tea with a small amount of sugar added (but it's best to avoid Indian-style milky sweet tea), purified water or, if nothing else is available, soft drinks allowed to go flat and diluted with purified water (but avoid colas if possible).

Alcohol, strong tea, coffee and other caffeine-containing drinks (such as colas) are all best avoided because they can irritate the gut and also promote fluid loss through a diuretic action. It's best to steer clear of dairy products while you have diarrhoea – you can get an intolerance to the sugar in milk when you have diarrhoea, which then exacerbates the problem.

FLUID BALANCE

If you're vomiting or feeling sick, try taking small sips of fluid regularly rather than forcing yourself to down a whole glass in one go. You need to drink the equivalent of two average-sized glasses of fluid every time you have diarrhoea. You should aim for a total fluid replacement of at least 3L over 24 hours, or more if you're not eating anything at all.

Use how much urine you're passing as a rough guide to your fluid balance. Small amounts of dark urine suggest you need to increase your fluid intake. Passing reasonable quantities of light yellow urine indicates that you've got the balance about right. As a rough guide, aim to produce a reasonable quantity of light-coloured urine every three to four hours while you're awake.

What to Eat

It's easy to get hung up about what, if anything, to eat when you have diarrhoea. But relax, use your common sense and try to tune in to what your body is telling you – if you feel like eating, go ahead, especially starchy foods which are known to promote salt and water absorption (such as bread, rice, potatoes, plantains or crackers).

Although eating may increase the bulk of the diarrhoea you pass, it won't generally prolong or worsen the illness, so there's no need to starve yourself deliberately. But if you don't feel like eating, don't force yourself to. Unless you've been travelling hard for some time, you're going to be basically well nourished and well able to withstand a couple of days with little or no food. It may make you feel a bit wobbly, so make sure you add a bit of sugar or honey to your drinks to keep your energy levels up.

Your overworked guts will appreciate small amounts of food at regular intervals rather than great big meals, and this may help make you feel less nauseated, too. You may find that eating brings on cramps and you have to dash to the toilet. We all have a natural physiological reflex whereby eating increases the activity of the gut, but this can get exaggerated in a diarrhoeal illness. It doesn't make you a great dinner companion, but you'll probably find that once you've answered the call of nature you can return to finish your meal! (But remember to wash your hands very thoroughly...)

It goes without saying that it's best to stick to a bland diet while you have diarrhoea and as you recover, and to go easy on fibre providers like fruit, vegetables and nuts. Bananas are good, as they tend to stop you up, and are a source of potassium and glucose. As the diarrhoea clears up and you start to get your appetite back, add in more foods gradually until you're back to normal – this can take some time, up to a week, but if you feel otherwise well, there's no need to worry.

Antidiarrhoeal Remedies

There are remedies you can take to stop you up if you get diarrhoea (antimotility drugs and bismuth), but you're generally better off allowing the illness to run its course.

Antimotility drugs ('stoppers') like loperamide, diphen-oxylate (with atropine) and codeine phosphate slow down your guts, reducing the number of times you have to visit the little room. These are sold under a wide variety of brand names.

Stoppers can be useful if you have to travel on a toilet-less mode of transport or attend an important meeting, but you should treat them with a bit of respect. If you do need to take them, be careful not to take more than the recommended dose. It's usually best not to take stoppers for more than 24 hours because of the risk of side effects (toxic dilatation of the gut and constipation).

Another reason not to take them for longer is that diarrhoea is nature's way of flushing out bugs and their poisons, and stopping this may prevent the illness from settling.

FIT TO EAT

While you have diarrhoea, it's good to eat:

- any of the sub-Saharan African starchy staples (mashed plantain, mealie meal, cassava, ugali etc), so long as they are not oily
- boiled potatoes
- couscous
- plain rice
- plain bread
- dry biscuits, salty or not too sweet
- bananas

If possible, it's best to avoid:

- fruit and vegetables, except bananas
- dairy products, including yoghurt
- spicy foods
- greasy foods

! Note that these drugs should be avoided in children because of the
  risk of side effects, and you shouldn't take them if you have a high
  ● fever or are passing blood or mucus (slime) in the diarrhoea.

Bismuth subsalicylate (trade name Pepto-Bismol) has been
shown to be effective at treating diarrhoea, although it is less
effective than the antimotility drugs and is probably better used
as a preventive. Bismuth shouldn't be taken if you have asthma
or if you are taking aspirin, are sensitive to aspirin or have been
told to avoid aspirin for any reason. It can cause ringing in your
ears and blackening of your tongue. Although it is relatively
safe, you'd be wise not to take large amounts over a prolonged
period of time (maximum three weeks).

 Alternatively, peppermint oil is an antispasmodic that may
be helpful if you're experiencing abdominal cramps. It has no
serious side effects. There are many homoeopathic remedies
for treating diarrhoea (see p82). If you have brought these
with you, take them as directed.

Antibiotics

Self-treating simple watery diarrhoea with antibiotics is one of
those issues that the medical profession can't agree on. There's
plenty of evidence to show that taking a dose of an antibiotic
(eg ciprofloxacin 500mg, single dose) with loperamide (an
antimotility drug) dramatically decreases the length of a
diarrhoeal illness (eg from four days average to maybe one
day) when taken as soon as you have diarrhoea.

Because of this, some doctors will advise you to carry a
treatment dose of an antibiotic to take as soon as you develop
diarrhoea. Others, however, argue that the benefits are not offset
by the risks (including possible side effects of the antibiotic and
the emergence of bacterial resistance) and that in any case
diarrhoea in travellers is usually a mild illness that will clear up
quickly enough on its own.

It's best to discuss this issue with your doctor before you
go, as it depends on how long you're going, how disruptive an
episode of diarrhoea would be, and your normal state of health.
On balance, it's probably worth having a course of antibiotics

with you, but keeping it for a bad attack of watery diarrhoea (eg dashing to the toilet more than about six times a day).

For more serious illnesses, you will probably need antibiotic treatment. See the sections on Dysentery and When to See a Doctor earlier in this chapter, and the following section on Prolonged Diarrhoea for more guidance on this. In this situation, you should seek medical care for a laboratory test to determine the cause of your diarrhoea and the most appropriate treatment.

Self-Treatment

If you're travelling in remote areas without access to medical care, you may need to treat your diarrhoea without a laboratory test, but bear in mind that it is notoriously difficult to make an accurate diagnosis on the basis of symptoms alone.

It would be appropriate to take a course of ciprofloxacin (500mg twice daily for five days) OR norfloxacin (400mg twice daily for three days) if you thought you had bacterial dysentery. If you thought you had a parasite like amoeba or *Giardia*, you could take metronidazole (250mg three times daily for five to 10 days) OR tinidazole (2g single dose).

PROLONGED DIARRHOEA

You may find that, perhaps after an acute attack, you just can't seem to get rid of the diarrhoea. Persistent diarrhoea can be a nuisance. You need to get it checked out by a doctor because you'll need a laboratory test to find out what's causing it so that if it's an infection (most likely), a course of appropriate treatment can be prescribed. Use your common sense, but as a rough guide 'prolonged' diarrhoea is anything lasting longer than about a week.

Infectious causes of persistent diarrhoea include:

- *Giardia*
- amoeba
- bacteria (eg salmonella or campylobacter)
- *Cyclospora* – a recently identified algal-like parasite

IRRITABLE BOWEL SYNDROME

This is a very common condition resulting from bowel dysfunction. You probably won't get it for the first time while you are travelling, but a change in diet and increased stress may make symptoms more likely. There is also some evidence to suggest you're more likely to get it following an episode of food poisoning or travellers diarrhoea. Although the symptoms can be troublesome, they aren't life threatening. The symptoms are variable in nature and severity but may include:

• abdominal pain and spasm (often in the left lower abdomen), relieved by passing wind or faeces

• abdominal bloating (due to trapped wind)

• diarrhoea or constipation

• passing ribbon-like or pellet-like faeces

Symptoms may last only a few days or can persist for a weeks; they often recur. Different people respond differently to treatment. If constipation is the major factor, an increase in dietary fibre will help. If bowel spasm and pain is the main problem, an antispasmodic such as mebeverine 135mg three times daily or peppermint oil capsules may help. Use your common sense and avoid any foods that make the symptoms worse.

If you are not sure of the diagnosis, the symptoms don't fit the pattern described, you have pain that is new or severe or you are unwell in any other way, you should seek medical advice.

Corinne Else

- tropical sprue
- intestinal worms
- TB (very unlikely)

Noninfectious causes include:

- post-infectious irritable bowel (see the boxed text 'Irritable Bowel Syndrome')
- inflammatory bowel disease (unlikely)
- temporary intolerance to lactose, the sugar in milk and milk products.

Tropical sprue is an uncommon condition thought to be due to persisting infection, agent unknown, of your small intestine (the top part), causing you to be unable to absorb nutrients properly. It can be very debilitating, with persistent diarrhoea and weight loss. It can be diagnosed by a laboratory test on a sample of your gut, and is effectively treated with an antibiotic, eg tetracycline and folic acid.

Giardiasis

This travellers favourite is caused by a parasite, *Giardia lamblia*, which you acquire by ingesting food or water contaminated by the hardy cysts of the parasite. *Giardia* can also infect animals, and may be found in streams and other water sources in rural areas, especially on trekking routes. The illness usually appears about a week after you have been exposed to the parasite, but it can appear several weeks after. It may cause a short-lived episode of typical 'travellers diarrhoea', but it can cause persistent diarrhoea. You often notice weight loss with giardiasis, as it can prevent food from being absorbed properly in the upper part of your gut.

Giardiasis can start quite suddenly, with explosive, watery diarrhoea, without blood. More often you get loose, bulky, foul-smelling faeces that are hard to flush away (assuming you have the luxury of flushing, of course), with lots of gas, bloating, stomach gurgling and cramps. You can sometimes get a mild fever and often feel nauseated, with little or no appetite, 'indigestion' (heartburn) and rotten egg burps. Although all these symptoms commonly occur in giardiasis, note that they are nonspecific symptoms and can occur in other types of diarrhoea too – eg you can't assume you've got giardiasis just because you've got rotten egg burps.

You should ideally have a laboratory test to diagnose your illness before starting a course of antibiotics, but if you are in a remote area away from medical help, you could take either metronidazole 250mg three times daily for five to 10 days OR tinidazole 2g single dose (tinidazole is not currently available in the USA).

Amoebiasis

Amoebic dysentery is worth knowing about because it can cause problems outside the gut and won't clear up without antibiotic treatment. It's caused by a protozoan parasite called *Entamoeba histolytica*, which you get by eating food and water contaminated by the parasite cysts. It causes dysentery, ie you get blood and mucus in the diarrhoea, which can be relatively mild and tends to come on gradually. Associated symptoms like fever, vomiting and stomach cramps are much less likely than with giardiasis or bacterial causes, although they can occur.

Complications can occur if the amoeba migrate to your liver or brain, where they can form abscesses, sometimes without diarrhoea beforehand. Signs of an amoebic liver abscess are pain in the right upper abdomen, fever and tenderness on pressing the right upper abdomen.

Treatment is as for giardiasis.

CHOLERA

This diarrhoeal disease can cause rapid dehydration and death. As a traveller you're thought to be at very low risk of getting it, unless you are staying in an area which is experiencing an epidemic. Epidemics tend to be widely reported in the media, so you shouldn't have trouble avoiding them.

Cholera is caused by a bacterium, *Vibrio cholerae*. It's transmitted from person to person (often via healthy carriers

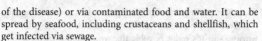

of the disease) or via contaminated food and water. It can be spread by seafood, including crustaceans and shellfish, which get infected via sewage.

Cholera exists where standards of environmental and personal hygiene are low, so it tends to affect the poorest of the poor in developing countries. Every so often there are massive epidemics, usually due to contaminated water in conditions where there is a breakdown of the normal infrastructure, eg in 1994 cholera decimated a Rwandan refugee camp in the Democratic Republic of Congo.

The time between becoming infected and symptoms appearing is usually short, between one and five days. The diarrhoea starts suddenly, and pours out of you. It's characteristically described as 'ricewater' because it is watery and flecked with white mucus. Vomiting and muscle cramps are usual, but fever is rare. In its most serious form, it causes a massive outpouring of fluid (up to 20L a day). This is the worst-case scenario – only about one in 10 sufferers get this. It's a self-limiting illness, meaning that it will end in about a week without any treatment.

You should seek medical help urgently; in the meantime, start rehydration therapy with oral rehydration salts. You may need antibiotic treatment with tetracycline, but fluid replacement is the single most important treatment strategy in cholera.

Prevent cholera by taking basic food and water precautions, avoiding seafood and having scrupulous personal hygiene. The currently available vaccine is an oral vaccine requiring two doses and providing good protection for about two years.

OTHER GUT PROBLEMS

INTESTINAL PARASITES

Although high in yuck value, these infections are rarely life-threatening and often cause remarkably few symptoms. It can be some months or even years before symptoms appear, so if you've been on a long trip, especially if you've been roughing it or spending long periods of time in rural areas in tropical Africa, it's a good idea to get a stool test done to check for these when you get back. Throughout Africa, mind-boggling numbers of people are chronically infected with intestinal worms, and it's quite possible that you could pick up a light infection along the way.

Worms

Different worms are spread in different ways, but the common factor is faeces. Intestinal worms are more common where

---

SUCCULENT SEAFOOD?

Fish and other seafood is an important part of the diet of most coastal communities in Africa and can be a highlight of a trip here. However, you might not be quite so tempted when you realise how many ways fish and shellfish can poison us. Shellfish and crustaceans are filter feeders, so they concentrate any disease-causing bugs (eg cholera and hepatitis) that might be in the water and often thrive near sewage outflows. Fish and shellfish can also cause disease via toxins they can contain.

If tuna and related species are not kept properly refrigerated, they can cause scombroid poisoning, a histamine-like (allergic-type) reaction. Often the fish will taste peppery or sharp, then within half an hour of eating it you get headache, flushing, nausea, vomiting, diarrhoea, dry mouth, and sometimes an allergic rash and wheezing. The syndrome doesn't last long (eight to 12 hours) and it's rarely dangerous. However, if your symptoms are severe, especially if you experience difficulty breathing, you must seek medical advice urgently as you may need adrenaline (epinephrine) treatment.

Ciguatera poisoning occurs when you eat normally edible reef fish that contain ciguatoxin. Symptoms sewage disposal systems are inadequate or nonexistent and water supplies are likely to be unsafe. Flies contribute to their spread by carrying infective eggs or larvae on their feet.

The larvae of **hookworms** and a worm called **strongyloides** develop in the soil after being passed in the faeces of an infected person and can penetrate the skin of bare feet. Both types of worm find their way to the gut, sometimes causing a cough as they pass through the lungs.

usually come on two to six hours after eating the fish, and include some bizarre sensory alterations involving hot/cold sensations, as well as gastro. Rashes are common, and you can get quite severe symptoms, including paralysis, transient blindness and sometimes death. Seek medical help urgently if you think you may be affected.

Shellfish also do their bit to encourage us to leave them alone. In the presence of **red tides** (caused by a type of plankton at certain times of the year) eating shellfish like clams, mussels and oysters can cause numbness and paralysis within half an hour of eating them.

All in all, you'd be wise to give seafood a wide berth, but if you can't resist the temptation:

- seek local advice on the risks of eating seafood (eg ask about any red tides in the last year or so)
- avoid raw seafood (but remember that steaming doesn't necessarily make it safe)
- remember that you can't tell if seafood is toxic by looking or smelling
- get medical help urgently if you experience pins and needles, numbness or paralysis after eating seafood

Untreated, they can live in your gut for years. Hookworms suck blood, so if the infection is heavy (unlikely in travellers), it can cause anaemia.

Roundworms are acquired by ingesting their eggs, often on vegetables. A light infection rarely causes any symptoms, but should be treated because the worms can sometimes get caught in narrow openings (eg into the gall bladder) and cause blockages.

Threadworms are readily passed from person to person via contaminated hands or food, and they cause intense anal itching, especially at night. They are very small and white, and you may notice them wriggling in your faeces or on toilet paper.

Treatment

Treatment of hookworm, strongyloides and roundworm is with an anti-worm medicine like mebendazole or albendazole. Threadworm can be treated with mebendazole or piperazine. Note that mebendazole is not suitable in pregnancy or in children under two years of age.

Tapeworms

Tapeworms have a very high yuck value; worse still, they can make you seriously ill. They are acquired by eating raw or lightly cooked infected meat (eg pork) or fish, or directly swallowing the eggs in the case of the pork tapeworm. Larvae of the pork tapeworm hatch out from the eggs and migrate through the body, forming cysts in the muscles and brain. This condition is called cysticercosis and it's widespread in Africa, especially south of the Sahara. The symptoms are variable, depending on what part of your body is affected, eg if your brain is affected, you can get seizures. This can be a serious condition, so seek medical advice urgently if you think you may be affected. Treatment is with a drug called niclosamide or praziquantel.

Hydatid disease is caused by the larvae of an animal tapeworm and is acquired by stroking dogs which are infected with the adult tapeworms. Eggs may be present in the fur and can stick to your fingers. The eggs hatch into larvae which form cysts in different parts of your body, including the liver, lungs, brain and bones. Treatment can be difficult (it usually involves surgery), so prevention is particularly important.

Lung Fluke

In some parts of West Africa, you may be at risk of acquiring a parasite called a lung fluke from eating raw freshwater fish and crustaceans. Lung flukes cause a cough, fever and chest pain. Other problems are caused if the parasite settles outside the lungs, eg they can cause blindness if they lodge in the eye.

Infection is diagnosed by a laboratory test on a sample of your faeces. Effective and simple treatment is available (praziquantel 20 to 30mg per kilogram twice daily for three days).

Prevention

With all intestinal worms, prevention is the main aim:

- don't walk barefoot
- take care with your food and water and wash your hands before eating
- avoid undercooked meat and fish
- steer clear of dogs

If you think you may have been infected, get this checked out when you get back, or, if you are on a long trip, get a stool test done when you reach somewhere with good medical facilities.

CONSTIPATION

Far less has been written about travellers constipation, but it is a least as common as travellers diarrhoea. Plenty of factors conspire to stop you up while you're travelling, including immobility if you're stuck on a bus, plane or train for hours on end, not drinking enough fluids, disruption to your normal routine, jet lag and a change of diet. A lack of privacy and time to relax can be enough to bring on constipation if you have a shy bowel, or you may find it difficult to get used to squatting (although this is supposed to be a more 'natural' way of defecating). Drugs you have been taking, eg antidiarrhoeals, can cause relatively intractable constipation.

The end result is being unable to defecate as often as normal, which can make you feel bloated and uncomfortable, with no appetite and no energy. If you have piles, this can worsen them.

Tackling Constipation

If you know you are prone to constipation, consider bringing your own supply of bran with you or a reliable remedy you know. Otherwise, try a few simple measures before diving into the nearest pharmacy or your medical kit.

Make sure you're drinking plenty of fluids, especially if it's hotter than you're used to. Try to increase the fibre in your diet by eating more fruit (peeled) and vegetables (cooked and peeled) but avoid bananas, which can stop you up. Porridge, pulses, nuts and dried fruit are also good fibre providers. Prune juice is an old favourite, if you can find it. A cup of hot, strong coffee can get things moving, especially first thing in the morning, while a large meal can have the same effect (remember that if you're not eating much for any reason, there's not going to be much coming out, either). Alcohol has a laxative effect but don't overdo it. Finding a decent toilet may help – perhaps consider changing hotels. Exercise is beneficial in many ways, including stimulating your guts. Finally, if you feel like going, don't be tempted to hang on or the moment will pass.

If simple measures fail, you could consider taking something fairly gentle like lactulose syrup (15mL twice daily, takes about 48 hours to work) or senna, a gut stimulant (two to four tablets at night, works in eight to 12 hours).

PILES (HAEMORRHOIDS) & OTHER ANAL PROBLEMS

Piles are swollen veins around the anus, either on the outside (external) or inside, occasionally popping out (internal) when you strain. Both are more common in constipation (because of straining) or diarrhoea, or by carrying heavy packs, especially up mountains. External piles can be excruciatingly painful.

The pain can be relieved by cutting them open (still with us?) but this needs to be done by a medic, ideally under sterile conditions. Otherwise, you may need to take painkillers and hotfoot it down the mountain.

Internal piles can be uncomfortable, with a feeling of something popping out when you strain and may cause itchiness around the anus. Local anaesthetic creams can help, eg those containing lignocaine.

If you get excruciating pain when you pass faeces, especially if you've been constipated, often with bright red blood on the toilet paper, you probably have an anal fissure, a small split in the anus. It can be very painful, but there's no specific treatment apart from taking care to keep the area clean and dealing with any constipation you may have.

Anal itching may be caused by threadworms. The way to test for these, apart from studying your faeces carefully, is to put a piece of tape across your anus at night and examine it in the morning for the tiny white thread-like worms. Treatment is with an anti-worm medicine, as described earlier in this chapter. Other causes of anal itching are chafing and poor hygiene.

INDIGESTION

A change in diet, stress, anxiety and spicy foods can all make 'indigestion' (burning pains in your upper stomach) and heartburn (burning in your gullet, often with an acid taste in your mouth) more likely when you're travelling. The discomfort is often worse when you're hungry and just after meals. Smoking and alcohol exacerbate it.

Simple measures you could try are to eat small, regular meals – eg don't eat a huge meal just before you go to bed. Consider stopping smoking and cutting back on alcohol or at least giving yourself a break for a few days. It can be difficult in some places, but try to avoid spicy, hot foods. Milk and yoghurt can be soothing, as can eating plain, starchy foods like bread, chapattis or rice.

You could consider trying antacids (there are many products available without prescription; take them between meals and at night), although stomach acid has a protective effect against infective agents, so this may make you more vulnerable to gut infections.

! You need to seek medical help urgently if the pain is severe and not relieved by any of these measures, if it wakes you at night, if it seems to go through to your back, if you have had a stomach or duodenal ulcer in the past or if you vomit blood.

If you have a gastric or duodenal ulcer, or are taking treatment for one, this may make you more susceptible to gut infections, so it's best to discuss this with your doctor before you go, as you may be able to change to a different anti-ulcer medicine.

APPENDICITIS

If you've still got your appendix, acute appendicitis is a possible cause of severe abdominal pain. It's reasonably common in both adults and children, and you should consider it if you've got abdominal pain that's colicky or constant, and increases in severity over a short period of time (12 to 24 hours). Symptoms can vary, but typically they're as follows:

- central abdominal pain that may be colicky (comes and goes) or constant, and which moves to the right lower abdomen after a few hours, becoming constant
- nausea, loss of appetite and sometimes vomiting
- mild fever but not usually very high
- diarrhoea in some cases, but it's not usually very severe
- the right lower abdomen is tender when you press on it

Seek medical help urgently if you think appendicitis may be a possibility, as you'll need surgery if the diagnosis is confirmed. It's potentially extremely dangerous if it's not treated quickly.

KIDNEY STONE

Dehydration (and other conditions) can cause chemicals in the urine to harden and form small stones in the kidney. A stone can become stuck in the tube leading from the kidney to the bladder and, if it does, you experience excruciating pain. The pain usually starts suddenly on one side, in the back just below the ribcage, spreading round to the groin in the front. Characteristically, the pain is gripey (ie it comes and goes in waves) and you can't stay still with it. It can be so severe that it makes you vomit.

Most (95%) kidney stones eventually work their way down to the bladder and get passed out within about a day or so. However, you should seek medical help if possible, as you will probably need a strong painkilling injection.

• If you have a fever, this indicates that the kidney is infected, which is a medical emergency.

If the pain subsides and has not returned after 12 hours or so, this means that you've probably passed the stone, but it's a good idea to get this checked out as soon as possible, or when you get back if you're on a short trip. Make sure you drink plenty of fluids to prevent further problems.

Respiratory System...

Coughs and colds can be troublesome when you're travelling and can sometimes lead to worse problems, so make sure you recognise the symptoms and don't let complications get a hold.

COLDS

It's not just the culture that's different and exciting, the viruses are too. The common cold is common the world over. Because colds are spread by droplets (eg sneezing) and close personal contact, you're more likely to get them in crowded urban environments, by travelling on crowded public transport or by eating in crowded restaurants. Air pollution in big cities, and hawking and spitting compound the problem.

As for symptoms, you know the score – slightly raised or normal temperature, runny nose, sore throat and maybe cough. Colds usually go away in a few days without any special treatment, but when you're travelling you're more vulnerable to complications like sinusitis, bronchitis and ear infection.

Recognise the symptoms of a cold as a sign to take it easy for a day or two. Unless you get complications, antibiotics are no use because colds are caused by viruses, not bacteria. Drink plenty of fluids, treat yourself to some good meals and take simple painkillers if necessary for any aches or pains. You can make your own cold remedy by adding honey or sugar to lemon or lime juice and top up with boiled water.

 If you've got homoeopathic remedies with you, try taking gelsemium or allium cepa. Helpful naturopathic remedies include Combi Q tissue salts, thyme and sage tea or, perhaps most popular of all, echinacea tincture or tablets with or without zinc.

SINUSITIS

This usually follows a cold, and can be a pain – literally. The sinuses are air-filled cavities in the skull above the eyes and on either side of the nose, designed to make our heads lighter so that they don't drag on the ground. If the lining of the cavities becomes infected and the normally empty spaces fill with mucus or pus, it causes you pain.

Symptoms are headache (usually over your forehead) or face pain, which is worse when you strain or bend over. Your forehead or cheeks may feel tender when you press them, and you feel something dripping down the back of your throat. Typically the pain isn't there when you get up, but comes on during the morning, reaching a crescendo about lunch time before gradually receding. It's possible to be quite ill, with a fever and aches and pains.

Try inhalations of steam, menthol, tiger balm or eucalyptus or tea tree oil as a first measure, together with simple painkillers. If this doesn't help, you could try taking a nasal decongestant like pseudoephedrine hydrochloride 60mg four times daily (though not if you have high blood pressure). Antihistamines may also help.

If you have a fever and you feel rough, you'll probably need a course of antibiotics – see a doctor if possible. If not, suitable antibiotics are co-amoxiclav 250mg three times daily OR cefaclor 250mg three times daily.

! Flying can make the pain worse, so start taking a nasal decongestant the day before you fly or use a nasal decongestant spray. Underwater diving also makes it worse, so avoid diving until you feel better.

HAY FEVER (ALLERGIC RHINITIS)

This common condition is usually due to an allergy to something in the air you're breathing, such as pollen. It can often be difficult to decide whether your symptoms are because of a cold or an allergy, although if they persist and you otherwise feel reasonably well, it's probably hay fever.

Hay fever involves lots of nose blowing. Other symptoms include sneezing, and itchy eyes, roof of the mouth and (sometimes) ears. Your chest may feel tight as you can get asthma with it (see the section on Cough later in this chapter).

INHALATIONS – HOW TO DO IT

In case you don't know, here's how:

- get hold of a washing up basin, bucket or bowl, or use a washbasin (you'll need that universal plug)
- fill it with boiling water
- optional – add a few drops of menthol (which should be widely available), tiger balm, eucalyptus or tea tree oil
- once the heat is bearable, put your face in the steam rising from the bowl and drape a towel over your head
- stay like this for as long as you can bear it or until it has stopped steaming

If you know you're susceptible to hay fever, it's a good idea to bring all your usual remedies with you. If it's being a real nuisance, try antihistamine tablets to start with (see the Buying & Using Medicines appendix for more details), but if this doesn't control it, you could try a nasal spray containing steroids (the amount used won't cause any general problems) such as beclomethasone dipropionate spray. It needs to be taken regularly to have the best chance of working.

INFLUENZA

Influenza is often called flu, and with other similar viral illnesses is spread in the same way as colds and, for the same reasons, infection is more likely when you're travelling. Although we tend to think of colds and flu as the same thing, they actually have very different symptoms. Influenza is a more severe disease. Flu tends to start quite suddenly, often with a high temperature, and it can make you feel pretty dreadful, with headache and generalised aches and pains. You may have a runny nose and sore throat with it, and often a dry cough that can last for several weeks. Although the illness usually lasts a few days, it can leave you feeling tired and out of energy for some time. The good news is that there's a vaccine against flu which is recommended for travellers. It is new each year, and contrary to popular belief, cannot give you flu.

There's no specific treatment for flu but, as for colds, complications such as a chest infection may be more likely when travelling, so it's worth taking care of yourself. You probably won't feel like doing much for a day or two anyway, so rest up. Paracetamol (acetaminophen) can help lower the fever and relieve aches and pains, and any of the remedies discussed under Colds may help your symptoms. Drink plenty of fluids because it's easy to get dehydrated with a fever, and once the fever is down, step up the food as you start to feel better. As flu is a viral illness, antibiotics won't do you any good unless you get complications.

The trouble with flu is that the symptoms are so nonspecific that lots of diseases can mimic it, and it can be hard to tell if it's flu or something more serious like malaria. To give you some guidelines, you need to see a doctor if:

- your temperature is over 39°C (102°F) and it can't be lowered by any of the measures suggested on p121
- you try all of these measures, but you don't feel better after two days – it may not be flu after all
- you feel breathless, start to cough up green spit or have chest pain – this may indicate a chest infection
- you think it could be malaria or dengue fever – the symptoms can be identical
- you have a severe headache, neck stiffness and hypersensitivity to light – you may have meningitis

SORE THROAT

You can get an uncomfortable throat if you're travelling in dry and dusty situations, if you're mouth-breathing because your nose is blocked or you're doing strenuous exercise. Drink plenty of fluids, eat moist foods like fruit and vegetables, and consider chewing sugar-free gum if you can get hold of it. Your lips can get very dry under these conditions and cracked lips are uncomfortable (and an infection risk). The tender skin of your lips is also very sensitive to the sun, so use a lip salve with sunblock, and reapply it regularly throughout the day. Keep 'em luscious by using a lip balm or plain paraffin jelly at night.

Sore throats can also be caused by infection, usually viral, often with a viral eye infection (conjunctivitis – see p187) as well. They can occur on their own or as part of other illnesses like colds, flu and glandular fever (see that section in this chapter). They usually clear up on their own after a few days without any special treatment. Simple measures for treating sore throats are to gargle regularly with salty water (buy some table salt and put a few spoonfuls into a glass of purified water) or a solution of soluble aspirin or paracetamol (acetaminophen). Having lots of warm drinks will also help: add some grated ginger, lime juice and sugar (honey is better if you can get it) to a cup of hot water.

About a third of sore throats are caused by a bacterial infection. The reason this matters is that some bacterial throat infections can occasionally lead to serious complications, especially in children. Unfortunately, the only sure way to tell bacterial and viral sore throats apart is by a laboratory test, but as a rule of thumb, you need to seek medical advice for severe (eg if you can't swallow solids) or persistent (more than five days without any improvement) sore throats, as they will need to be treated with antibiotics. Suitable antibiotics are co-amoxiclav 250mg three times a day OR cefaclor 250mg three times a day.

Note that if you've been having oral sex, especially with a new partner, gonorrhoea can cause a sore throat. If you think this is a possibility you should seek medical advice to get it checked out, as you'll need a course of antibiotics.

GLANDULAR FEVER

Glandular fever (infectious mononucleosis), also known as the 'kissing disease' because it can be passed by saliva, causes a severe sore throat. Suspect this viral disease if you have a severe sore throat that doesn't settle with antibiotics.

Symptoms include a sore throat, swollen glands (lumps in your neck, armpits and groins) and fever. You may also notice that you're jaundiced (yellowed skin and whites of the eyes). Very occasionally, it can lead to a serious complication – bursting of the spleen (one of your internal abdominal organs). If you have glandular fever and you develop abdominal pain, particularly in the left upper part of the abdomen, you need to seek medical advice urgently.

Glandular fever can only be confirmed by a blood test; there's no specific treatment. It can leave you feeling weak and washed out weeks, sometimes months, afterwards. Other viral infections can cause similar symptoms.

CAUSES OF SORE THROAT

- heat and dust
- viral infections, colds and flu
- bacterial infections ('strep' sore throat)
- glandular fever (infectious mononucleosis)
- toxoplasmosis
- sexually transmitted infections (eg gonorrhoea)
- diphtheria (p229)
- Lassa fever (p224)

COLD SORES

Cold sores are caused by a herpes virus infection which recurs periodically. If you've had these before, the stresses of travel are quite likely to make them recur. Other factors that make recurrences more likely include sunlight, fever and menstruation. You usually know when one is coming on because you'll feel a burning sensation on the edge of your lip followed by a blister, usually the next day. They take about a week to clear up. Acyclovir cream (5%) can be effective if you apply it as soon as you feel the burning starting, but it may be difficult to get hold of locally, so take a tube with you. Using a lip salve with sunblock can help prevent recurrence.

Secondary bacterial infection is a risk, so try to avoid touching the sore with your fingers. This is good practice anyway, as you can introduce infection in your eye if you then rub your eyes.

MOUTH ULCERS

These are more likely to occur if you're stressed or if you're taking proguanil as an antimalarial; otherwise, they're a bit of a mystery. Regularly swishing your mouth out with salty water or an antiseptic mouthwash (eg chlorhexidine), or even just applying a small amount of toothpaste to the ulcer can help, although all these measures will sting at first.

COUGH

Lots of things can make you cough in this part of the world, including physical hazards like dust, smoke and air pollution, as well as infections like colds and flu, chest infection (bronchitis), asthma and even malaria (p125). There are some much rarer causes of cough which you don't need to worry unduly about, including lung flukes (p167), hydatid disease (p166) and various worm infestations (p164).

Many chest infections are caused by viruses, unless you've got a chronic lung condition or it follows another illness like flu. We know you know, but it should be pointed out that all chest infections are more common in cigarette smokers.

Bronchitis usually begins with an irritating, dry cough and a feeling of tightness in the chest. You may have a mild fever. After a day or so, you start coughing up yellow or greenish gunk. It usually clears up on its own in about five to seven days.

PASSIVE SMOKING

Cairo is one of the most polluted cities in the world. Air pollution here in the mother of all cities is so bad that breathing the atmosphere in the city centre is said to be to be equivalent to smoking a packet of cigarettes a day. It's worse in the summer heat – something to bear in mind if you suffer from asthma or other respiratory diseases.

The main culprit is the almost two million vehicles on Cairo's roads. Levels of lead and other pollutants in the air are some of the highest in the world, and hundreds of infants die each year because of their mother's exposure to lead during pregnancy, and many more children suffer reduced IQ and other health problems because of exposure to high lead levels in the air. However, the Egyptian government has become sufficiently alarmed to do something about it: laws have been passed requiring factories to install filters, there's a small fleet of buses that run on natural gas and in 2006 a fleet of eco-friendly taxis was introduced (albeit with higher fares).

Antibiotics aren't usually needed (they don't work against viral infections), but there are some situations when you do need to see a doctor:

you're pretty sick, with a high fever – it may be malaria or a more serious chest infection

you're still coughing a week later

you're feeling increasingly short of breath

you have pain in your chest on coughing or taking a deep breath

you cough up blood

If you do need antibiotics, appropriate treatment would be amoxycillin 250mg three times a day OR, if you're allergic to penicillin, erythromycin 250mg four times a day.

If you're asthmatic, you'll probably know about it before you go travelling, and you should take a plentiful supply of your usual medicines with you. Symptoms include a cough, wheeze, chest tightness and shortness of breath, which may be worse at night or brought on by exercise.

It is possible that asthma may start for the first time while you are travelling, especially if you are travelling in polluted urban areas. It's very common in children and young adults, and appears to be a disease of 'Westernisation'. Some drugs can make it worse and should be avoided, the most common one being aspirin.

If you're worried, seek medical advice so that appropriate medication can be prescribed if necessary. If you are very short of breath or wheezy, you should seek help urgently.

Ears, Eyes & Teeth...

Grouped here are three parts of the body you probably wouldn't normally give much thought to. However, they can be troublesome if they go wrong, and some aspects of travelling can make this more likely.

EARS

FLYING

Cabin pressure is normally kept at levels equivalent to those at altitudes of 1800 to 2400m (6000 to 8000ft). At these pressures, gas in body cavities (like your ears) expands by about 30%. Normally, this isn't a problem because you can equalise the pressure between the cabin and your ears by swallowing, yawning or sucking on a sweet. However, if your ear is blocked for any reason (eg if you've got a cold or hay fever), you can get a pressure build-up which is very painful, and sometimes your eardrum can burst.

It's best not to fly if you've got a cold or severe hay fever, and you shouldn't fly at all if you've got a middle ear infection. If you have to fly with a cold, the following measures should help:

- take a decongestant, such as pseudoephedrine hydrochloride 60mg four times daily (but not if you have high blood pressure), starting the day before you fly
- take an antihistamine before and during the flight (follow the dose instructions on the packet)
- try a nasal decongestant spray – use it an hour before the expected time of arrival, and every 20 minutes after this
- during the descent, pinch your nose firmly and blow hard down it – this should force the pressure to equalise, and you should feel your ears pop; do this as often as necessary

If these measures don't work, your eardrum may burst. You'll get a gradual build-up of severe pain, followed by sudden relief. You may notice a bit of bleeding from the ear.

If this happens, ideally see a doctor to get it checked out. If it
has burst, it'll take about six weeks to heal up. During this time,
you should avoid getting water in the ear – use ear plugs or a
cottonwool ball covered in petroleum jelly when you shower or
wash your hair. It's best to avoid swimming altogether until it's
healed, and you should definitely avoid swimming underwater.
If you do swim, take care to protect your ear with earplugs. If
possible, you should get your ear looked at again in about six
weeks. If you have any persistent symptoms (eg discharge from
the ear), you should seek medical advice before this.

EARACHE

The most common cause of earache is fluid build-up behind
the eardrum during or just after a cold. This will respond to
simple painkillers and doesn't need antibiotic treatment.

Sometimes earache is due to infection, either in the outer
ear (the bit you can stick your finger into) or in the middle ear
(the bit behind the eardrum). The causes and treatment differ
depending on where the infection is. You can tell them apart by
pulling on your ear lobe – if the pain increases, it's a problem in
the outer ear; if there is no pain, it's a middle ear problem.

Outer Ear Infection

This is very common in swimmers, and is sometimes called
'swimmer's ear' or 'tropical ear'. It's caused by swimming in
dirty water, especially in hot, humid conditions. Bugs thrive
in these conditions, and you can get an infection even if you
haven't been swimming in dirty water.

'Tropical ear' is very itchy, and you may notice a discharge,
as well as earache. If it's very painful, it may indicate that you
have a boil in the ear canal.

Simple painkillers will help relieve the discomfort. Warmth
also helps – you could try putting a water bottle filled with
warm water and wrapped in a towel against your ear. If you
can get hold of some eardrops, appropriate treatment is either
aluminium acetate drops (this helps to toughen the skin) OR
antibiotic drops, usually combined with a steroid and ideally

with an antifungal too (eg neomycin with hydrocortisone and polymyxin B sulphate).

Note that antibiotic eardrops shouldn't be used for longer than a week because long term use can lead to secondary fungal infection. If your symptoms haven't settled in a week, seek medical advice, since you may need a change of antibiotic or treatment to clean out your ear canal.

> To give the infection a chance to get better, make sure you don't get water in your ear for at least two weeks; use earplugs if you're washing your hair, taking a shower or swimming, and avoid swimming underwater.

Allergic reactions, eg to eardrops or swimming pool water, can also cause itching. If so, try to keep your ears dry and think about stopping the eardrops.

> It's tempting, but avoid cleaning your ears out with the corner of a towel, a cotton bud or anything else, as this makes infection much more likely.

Middle Ear Infection

Typically, you get this during or just after a cold. It starts as a blocked feeling in the ear and progresses to pain, often with a fever. Later, you may notice a discharge from the ear (eg on your pillow) if your eardrum bursts, followed by relief from the pain.

If it doesn't start to get better in 48 hours, seek medical advice, as you'll probably need a course of antibiotics (usually amoxycillin). In the meantime, simple painkillers will help the discomfort and to bring any fever down. Warmth against your ear may help. You should avoid putting eardrops or getting water in your ear in case your eardrum has burst. See the previous section for guidance on this.

Note that earache in both ears is unlikely to be due to infection. It's more likely to be due to blockage by mucus, and it may respond to decongestants (eg pseudoephedrine) or antihistamines.

Earache sometimes isn't to do with your ears. Problems outside the ear – such as in the jaw, throat or teeth – can sometimes cause earache and may be the reason why the treatments described earlier don't work.

> **!** Diving into the water when you've got a cold may push germs into your ears and make infection more likely, so it's best avoided.

DEAFNESS WITHOUT PAIN

This is usually due to wax. Don't attempt to poke anything in your ear, as this makes infection more likely. Try wax-dissolving eardrops (eg Cerumol), or warm almond or olive oil. If this doesn't work, your ears may need to be syringed out, but you might want to wait until you get home before getting this done.

EYES

This section was compiled by Graeme Johnson, an ophthalmic surgeon based in Sydney, Australia.

If you use regular medications for a preexisting eye condition like glaucoma or diabetes, remember to make sure you take plenty of supplies with you, as well as a letter from your doctor saying why you need to carry them, to avoid any problems at customs.

If you have had recent eye surgery, get advice from your eye doctor on what you can and cannot do (eg diving into swimming pools is not advisable for some time after surgery).

When you're travelling it can be hard to keep your hands clean, and general environmental cleanliness can be far from ideal in many countries, so take care to touch your eyes as little as possible, especially when you're out and about. Don't wipe your eyes with cloths or towels that could be dirty – if necessary, use a clean tissue.

SPECTACLES

If you wear glasses, remember to take a spare pair with you and consider having a pair tinted as sunglasses. Optical prescriptions are understood in all languages, so if you take a copy, you can always have a new pair made. You could consider carrying one of those miniature screwdrivers which will tighten the screws in glasses frames; these always work loose at the most inopportune times.

CONTACT LENSES

If you wear contact lenses, you will know what to take – remember that the various solutions and cleaners can take up a fair bit of luggage space. It's a good idea to take back-up glasses. Maintaining your usual hygiene standards could be difficult, especially if you're roughing it. If necessary, you can use boiled and cooled water in place of your usual cleansers. Take extra care to wash your hands with soap and water before handling the lenses.

If your eye becomes red or irritated, remove the lens, clean and sterilise it and leave it out until your eye is better. Bathing your eye in clean salty water may help. If your eye hasn't improved after 48 hours, you should seek medical advice, as it may indicate an infection that needs to be treated appropriately.

ANTIMALARIALS

If you're taking chloroquine, you may notice some blurring of vision – this doesn't indicate any permanent damage. A more serious, but rare, complication is permanent damage to the retina (the back of the eye), but this is only likely to occur if you take chloroquine in high doses for a long time (usually for more than three years).

SUN

Sunlight can damage your eyes, so make sure you take good (but not necessarily expensive) sunglasses, and wear them. Sunglasses that block out light from the sides (ie wraparound ones, or ones with side pieces) are best. Sunlight is reflected off water and snow. If you're going to be trekking in snowy conditions, ski goggles may be better. Snow blindness, or sunburn of the surface of the eyes, can be excruciatingly painful and may take a couple of days to resolve. It doesn't have any lasting effects.

BATHING YOUR EYES

If you've got an eye bath, this is obviously designed for the purpose, but good substitutes include any small container or glass, or an egg cup. If you have a ready-made saline (salt) solution, you can use that; or you can make up your own by dissolving a level teaspoon of salt in about 600ml (a pint) of boiled and cooled water or by adding a pinch of salt to a cup of water.

Fill the eye bath or container, bend your head over it with your eye open and blink rapidly in the water. You could get someone to pour the water into your eye if you prefer, but you'll get pretty wet. Alternatively, get someone to soak a tissue or a clean cloth in the water and squeeze it into your eye from a height of a few inches while you are lying down.

DRY OR ITCHY EYES

Air conditioning, especially in aircraft, can exacerbate dry eyes and allergic eye conditions. Take lubricant drops with you (available without prescription from pharmacies) and use them frequently. Note that anti-allergy drops containing a decongestant ingredient shouldn't be used more than every few days – these are eyedrops that usually claim to make red, tired eyes look white.

SOMETHING IN THE EYE

Dust, particles of sand and insects can get blown into your eyes. If you need to, get a travel companion to wash the particle out with copious amounts of water – see the boxed text for guidance on how to do this. Salty water is better in theory, but clean water is fine if nothing else is available.

If a particle can be seen on the white of the eye or under the upper eyelid (turn the eyelid over a match or a small key), it can be gently removed with the corner of a tissue or (even more gently) a cotton bud. The clear central part of the eye is too sensitive for you to be able to do this. If you can't wash the particle away, you'll need to go to a doctor, who may be able to remove it after anaesthetising the eye.

RED EYE

If your eye is red and sticky, with a discharge, you've probably got an infection (conjunctivitis). Another cause of red eye is a haemorrhage on the surface of the white of the eye. It can look fairly spectacular, but if your sight is unaffected and you don't have any pain, there's nothing to worry about. You don't need any specific treatment and it will clear up in a week or so.

Conjunctivitis

This eye infection is quite common, especially in children. When you're travelling, it can be difficult to keep your hands clean, which is a source of infection if you then put them up to your eyes. You can also get conjunctivitis by swimming in crowded pools or dirty rivers, or through flies landing on your eyes (although you usually have a reflex blink that prevents flies landing).

Conjunctivitis can be caused by bacteria or viruses. Bacterial conjunctivitis usually quickly affects both eyes, whereas viral conjunctivitis is more likely to affect one eye only, and you don't usually get such a copious discharge. Viral conjunctivitis often comes with flu or a cold.

In addition to looking red, your eye may feel very irritated, as though there's something in it. If you have a bad infection, your eye can be quite uncomfortable, and you'll find bright light difficult to tolerate.

Treatment

If you've got a red, sticky eye, bathe it frequently in clean (boiled and cooled) plain or salty water. Try not to touch or rub your eye, as this makes the infection more likely to spread to your other eye – or to other people.

If the redness doesn't clear up in a couple of days or you've got ready access to medical care, see a doctor, as you will probably need a course of antibiotic eyedrops or ointment.

A common and effective antibiotic for eye infections is chloramphenicol (eyedrops or ointment); other commonly used antibiotic eyedrops and ointments that may be available include neomycin, gentamicin or sulphonamides. Start by putting one drop in every two hours, decreasing this as the redness and irritation improve. If you've got an ointment as well, apply the ointment at night before you go to sleep. If you've got ointment alone, apply it three to four times daily.

Ointment should be put directly into the eye, as follows: hold out the lower eyelid and squeeze about 1cm of cream into the pouch made behind the lid, then close the eye on it.

Bacterial conjunctivitis usually improves (ie the redness clears up) in two to three days, but you need to continue using the drops or ointment for three more days to make sure. If you don't notice any improvement within 48 hours of using the antibiotic, it may be that the cause is not bacterial. Viral conjunctivitis won't respond to antibiotics – it will clear up on its own, although it may take a week or two.

> As a rule, you should avoid using eyedrops containing a combination of an antibiotic and steroids (the names of these usually end in '-sone' like betamethasone), as this can sometimes cause a serious problem if the infection is not bacterial.

Trachoma

This type of conjunctivitis, spread by flies, is most common in dry, rural areas of Africa (especially North Africa), as well as in other parts of the world. Untreated and repeated infection results in serious damage to the eyes, and it is a major cause of blindness worldwide. Before you get too alarmed, it's not likely to be a big problem for you as a traveller in the region, as you'll generally wave off any flies that approach your eyes. Treatment is with antibiotic eyedrops (chlortetracycline) or tablets (eg a single dose of azithromycin).

STYE

If you develop a painful red lump on the edge of your eyelid, it's probably a stye. This is a bit like a pimple anywhere else. It usually clears up in a couple of days without any special treatment. Try putting a clean cloth soaked in clean hot water (not scalding) on your closed eyelid, and do this several times a day.

If it doesn't go away, it might be something called a chalazion. This is a blocked and infected gland in the eyelid, and you'll need to see a doctor about it.

BLACK EYE

If you receive a blow to the eye, you may get a black eye. This is due to bruising around and behind the eye, usually with swelling of the eyelids, but your sight is not usually affected (unless your eyelids are so swollen, that you can't open them, of course). If your sight is not normal, then you need to get medical advice as soon as possible. Minimise the bruising by putting an ice pack (or anything cold, including snow) on your closed eye.

OTHER EYE INJURIES

You can get a scratch on the eye if the branch of a bush or tree whips back in your face after the person in front passes it and bends it forward. You usually get pain straight away, which may become worse after an hour or two. If you put a pad on the eye, this makes it more comfortable, although if you're trying to walk on rough ground, this is not easy with one eye! Keep the pad on for a few hours or even a couple of days if the pain persists, although you might find it's more trouble than it's worth.

If you've got a tube of antibiotic eye ointment (such as chloramphenicol), you could use that. If the abrasion is not too deep, it should heal in one or two days.

A blow to the eye can cause bleeding inside the eye, which your travel companion may see as a fluid level of blood in the iris (the coloured part of the eye). This is a potentially dangerous situation – seek medical help urgently; in the meantime, rest in bed with the eye covered.

SIGNS OF SERIOUS EYE PROBLEMS

If you experience any of the following symptoms, you should seek medical advice urgently:

- any blurred vision or loss of vision that can't be improved by blinking or washing your eye
- sudden loss of vision
- painful eye, especially if it is also unusually sensitive to light
- double vision
- eye injury followed by loss of vision or blood in the eye

LOSS OF VISION &/OR PAIN IN THE EYE

! If you lose your sight, partially or totally in one or both eyes, you need to seek medical help urgently.

If you suddenly lose your sight (from blurring to total loss) without any pain, it could be due to a haemorrhage inside the eye or detachment of the retina (the back of the eye). You may notice a curtain obstructing part of the vision in one eye, which may be preceded by seeing lightning flashes on one side of the vision. Retinal detachment can also follow injury.

If you have blurring or loss of vision associated with intolerance to light and severe aching pain in the eye, it could be due to inflammation inside the eye (iritis) or glaucoma (where the pressure inside the eye is abnormally high). Glaucoma is more likely to occur in older people. Both of these conditions need urgent medical attention.

Partial loss of vision associated with giddiness (especially if you experience weakness in an arm or leg) is likely to be a stroke – a blockage of the blood vessels in the brain. This is also more likely to occur in older people.

MIGRAINE

Bear in mind that migraine headaches can be associated with flashing lights or other eye symptoms like tunnel vision. The visual symptoms usually last about 20 minutes, and may or may not be followed by a headache. If you have had it before, you will know what it is, but if it is the first time, it can be frightening.

All sorts of factors can trigger migraines when you're travelling: tiredness, movement, stress and sunlight. Try taking simple painkillers as early as possible to prevent the attack worsening. Natural remedies like feverfew can be helpful (although you will need to have a supply with you).

TEETH

UK-based dentist Iain Corran gives you the low-down on staying out of the dentist's chair while you're away.

There are lots of reasons why dental problems are more likely when you're travelling. You tend to consume sugary drinks (soft drinks or sweet tea or coffee) in much larger quantities than you would at home, while practical difficulties with water supplies – or simply the lack of a washbasin – may mean that you take a break in your usual dental hygiene routine just when it's needed most. You'll probably want to avoid having to get dental treatment while you are away because it may be unreliable, expensive and could carry a risk of hepatitis B or HIV if instruments are not properly sterilised.

BEFORE YOU GO

It's a good idea to have a dental check-up about four to six weeks before you plan to travel, as this allows time for you to have any necessary treatment. Let the dentist know you're going away so you can have a really thorough examination. If you wear a brace, be sure to get it checked before you leave, and let your dentist know how long you are going to be away so any necessary alterations can be made.

DENTAL KIT

Consider taking a dental kit with you, or ask your dentist to provide you with a small tube of temporary filling material (which is a bit like chewing gum) or even a plastic filling tool (a spatula thing to help you put the filling in), but make sure you're clear about when and how to use these. Commercial dental kits are available from many travel health clinics, and usually include a dental mirror and temporary filling material, as well as instructions on how to use them. They tend to be quite expensive, but are probably worth considering if you're planning to be away for a long time or trekking in remote areas. Other useful items for dental emergencies include painkillers (eg co-codamol), a course of antibiotics (discuss this with your doctor) and oil of cloves (for toothache).

If you have been advised to have antibiotic cover for any dental treatment, eg because you have heart valve disease, then remember to carry the necessary medication with you (ie amoxycillin 3g sachet, or erythromycin if allergic to penicillin).

AVOIDING DENTAL PROBLEMS

The two main preventable causes of dental problems are tooth decay and gum disease. Tooth decay arises when refined sugars are turned into acid by bacteria in the mouth. The acid erodes the outer layer of the tooth, called enamel, eventually resulting in a cavity. Gum disease is caused by a build-up of plaque (a layer of bacteria and food gunk) on the tooth surface near the gum margin. This can cause sensitivity, particularly to hot and cold foods, and you may notice bleeding from the gums, especially when you brush your teeth.

As a general rule, try to avoid sweet sugary foods and drinks, especially carbonated soft drinks and local-style tea (which is often extremely sweet), and rinse your mouth out with clean water after you eat. In hot climates, you may find your mouth gets really dry. Keeping your mouth moist, eg by chewing on a sugar-free gum, helps reduce the risk of tooth decay, as the saliva neutralises the acid by bacteria in the mouth.

Avoid plaque build-up by brushing your teeth, ideally with a fluoride toothpaste, at least once a day. Remember to take generous supplies of your favourite toothpaste with you, as it may not be available locally. If you run out of toothpaste and you can't get any more, you can use a small amount of salt instead on a moist brush. If you're on a long trip, remember to pack a spare toothbrush. However, if you can't get a replacement, you can use your finger as a toothbrush, possibly with a small piece of clean cloth around it.

In some places making a toothbrush from a piece of wood, by splitting the end to make bristles, is quite common, but beware of splinters in the gums.

It's also a good idea to use dental floss or tape to clean the areas between your teeth where the toothbrush doesn't reach. If you run out of floss, toothpicks can do the same job, and are widely available. Dental floss can come in handy for a multitude of minor repairs, so is well worth tucking into your pack.

Remember that you need to use clean (bottled or purified) water for brushing your teeth or flossing – it's obvious, but surprisingly easy to forget!

If you wear a brace, it's particularly important to avoid sticky or hard foods which may damage it, as specialist treatment may be required to fix it.

DENTAL PROBLEMS

In spite of your best efforts, you may experience some teeth problems while you're away.

Broken or Lost Fillings

This can happen if you bite on something hard such as nuts or the ubiquitous crunch in a rice dish. You may feel a sudden pain, a gap where the filling was, and pieces of the filling in your mouth. As an immediate measure, rinse your mouth out with some warm salty water (add a couple of teaspoons of salt to a glass of boiled and cooled water) to clear any debris from your mouth.

If you have some temporary filling material (from your dentist or a commercial kit), you can use it to plug the hole up or you can use a piece of sugar-free chewing gum. It's important to plug it up so that the hole doesn't get filled with food, which can cause more problems. You'll need to get dental treatment for a permanent filling as soon as possible. If you're on a short trip, and it's just a small surface filling, it could wait for a week or so until you get back.

If the filling has cracked rather than fallen out, you may notice that it's sensitive to hot/cold/sugary foods and drinks. A cracked filling can lead to toothache, so try to get a permanent filling placed in the tooth as soon as is convenient.

As a general rule, avoid sugary, hot and cold foods in all these situations.

Toothache

There are lots of causes of this most unpleasant of symptoms: an injury to a tooth, a filling breaking or falling out, or tooth decay can lead to a tooth abscess.

Unless it settles quickly, you're going to need to find a dentist or doctor. In the meantime, take painkillers (eg co-codamol) regularly. Note that you shouldn't put aspirin directly on a painful tooth, as this can cause a sore patch on the gum. If you have oil of cloves with you, it can help relieve the pain when applied to the offending tooth on a clean cotton bud, although applying it may be uncomfortable.

Wash out your mouth regularly (after meals) with warm salty water. Try to avoid sugary foods, hard foods (ie nuts) and hot and cold foods. It goes without saying that you should avoid biting on the tooth.

If the pain is severe and unrelieved, perhaps with a bad taste in your mouth, you've probably got a tooth abscess, and you may need to have the tooth extracted eventually, although root treatment may save the tooth (but you'll need a good dentist). Seek medical or dental help urgently, but if you're in a remote area away from help, start taking a course of antibiotics, for example amoxycillin OR erythromycin OR metronidazole, or whatever you have with you (so long as you're not allergic to it).

> If your face becomes swollen or you develop a fever, you must seek medical help as soon as possible, as it means that the infection is spreading. In the meantime, drink plenty of fluids and start a course of antibiotics.

Another cause of pain in the mouth is a gum abscess, which can occur around a partially erupted wisdom tooth or when the gum has receded around a tooth, but hopefully both of these will have been picked up by your dentist before you left. Treatment is the same as for a tooth abscess.

Chipped Teeth

This can be caused by a fall, or a direct blow to the tooth. It can cause toothache immediately or after a delay, and an abscess can develop. You need to seek treatment as soon as possible, as you may need root canal treatment or extraction of the tooth. In the meantime, take painkillers if necessary.

Crowns & Veneers

If a crown comes out, stick it back in and then find a dentist to glue it back on. If a crown breaks (usually front porcelain ones), it's unlikely that you'll be able to get a new one made, but you should be able to find a dentist to put on a temporary crown, which should last you till you get home.

If a veneer cracks, chips or breaks off, you probably don't need to get dental treatment until you get home, as it's not likely to cause any damage to the tooth if it is not replaced in the short term. A rough edge may initially cause some irritation.

If a Tooth is Knocked Out

If you can find the tooth, wash it in milk (better) or clean water and, if practical, place it back in the socket to reimplant it. Get dental help as soon as possible. If it's in a child, remember that milk teeth won't need to be replaced.

If it is not practical to attempt to reimplant it (eg if it's chipped or broken or you've got other injuries in your mouth), keep the tooth in milk, and try to get a doctor/dentist to attempt to reimplant it.

Reimplantation may not be successful, but it is worth trying. If more than two hours have passed between the tooth being knocked out and reimplantation, the chance of success is slim.

If you are left with an open socket, rinse your mouth out with warm salty water. Don't rinse too vigorously, as this may dislodge the clot forming in the socket. Avoid strenuous exercise for a few hours.

If there is persistent bleeding from the socket, place a clean piece of cloth across the top of the socket and bite onto it for 20 to 30 minutes. If bleeding persists, seek expert advice as soon as possible, as the socket may need stitching. Make sure you know what type of stitches have been put in, and whether or not you need to go back to have them removed.

Sometimes the socket can become infected and very painful. Use warm salty water mouthwashes and take painkillers as an immediate measure. Seek treatment as soon as possible for specialist treatment and possibly a course of antibiotics.

GETTING DENTAL TREATMENT

The same rules apply to finding dental treatment as for medical treatment, and a personal recommendation from a reliable source is probably the best way to go. Five-star hotels, the local expatriate community and embassies may be able to point you in the right direction. If possible, try to find a dental teaching hospital – most capital cities should have one. Charges for treatment vary, but it's probably best to negotiate the price before treatment starts.

A major concern when receiving any dental treatment is the risk of contracting infections like HIV or hepatitis B from the dentist or the instruments being used, but there are some basic precautions you can take. Check that the dentist is wearing a clean pair of dental gloves, and make sure they wash their gloved hands if there's any doubt in your mind. Ideally, they should put on a new pair for each patient, but this may not be possible in some areas. You should consider taking a pair of disposable surgical gloves in your medical kit. If you need an injection, make sure the dentist uses a new, sterile needle.

Always tell anyone who is going to give you dental treatment about any existing medical condition or medication you may be on, before they start treatment.

Skin...

✚ For details on the effects of the sun on the skin, see p311

✚ See the First Aid appendix for treatment of cuts, burns and scalds

✚ For bites and stings, see p359

✚ For information on looking after your feet, see p97

The skin is your body's first line of defence against the outside world. When you're travelling it's subjected to assaults from all directions: physical hazards like the sun, wind and cold; insects and parasites of all shapes and forms which attack it with glee; and bacterial and fungal infections which thrive in hot and humid conditions. Although there's a great line-up of weird and wonderful 'tropical' skin diseases, your skin problems are likely to be much more prosaic: sunburn, bacterial infections and allergic rashes are the most common afflictions.

RASHES

Skin rashes can occur as part of a more generalised disease. In this case it will usually be obvious, because you'll usually have a fever and other symptoms such as sore throat or nausea, as well as vomiting. Some diseases that are associated with a skin rash include:

■ the 'childhood' illnesses (which can occur at any age if you haven't had them before) – measles, rubella and chicken pox (p229)

■ glandular fever and other viral infections (p177)

■ food poisoning or allergies (p149)

■ dengue fever and other viral haemorrhagic fevers (p132)

■ meningococcal meningitis (p135)

■ tick-transmitted fevers (p366)

■ schistosomiasis (Katayama fever, p338)

■ worm infestations of the gut (p164)

■ river blindness (p362)

PRICKLY HEAT

This uncomfortable rash is caused by blockage of the sweat ducts. It's called 'prickly heat' because as sweating tries to occur in the blocked glands, you get an uncomfortable prickling sensation. Common in hot, humid conditions, it can strike you when you first arrive or further down the track. It's very common in babies and children.

! Nappy rash can be a big problem in hot climates – see the Babies & Children chapter for more guidance on dealing with this.

At its mildest, prickly heat consists of a rash of painless clear blisters without any redness. These usually burst quickly and don't cause any other problems. The next step up is prickly heat proper. You get itchy areas of redness, with spots and small blisters, usually in covered, sweaty areas like around your waist, chest or back, under your breasts or in the groin. You may get it on the backs of your knees or in the elbow creases. Babies and young children commonly get it on their heads.

Because the problem is the build-up of sweat in blocked ducts, treatment is aimed at preventing sweating:

- stay cool – rest and use fans, cool showers, cover yourself with damp cloths or move to an airconditioned hotel
- wear loose cotton clothing
- wash with water – overuse of soap may destroy the skin's natural oils and defences and is thought to be a contributory factor
- calamine, calendula or comfrey cream on the rash can be soothing
- antihistamine tablets will help stop the itching
- watch for signs of secondary infection (see p422)

Prickly heat usually clears up in a few days. Rarely, the rash refuses to go away and becomes widespread. Because your sweat ducts are blocked all over, this affects your heat controlling mechanisms and you can get heatstroke because of it. This type of heatstroke is more likely after you've been in a hot climate for several months.

ITCHY SKIN RASH – CAUSES

- dermatitis (allergic or irritant reactions) – often on hands or other exposed areas
- prickly heat (p199) – armpits, waist, groin, head (in babies and children)
- fungal infections (p202) – sweaty areas: armpits, groin, under breasts, between toes
- insect bites (p359) – any exposed area
- scabies (p204) – intense itchiness, especially at night
- reaction to medicines – rash all over
- swimmer's itch (p338) – anywhere that was in contact with water
- creeping eruption (cutaneous larva migrans, p207) – moving red tracks, usually on feet and legs
- river blindness (onchocerciasis, p362)

DERMATITIS

Dermatitis is a general term for an itchy skin rash. It's very common worldwide and can be caused by a whole range of factors, from simple chemical irritation to reactions to plants and insects. It may be an in-built tendency in some people, when it can occur without any obvious cause. In this situation it's known as atopic dermatitis or eczema, and may be associated with asthma or hay fever. Most people with eczema will have had it for some time, often since childhood, and it is unlikely to develop for the first time on your travels.

Itching is the main feature of any dermatitis, which appears as thickened, red and often cracked skin. There may be some blistering, particularly if it has been caused by contact with a plant. Where you get it depends on what's causing it: eczema usually affects your hands, inside of the wrists and backs of the knees; while contact dermatitis, caused by something you've touched, will appear wherever contact was made.

If you haven't had dermatitis before and it suddenly appears when you're travelling, it's most likely to be due to contact with something...the question is what. It may be a chemical irritant, eg soaps or detergents, or something that you are allergic to, eg an ingredient in a new skin lotion or a plant you've touched or brushed past.

Some unlucky people can get dermatitis, often with blistering, as a result of mild to moderate sun exposure – consider this possibility if it only occurs on parts of your body that have been exposed to the sun. Alternatively it could be a reaction to the sunscreen you're using, or it could just be sunburn.

It's not always easy to work these things out, but a bit of common sense and a certain amount of trial and error can help. For example in this case, you could see if covering up or changing sunscreen helps. Don't forget that you can develop a sensitivity or allergy to something you have used without problems in the past.

Treatment

Most contact dermatitis will gradually settle once the irritant or allergy-causing substance is removed. If you can work out what the culprit is, avoid it! Otherwise, finding the cause only really matters if it doesn't go away.

If the rash is mild, try liberally covering it with a simple moisturiser (like aqueous cream or white soft paraffin). The trouble with 'cosmetic' moisturisers is that they can contain ingredients that may exacerbate the rash, but if you've got nothing else, it may be worth giving them a try.

 Calendula or comfrey cream may help to soothe an itchy rash.

If this doesn't work, a weak steroid cream can help, such as hydrocortisone 1% cream or ointment, and is quite safe to use for a short period of time. You may find that if the skin is thick, eg on the palm of your hand, a stronger steroid cream is needed, such as betamethasone 0.025% or 0.1% cream.

If the skin is cracked and weeping, it's likely to be infected and an antibiotic cream will be helpful.

Note that all steroid creams should be used as sparingly as possible, twice a day. Don't use anything stronger than hydrocortisone 1% on the face or genital area. If you're using these creams for the first time, discuss it with a doctor or pharmacist if possible.

If a steroid cream makes a rash worse, stop using it – you've probably got the diagnosis wrong! Steroid cream on its own will make fungal and bacterial infections much worse.

FUNGAL INFECTIONS

These are common diseases worldwide, but are even more common in hot, humid conditions. (A piece of bread in a plastic bag quickly goes mouldy in the heat, and it's the same principle with your skin and fungal infections.) If you've already got a fungal infection before you leave, you'll probably find it gets worse when you're travelling.

Fungal infections can affect different parts of your body, but the basic principles for preventing them are the same:

- wear loose fitting, cotton clothing
- wash regularly and dry yourself carefully, especially between the toes, around the groin area and under the breasts

You can get fungal infections from other people, animals or the soil, and they can affect different parts of your body.

Treatment of these rashes is generally with an antifungal cream – there are many different creams available (eg clotrimazole, ketoconazole, miconazole, nystatin, terbinafine and amorolfine) but all need to be applied daily or twice daily and used for at least a couple of weeks.

Scalp

Ringworm of the scalp (tinea capitis) gives you flaky, round lesions and is more common in children. Treatment is with antifungal tablets, such as fluconazole 50mg daily for two to four weeks OR griseofulvin 500mg (10mg/kg/day in children) daily for six to 12 weeks (avoid in pregnancy).

Body

Ringworm on the body appears as flaky, red areas which spread outwards, leaving a clear patch in the middle. Treatment is with antifungal cream.

Another fungal infection that is common in the tropics is tinea (also called pityriasis) versicolor. It often affects young adults and can be difficult to get rid of. You get round slightly scaly, itchy patches which may be lighter or darker than the surrounding skin, usually over your shoulders, chest and back. Seek medical advice, but treatment options include selenium sulphide shampoo OR an antifungal cream OR itraconazole 200mg daily for seven days OR fluconazole 50mg daily for two to four weeks for persistent problems.

Crotch

Tinea cruris, or 'jock itch', appears as a red, flaky rash in the groin crease, especially in men; there's often a fungal infection of the feet too. Treatment is with antifungal cream.

Feet

Athlete's foot is extremely common in hot, humid climates. You get a flaky rash between the toes, which can progress to splitting of the skin. Dry carefully between your toes and use an antifungal cream or powder, or calendula tincture.

BACTERIAL INFECTIONS

✚ For more guidelines on preventing and treating bacterial skin infections, see the First Aid chapter (p419).

Warmth, humidity, dirt and dust make bacterial infections of the skin very common when you're travelling. They're extremely common in local populations too, occurring in one-tenth of adults and up to one-third of children in the tropics.

Bacterial infections usually have pus as their main feature. Any break in the skin, however small and insignificant it may seem at first, can get infected if you don't take steps to prevent it. If the infection spreads, it can make you seriously ill with blood poisoning. Boils and abscesses (collections of pus under the skin which form hot red swellings, often with a head of pus) are also more common. Folliculitis, a rash of pimples caused by infection of the hair follicles, is more common in hot, humid climates, especially if you swim in dirty water.

> **!** Surfing abrasions and cuts should be treated quickly with iodine antiseptic as the germs in corals can cause serious infections if left alone.

Impetigo is an extremely common bacterial skin infection, especially in hot, humid climates. It typically affects children but is common in adult travellers too. It usually starts on the face, often around the mouth or from a mosquito bite. The first sign of this infection is the appearance of blisters on the face, looking a bit like a cold sore at first. These then burst, forming golden, crusty sores, which can spread quickly to different areas of the skin. Impetigo is very contagious, and can easily be spread by fingers and towels or face cloths. Treat impetigo as follows:

- wash the crusty sores regularly (eg twice a day) with soap and water or an antiseptic solution like povidone-iodine

- apply an antibiotic cream (eg fusidic acid three times daily for five to seven days) on the sores after washing the crusts off

- take a course of antibiotics (eg flucloxacillin OR erythromycin if penicillin-allergic) if it's very severe or doesn't respond quickly to treatment

SCABIES

You're not that likely to get this infestation unless you're planning on intimate, prolonged contact with a sufferer. The villain is the scabies mite, which burrows into your skin, usually between the fingers, the wrists and genital areas, where it lays its eggs.

SKIN LESIONS

Skin lesions, especially wound infections, are extremely common in the tropics and can be a nuisance. Some causes of sores include the following:

• bacterial infection
• insect bite
• tropical ulcer
• leishmaniasis (p224)
• Buruli ulcer (p221)
• guinea worm ulcer (p221)
• cutaneous diphtheria (p229)

It causes intense itching, which is much worse at night, and has a high risk of secondary bacterial infection. The itching isn't actually due to the mites themselves but is a sensitivity reaction they produce in you six to eight weeks after you've been infected. It can persist even when the mites have gone. You may see typical burrows between the fingers. It's not a tropical disease as such but is encouraged by poor personal hygiene, eg when water isn't readily available for washing.

Treatment is with malathion or permethrin lotion (preferably); benzyl benzoate lotion may still be available locally but should be avoided in children. You need to cover your whole body apart from your head (except in young children) and leave it ideally for 24 hours, but overnight treatment (10 to 12 hours) is probably adequate.

Itchiness may persist for 10 to 12 days even after successful treatment of the mite, so try to soothe it with calamine lotion or antihistamine tablets. You need to wash all your clothes and anything you've been sleeping in (eg your sleeping bag and liner) to prevent reinfection. Anybody who has shared a bed with you will also need to be treated. It's not very pleasant but at least scabies mites are not known to transmit any diseases.

LICE

Contact with lice is a definite possibility in many countries, especially if you're roughing it. There are three types of lice which infest different areas: head, body and pubic areas (crab louse). They all cause itching due to bites. You may not see the lice themselves, as they're transparent, but they lay eggs that look like white grains attached to hairs. Lice are passed by close contact between people (sexual intercourse for pubic lice) and via infected bedding or clothing for body lice.

Head lice can be treated with carbaryl, malathion, permethrin or phenothrin lotions – apply the lotion to your head and wash it off after 12 hours. Alternatively, use any hair conditioner and get a (good) friend to comb through your hair – the lice just slip off. You'll need to repeat this every three days or so for two weeks after the last louse was spotted. Treat anyone you share a bed with as well. The empty egg cases can stick around after the lice themselves have gone.

Treat body lice by getting rid of them: wash all bedding and clothing in hot water, which kills the lice. Body (clothing) lice can, rarely, transmit typhus via their faeces.

Pubic lice should be treated by applying malathion OR carbaryl lotion all over your body (not just the pubic area) and leaving it overnight. You'll need a second treatment after seven days to zap any lice appearing from surviving eggs.

BEDBUGS

You're very likely to get acquainted with these, especially if you're on a shoestring budget. Bedbugs are 3mm x 4mm oval insects that live in mattresses, cracks in the walls etc, but not on you. They merely visit you when it's dark for a meal. Bites, which can be itchy, are usually in a line of two or three on your face, arms, buttocks or ankles: anything accessible. If bites are itchy, try some calamine lotion.

The best way to get rid of them is to spray furniture and wall cracks with an insecticide, or to use a permethrin-impregnated mosquito net. Better still, find another hotel.

There's been much debate about whether bedbugs can transmit HIV – in theory at least it's a possibility but there is no evidence to suggest they do.

CREEPING ERUPTION

This moving rash (also called cutaneous larva migrans, because it migrates, or geography worm) is caused by the larvae of various worms, usually the dog or cat hookworm, which are passed in their faeces. It occurs worldwide, but it's much more common in hot, humid environments which encourage development of the larvae. You're at risk anywhere contaminated with dog and cat faeces, usually by walking barefoot or sitting on sandy beaches (you should always wear thongs or sandals).

You can get mild itching and a rash when the larvae first enter your skin, but the real fun begins when they start to migrate a few days later. They produce intensely itchy red tracks that advance slowly day by day. They're desperately hoping you're a cat or dog, as they can't live in humans and will die after a few weeks.

You could just wait for them to die naturally, but you're probably not going to want to leave it that long. Treatment is by freezing the head of the track with ethyl chloride spray or applying an anti-worm medicine like thiabendazole (made up into a 10% solution) directly to the track. Alternatively, albendazole 400mg twice a day for five days is very effective. As with any skin condition in the tropics, look out for secondary infection.

A similar rash can be caused by intestinal worms (see the Digestive System chapter), but they tend to be much speedier.

JIGGER FLEA (TUNGIASIS)

These fleas live in sandy soil and infest pigs, humans and other mammals. They occur throughout tropical Africa and you're quite likely to pick them up if you go barefoot or wear open sandals.

The flea burrows into your skin, commonly the soles of your feet or on your toes, under the toenails. It forms a swelling the size of a pea with a central black spot (the back end of the flea).

Treatment is aimed at getting rid of the flea and preventing any secondary bacterial infection. Textbooks talk of microsurgery but it is possible to dig it out relatively painlessly using a sterilised needle and plenty of antiseptic solution. You should make sure you remove it whole and take care to keep the open wound clean afterwards.

TUMBU FLY BOILS

This is a risk in some parts of Africa, including most of West and Central Africa, as well as other areas like Malawi.

The tumbu fly lays its eggs on the ground and on laundry put out to dry. The larvae burrow into the skin of humans (and other mammals), where they mature, breathing through an opening in the skin. Once mature, after about a week, they exit through the opening.

They cause multiple boils, often on the thighs or buttocks (and worse). The boils have a central black mark which is the breathing hole of the larva, and a characteristic symptom is feeling the larva moving about in the swelling. The larvae don't cause any diseases, but secondary infection is very common.

The aim of treatment is to extract the larva. Blocking the larva's breathing hole with something like petroleum jelly can cause it to come up for air, at which stage you can grab hold of it. Alternatively, you could try tempting it out with a piece of raw meat: just place the meat over the hole and wait for the larva to bite...

Other options are to perform minor surgery to open up the hole so that the larva can be extracted with forceps. You could be kinder to the larva and apply a small bandage over the boil to suffocate it (leave it in place for three to four days to be sure), then remove it and the larva. It's important to remove the larva intact, as half a worm can cause an intensely irritant reaction.

Prevent infection by not going barefoot in risk areas and not hanging your washing out to dry. If you happen to have an iron with you, ironing your clothes kills the larvae.

HIV/AIDS & Sexual Health...

✚ For a general discussion about sex and travel, including how to avoid sexually related health problems, see the section on Sex & Travel in the Staying Healthy chapter earlier in this book.

HIV/AIDS

AIDS stands for acquired immunodeficiency syndrome, and it describes the collection of diseases that result from suppression of the body's immune system by infection with the human immunodeficiency virus (HIV). HIV targets cells in the blood that are an important part of your immune system, which protects you from infections. At present, although there are effective (but toxic) treatments that can keep AIDS at bay for a period of time, there is no known cure.

TRANSMISSION

In Africa, heterosexual intercourse is the most common way in which HIV is passed from person to person. HIV can be transmitted through vaginal, anal or oral sexual intercourse between men and women or between men.

Transmission from mother to unborn child and via infected blood transfusions are the second and third most important ways in which HIV is spread in Africa and other parts of the world. In many Western countries, the risk of getting HIV from blood transfusions is practically zero because of stringent screening procedures, but in most African countries, blood for transfusions is not screened or is inadequately screened – see p102 for more discussion of this issue.

Other ways in which HIV is transmitted are through needle sharing among injecting drug users and inadequate sterilisation or reusing of needles, syringes and other equipment in medical and dental procedures, as well as tattooing, ear and body piercing, and using cut-throat razors.

FACT OR FICTION?

It can be confusing trying to separate fact from fiction with HIV, but here's the current wisdom on it:

- a vaccine against HIV is looking promising, but there's a long way to go, so don't throw away those condoms just yet
- worldwide, most HIV infections are acquired through heterosexual sex
- the more sexual partners you have, the more at risk you are for HIV/AIDS
- you can be perfectly healthy for 10 years or more after infection before any signs of the disease show up
- you can't tell by looking at a person if they are infected or not
- HIV can be transmitted through infected blood transfusions
- HIV is not thought to be transmitted by saliva
- acupuncture, tattooing, ear and body piercing, injections and other medical and dental procedures with unsterilised equipment can all transmit HIV infection
- HIV is a sensitive little virus and needs pretty intimate contact to be transmitted – it's not transmitted by hugging, social kissing, using the same toilet seat or sharing a cup
- it's not passed in swimming pools
- insects like bedbugs and mosquitoes do not transmit HIV

RISKS

The risk of acquiring HIV per exposure varies enormously, from one in 20 to one in 1000 for different types of sexual intercourse, one in 20 for needle sharing, to near certainty for a contaminated blood transfusion. In general, it's twice as easy to transmit HIV from men to women than the other way round, and receptive anal intercourse is especially risky. Many other factors can affect the risk, including the stage of infection (early and late are the most risky), the strain of HIV and whether you have another STI. Having another STI increases your risk of getting HIV, and if you are already infected, it increases the chance of you passing it on.

HIV INFECTION & AIDS

There aren't any immediate signs of infection, although you may get a glandular-fever-like illness a few weeks after infection, with fever, aches and pains, a skin rash and swollen glands. After this you may have no more symptoms for 10 years or more, although this time of being HIV-positive is very variable. This is the danger period in terms of passing the infection to others, because, to all appearances, you seem healthy and you may not realise that you've got HIV. Eventually, your immune system starts to show signs of strain, and the syndrome of AIDS starts.

A blood test can show if you're infected or not, but it won't show positive for about three months after you may have been exposed to HIV.

HIV & YOU

While you are away, you could put yourself at risk of HIV infection if you:

- have sexual intercourse with an infected person
- receive an infected blood transfusion or injection
- share needles with HIV-infected injecting drug users

You're obviously going to want to take steps to avoid these risk situations – always practise safer sex; avoid getting into situations where you might need a blood transfusion; never share needles with other injecting drug users.

If you're worried that you've put yourself at risk of HIV infection:

- don't sit and brood on it – phone an AIDS helpline as soon as possible to talk about your concerns; either wait until you get back home if you're on a short trip, or check your guidebook or a phone book for the local number
- play fair with partners and always practise safer sex
- make an appointment with your doctor or a sexual health clinic when you get back to discuss your best course of action

Remember that an HIV test won't be able to tell you either way for about three months after the risk situation; in the meantime you will need to practise safer sex.

You may have heard about a 'morning after' treatment for HIV, called post-exposure prophylaxis. It's a cocktail of antiviral drugs that, in theory, stops HIV infection getting a hold after you've been exposed to it. Although it may be of value for health workers who accidentally get jabbed by contaminated needles, its use after sexual exposure is very controversial. It's not guaranteed to work, and there are enormous practical problems associated with its use – it's extremely expensive, several different drugs have to be taken every day for at least six weeks and it can cause unpleasant side effects. For most travellers, this isn't an option, and you shouldn't rely on it.

WHAT IS SAFER SEX?

Using a latex (rather than natural membrane) condom is extremely effective at preventing transmission of HIV and other STIs. Use only water-based lubricants, as petroleum or oil-based lubricants can damage rubber.

You may feel awkward about discussing condoms because of cultural differences or a worry that you might be seen as 'forward' or as having planned it, but it's a small price to pay for peace of mind and your good health.

Your local health centre, any travel health clinic and any sexual health clinic will be able to provide you with more information on safer sex or, if you have access to the web, you could check out the UCSF safer sex site (http://hivinsite.ucsf.edu/InSite?page=kb-07-02 -02#) for more info. The Terrence Higgins Trust web site (www.tht.org.uk/index.htm) also has loads of information on all aspects of preventing and living with HIV/AIDS – its Africa links in particular are excellent.

AIDS IN AFRICA

You can't go to sub-Saharan Africa without at least some idea of the magnitude of the AIDS problem here. The statistics certainly make grim reading: currently, of the 40 million or so adults living with HIV/AIDS worldwide, about 25 million live in sub-Saharan Africa. Of every 10 children living with HIV/AIDS, nine live in sub-Saharan Africa. The epidemic has left around 12 million African children orphaned.

When AIDS first surfaced in the 1980s (in the West at least – some experts believe that AIDS was present in Africa several decades earlier; others consider the hypothesis that HIV originated in Africa from contact with a monkey in Gabon to be a form of colonial racism), it spread rapidly, mostly via heterosexual contacts and mother to infant transmission. Transmission through unscreened blood transfusion (about a quarter of all transfusions performed are thought to be with unscreened blood) is also a major problem in sub-Saharan Africa.

Why did the infection take such a hold so rapidly? There's no simple answer, although some contributory factors are obvious, like the fact that people tend to move around a lot in search of work or to escape wars and natural disasters such as famine, compounded by a general lack of adequate health care and prevention programs. Social and cultural factors are important too, and mainly stem from the low status of women and their lack of empowerment in many African societies.

Africa isn't uniformly affected by the epidemic, and although no country has escaped HIV/AIDS, some nations are much less severely affected than others; even within countries, some areas and populations are worse affected than others. For example, North Africa has fairly low rates of infection at present, while many of the southern African nations have alarmingly high rates of infection (more than one person in five is currently living with HIV/AIDS in Botswana and Zimbabwe, and Swaziland currently has the highest HIV prevalence rate of any country in the world, at over 33%). Life expectancy in these countries is less than 40, whereas without AIDS it would be closer to 60. Urban areas tend to be worse hit than rural areas, as are border posts and trading stops along major transport routes.

In nations with high infection rates, the socioeconomic effects can be devastating. HIV/AIDS hits the most productive members of society (young adults) which has knock-on effects on food production and local economies. The growing numbers of orphans puts great strain on carers, compounding the economic problems. Hospitals, already overstretched, are unable to cope with the increased burden.

It's not all bad news, though – some countries have achieved significant success with programs to halt the spread of AIDS, particularly Senegal and Uganda. Kenya and Zimbabwe are also seeing declines thanks to effective prevention campaigns.

This is not intended to put you off visiting badly affected areas; it just means that you should be aware of the problem and to take sensible precautions to avoid exposing yourself to risk. In particular, it's a good idea to avoid any skin piercing procedures (medical, dental or otherwise) and blood transfusions as far as possible, although you'll find that local health care workers are well aware of the risks – and of Western fears. It should go without saying that it's always best to avoid unsafe sex, especially with sex workers, wherever you go.

OTHER STIS

Although some of the 'traditional' STIs like syphilis and gonorrhoea have faded from the picture somewhat in developed countries, they're alive and kicking in most other parts of the world, including Africa.

Why do you care? Because travellers tend to regularly roll up at STI clinics back home with infections they've acquired while they were away. There's a long history of an association between itinerant populations (sailors, soldiers and long-distance truck drivers) and the spread of STIs. Most famously, Christopher Columbus and his crew have been accused of initiating an epidemic of syphilis that spread through Europe in the 16th century. The two world wars were both associated with epidemics of STIs and, more recently, the spread of HIV through Africa can be directly related to long-distance truck routes.

Many STIs (including gonorrhoea and syphilis) can be simply and effectively treated with antibiotics if they're caught early. However, others (eg chlamydia and gonorrhoea) can make you seriously ill and may have long-term effects – especially if they are not treated early – including infertility, liver disease (eg hepatitis) and an increased risk of cervical cancer (eg genital warts).

> Note that hepatitis B is the only sexually transmitted infection for which there is an effective vaccine. Discuss with your doctor, but consider getting vaccinated against hepatitis B if you think you're at high risk of infection (see p141 for more details).

Some STIs cause no symptoms or only mild symptoms that may go unnoticed; sometimes fertility problems are the first sign you have an infection. If STIs do cause symptoms, these are usually an abnormal vaginal or penile discharge, pain or irritation during intercourse or when you urinate, and any blisters, lumps, itches, rashes or other irritation on/around your genitals or anus.

> Because STIs can go unnoticed, it's best to get a check-up when you get home if you had unprotected intercourse while you were away.

If you notice any symptoms, it's best to get expert help as soon as possible. You can't tell accurately from your symptoms what infection you're likely to have, and you can often have more than one STI at the same time. Taking the wrong treatment or inadequate treatment leaves you at risk of future complications like infertility, or you may think you're cured when you're not. Try to find a reputable doctor or STI clinic for a thorough examination and laboratory tests, and see your doctor when you get back so they can confirm that the infection is gone and there are no other problems.

If you think you may have an STI:

- seek medical advice for investigation and treatment
- remember that self medication is best avoided, as it can be disastrous
- your partner will need treatment too
- avoid intercourse (assuming you still feel like having sex) until you have finished a course of treatment
- play fair, and don't spread it around

Bear in mind that STI clinics are probably not going to be called this in Africa – they are more likely to be called by the bad old names like VD clinic or venereo-dermatology clinic. Alternatively, you could try a family planning clinic.

SOME DETAILS

In this section we've summarised a few details about some of the STIs you may be at risk of acquiring. We haven't included specific antibiotic treatments because the sensitivity of infections to antibiotics varies from region to region and with time, and it's near impossible to diagnose STIs without a laboratory test. In any event, you always have time to find medical help.

Trichomoniasis is another STI that women may be at risk for – we've covered this in the Women Travellers chapter (p243).

Gonorrhoea

Caused by bacteria, this STI occurs worldwide, affecting hundreds of millions of people. It usually causes a penile or vaginal discharge and burning on urination. You can also be infected in the throat or rectum. It can lead to serious complications like pelvic inflammatory disease and infertility if it's not treated promptly.

Gonorrhoea used to be effectively treated with high-dose penicillin, but multiple antibiotic resistance is a major problem worldwide, and treatment is now usually with one of the newer antibiotics. You'll need a couple of check-ups to make sure it has gone completely.

Syphilis

This ancient disease occurs in three stages, and can cause serious complications in a proportion of sufferers if it's not treated early. Initially it causes a painless ulcer (on your genitals, rectum or throat) and a rash. Later you may get a feverish illness with painful ulcers and rashes, and later still (up to 50 years) you can get problems involving major blood vessels or the brain. Diagnosis is by a blood test.

Treatment needs to be administered and monitored by an expert, and usually involves multiple injections of penicillin.

Chlamydia

Known as the silent STI because it often causes mild or no symptoms, this infection is extremely common worldwide. It's also known as NSU, and if symptoms are present they're similar to gonorrhoea but milder. It's a major cause of pelvic inflammatory disease and infertility in women. Antibiotic treatment is effective at treating this condition.

CONDOMS

What condoms won't protect you against:

- genital herpes
- genital warts
- pubic lice
- scabies

Condoms do help protect against STIs transmitted through the exchange of body fluids. These infections include:

- HIV
- hepatitis B and C
- gonorrhoea
- chlamydia
- syphilis

Genital Herpes

This is a very common cause of genital ulceration. Ulcers can be very painful, occur in clusters and may recur. It's caused by a similar virus to the one that causes cold sores on your lips, and if your partner has a cold sore, it can be transmitted to your genitals by oral sex.

The initial infection is usually the worst, and can last about three weeks. You can feel quite miserable with it, with a fever, aches and pains, and swollen glands. Once you have herpes, you are liable to have recurrences, but subsequent attacks are usually less severe, and you may recognise and be able to avoid triggers like stress or being rundown. Note that any genital ulcers make transmission of HIV more likely.

Treatment is with simple painkillers and bathing the ulcers in salty water or a mild antiseptic solution; a local anaesthetic jelly applied to the ulcers may help. Antiviral drugs (eg acyclovir 200mg five times daily for seven days) can help shorten the length of an attack and reduce the severity, but they are expensive and only moderately effective.

GENITAL ULCERS

Causes of these lesions include:

- chancroid (common in tropical regions)
- genital herpes
- syphilis
- lymphogranuloma venerum
- granuloma inguinale (donovanosis)

Genital ulcers make transmission of HIV infection more likely.

> **!** It's best to avoid any sexual contact while you have an attack of herpes or if you notice a sore or ulcer on your genitals.

Genital Warts

These are usually painless, and can appear on the vulva, vagina, penis or anus. Warts can be painted with an acid solution that makes them dry up and fall off, or you sometimes need to have them removed in hospital, where they can be frozen or burnt off. Occasionally they may need to be surgically removed. They can recur and often there's no obvious trigger, although smoking and stress are sometimes thought to be factors.

Fortunately, genital warts usually disappear completely, but in women they are associated with cancerous changes in the cervix, so it's important to have regular cervical smear tests if you have been infected.

Chancroid

This highly infectious STI occurs in tropical and subtropical areas, where it is the most common cause of genital ulcers. Worldwide, it's more common than syphilis. It is endemic in eastern and southern Africa. The ulcers are painful (and can get secondarily infected) and you often get swelling of the glands in the groin. It is much more common in men than in women, and it often occurs with syphilis. Antibiotics are effective against chancroid.

Lymphogranuloma Venerum

This is caused by types of chlamydia (see earlier in this section) and occurs worldwide. It's endemic in eastern and West Africa. Symptoms are variable, but you may notice a blister or small painless ulcer or, more commonly, tender swelling of the lymph glands with fever and general aches and pains. Later problems, if it's not treated, include bladder and rectal problems and swelling of the genitals (genital elephantiasis). Antibiotic treatment is effective in the early stages.

Donovanosis (Granuloma Inguinale)

You probably don't need to worry about this one as it's pretty rare, but hot spots in Africa include Zambia and South Africa. It causes a persistent genital ulcer. Antibiotic treatment is effective, but may need to be prolonged over several weeks.

Other infections

Just be aware of some other infections that can be transmitted through sexual intercourse:

- viral hepatitis (p141)
- pubic lice (p206)
- scabies (p204)
- intestinal infections (p147)

Rarities...

Grouped here are some infections you're generally going to be at very low risk of getting, except under special circumstances or, in the case of the 'childhood' infections, if you are not up to date with your immunisations. We've listed these infections in alphabetical order. If you think you might have one of these diseases, see a doctor.

EXOTIC INFECTIONS

If you get one of these, you're either exceptionally unlucky, or you were just in the wrong place at the wrong time.

AVIAN INFLUENZA

This is an infection of birds, is extremely rare, and occurs in humans who have close contact with infected birds or bird products. Stay away from birds is the message. Scientists are concerned that if the virus gets into humans and becomes easily transmissible, it will cause a human influenza pandemic. Watch this space!

BURULI ULCER

Named after the place in Uganda where it was first diagnosed, this condition is rare and extremely unlikely to affect you. It is caused by a relative of the tuberculosis bacteria.

Firstly, a firm, painless lump appears, usually on the limbs. It then breaks down and spreads rapidly, causing huge damage to the skin. The ulcer tends to heal spontaneously after some months or years but it leaves extensive scarring and deformity.

Treatment is with antiseptic solutions and skin grafting; some anti-tuberculosis drugs have also been found to be useful.

GUINEA WORM

This ancient scourge, described in the Bible and by Hippocrates, has been the target of a successful World Health Organization (WHO) eradication program, which has reduced the number of cases from several million a year in the 1970s to about 10,600 at the most recent estimate. The majority of sufferers are in rural areas among the poorest communities without access to clean water. As a traveller, you'd be extraordinarily unlucky to get it.

Larvae of the guinea worm live in small freshwater crustaceans called Cyclops. When you swallow water in which these tiny crustaceans live, you swallow the larvae. Once in your gut, the larvae are released from the Cyclops and develop deep in your body tissues. The female worms are the ones that cause the problems and can grow up to 1m long.

When the female is mature, she migrates towards the skin to release the larvae from her uterus. Most (90%) worms emerge from the legs but they can emerge from anywhere (yes, anywhere). Symptoms occur as the worm matures and include pain at the site of emergence, swelling, itching and fever. A blister appears over the end of the worm and then bursts, leaving a small ulcer. You can usually see the swollen uterus of the worm in the centre of the ulcer.

The aim of treatment is to remove the worm and to prevent secondary infection, although worms that are left just die and the wound usually heals up without any other problems. Surgical removal is effective but the traditional method is more fun to describe – and may be the only option available:

- first, empty the uterus of the worm by repeatedly washing the ulcer in clean (boiled) water (this makes the worm easier to extract)
- pull the worm out a little way, taking care not to pull too hard
- attach the worm to a preferably sterile piece of wood with thread
- gently draw the worm out by rolling it round the stick until you feel resistance
- cover the wound with a sterile dressing to prevent it from getting secondarily infected
- it's important to remove the worm intact because it can cause a severe reaction if it breaks
- roll the worm up a little bit day by day – it can take up to two weeks to remove it this way

The life cycle of the guinea worm is completed when sufferers bathe ulcers in water, which releases the eggs into the water, and so the cycle starts again.

VIRAL HAEMORRHAGIC FEVERS

These are a group of diseases that are notable chiefly for their impact on the public psyche rather than their importance to travellers health, and for that reason it's worth briefly mentioning them. We should stress at the outset that the risk of a traveller acquiring any of them is minuscule.

The diseases in question are haemorrhagic (bleeding) diseases that have high fatality rates and can be transmitted from person to person probably via body fluids, usually in the hospital environment. These include Lassa fever and the illnesses caused by the infamous Ebola and Marburg viruses. These are animal illnesses that are occasionally transmitted to humans. As an ordinary traveller (and not, for example, a medical worker), you are at an incredibly low risk of any of these illnesses and can minimise this risk further by avoiding areas which report outbreaks (the CDC and WHO web sites listed under Information Sources in the Before You Go chapter both have disease outbreak registers).

Ebola & Marburg Viruses

Outbreaks of Ebola virus infection have occurred in equatorial Sudan and the Democratic Republic of Congo, amid much media scrutiny and public hysteria. Hospital staff in close contact with patients suffering from haemorrhage had a high mortality rate. Infections with Marburg virus have occurred in eastern and southern Africa.

Symptoms are high fever, with headache and muscle and joint pains, nausea and vomiting. Other symptoms include discomfort in the throat, diarrhoea, stabbing chest pains and abdominal pains. Some sufferers develop uncontrolled bleeding about a week after the start of the illness, which can be rapidly fatal.

Lassa Fever

This viral infection is present in rural areas of West Africa and is transmitted via the urine of a rat found only in these areas. You may come into contact with it by going into huts where rats have urinated on the thatched roof.

Symptoms include fever, a general feeling of not being well, with aches and pains and, very characteristically, a sore throat. It can lead to death in a proportion of cases. There's no vaccine available and treatment is nonspecific.

If you develop a sore throat beyond three days of arrival in a rural area or within three weeks of leaving it, and think you may be at risk, you should seek medical advice.

LEISHMANIASIS

This parasitic disease is rare in travellers but is an important cause of illness and disfigurement worldwide, occurring in parts of North Africa and sub-Saharan Africa. Leishmaniasis is caused by parasites of the *Leishmania* family and is spread through the bite of infected sandflies. There are three main forms of the disease: skin (cutaneous or CL), visceral (VL – which affects the internal organs) and mucocutaneous, which occurs in Latin America only.

Development of a vaccine seems likely in the near future, although one isn't available commercially yet. Recovery from an attack gives lifelong immunity to both forms of the disease. The best prevention is to avoid sandfly bites. Animals such as dogs can act as reservoirs of infection in certain areas.

CL is the most common form of the disease, with approximately 1.5 million new cases occurring every year. It occurs in North Africa and drier parts of sub-Saharan Africa and causes a skin lesion or sometimes lots of lesions that usually heal spontaneously, although they can cause scarring.

VL is a more serious form of the disease and can be fatal. There is an ongoing epidemic of VL in parts of Sudan, where it has killed more than 50,000 people. The increase in VL in some areas of the world has been linked to levels of HIV infection, as

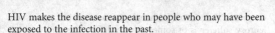

HIV makes the disease reappear in people who may have been exposed to the infection in the past.

Symptoms

VL develops anything from three to 18 months after you get bitten, and sometimes the parasites can persist in a dormant state for many years. Initially a nodule called a leishmanioma may appear. Later you get a fever, usually irregular and intermittent, and massive enlargement of the spleen and liver. You may also get enlargement of your glands, which is a feature of the African form of VL.

Diagnosis & Treatment

Leishmaniasis isn't something you are going to be diagnosing in yourself. It can be diagnosed by laboratory examination of a sample of tissue. Seek medical advice if you think you may have it, and remember that it can have a long incubation period.

Diagnosis of CL is by laboratory examination of a small piece of tissue from the ulcer. Treatment of simple, single ulcers is nonspecific – just the usual measures to prevent secondary bacterial infection.

Drug treatment is available with antimony drugs, and is used for multiple ulcers and for kala-azar.

LEPROSY

Although you're almost certain not to get this disease, you'll probably see sufferers on your travels through Africa. Leprosy is an important cause of permanent and progressive disability worldwide and occurs throughout Africa.

Leprosy was well known to the ancient world and used to be widespread in Europe in the Middle Ages. Crusaders returned with it from the Middle East. It's now estimated to affect 15 million people worldwide, over half of whom live in Africa and India.

The disease is caused by a bacterium, *Mycobacterium leprae*, which attacks the nerves. This deadens feeling in the extremities, so sufferers damage themselves without realising it. The secondary infection of wounds due to poor hygiene completes the picture. Although the stereotypical image of a leprosy sufferer is of someone with deformities and weeping sores, in reality leprosy causes a wide spectrum of disease, from simple depigmented patches of skin to characteristic deformities like claw hand.

You won't catch leprosy by touching a sufferer. Prolonged contact with a sufferer (eg living in the same house) is needed for the disease to spread (possibly by droplets from the nose and mouth). Socioeconomic conditions are thought to play a big part in determining spread – malnutrition, for example, can increase susceptibility to the disease. An animal reservoir may be important – the nine-banded armadillo is the only animal known to be affected by leprosy and may act as a reservoir of the disease in some areas.

Specific treatments are available and, if started early, the disease can be halted before deformities occur. The problem is that diagnosis is often delayed because of fear of the disease and its social stigma. Leprosy is unique as a disease in its status in society – sufferers have been stigmatised to an extraordinary degree, shunned by society and banished into ghettoes. Because it's such an emotive term, leprosy is now officially known as Hansen's disease, after the person who first identified the causative organism in 1873.

LOA LOA

This disease occurs in forested areas of West and Central Africa. It's caused by a parasitic worm and is spread via a type of fly called a mango fly that bites during the day. The worms roam around in the skin happily for many years (possibly up to 15 years). Every so often itchy painful swellings appear; they are called Calabar swellings after the town in coastal Nigeria. They don't need any specific treatment and generally subside in a few days.

Occasionally a worm migrates across the surface of the eye, which can be pretty scary when you look in the mirror and see the parasite moving. This causes redness and irritation but there are no long-term consequences.

Effective treatment is available with the drug diethyl-carbamazine, or, if a worm has been unwise enough to reveal itself, by removing the offending parasite through minor surgery.

If you're in a risk area, protect yourself against bites. It's also possible to take a preventive dose of diethylcarbamazine (300mg weekly) if you are planning on spending some time in the area. It would be best to discuss this with a doctor locally or before you go.

LYMPHATIC FILARIASIS

This parasitic disease is transmitted by mosquitoes and occurs in sub-Saharan Africa and Egypt. You've probably heard of the most severe form of this disease, elephantiasis, when male sufferers have to carry their enormously enlarged genitals in wheelbarrows – an image that is bound to stick in your mind. However, the risk to you is very, very small, as it takes prolonged (three to six months at least) and intense exposure to the parasite for infection to become established, and elephantiasis only occurs in a small proportion of heavily infected people living in high risk areas. However, it's sensible to avoid insect bites in these areas. There's no vaccine available against lymphatic filariasis.

Filariasis is caused by blockage of the lymph channels by long thread-like worms (filaria) which are transmitted by the bite of several varieties of mosquito. There may be no symptoms at all with light infections, or you may get fever, painful swellings of the lymph glands (eg in your armpits, groin or elbows) and, for male travellers, swelling of the testes with scrotal pain and tenderness. Note that symptoms usually develop about six months after infection.

If the infection is not treated, you can get permanent damage to the lymph system, leading to swelling of the arms, legs, breasts or scrotum, with associated thickening and wrinkling of the skin that's supposed to resemble elephant skin, hence the name 'elephantiasis'.

If you think you may have filariasis, you need to seek medical advice as soon as possible for appropriate treatment. Infection can usually be diagnosed with a blood test, although this can sometimes be tricky. An effective treatment is available with diethylcarbamazine or, possibly, ivermectin.

RIFT VALLEY FEVER

This viral disease usually occurs in domestic animals but it can be transmitted to humans by mosquitoes. Epidemics occur periodically, the latest being in Kenya in 1999. As a traveller, you're at pretty low risk of getting this disease. It causes fever, encephalitis (inflammation of the brain) and bleeding. There's no specific treatment and no vaccine. Prevention is by avoiding mosquito bites.

FILARIAL WORMS

Several varieties of these worms occur worldwide, causing different diseases. About 300 million people are infected with filarial worms but, although they can cause significant disability, they rarely cause death, and infection can be cured if treated early enough.

Diseases caused by filarial worms include lymphatic filariasis, river blindness, loa loa and guinea worm, from the largest of the filarial worms.

All these diseases are transmitted via biting insects – mosquitoes, blackflies or midges. They are not a big risk to you because you need prolonged and intense exposure for disease to develop, but it's worth minimising your risks by avoiding bites. If you have spent a long time in a risk area, it may be worth getting this checked out when you return home.

INFECTIONS COVERED ROUTINELY BY IMMUNISATION

In most Western nations, national immunisation programs ensure that you are usually protected against the infections listed here. See the Immunisations section of the Before You Go chapter for details.

DIPHTHERIA

Vaccination against this serious bacterial disease is very effective, so you don't need to worry if you've been properly immunised against it.

Diphtheria occurs worldwide, but has been controlled by vaccination in most developed countries. It mainly affects children and causes a cold-like illness which is associated with a severe sore throat. A thick white membrane forms at the back of the throat which can suffocate you, but what makes this a really nasty disease is that the diphtheria bug produces a very powerful poison which can cause paralysis and affect the heart. Otherwise healthy people can carry the disease-causing microorganism in their throats, and it's transmitted by sneezing and coughing.

It can also cause a skin ulcer known as a veldt sore, and vaccination protects against this form too.

Treatment is with penicillin and a diphtheria antitoxin, if necessary.

INFLUENZA

The commonest vaccine-preventable disease, influenza is a very common travellers ailment. While mostly a nuisance spoiling one to two weeks of any trip, it occasionally causes serious complications. The annual vaccine protects against circulating strains and is recommended for travellers every year.

MEASLES, MUMPS & RUBELLA

These diseases are now much less common in most Western nations because of widespread immunisation programs, but they are still prevalent throughout much of Africa, especially in countries with limited resources for adequate immunisation programs. You (and your children) are generally at low risk of these diseases, especially if you have been fully immunised. Although they are thought of as 'childhood' illnesses, all these diseases can occur in adults and tend to be much more serious when they do.

Measles starts a bit like a cold, then appears to get worse, and a fever develops. At about the third or fourth day, a rash appears on the skin, starting on the face and moving down. The rash is red, raised and tends to conglomerate together. It starts to fade after about five days. You can get ear and chest infections with measles, and also diarrhoea. Occasionally, severe complications (affecting the brain) can occur, which is why you should seek medical advice if you think you may have measles.

Mumps is a viral infection of the salivary glands. You feel generally unwell and you may notice swelling around the jaw, extending towards the ear and associated with pain (especially when eating). It usually resolves after about a week without any special treatment. There is a risk of infection affecting the testicles in adult men who get mumps, although not in children.

Rubella (German measles) is generally a very mild illness, a bit like a mild cold, associated with a pink, non-raised rash that starts on the face and spreads downwards. It can, however, cause severe problems in unborn children, so it is extremely important that you are immunised if you are a woman of child-bearing age.

POLIO

Polio used to be an important cause of disability, but thanks to the Global Polio Eradication Initiative launched in 1988, which aims to eliminate the disease worldwide through vaccination, cases now only occur in parts of Africa (particularly Nigeria) and south Asia.

The polio virus is spread from person to person by coughing and sneezing, or by contamination of food and drink with faeces from an infected person. Polio attacks the nerves, causing paralysis of muscles, and commonly affects young children. At first, infection causes a flu-like illness with fever, headache, muscle aches and pains, nausea, vomiting and sometimes diarrhoea, then it appears to settle for a few days before you get more muscle pains and paralysis of a limb, or more generalised paralysis. Paralysis occurs in less than one in 100 infected people. It can be dangerous if the muscles controlling breathing are affected – you may have seen old photos of polio sufferers in 'iron lungs'; the technology is a bit more sophisticated these days, but the principle is the same. The paralysis does improve with time but a proportion of people are left with some disability, often a wasted, paralysed limb. Polio can be diagnosed by a blood test.

If you are up to date with your immunisation, it's very un-likely that you will get infected. Prevention is through immunisation and taking care to avoid contaminated food and water.

TETANUS

You probably know that you have to be up to date with this vaccination, but do you know what you're being protected against? Spores of the tetanus bacterium are widespread in soil and some animal faeces, and occur worldwide. They can be introduced into your body through injury, eg through a puncture wound (even a very trivial one), a burn or an animal bite. The tetanus bacteria produce a toxin in your body that causes severe, painful muscular contractions and spasm leading to death through spasm of the respiratory muscles. It's old name is 'lockjaw' because of the spasms of the jaw muscles.

Tetanus needs specialist treatment in hospital, but don't worry: you shouldn't get it if your vaccination is up to date.

Clean any wound immediately and thoroughly with soap and water or antiseptic and, if you haven't been vaccinated against tetanus within the last 10 years or the wound is particularly dirty, get medical advice on having a booster dose of the tetanus vaccination as soon as possible (you may need a booster even if your vaccination is up to date).

VARICELLA (CHICKEN POX)

Another disease of childhood, usually less serious than measles, varicella can be prevented by vaccination. Antibody tests can measure immunity – usually acquired during childhood, and two doses of vaccine can be offered to non-immune travellers.

Mental Wellbeing...

If you're jetting off to an exotic African destination, you probably don't expect stress or other mind problems to be high on the travel health agenda. Then again, heat, unfamiliar surroundings and lifestyle, and perhaps a lack of home comforts can mean that your holiday falls short of the stress-free nirvana you anticipated.

STRESS, PHYSICAL & MENTAL WELLBEING

You'll probably find that sooner or later, you get stressed out by the travel experience – you might say stress is the travellers diarrhoea of mental health.

Everything that makes travelling good is also a potential source of stress. There's a different physical environment to cope with, your lifestyle is completely different and you've lost all your usual points of reference; you're cut off from your usual support network of family and friends. Language difficulties combined with unfamiliar social and cultural cues can make communication problematic, even on a basic level.

Often the lead-up to the trip has been less than relaxing, as you rush around trying to get things done before you leave, and you may be jet lagged for the first week. And then you're expected to enjoy yourself ...

Unless you're on a short trip, you may find it helpful to factor in some time and emotional space for adjusting to your new situation. You might want to bear in mind the following points:

- high levels of stress can make you less able to cope, with even minor difficulties and setbacks seeming like insurmountable hurdles

- you may feel frustrated and angry, taking your frustrations out on your travelling companions and other people you have to deal with

- stress can make you feel anxious or depressed, irritable, tired, unable to relax, and you may have difficulty sleeping (although this is often due to external causes)

- because you don't feel 100%, you may think you are physically ill, especially as the physical manifestations of anxiety can easily be mistaken for illness

- stress affects your immune system, making you more vulnerable to infections. Conversely, being physically ill affects you emotionally, often making you feel low and less able to cope

- if you know you're sensitive to stress, or you've had emotional problems before (you may even have come away to escape them), you may find that, in the short term anyway, travelling can exacerbate your problems

Half the battle is recognising that the way you're feeling is because of stress rather than some worrisome physical disease you've caught. An acute stress reaction is to be expected to some degree at the start of your travels and will probably ease by itself over the course of a few days, but you might want to activate some damage-control measures:

- take some time off to unwind: quit the tourist trail for a few days and do something completely different

- rest and try to catch up on any missed sleep (as a result of jet lag, overnight bus journeys, noisy hotel rooms etc)

- on the other hand, exercise is a great de-stresser, and worth a try if you've been stuck in trains or buses, or you're on an overland tour

- catch up on missed meals – stress is very energy-consuming

- try a de-stressing routine like aromatherapy, massage, yoga, meditation or just lying on a beach

- talk with fellow travellers, who may be experiencing similar emotions

Cook's Traveller's Handbook Egypt and the Sudan (1929) contains some good advice on destressing: 'A Turkish bath will be found delightful after a fatiguing day of sightseeing … Combine this with a sip from the emergency flask of liqueur brandy it recommends taking with you as part of your medical kit and you'll be well away.

STRESS EFFECTS

Stress is thought to play a significant part in some conditions, including the following:

- tension headaches (by definition!)
- migraine
- asthma
- eczema
- irritable bowel syndrome
- premenstrual tension

CULTURE SHOCK & TRAVEL FATIGUE

People experience a well recognised set of emotional reactions following any major life event; when this occurs as a result of living (or travelling) for an extended period of time in a culture markedly different from your own, it's called culture shock. The culture shock syndrome is a well known hazard of living overseas for any length of time. It's unlikely to strike hard on a short trip, but you may notice it if you're on a long trip, especially if it is compounded by travel fatigue.

Culture shock can be thought of as a sort of psychological disorientation resulting from a conflict between your deeply ingrained cultural values and the different cultural cues and behaviours of the society you have relocated into. It seems that however broad-minded you may hope you are, deep down we all have a fundamental assumption that our own culture is right.

Four basic stages in adjustment can be recognised. Culture shock doesn't happen all of a sudden – it progresses slowly, and affects some personalities more than others. Sometimes it doesn't progress, and you may get stuck at one stage. If you've been travelling a while, you'll probably recognise some of the stages and symptoms, as identified by Myron Loss in *Culture Shock – Dealing with Stress in Cross-Cultural Living*:

- euphoria, when everything is new and exciting
- hostility as the novelty wears off and the differences start to irritate – you may feel critical of your host country, stereotyping local people; you may feel weepy, irritable, defensive, homesick, lonely and isolated, perhaps worried about your physical health
- adjustment is when you start to feel more comfortable in your new lifestyle and with the new culture
- adaptation occurs when you lose that 'us and them' feeling

Travel fatigue is bound to affect you after you've been on the road for many months. It's a combination of culture shock, homesickness and generally feeling fed up with the hassles and inconveniences of life on the road.

Some strategies you might want to try to minimise the impact of culture shock on you and people in contact with you are as follows:

- accept that everyone experiences some degree of culture shock, and be prepared to recognise the symptoms as such
- find out about the country, people and culture before you go and when you're away – surprisingly, it doesn't have a huge effect but there are other good reasons for doing it
- look after your physical health – it's easier to feel positive if you feel well
- friendships and keeping in touch with home can help you feel less isolated
- you don't achieve anything by succumbing to the temptation of disparaging everything local
- having a sense of humour can help you keep your head above water – just think what good stories you'll be able to tell later

ANXIETY

A certain degree of anxiety is a natural reaction to a change in lifestyle and environment, and you'll probably accept it as such. But there are situations when anxiety is a worry, either because it's over the top or because you misread the symptoms as something else.

Anxiety can take a number of forms, any of which can strike you for the first time when you're away, especially if you're a worrier by nature. If you have any preexisting anxiety-related problems, travel may exacerbate them.

FEELING ANXIOUS?

Anxiety is the body's way of preparing for an emergency: the so-called fight or flight reaction. Symptoms are a result of physiological changes that take place, and include:

- palpitations, missed heartbeat or discomfort in chest
- over-breathing, shortness of breath
- dry mouth and difficulty swallowing
- stomach-ache, bloating and wind, diarrhoea
- needing to pass urine frequently
- periods stop
- premenstrual tension
- tremor and aching muscles
- pricking sensations
- headache
- dizziness and ringing in the ears

For the conditions described, we've suggested some short-term strategies for coping; you'll probably want to discuss longer-term methods of anxiety reduction with your doctor when you get home, especially if the problem is new or persistent. This is important because some physical diseases like thyroid and diabetic problems can cause anxiety symptoms, and your doctor may want to test for these.

Generalised anxiety often affects worriers; you feel restless, irritable and tired, stretched to the limit, with tension headaches and sleep problems.

Any of the strategies listed earlier for stress reduction may help; also try cutting out coffee and strong tea, both of which make tension symptoms worse. Drug treatment is only indicated if your symptoms are very severe and disabling.

Remember that alcohol withdrawal, perhaps after a binge or if you're a habitually heavy drinker, can be a cause of acute anxiety; it's best to avoid binges in the first place, and if you are a heavy drinker, it's best to cut down gradually.

Panic attacks can occur without warning and can be terrifying. They're marked by frightening physical symptoms as well as thoughts, and there's rarely a recognisable trigger. You feel like you're suffocating, you can't get enough air, and have palpitations, light-headedness, faintness and pins and needles. Often you have a feeling of being outside yourself, and everything seems unreal.

You'll probably recognise the symptoms if you've had an attack before, but if it's the first time, you may think you're dying. Sounds silly, but breathing in a controlled way in and out of a paper bag for a short time can help the symptoms of a panic attack. This is because when you panic, you start to overbreathe, and this causes you to feel lightheaded and gives you pins and needles.

The main thing is to recognise what's happening, and to be reassured that you're not having a heart attack, and that it will pass eventually. Some general stress reduction is probably a good idea in the short term.

DEPRESSION

The blues can strike any time, even when you're on holiday. Stress, anxiety, disappointment, isolation and poor physical health can all make an attack of the blues likely. You know you've got it bad when you feel teary, listless and tired; you can't be bothered to do anything and nothing is enjoyable any more. You lose interest in sex and food (although sometimes you over-eat instead), you may have trouble sleeping and you just want to withdraw from the world.

Any physical illness can make you feel low, but some diseases are known for causing depression and fatigue, often for prolonged periods of time. Some notable culprits are viral diseases like flu, glandular fever and hepatitis; dengue fever is also notorious for this, and malaria. Other causes are anaemia and low thyroid function.

If it's just a simple case of the blues, and you'll probably find that you bounce back in a few days, especially if you can identify and deal with the cause.

- Try any or all of the de-stress strategies mentioned earlier and reassure yourself that it will pass.
- If you know you suffer from depression, try anything that has worked in the past.
- Exercise is known to stimulate the production of endorphins, which are natural feel-good factors.
- Maybe it's time to stop and re-think what you're doing, and perhaps to head home.

If your depression is a follow-on from a physical illness, it may be reassuring to recognise that this is the reason you are feeling low. It's also worth seeking medical advice, as antidepressant drug treatments may be helpful in this situation.

If you think you may be depressed and things haven't improved over a couple of weeks, you should think about getting medical help. Depression is an illness, and it can be successfully treated with medication ('conventional' antidepressants or the herbal remedy St John's wort) or counselling. Severe depression can be very frightening and if it's not treated, you're at risk of suicide.

PHYSICAL DISEASES & MIND PROBLEMS

Depression and tiredness can follow several diseases, as discussed earlier under Depression. Any serious physical illness, but especially infections, can cause delirium. This shows itself as confusion, restlessness, disorientation, sometimes hallucinations, and it can be difficult to persuade someone who is delirious to stay in bed or to take treatment. Treatment of the underlying illness will settle it. If you or someone you are with is this ill, you need to seek medical attention urgently; in the meantime, take steps to bring down a fever and make sure the person doesn't hurt themselves.

Alcohol withdrawal is a specific form of delirium, and strikes people who are habitually heavy drinkers who suddenly stop (eg if they're ill and miss their usual alcohol intake). It's a serious, life-threatening condition, and you must seek medical advice urgently.

Some therapeutic drugs can cause problems with your mind. You may be aware that the antimalarial mefloquine can cause a variety of symptoms, from abnormal dreams to panic attacks, depression and hallucinations. They're all more likely if you've had emotional problems in the past, and your doctor will usually have recommended an alternative drug in this case. If you're taking mefloquine, it will probably have been prescribed well before you leave, and you'll have had a chance to deal with any potential problems before you go. However, if you do experience problems while you're away, stop taking it and seek medical advice about alternative protection. Since mefloquine is only taken once weekly, you should be able to organise an alternative antimalarial without any break in protection. For more details on antimalarial medication see p44.

Some diseases affect the brain and can cause changes in behaviour or level of consciousness, such as concussion following a head injury (p431) or meningitis (p135).

STRANGE EXPERIENCES

Some serious illnesses like schizophrenia could theoretically be kick-started by the stress of travelling. If someone you are with starts experiencing signs like visual or auditory hallucinations, and delusions, they may need urgent medical help. They may not recognise that they are ill, which can make it frightening and confusing.

ALCOHOL & RECREATIONAL DRUGS

It's not just a question of what these substances can do to you, it's also what they make you do to yourself. Before you begin a session, assess your situation for potential risks. You're much more likely to have an accident while under the influence of alcohol or other drugs, and you're more likely to take unnecessary risks that you might regret later (such as having unprotected sex with a new partner).

It's probably a good idea to be wary of some local brews, especially distilled spirits, as they can contain additives you might not want to treat your system to (eg in Egypt, a couple of deaths due to locally brewed whisky have been reported). They can also contain methanol, a highly toxic form of alcohol which has the potential to cause permanent blindness, among other things.

In many tourist haunts in Africa, drugs are easy to come by. Marijuana and hashish are widely available, and harder drugs are in circulation too. It's a personal decision whether or not you take drugs, and it makes sense to inform yourself of the legal and health consequences if you do.

By definition, these substances affect your mental state – this is after all the reason for taking them – but they can have effects that are unwanted or unexpected, especially if you're taking them for the first time.

- Acute anxiety or panic attacks are common with marijuana (also LSD or mescaline), and are more likely if you're taking it in a stressful situation or for the first time.

- Acute paranoia ('persecution complex') can be a result of taking cocaine, crack, amphetamines or ecstasy, and can be very frightening.

- Overdose can be fatal anywhere, but especially where you can't rely on the emergency services.

Anxiety attacks or acute paranoia are likely to resolve themselves without any specific treatment, although they may be pretty unpleasant at the time.

Just be aware that there's no quality control on the drugs you buy, and locally available substances can be unexpectedly strong or may be mixed with other harmful substances. You are at the mercy of sellers when it comes to quality of ingredients, and their main concern is unlikely to be your good health. Because unexpected reactions – including accidental overdose – can occur any time, you should never take drugs when you are alone.

Women Travellers...

Travelling can present some particular problems for women, and some women's health issues are a bit trickier to cope with on the road.

RESOURCES FOR WOMEN TRAVELLERS IN AFRICA

Although primarily for women planning to stay for long periods in Africa, you could try contacting an organisation called Tam Tam Femme (email info@tamtamfemme.it), which offers support and information on a variety of issues of relevance to women, including security and health. Check out its web site (**www.tamtamfemme.it**), or write to Tam Tam Femme, Via Giacomo Carissimi 28, 20123 Milano, Italy.

IPPF (see the boxed text 'Women & Health in Africa' for contact details) can provide information on local availability of contraceptives, and attitudes (and laws) on abortion and other reproductive issues.

MENSTRUAL PROBLEMS

PRACTICALITIES

Although you shouldn't have a problem finding tampons and sanitary pads, especially in urban areas, it's probably best to take all you think you'll need with you. Disposal of used tampons and sanitary towels can be a major concern (and not just when you are travelling), especially in remote or environmentally sensitive areas. So what do you do?

- You could burn them; this is environmentally the best option, but it's hardly practical.
- If you're in the wilderness, you could bury them, but you will need to dig a decent-sized hole and cover it well.
- You could carry them out with you and dispose of them somewhere more convenient later.

- Reusable items are available from specialist shops selling environmentally friendly products, but they do rely on you having access to adequate water and washing facilities.

- Some women travellers recommend using a rubber cap device, worn in the vagina and similar to an upside-down diaphragm. It has to be removed every six to 12 hours to be rinsed and emptied then replaced. Between periods you carry it in a cotton bag in your luggage. The Keeper is one brand, and (wouldn't you know it) there's a web site (www.keeper.com) where you can find out more.

Cleanliness is obviously even more important when you're travelling; wash your hands carefully before and after changing tampons, and change them regularly.

WOMEN & HEALTH IN AFRICA

In general, the quality of health care in Africa is low, and women, because of their lack of social and financial empowerment, tend to get the worst level of health provision. The maternal mortality rate is among the highest in the world: an African woman, for example, is 500 times more likely to die of pregnancy-related causes than a woman in Scandinavia.

Malnutrition and anaemia are major causes of ill-health in women between the ages of 15 and 44. Women in Africa have an average of five or six children, and the death rates for babies are also among the highest in the world.

Sub-Saharan Africa has the lowest rate of contraceptive usage in the developing world, and unwanted pregnancies, especially among teenagers, often end up in unsafe abortions, which account for up to 40% of maternal deaths. Sexually transmitted infections, including HIV/AIDS, are the second-most common cause of ill health in women in Africa (after pregnancy-related illness).

In recognition of the magnitude of these problems, WHO has called on African governments to help implement a 10 year reproductive health strategy aimed at addressing these problems. ('Reproductive health' is a relatively new concept, and represents a deliberate shift away from the idea of 'population control'.) There are complex social and cultural issues surrounding population issues, fertility and sexuality in Africa, making make this an enormously challenging health issue. (In a National Geographic article on 'Women and Population', a Kenyan man is quoted as saying 'When my wife didn't want to have more than three children, my mother told her, 'You're just lazy'.)

It's now recognised that reproductive health is inextricably linked to issues such as the education and empowerment of women, and financial and political security in the region.

If you want to find out more about the issues surrounding women and health in Africa, and how you may be able to help, contact any of the aid organisations mentioned in the boxed text 'Africa's Health' in the Staying Healthy chapter earlier in this book. You can get a copy of the latest United Nations Population Fund report, The State of the World's Population, from UNFPA, 220 East 42nd St, New York, NY 10017, USA.

Another good place to look is the International Planned Parenthood Federation (IPPF), a voluntary organisation concerned with all aspects of sexual and reproductive health worldwide. IPPF has an excellent web site (www.ippf.org) with heaps of information on a wide variety of relevant issues, as well as comprehensive links to related sites; or you can contact it in the UK on ☎ 020-7939 8200 or by mail at 4 Newhams Row, London SE1 3UZ..

MENSTRUAL-FREE TRAVEL

If all this sounds too daunting for words, it is possible to take measures to temporarily prevent menstruation, for example if you're going on a trek in a remote area. Discuss this with your doctor before you go, but some options include the following.

- If you're taking the combined oral contraceptive pill, you could carry on taking the pill without the usual break (or skip the seven days of inactive pills), although it's not advisable for more than three cycles at a time and, if you're unlucky, you may have some breakthrough bleeding.

- For a short trip, norethisterone (a progesterone) can be used to postpone a period. You need to start taking it three days or so before menstruation is due to begin and continue until the end of the holiday (for up to two to three weeks); menstruation occurs again two to three days after stopping. The dose is 5mg three times daily and side effects are rare, but it's not suitable for long term use. It's not a contraceptive.

- An injected progesterone contraceptive produces light, infrequent periods or none at all in most women – great for when you're travelling. However, you need to have injections every eight to 12 weeks and the effect on menstruation is initially unpredictable.

PREMENSTRUAL SYNDROME

If you normally get period pains and premenstrual bloating, you may find these are worse while you are travelling, for a variety of reasons – physical and psychological stresses, unaccustomed heat and prolonged immobility (on long bus or plane journeys). If you think this could be a problem, take a good supply of a painkiller or any other remedies that you know work for you. Alternatively, you could consider starting the oral contraceptive pill before you leave, but it's best to sort this out in plenty of time before you go.

Remedies that may be helpful include evening primrose oil, which can be taken in capsule form or as the oil, and vitamin B6, magnesium or calcium supplements. Or you could try the delightfully named Chaste tree (Vitex agnus castus) or dong quai, a herbal treatment widely used in Asia for 'women's problems'.

MENSTRUAL MYTHS

Heard the one about menstruating women being attacked by wild animals? Be reassured that predators like lions are not thought to be attracted to menstruating women in any situation travellers would be likely to get themselves in to.

Leaving aside the 'blood myths', the accepted wisdom is that many animals can detect menstruation in humans, eg some monkeys are thought to be able to detect hormone cycles in humans and can react accordingly, although it's not to menstruation as such.

In Africa, monkeys are probably the most likely hazard to you, as you may find yourself in close contact with them on safari (where they can be quite aggressive) and in urban areas. Monkeys can transmit rabies, so take care around them – never be tempted to feed them or to walk around eating food when they are in the vicinity.

As for sharks, you'd probably want to avoid swimming in shark-infested waters anyway!

LIGHT OR ABSENT PERIODS

You often find that your periods disappear or become irregular when you're on the road, probably because of the mental and physical stresses of travel and the change to your usual routine. Other causes are pregnancy, drastic weight loss and hormonal contraceptive problems. Obviously the most important cause to exclude is pregnancy – see the section 'Am I Pregnant?' later in this chapter for more guidelines.

There's usually nothing to worry about, although if you don't have a period at all for more than about three or four months, it's a good idea to get a check-up. Periods usually get back to normal once you have finished your travels.

New, severe period pains can be a result of a vaginal infection or a tubal pregnancy (if there's a chance you may be pregnant), so seek urgent medical advice in this case.

HEAVY PERIODS

Light or absent periods are great, but you can find that your periods become heavier or more frequent while travelling, so be prepared for either possibility!

If your periods are heavier than usual, you may develop a mild anaemia; boost your diet with fresh fruit and green vegetables, or consider taking a multivitamin and iron supplement.

Heavy bleeding is often due to hormonal problems. If you suffer heavy persistent bleeding for more than seven days which shows no sign of lessening and you are in a remote area and unable to get medical advice, you could try taking norethisterone (a progesterone tablet) 5mg three times daily for 10 days (if you can find it). If you're prone to unpredictable bleeding, you might want to discuss taking a supply of norethisterone with you before you go.

Bleeding should stop by the end of the course and you should expect to have a period after about seven days of finishing the course. If the bleeding does not stop, you will need to seek medical advice urgently.

Note that this is only for emergencies, and you should not take it if there is any chance you may be pregnant, or if you have a history of gynaecological problems or are otherwise unwell – you must seek medical advice in all these cases.

Abnormally heavy periods can be an indication of problems with the cervix or womb (such as pelvic inflammatory disease, fibroids, miscarriage), so you should try to find a doctor to get it checked out as soon as possible.

MENOPAUSAL & POSTMENOPAUSAL TRAVELLERS

Hot flushes can be worse while you are travelling, as hot weather, spicy meals and any sort of emotional upset can trigger them. It's probably worth discussing this with your doctor before you go so you can work out ways of dealing with it. If you're not taking hormonal replacement therapy, this could be an option to consider. Try simple measures to keep cool, such as wearing loose cotton clothing, not overexerting yourself, resting during the heat of the day and, if evening flushes are a problem, it may be worth making sure you have a room with a fan or air-conditioning. Cool drinks and eating small, frequent meals may also help.

 Many natural remedies can be helpful for menopausal symptoms, including the herb dong quai (for flushes), St John's wort (Hypericum perforatum, for depression), ginseng (to reduce sweating) and Bach flower remedies, so check these out with your practitioner before you go, and take a good supply with you.

Dry, itchy skin can be a problem at and after menopause. The physical hazards of travelling can exacerbate this, so take care to protect your skin from the sun and wind by using sunscreen and moisturisers.

Cystitis (see that section later in this chapter) can occur at any age but is very common after menopause, and travelling can make an attack more likely.

If you're postmenopausal, and you're not on HRT, you need to seek medical advice for any vaginal spotting or bleeding that occurs, although if you're on a short trip, this can probably wait until you get back.

HRT & TRAVEL

As for any medication, it's best to take all you'll think you'll need with you. If you have an implant, will it be due for renewal while you are away? If you're going to be travelling in the heat, sweating and swimming may mean your patches stick less well, so you might want to consider changing to a tablet or gel preparation before you go.

If you're taking a preparation that induces bleeding, it may be possible to change to a different one that induces periods every three months instead of every month if a period is going to be inconvenient while you're travelling. Periods can be postponed by manipulating your progestogen dose, but this can sometimes lead to heavy bleeding, so it's best to discuss this with your doctor before leaving.

HRT makes you slightly more prone to thrombosis (blood clots) in your leg veins, especially if you're immobile for long periods of time, for example on a long flight or bus journey. A few things to try:

- take regular walks
- when you're sitting, wriggle your toes and flex your calf muscles
- support stockings or tights are an option but not a very attractive one in a hot climate
- drink plenty, as dehydration makes clotting more likely

If you're going to be at high altitude for any length of time, discuss this with your doctor before you go because you may be at greater risk of blood clots.

If you have been on HRT for some time and you develop heavy or irregular bleeding while you are away, it could indicate a problem with the lining of your womb (such as thickenings called polyps or even early cancer), and you should seek medical advice as soon as possible.

BLADDER INFECTION

Also called cystitis, the main symptom is having to empty your bladder frequently – great when you're travelling! Although you have to go more frequently, you only pass small quantities of urine, often with pain or a burning feeling and sometimes an ache in your lower abdomen.

Cystitis is often due to infection by bacteria that normally live in the bowel. It's very common in women. The reason for this is that, compared with men (who relatively rarely get cystitis), the tube leading to the bladder in women is short, making it easy for bacteria to enter the bladder. This is also why bladder infections often occur after sexual intercourse, and are more likely if you use the diaphragm for contraception.

If you think you've got cystitis:

- drink plenty of fluids to help flush the infection out; citrus fruit juice or cranberry juice (if you can find it) can help relieve symptoms
- take a non-prescription cystitis remedy (these usually contain an alkalinising agent like potassium citrate, sodium bicarbonate or sodium citrate) to help relieve the discomfort; alternatively, add a teaspoon of bicarbonate of soda to a glass of water
- if there's no improvement after 24 hours despite these measures, you may need a course of antibiotics

Get medical advice, but there are several antibiotic options for cystitis, including single dose treatment with trimethoprim 600mg, norfloxacin 800mg or ciprofloxacin 500mg (avoid all three in pregnancy). Other antibiotics (suitable in pregnancy) include amoxycillin (take two 3g doses 12 hours apart) or nalidixic acid (1g four times daily for seven days). Avoid any antibiotic you are allergic to – see p406 for more details.

If you have the symptoms described earlier, you almost certainly have cystitis, and it will almost certainly respond to a course of recommended antibiotics. If it doesn't, or if the symptoms recur quickly, you should seek medical advice so a urine test can be done to clarify what's causing your symptoms.

If cystitis is left untreated, there's a risk of the infection spreading to the kidneys, which causes a much more serious illness.

Symptoms of a kidney infection include a high temperature, vomiting (sometimes) and pain in the lower back – you should seek medical attention in this case.

Just to confuse the issue, about a third of women with symptoms of cystitis don't have an infection at all (it may be a sort of 'irritable bladder' syndrome), so it's definitely worth trying some simple non-antibiotic measures first. It's worth bearing in mind that 'cystitis' can be caused by a sexually transmitted infection, so you should get this checked out if you are concerned, especially if you have any other symptoms such as an abnormal vaginal discharge.

> Help prevent cystitis by drinking plenty of fluids and making sure you don't hang on too long – empty your bladder at regular intervals. If you know that you are prone to cystitis, arrange to take a couple of courses of treatment with you in your medical kit.

VAGINAL INFECTIONS

If you've got a vaginal discharge that is not normal for you (more copious, abnormal colour, smelly) with or without any other symptoms, you've probably got an infection.

- If you've had thrush before and you think you may have it again, it's worth self-treating for this (see following section).

- get medical advice as you will need a laboratory test and an appropriate course of treatment.

- It's best not to self-medicate with antibiotics because there are many causes of vaginal discharge, which can only be differentiated with a laboratory test.

Although candidiasis ('yeast' infection) is probably the best known cause of vaginal problems, and the one women are most likely to self-diagnose, it's worth remembering that it probably accounts for only 20% to 30% of all vaginal infections, which is a relatively small proportion. Sexually transmitted infections (such as gonorrhoea) are an important cause of vaginal discharge.

THRUSH (VAGINAL CANDIDIASIS)

If you don't already know, symptoms of this common yeast infection are itching and discomfort in the genital area, often in association with a thick white vaginal discharge (said to resemble cottage cheese). It's due to an overgrowth of the vaginal yeasts, usually the species called *Candida albicans,* which are present normally in the vagina and on the skin.

Many factors, including diet, pregnancy and medications, can trigger this infection, which is normally kept at bay by the acid conditions in the vagina and the normal balance of organisms. Heat, the oral contraceptive pill and antibiotics can all make an attack more likely, so it's no surprise that it's even more common when you're travelling.

Although candidiasis is not a sexually transmitted infection as such, it makes sense to treat your regular partner with an antifungal cream on the genital area for five days.

You can help prevent thrush by wearing cotton underwear and loose-fitting trousers or a skirt; it's a good idea to wash regularly but some soap and bath salts can make vaginal irritation and candidiasis more likely, so are best avoided.

If you have thrush, a single dose of an antifungal pessary (vaginal tablet), such as clotrimazole 500mg is an effective and convenient treatment. Short courses of three to 14 days are also available but are less convenient. Alternatively, you can use an antifungal cream (eg clotrimazole 1% or econazole nitrate 1%) inserted high in the vagina (on a tampon) instead of a pessary. The treatment can be used even if you're on a period. Antifungal cream can be used in addition to a pessary to relieve vulval itching. A vaginal acidifying gel may help prevent recurrences.

If you know you are prone to thrush, take a supply of pessaries or cream with you in your medical kit.

If you're stuck in a remote area without medication, you could use natural yoghurt (applied directly to the vulva or on a tampon and inserted in the vagina) to soothe and help restore the normal balance of organisms in the vagina. Sitting in or washing with a weak solution of vinegar or sodium bicarbonate may also help. If thrush is really being a nuisance, some nonspecific strategies you could try are cutting down on sugar and alcohol, and eating more plain live yoghurt.

BACTERIAL VAGINOSIS

Also known as nonspecific vaginitis or *Gardnerella* vaginitis, bacterial vaginosis is the most common cause of abnormal vaginal discharge. It can cause a range of symptoms, but the most common are odour (fishy) and discharge (white-grey).

Although it is more likely if you are sexually active, there's no evidence that it is transmitted by intercourse. It's not caused by any one organism – instead there's a general change in the whole vaginal environment, with the good guys, the lactobacilli that normally keep the vagina healthy, being replaced by a variety of bad guys.

Treatment is with an antibiotic, usually metronidazole 500mg twice a day for seven days.

SEXUALLY TRANSMITTED INFECTIONS

✚ For a more detailed discussion of STIs, see the HIV/AIDS & Sexual Health chapter earlier in this book.

Prevention is definitely the aim with sexually transmitted infections (STIs). Symptoms include sores in the genital area, an abnormal vaginal discharge and sometimes cystitis symptoms.

- Signs of an STI are usually an abnormal vaginal discharge or sores in the genital area; sometimes it can cause symptoms of cystitis (see earlier in this chapter).

- Casual intercourse is risky anywhere in the world; asking your partner to use a latex condom helps prevent transmission of STIs, but is not 100% effective.

- Having an STI can make you more vulnerable to HIV infection.

- STIs need to be diagnosed and treated properly, as they can cause chronic pelvic inflammatory disease (in women) or infertility (women or men) later, so it's worth finding a doctor or clinic to get it checked out.

- It's important that your partner is treated for the STI as well.

- You may have an STI even if you have no symptoms – if you think you may have put yourself at risk, get a full check-up when you get home.

Trichomoniasis

This sexually transmitted infection often occurs together with other STIs. Symptoms include vaginal discharge (thick yellow), itchiness and sometimes discomfort on passing urine. About 50% of women with the infection don't have any symptoms. Men rarely have any symptoms, but partners must be treated to prevent reinfection. Treatment is with an antibiotic, usually metronidazole either in a single dose of 2g or 250mg three times daily for seven days.

CONTRACEPTION

It makes sense to discuss your contraceptive needs with your doctor or a specialist family planning clinic well in advance of travelling. Even if you're planning on celibacy, it's always worth being prepared for the unexpected.

There's a whole range of options available to you, so if one method doesn't suit, there's plenty more to choose from. Seek professional advice, but the following table summarises the major players, with some of the pros and cons for travellers.

> New sexual partner? Go 'double Dutch' – use a barrier method in addition to a non-barrier method to protect yourself against HIV and STIs (and babies).

Contraceptives (including condoms) are generally widely available, but it's best to take your own supplies, as you may not be able to find exactly what you want when you want it. If you need contraceptive advice while you're away, you could try a local doctor, hospital or family planning clinic. If you do have to see a doctor, use common sense and choose someone you can trust. If you can't find a reputable female doctor, insist on having a chaperone present if you need to be examined.

HEALTH TIPS FOR LESBIANS

Lesbians around the world have created some of the many resources that are now available to make your trip easier – it's worth the effort to do some research before leaving home. Wondering what to do miles from home when symptoms are already presenting is definitely a situation to be avoided.

If you can, make sure you are as healthy as possible before leaving home. Improving your fitness and general wellbeing can provide a buffer to the demands of travel and the health challenges in front of you. You might want to check out a lesbian health guide like *Caring for Ourselves – The Lesbian Health Book* (Jocelyn C White & Marissa C Martinez, eds) or any general women's health guides.

Enjoy your travel experience, but remember that simple safe sex precautions are even more vital when you don't know your partner's medical history. Lesbian sex is low risk, but this doesn't mean that it's no risk.

Avoid touching or tasting blood or body fluids. Use gloves and dental dams or another latex barrier with plenty of wet stuff and your favourite water-based lubricant. Note that extremes of heat can melt dental dams in their packaging.

Depending on where you are travelling, you may need to be creative, but never be careless. Don't share sex toys without washing them between each use; alternatively, cover them with condoms. Travelling into some countries with your toys on board can be a bit embarrassing, but let's face it, if tampons are in short supply, other womanly essentials will be totally out of stock. So plan ahead if you intend to play around.

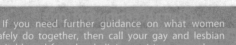

If you need further guidance on what women safely do together, then call your gay and lesbian switchboard for a local clinic, or visit any good gay and lesbian bookstore before you leave.

And a final warning…beware the dreaded love bug. The authors of this section, one European and one Australian, met in North America, fell in love and have never recovered…

Leonie Englefield & Caz Price

ORAL CONTRACEPTIVE PILL

As for any medication, take enough (and some more) to last the entire trip, as your brand may not be available locally. If you are crossing time zones, or travelling at night, it can be easy to forget to take a pill:

- combined oral contraceptive (COCP) – make sure that you do not leave more than 24 hours before taking the next pill; take it earlier rather than later
- progesterone-only pill (POP) – the timing needs to be much more precise with this; if you're more than three hours late, you'll need to take additional contraceptive precautions for the next seven days

Vomiting or diarrhoea can mean the hormones are not absorbed properly and therefore that you are not protected. For either the COCP or POP:

- if you vomit or have severe diarrhoea less than three hours after taking the pill, take another pill
- if more than three hours, or if vomiting and diarrhoea persists, take the pill as normal, but take additional contraceptive precautions for the rest of the cycle

You should stop taking either the COCP or POP and use an alternative method of contraception if you get hepatitis (jaundice), as the jaundice can interfere with the usual way in which the body deals with the pill.

CONTRACEPTION OPTIONS

Method	Advantages on the road
Combined oral contraceptive pill	effective and reliable; periods may be lighter and PMT less
Progestogen-only pill	useful for a selected group of women (eg older women, heavy smokers, migraine sufferers); not affected by antibiotics
Hormonal implants	effective and reliable; nothing to remember or lose; not affected by diarrhoea and vomiting or antibiotics; periods usually lighter and may disappear altogether; injection lasts eight or 12 weeks
Intrauterine copper devices ('the coil')	convenient – nothing to remember or lose; reliable
Intrauterine progestogen	convenient and reliable; period pains are improved and periods are usually lighter and may disappear; STIs less likely to cause problems than with the coil and there's less risk of tubal pregnancy
Diaphragm or cap	no hormonal side effects
Female condom	available over the counter; less likely to rupture than male condoms
Male condom	readily available; no mess – important if washing facilities are in limited supply; can be carried just in case

Disadvantages on the road	Protects against HIV, hepatitis B & STIs?
only effective as long as you remember to take it! diarrhoea and vomiting, and some antibiotics, can reduce effectiveness; fluid retention side effect may be worse in hot climates	No
effectiveness reduced by diarrhoea and vomiting; small margin for error if you forget to take it	No
irregular bleeding can be a problem, especially at first; if you're going to be away on a long trip you will need to arrange when and where to have the next injection	No
STIs more likely to cause long term problems, so this method is not advisable if casual sex is likely; tubal pregnancy may be more likely	No
periods may be unpredictable at first	No
hygiene may be a problem when travelling; difficult to replace if lost; you need a refit (diaphragm) if you lose a lot of weight (4kg)	protects against some STIs, but not HIV
useability could be improved, but sense of humour may help	Yes
can split or leak – needs to be used correctly to be effective	Yes

Some common broad-spectrum antibiotics (such as ampicillin) can reduce the effectiveness of the COCP (but not POP); the UK Family Planning Association advises you should use additional contraceptive methods during a short course of these antibiotics and for seven days afterwards (the leaflet accompanying the pill packet will give you more guidance on which drugs to be careful with, but if in doubt, take extra precautions anyway). If you get to the end of the pill packet during the week after finishing the antibiotics, you should start the next packet straight away and take additional precautions.

At high altitude you get an increase in circulating red blood cells so there's a theoretical risk that side effects of the COCP like blood clots in the leg veins or lungs may be more likely. If you think this may be a problem for you, it's a good idea to discuss the issue with your doctor before you go.

MISSED A PILL?

If you miss a pill (either the combined oral contraceptive or progestogen-only pill), take the missed pill straight away, and take the next pill on time, even if it is the same day.

You'll need to use a different form of contraception for the next seven days in the following situations:

• progestogen-only pill: if you took it more than three hours late

• combined pill: if you took it 12 or more hours late

In addition, for the combined pill, if the seven days extend into the pill-free gap (or into the inactive pill interval), you should start the next course straight away without the usual break.

INTRAUTERINE DEVICES (IUD)

If you can't feel the strings, you should assume you are not protected and use an alternative contraceptive method until you can get it checked out by a doctor.

> **!** You should seek medical advice urgently if you develop low abdominal pain, especially with a fever and vaginal discharge; if you miss a period; or if you develop unusually heavy or painful bleeding.

BARRIER METHODS

See also Contraception in the Men Travellers chapter for more details on condoms. A couple of points to bear in mind:

- heat can cause rubber to perish so check your diaphragm for holes periodically, and try to keep it in a cool place

- consider taking a second diaphragm with you, especially if you are going to be away for a prolonged period of time

EMERGENCY CONTRACEPTION

In an emergency, you can try to prevent pregnancy following unprotected intercourse by taking a couple of high doses of oestrogen, which helps prevent the fertilised egg from settling in the lining of the womb.

Ideally, you should see a doctor who can prescribe the so-called 'morning-after' pill. You need to take two doses 12 hours apart, and you need to take the first dose as soon as possible within 72 hours of unprotected intercourse. The high dose of oestrogen may cause nausea and vomiting. If you vomit within two hours of either dose, the dose should be repeated. You should not take the morning-after pill if you are suffering from a severe migraine at the same time. Your next period may be either early or late. If you are taking the oral contraceptive pill, continue taking it as normal.

> **!** The morning-after pill is not 100% foolproof; it's for emergencies only not for use as a regular method of contraception.

The morning-after pill usually prescribed contains ethinyl-oestradiol 50 micrograms and levonorgestrol 250 micrograms. The dose is two tablets followed by another two 12 hours later. The important ingredient is oestrogen (usually in the form of ethinyloestradiol). If it's not practical to seek medical advice, then see if you can buy a pill containing the same dose of oestrogen (check the packet or ask the pharmacist to tell you), and treat yourself as indicated in the previous paragraph. If you can't find a high-strength pill, you could use a 'normal' contraceptive pill, as follows:

- if the pill contains 20 micrograms of oestrogen,
  take five pills and then another five 12 hours later

- if the pill contains 30 micrograms of oestrogen,
  take three pills and another three 12 hours later

Another method of preventing pregnancy is to have an intrauterine contraceptive device inserted within five days, but you'd want a reliable doctor for this.

AM I PREGNANT?

If you have reason to be concerned about pregnancy, be suspicious if you miss a period (or have an unusually light one); other signs are enlarged, tender breasts and, although this is usually a later sign, nausea ('morning sickness'). So what do you do if you think you may be pregnant?

It's probably best to continue (or start) using a reliable contraceptive method (there is no evidence that the contraceptive pill harms the foetus, for example, so it's probably best to continue taking it until you know for certain that you are pregnant, especially if you are still sexually active).

Get a pregnancy test as soon as possible so that you have plenty of time to make arrangements – you may be able to buy a kit from a pharmacist in some big cities; otherwise, go to a doctor, clinic or hospital and ask for a pregnancy test to be done (note that a pregnancy test won't show positive before the first missed period). If it's negative, but you still think pregnancy is a possibility, wait two weeks and then repeat it.

If you're happy to be pregnant, you should see a doctor as soon as possible for blood tests and advice on optimising the outcome for you and the foetus. Some medications you may be taking (such as antimalarials) are known to be harmful to the foetus, also some diseases (including malaria and hepatitis A and E) may be more serious in pregnancy. For more details on travelling while pregnant, see that section later in this chapter.

If you decide you want to terminate the pregnancy, timing could be important: abortions are best done before (and in many Western countries can be difficult or impossible to obtain after) the 12th week of pregnancy (counting day one of pregnancy as the first day of your last menstrual period). In many developed countries, abortion is effectively available 'on demand' but this is not the case in many parts of the world, including here. In addition to social and ethical constraints, it may also actually be against the law of the country, so you should check this as soon as possible.

In addition, consider carefully where you would want to have the procedure done; it may be worth changing your travel plans to accommodate this. Remember that any surgical procedure carries a risk of HIV or hepatitis B transmission in a country with less developed medical services. In less competent hands, abortion carries significant risks of infection, blood loss and permanent infertility.

! You should avoid a 'back street' abortion at all costs – these are notoriously dangerous, and can result in long-term problems or even death.

FEMALE GENITAL MUTILATION

This practice affects millions of women, mostly in the Sahel zone nations of sub-Saharan Africa, and has a significant impact on women's health in Africa. It's a complex issue that can be hard for non-Africans to fully understand. African women have been working over the last couple of decades to sort this issue out, and much progress has been made. Egypt was the first country to pass a law banning it in 1978; it's now also banned in Kenya and Senegal, although there are doubts as to the effectiveness of the bans.

Contrary to what you might think, FGM is not a practice required by any religion, it's a cultural rite. One of the more perplexing aspects is the fact that it is generally performed by women, and many women support the practice. The justification behind the rite is that removal of a woman's genitalia purifies women and makes them more likely to be faithful to their husbands because this diminishes sexual desire.

However, the procedure is associated with significant health risks, and is thought likely to have powerful psychosexual effects on girls who have undergone it. There are three types of FGM, varying in the amount removed. The most severe form, infibulation or pharaonic circumcision, leaves the girl with only a small hole through which urine and menstrual blood can pass.

The procedure is usually performed on girls and young women by birth attendants, often without anaesthesia and with a razor blade or knife. Immediate risks are extreme pain, bleeding, infection, tetanus and HIV or hepatitis B infection from unsterilised instruments. Immediate risks are extreme pain, bleeding, infection, tetanus and HIV or hepatitis B infection from unsterilised instruments. Possible long-term health effects include scarring and infections of the bladder and kidneys, infertility, sexual problems and difficulties during childbirth. Although this is clearly an issue that African women need to reach a solution on themselves, if you want to find out more, there are some excellent resources available to you on the web: try IPPF (**www.ippf .org**). Alternatively, *Desert Flower, the Waris Dirie Story* provides a heart-wrenching account of the procedure by the now internationally famous Somalian model and United Nations spokesperson on women's rights in Africa.

PREGNANT TRAVELLERS

The days of seeing pregnancy as an 'indisposition' are long gone, and many women either choose or end up having to travel while they are pregnant, without any adverse effects on mother or foetus. However, there are some important considerations to bear in mind if you are planning to travel while you're pregnant, and these are summarised in this section. We should stress that this is to give you an idea of the issues that may be involved – you should seek expert medical advice well before you plan to go on any trip.

 If you've had complicated pregnancies before, or you're expecting twins, it would be best to postpone your trip.

WHEN?

Most doctors would suggest that the best time to travel in pregnancy is during the middle 12 weeks, when the risk of complications is less, the pregnancy is relatively well established and your energy levels are getting back to normal.

Before the 12th week, there is a relatively high risk of miscarriage (which could require surgical treatment like a scrape of the womb lining or even a blood transfusion) or a tubal pregnancy, which occurs in about one in 200 pregnancies and nearly always requires surgical treatment; it is an emergency situation. In addition, many women experience morning sickness in the first three months (sometimes for longer), which could make travelling less than enjoyable. Occasionally, it can be severe enough to require treatment in hospital. More mundane, but just as incapacitating for travelling, is needing to empty your bladder more frequently as the enlarging womb takes up more room in the pelvis and presses on the bladder.

> Note that most airlines prohibit flying after the 35th week of pregnancy (sometimes this can be waived if you have a doctor's certificate to say that there are no complications) – this is because they don't want to risk a woman going into premature labour on a flight, not because there's thought to be any intrinsic danger to the pregnancy.

In the last three months, major complications such as premature labour, blood pressure problems and problems with the placenta can all occur, so you would probably not want to risk a trip of any length during this time.

WHERE?

> It's best to avoid travelling to a high-risk malarial area if you're pregnant because malaria is very much more serious in pregnant women, and can have disastrous effects on the foetus. Some of the more effective antimalarial drugs are not suitable to take in pregnancy, which makes it even riskier.

You need to take into account the standard of medical facilities and the safety of blood for transfusion, in case any complications occur while you are away. For the same reason, it's probably not a good idea to plan a trip to remote areas while pregnant, in case complications occur that need to be treated urgently. High altitude trekking or scuba diving, assuming you'd want to do either of these activities in mid-pregnancy, are not advisable either.

IMMUNISATIONS & MALARIA PREVENTION

Your best bet is to make sure you're up to date with all your vaccinations before you get pregnant. Generally, it's best to avoid all vaccinations in the first 12 weeks of pregnancy, as there's a theoretical risk of harm to the foetus and miscarriage. In addition, 'live' vaccines ideally should be avoided at any time during pregnancy. Live vaccines include yellow fever and oral typhoid. You may be able to get a certificate of exemption for yellow fever if necessary. Hepatitis A is a much more serious illness in pregnancy, so it's important to be protected against it with the hepatitis A vaccine, and to take food and water precautions. An inactivated polio vaccine can be used instead of the usual oral live vaccine in pregnant women if necessary. A tetanus booster can be given safely in pregnancy, and tetanus protection is conferred to the newborn.

Travel to malarial areas is not recommended but if necessary, preventive medication is considered safer than risking the disease in pregnancy. Chloroquine and proguanil are considered safe in pregnancy, although you may need a folic acid supplement with proguanil, and this combination is not highly protective as resistance has increased. Mefloquine can be used in the last 24 weeks of pregnancy, although it should be avoided if possible for emergency treatment. If prevention fails, quinine is known to be safe in pregnancy for emergency treatment (for more details, see Malaria in the Fever chapter earlier in this book).

SPECIAL CONSIDERATIONS

All the predeparture preparations discussed in the Before You Go chapter apply if you're pregnant, but there are some special considerations for pregnant travellers. Be prepared, especially if this is your first pregnancy. It's a good idea to read up on pregnancy before you go so you have an idea of what to expect (such as tiredness, heartburn etc) and are familiar with any minor problems that may arise. Discuss these with your doctor, and work out strategies for coping in advance.

! Make sure you are clear on what your travel health insurance covers you for during pregnancy.

As a general rule, you should avoid unnecessary medications when you are pregnant. Don't take any medications while you are away unless you know they are safe in pregnancy (read the information leaflet or packaging, or ask a reliable doctor or pharmacist). It's a good idea to take a well stocked medical kit with you, with suitable medications for common problems, so that you are clear on what you should and shouldn't take while you are away.

Long flights or bus rides increase the risk of blood clots in the legs, so if possible try to get up and walk around, drink plenty of water and consider wearing support stockings to reduce this risk on a long flight.

Every traveller should take steps to avoid illness, but it's even more important in pregnancy, when illnesses can have more severe effects both on your health and your baby's. Prevent insect bites, take food and water precautions, and avoid risk situations for accidents.

During pregnancy, your immunity is lower; infections, such as cystitis and chest infections, can be more severe and should be treated with antibiotics early – get medical advice. In the tropics you may be less tolerant of the heat. Rest, drink plenty of fluids and give yourself lots of time to adjust.

It's a good idea to make sure you eat a well balanced, nutritionally sound diet during the trip. Avoid potential problem foods like raw or partially cooked eggs, peanuts and peanut products, and soft cheeses. You can get toxoplasmosis by eating undercooked meat in many countries in the region. It can cause a mild flu-like syndrome in adults, but result in birth defects in unborn children.

And all the general advice about not smoking and being careful with alcohol obviously holds true wherever you are.

Men Travellers...

There are some conditions that only men travellers are in line for...besides, we didn't want you to feel left out.

JOCK ITCH (CROTCH ROT)

Hot, humid climates, tight underwear and infrequent washing all make this fungal infection more likely while you're travelling. It can occur in women, but it more usually affects men...as you might have guessed from these affectionate terms.

It produces itching and soreness in the groin area and inner thighs. Inspection reveals a red, flaky rash, sometimes with blisters.

Keep the area clean and dry, but do not over wash with soap, as this may increase the irritation. Wearing cotton shorts rather than close-fitting underpants can also help. An antifungal powder or cream (such as clotrimazole, econazole or miconozole) should be applied twice a day for at least seven days.

PAINFUL TESTICLE

You should seek medical advice urgently if you develop a sore testicle. If the pain started suddenly, and the testicle is swollen and red, it may be due to torsion. This is when the testicle gets twisted, which cuts off its blood supply – with the risk of irreversible damage. This is an emergency situation, as you may need surgery to fix the problem. While not specific to travellers, it demands attention if it occurs.

If the pain has come on more gradually, it may be due to an infection, often a sexually transmitted one like chlamydia (common) or gonorrhoea (less common). You may have noticed other symptoms, such as a discharge from the penis, and the testicle will feel hot and tender. You may have a fever. You will probably need a course of antibiotics to treat the infection, so it's best to seek medical advice.

Pain in the testicle can be due to a problem elsewhere, eg stones in the urinary tract (see p171), when the testicle will look and feel normal to the touch.

LUMP ON TESTICLE

Feeling your testicles for lumps is a good habit to get into, although travelling may not provide the ideal environment for doing it in – it's usually best in a hot bath or shower. If you do feel a lump, or you think one of your testicles has changed in shape or feel (eg it feels harder), you should get this checked out as soon as possible. Testicular cancer, although uncommon, tends to strike younger men. If diagnosed and treated early, it often has a very good outlook. Note that it's normal for one testicle to be larger than the other, so you should be looking for any change in either testicle.

CONTRACEPTION FOR MEN

If you're planning on being sexually active with a new partner (or even if you're not), you'll probably want to make some preparations in this department. Your choices are limited, admittedly, and probably boil down to condoms, which are sensible anyway, as you will need to protect yourself from STIs and HIV. Condoms are generally widely available throughout the region, although they may be difficult to obtain in rural areas. Some points to bear in mind about condoms include:

- rubber condoms can disintegrate in the heat – try to keep them cool if possible and check them carefully before use
- if buying locally, check expiry dates and buy only items that are likely to have been stored properly (out of direct sunlight)
- local brands may be less reliable than international brands, and sizes can vary, so you may want to take a supply with you
- many commonly available lubricants cause rubber to perish, so be careful with what you use

SEXUALLY TRANSMITTED INFECTIONS (STIS)

These infections can cause genital sores, discharge from the penis and/or burning when you pass urine, but be aware that you can have an infection even if you don't have any symptoms. You need to seek medical advice if you notice any of these symptoms, so that the most appropriate antibiotic treatment can be given. For more information on STIs, including HIV/AIDS, see the HIV/AIDS & Sexual Health chapter earlier in this book, or visit your local sexual health clinic before you go.

'DECENT' WOMEN

Just be aware of the way cultural differences can impact on your health. For example, in most African societies, 'decent' women are ensconced in their homes by nightfall. This means that most of the women you'll meet in bars, cafes and nightclubs in the evenings are likely to be sex workers to some degree, even if it is just a question of buying her drinks. It's impossible to tell who is and who isn't, but you should bear the possibility in mind if a woman approaches you in this situation. We're not suggesting you should assume that every woman who exchanges a word with you in Africa is after your body (or at least the part attached to your wallet), but use a bit of common sense and be prepared!

PROSTATE PROBLEMS

While there's no reason why you shouldn't travel if you've got symptoms of prostate enlargement, it's probably a good idea to discuss this with your doctor in advance, especially if you are going to be travelling in remote areas. That way, you can work out strategies for dealing with any problems that might arise while you're away. The main concern is if you become unable to pass urine at all; in this scenario you will need to have a tube (catheter) inserted up the penis into the bladder to drain it manually. It's not something that you can accurately predict, so in certain situations it might be appropriate to take a sterile catheter set with you.

> ❗ If you are unable to pass any urine at all for more than 24 hours
> (you'll probably feel very uncomfortable before this) seek medical
> advice urgently.

TRAVEL HEALTH FOR GAY MEN

Glen Monks, UK-based Health Promotion Specialist for gay men and drugs, has the following tips for gay men.

BEFORE YOU GO

Try to get hold of the telephone number of a gay advice/support agency in the country(ies) you are visiting and also the number of an HIV/AIDS advice/support service or helpline. Try your travel guidebook or *Spartacus*, the international gay guide, which has listings for each country. Your local service at home should also have listings.

If you're HIV-positive, it's a good idea to consult your specialist for advice on possible risks before you travel as vaccination advice (eg Yellow Fever vaccine) can be more complex.

➕ For more information on travelling with HIV, see the Travellers
   with Special Needs chapter.

CONDOM CARE

Extra-strong condoms and water-based lubricant form the essential safer sex toolkit for gay men. You need to protect yourself from HIV and other sexually transmitted infections (STIs) even more when travelling than you do when you're at home.

For more information about condom availability and care, see that section in this chapter. Note that in some countries it is impossible to find extra-strong condoms and water-based lube, so it's best to take a plentiful supply with you.

IMMUNISATIONS

See the section on Immunisations in the Before You Go chapter for general recommendations on this, but note that hepatitis A and B can both be transmitted through sex and are fairly common among gay men. Hepatitis A is passed on through human faeces, so sex or even handling used condoms may present a risk.

GAY ABANDON

Everyone, no matter their sexuality, tends to be less inhibited away from home. Letting you hair down and having some fun is fine, so long as you don't put yourself and others at risk.

Personal safety is paramount. If you're the new boy in town and agree to go back to some other guy's place, are you getting into a vulnerable position? Is there someone else who knows where you'll be? How will you get home?

Remember that the law on sex between men varies greatly around the world, as does the policing of public sex venues and cruising sites. Public attitudes differ too, so find out about this before you go – try your travel guidebook or gay groups at home for information on this.

Be prepared: some people will be very upfront about safer sex and others very coy. The key thing, whatever your cultural disposition, is to avoid getting or passing on HIV and other STIs. To do this, however awkward it might feel and however many language barriers there seem to be, you will need to raise the subject of condoms and lubricant and make sure that you use them. Remember, you're the one on vacation, not HIV.

AFTER THE FUN

Few of us are saints all the time. If you have any concerns at all, it's a good idea to pay a visit to your sexual health or HIV clinic when you get back home.

Babies & Children...

The whole of this book applies as much to children as it does to adults, (except where we've indicated otherwise), but in this chapter we've highlighted some of the health issues that are especially relevant when you're travelling with babies or young children. Children can be surprisingly adaptable to climate and time changes, but you need to bear in mind that they are more susceptible to disease and accidents, and to take appropriate precautions to protect them. Children also change very quickly – they can deteriorate or improve within a matter of hours – so it's important to be vigilant, especially with young children.

BEFORE YOU GO

Good preparation is the key to a successful trip with babies or children, so it's worth putting a bit of effort into this before you go.

SOME CONSIDERATIONS

You might want to consider some of the following issues before you go.

Age

On the plus side, babies are easy to feed if they are exclusively breastfed, they're relatively easy to carry around in a sling and you don't need to worry about them getting bored by sightseeing. But they are a concern if they get sick, they can quickly become dehydrated and are very sensitive to heat and sun. Toddlers are more complicated to feed, transport around and to keep amused and safe, particularly around water! Obviously it's best to avoid travelling during toilet training …

Type Of Holiday

Staying in a resort is probably going to be easier than a backpacking-type holiday involving lots of long journeys, although this may depend on your children's temperament and ages. It's worth researching exactly what is available for the children before you go.

Health Risks

This can depend as much on the type of holiday you're planning as on the location. Backpacking through remote areas exposes you to more risks than staying in an upmarket hotel in a resort area. Don't assume that international-type hotels will necessarily have the standards of water quality and general cleanliness that you are used to. You may be able to get away with taking a few risks with your own health, but you may not want to take the same risks with your children's.

Medical Facilities

This is especially important if your child has an ongoing condition like asthma, diabetes or epilepsy that may need treatment while you are away.

SOURCES OF INFORMATION

For up to date information on current health risks of your destination and advice on immunisations, go to your family doctor or a travel health clinic at least six weeks before you intend to travel. It's best not to rely on your travel agent for health advice. See the earlier Before You Go chapter for contact details of travel health clinics and other information sources.

Some travel health providers and other commercial organisations have good leaflets and information sheets for travelling parents, including Nomad Travel Stores & Travel Clinics (listed under Information Sources in the Before You Go chapter) and the UK-based chain of pharmacies, Boots the Chemist.

Many of the travel health websites listed in the Before You Go chapter have items on travelling with children, some more informative than others. Try the Travel Doctor-TMVC website for a good, helpful summary written from personal experience.

If your child has an ongoing condition (such as diabetes or asthma), contact your national organisation or support group, as they often have good information for travellers – for more

BABY BASICS

We were delighted to hear from a Canadian family who travelled for six weeks in Senegal, Guinea and Guinea-Bissau with a one-year-old baby, and sent the following tips for tiny travellers:

In West Africa, travelling with a baby was not too difficult, even though life is different. People constantly wanted to touch him, and even though this bothered us on occasion, it was not serious. Most of the time we enjoyed the contact. We learned to travel light, and went with one 50 litre backpack and a baby carrier which also carried another 10 litres of luggage. Clothes could be washed every day, and dried while wearing them.

- *We used small chlorine pills to clean water that was not bottled – apparently iodine may be harmful to children.*

- *In every capital, we found nappies at grocery stores selling imported items. Sometimes the quality was poor so we secured them with strong sticky tape.*

- *Baby cereal and powdered milk were available in most towns, even small villages, and prices were similar to those at home.*

In Senegal our baby got heat rash caused by humidity (even local babies get it) – which gave his skin red spots. This was not dangerous, and with soothing powder it was gone in two days.

After the hot and humid temperatures of West Africa, we went to Europe and spent another six weeks hiking in the Alps and Pyrenees before returning home.

Gino Bergeron, Julie Morin & 'little Thomas'

details, see the section on Travellers with Special Needs in the Before You Go chapter.

An excellent, comprehensive guide for parents is *Your Child's Health Abroad* by Dr Jane Wilson-Howarth & Dr Matthew Ellis. For a useful insight into travelling with children of various ages, Lonely Planet's *Travel with Children* has loads of practical suggestions.

DOCTOR & DENTIST

It's a good idea to make sure your child is as healthy as possible before you go. When you see your doctor to discuss any immunisations and malaria preventives, your child may need, take the opportunity to discuss basic preventive strategies and to work out a plan of action for problems that are likely to occur, like diarrhoea or fever.

If your child has an ongoing condition like eczema, diabetes or asthma, it's best to be clear about what to do if the condition worsens while you are away, and to make sure you have a plentiful supply of any medications they normally take.

It's worth making sure your children have a dental check-up before going away, but remember to leave enough time for any treatment to be carried out if necessary.

IMMUNISATIONS

It's just as important for children to be protected against diseases through immunisation as it is for you. They should be up to date for all routine childhood immunisations and, in addition, they'll need the same travel-related vaccines as you – see the Immunisations section in the Before You Go chapter for more guidance on this. This is especially important if your child is going to be in close contact with local children while you are away.

Most fully immunised school-age children won't need further doses of routine immunisations, but babies and younger children who haven't completed their normal childhood immunisations may need to complete the schedules earlier than normal. You should discuss this with your doctor when you start planning your trip.

Note that some vaccines have age limits or are best avoided in childhood. Discuss this with your doctor, but to give you some idea:

- diphtheria and tetanus (usually with pertussis, as DTP) – the first dose can be given at six weeks of age if necessary
- polio can be given at six weeks if necessary
- measles can be given at 6 months of age if necessary (it's normally given as part of the MMR vaccine at 15 months of age) – measles is common in many African countries and can be a serious illness; mumps and rubella are less of a worry

Travel-related vaccines your child may need include the following:

- hepatitis A vaccine can be given from the age of one year (two years in the US)
- typhoid and meningococcal meningitis vaccinations aren't normally given below two years of age; young children may be more susceptible to meningitis
- rabies (pre-exposure) vaccine isn't normally given before the age of one year; you should be aware that children are more at risk of rabies because they tend to want to pat animals and they may not tell you if they have been bitten; also they're more likely to get bites to the head and neck area, which carry a greater risk of rabies
- yellow fever can be given from nine months, although usually twelve months
- tuberculosis (rarely used in the US) and hepatitis B vaccines have no lower age limit
- influenza vaccine can be given to children from six months of age

If your child is going to have a reaction to an immunisation, this will usually occur about 48 hours after the injection and generally settles with a dose or two of paracetamol (acetaminophen) syrup or suppositories. Note that children can go on to have further reactions and sometimes develop rashes 10 days after the immunisation, so the earlier you get this organised, the better.

MALARIA PILLS

Malaria is very dangerous in children – you should think very carefully before taking children to malaria risk zones in Africa, and you should definitely discuss this fully with your doctor. For more general information on malaria risk and prevention, see the Malaria Prevention section of the Before You Go chapter earlier in this book.

If you do take children into a malarial area, it's absolutely vital to protect them by using malaria prevention medications and taking steps to avoid mosquito bites.

Chloroquine, proguanil and quinine are known to be safe in children of all ages, and mefloquine can be given to babies over three months. Mefloquine should be avoided if your child has any history of seizures. Doxycycline should not be given to children under 12 years because of potential side effects (may stain teeth and retard growth). Note that if you are taking antimalarials yourself and you are breast feeding your child, you will still need to give your child antimalarials.

! Be careful to keep antimalarials out of reach of children – even a few tablets overdose of chloroquine can be fatal in small children.

Getting your children to take their malaria pills can be a real challenge, as only chloroquine is available in suspension form (in some countries). You may have to resort to crushing the tablets into a powder and disguising them in a small amount of food or drink.

! If it's a battle to persuade your child to take the medication, it can be tempting to stop as soon as possible; however, it's very important your child carries on taking antimalarials for four weeks after leaving a malarial area – otherwise, they are at risk of getting malaria.

EMERGENCY TREATMENT FOR MALARIA

If you are going to a malarial area (not advisable – see the cautions in the previous section), it may be necessary to carry a dose of malaria treatment for your child. You need to discuss this fully with your doctor or travel health clinic before you go. Make sure you are clear about when you might need to use it.

NAPPIES, FORMULA FEED & BABY FOOD

It's worth taking a plentiful supply of nappies with you. Washable nappies and liners tend to take up less luggage space than disposable nappies and are much more eco-friendly. If you need them, you should be able to find disposable nappies in big cities or tourist centres in Africa (widely available in South Africa), but they are less easy to find, if at all, elsewhere, especially in rural areas. It's the same story for tins of baby food, although formula feed is widely available throughout most countries in Africa.

Disposing of nappies can be a headache as well as an environmental nightmare, especially in countries where waste disposal systems are less than ideal (most of Africa). Washable nappies (worn with a liner) rely on you having access to water and washing facilities, but are a good alternative. You could burn disposable nappies (not a very practical option); otherwise, it's probably best to take a supply of large plastic bags or nappy sacks with you and to dispose of them as thoughtfully as you can.

MEDICAL KIT & MEDICATIONS

It's a good idea to take a child-specific medical kit in addition to your own basic medical kit (for detailed suggestions on what to take for yourself, see the What to Take section in the Before You Go chapter). If your child takes any medications regularly (eg for asthma, eczema or diabetes), remember to take a good supply of these with you.

You'll need to include something for pain and fever, for example paracetamol (acetaminophen) syrup or suppositories for little ones, Junior paracetamol (acetaminophen) for older children or ibuprofen paediatric syrup.

Consider taking a course of antibiotics with you for treating common ailments like ear infections or coughs, especially if you are planning on going to less developed nations in

Africa, where you may not have ready access to medical care or supplies.

Discuss your individual needs with your doctor, but some suitable antibiotics include co-amoxiclav, cephalexin or clarithromycin (if your child is allergic to penicillin). See the section on Antibiotics in the appendix on Buying & Using Medicines for more details.

Take a plentiful supply of oral rehydration salt sachets, barrier cream for nappy rash, calamine cream or aloe vera gel for heat rash and sunburn, motion sickness remedies, sunscreen, antiseptic wipes and antiseptic liquid or spray. Sterilising tablets are a good idea for cleaning feeding utensils, or you might want to consider taking a sterilising unit with you.

If you do need to give your child medication, remember that they will generally need a child-sized dose, and that some medications are best avoided in children. Follow the dosing instructions given by your doctor or on the packet. Doses are generally worked out from how much your child weighs, so it's a good idea to have a rough idea of this before you go away.

It's a good idea to carry plastic spoons (eg 5mL and 2.5mL capacity) with you for measuring out doses of liquid medications. A plastic syringe (5mL or 10mL) can be handy for giving medicine (and fluids) to a reluctant patient.

ON THE MOVE

Long journeys aren't always going to be a bundle of fun with children, so be prepared! Consider arranging your itinerary to minimise the number of long journeys you have to do, or consider alternative means of getting around (such as flying instead of taking a two day bus journey). For toddlers or older children, travelling at night may be one solution, although it might be exhausting for you. Take plenty of travel games, puzzle books, reading books, colouring books and electronic games. A new toy might just provide enough interest to last a journey.

MEDICATIONS TO AVOID

Some drugs you might be prescribed if you get ill should be avoided in children under the age of 12 years because of the possibility of side effects. Drugs to avoid in children include:

• for pain and fever – aspirin and aspirin-like drugs
• antibiotics – ciprofloxacin and doxycycline
• antidiarrhoeals – loperamide, diphenoxylate, bismuth
• antimalarials and malaria treatment – mefloquine before the age of three months; doxycycline in children below 8 years

If you are at all uncertain about the dose or whether the medicine is suitable for children, check with a doctor before giving it.

Trains tend to have more scope for running around than buses. It might be worth checking on the toilet situation for any mode of transport you choose, although most bus drivers are likely to be sympathetic to the vagaries of children's bladders. It's always worth checking the seating arrangements for young children, as you may be expected to keep your child on your knees for the journey.

On flights, air pressure changes can cause ear pain in babies and young children – for more details, see the section on Ears in the Ears, Eyes & Teeth chapter earlier. Older children can be encouraged to blow their noses, which should help their ears to pop. Younger children and babies can be given decongestant nose drops if necessary, (get these from your doctor or pharmacist before you go) as well as paracetamol (acetaminophen) syrup to ease the pain. Give the syrup approximately one and a half hours before landing. If you are bottle feeding during the flight, try to sit the baby or toddler upright as far as possible, as feeding can sometimes increase the ear discomfort. Note that if your child has an ear infection or a bad cold, you should postpone flying until it is better.

You might also want to bear in mind that children can get thirsty and hungry on plane journeys very quickly, which is one preventable reason for bad temper.

Motion sickness is extremely common in children – if you know yours is prone to it, consider using an anti-sickness remedy like promethazine (follow the dosing guidelines, and note that it's not recommended for children under two years) or ginger. Promethazine has the added advantage that it often makes your child sleepy – possibly sanity-saving on a long journey – although the effects are very variable. A naturopathic alternative is chamomile, which can be soothing.

You might want to make up some milk beforehand if you're bottle feeding, although it will only keep for a limited amount of time, or you can get bottles with powder and water which you can mix up when you need. It's always a good idea to take a few snacks and cartons of drink for giving out to little ones on the journey. A change of clothing is always good to have on hand for the inevitable spills etc.

STAYING HEALTHY

FOOD, WATER & CLEANLINESS

For most destinations in Africa, apart from South Africa, you need to be particularly careful about food and water, and be meticulous about maintaining good cleanliness habits. If possible, breastfeed babies and young toddlers, as this reduces their risks of getting diarrhoea by ingesting contaminated food and water.

If you give babies and children water, use only boiled water (allowed to cool) or bottled water, and if you are bottle feeding, remember to use only boiled or bottled water to make up the formula. You'll probably want to avoid giving children carbonated and other soft drinks, but packet fruit juices and UHT milk are usually available and make safe substitutes.

If you can, try to prepare any food for babies yourself, making sure that the utensils you use are sterile (take sterilising tablets with you). For more details on food to avoid, see the Safe Food section in the Staying Healthy chapter earlier.

Children who are crawling or just walking are particularly at risk of diseases spread via dirt, so take care to wash hands and faces frequently throughout the day, especially if you're travelling on public transport, and discourage wandering hands in the mouth, eyes and nose as far as possible. A supply of wet wipes can be invaluable, especially on long journeys.

If you get sick with diarrhoea yourself, be extremely careful to wash your hands after using the toilet to avoid passing diarrhoea to your child. However, it works both ways: be careful with nappies and other sources of contamination if your child has diarrhoea to prevent it passing to you.

COPING WITH JET LAG

Travelling eastwards is potentially the most difficult for your child to cope with. Allow your child to get plenty of sleep. You could consider using a mild sedative, eg an antihistamine like promethazine. When you arrive, slot your child into their new routine immediately. Serve their meals at the correct time and put them to bed at the local time. Also spend plenty of time outside because light (particularly sunlight) and physical activity in the first half of the day will help the body clock to adjust faster.

Be aware that our body temperature falls during the night and initially this will occur in the middle of your new day. Even though you may have travelled to a warmer climate, your child may require warmer clothes for a few days before their body clock adjusts.

John Mason

DIET & NUTRITION

Several factors may make your child less inclined to eat while you are away. New foods can induce surprise and a reflex refusal, stress and new surroundings can distract children from eating and the heat can often reduce even the healthiest of appetites. Try to introduce new foods gradually, perhaps starting before you leave, and consider taking a supply of familiar dry foods with you to provide an element of continuity. If the local cuisine is not proving a hit, Western-style dishes are often available, especially in touristed areas.

If you're on a long trip, try to make sure your child has as balanced a diet as possible, including a source of protein (beans, meat or fish), fresh fruit (peeled) and vegetables (peeled and cooked). Even if they are not inclined to eat, fluids are a must, especially if it's hot.

INSECT BITES

Biting insects carry a number of serious diseases, including malaria, so it's extremely important to protect your child from this hazard. For more details, see the section on Insect Bites in the Staying Healthy chapter, but the main messages are to make sure your child is covered up with clothes, socks and shoes, and to use DEET-containing insect repellents or the new natural repellents containing lemon eucalyptus on exposed areas. Permethrin-soaked mosquito nets are very effective at preventing bites at night and during daytime naps (the mosquito that spreads dengue bites during the daytime).

Try to discourage scratching of bites if they do occur, as this often leads to secondary infection. Keep fingernails cut short and use calamine cream or a sting relief spray to ease irritation.

ACCIDENTS & OTHER HAZARDS

Children tend to be accident-prone at the best of times, but the hazards are even greater when you're travelling, so you need to be even more vigilant than normal. Road traffic is often chaotic and unpredictable, and pavements (sidewalks) nonexistent.

If you're travelling in a motor vehicle, seat belts and child safety seats are often absent. Most hotel rooms and restaurants are not built with children in mind and may have a nightmare-inducing lack of safety features, particularly where windows and balconies are concerned.

Some sensible precautionary advice:

- be on the look out for potential risk situations and unsafe features
- keep all medications in child-proof containers and out of reach of prying fingers
- try to be aware of what your child is doing at all times, especially if they're playing outside
- consider using a harness for toddlers when you're travelling or walking in crowded places
- make sure your child has some form of identification on them at all times, including details of where you are staying
- never let your child touch any domestic or other animals
- if you're planning to travel by car, consider taking a child safety seat with you
- drowning is surprisingly common – be particularly vigilant around swimming pools or at the beach, and remember that drowning can occur in shallow water as well as deeper water
- check new beaches for debris, discarded hypodermics, glass and tins, as well as various offerings left by people and animals

In addition, children's natural curiosity and fascination with all creatures great and small make them more vulnerable to insect and scorpion stings, snake bites and animal bites. For more details on these hazards, see the Bites & Stings chapter later in this book.

CUTS & SCRATCHES

This is something else that's worth being particularly vigilant about, as it can be difficult to keep children clean, especially if they are running or crawling around. Any break in the skin can rapidly become infected in warm, humid climates – wash any break in the skin carefully with soap and water or antiseptic solution (or an antiseptic wipe if you haven't got access to water) and keep it covered with a sterile, non-fluffy, non-adherent dressing (eg a sticking plaster if the wound is small). It's probably worth checking your child carefully at the end of each day for cuts, scratches and potentially problematic bites. Itchy insect bites are a common cause of infection – another reason for making a strenuous effort to avoid them in the first place.

POISONOUS PLANTS

Small children are attracted like magnets to plants, particularly if they are colourful and look appetising. Toddlers will eat almost anything, regardless of taste. Children need to be supervised, especially if they are somewhere outdoors with access to plants and bushes. Contact with some plants and grasses may go unnoticed until a reaction occurs.

Some plants and grasses can cause toxic or allergic reactions when they come into contact with bare skin, so it's best to make sure your child is covered up if they are playing in grassland. This will help protect them from insect bites too.

If you catch your child eating a plant, keep a sample for identification. Watch for any symptoms, and encourage your child to drink plenty of fluids to help dilute any potential toxic effects. If possible, seek expert advice. If this is not available, you can induce vomiting by giving your child ipecacunha syrup (if you can find it) – but be aware that some experts believe children should never be given ipecacunha. This is usually only effective within four hours of eating a suspect plant, but it may be worth trying while you find medical help.

John Mason

SUN

Anyone can get sunburnt but little ones are especially vulnerable and need to be protected as much as possible from the sun's harmful rays. Keep them covered up (for example with a long-sleeved T shirt and long trousers or skirt and hat, or an all-over sunsuit – popular in Australia and available elsewhere). Apply liberal amounts of the highest factor sunscreen you can find on any exposed skin and re-apply it frequently. Avoid the sun during the middle of the day when it is at its fiercest. Beware of the strong reflections of the sun from sand and water. Not only is sunburn miserably painful for your child, it's thought to be a major risk factor for skin cancer in later life.

HEAT & COLD

If your child is not used to a hot climate, they will need time to acclimatise. Children tend to acclimatise relatively easily, but young children (with their greater surface area relative to their body mass) can lose fluid through sweating very rapidly and become dehydrated and vulnerable to heatstroke (see p316). Babies and young children may not be able to tell you how hot they're feeling, so if you're feeling the heat, check to see how your child is coping, and in particular whether they are dressed appropriately. Discourage mobile youngsters from rushing around in the heat of the day.

Because babies and children can become dehydrated relatively easily, they require a significant increase in their fluid intake. As a general rule you can double their fluid intake. Consider sprinkling a little extra salt on their food, as salt can be lost through sweating, especially to start with. You could also encourage them to eat lots of juicy fruit and vegetables. Keep an eye on how much urine they are passing – small amounts of dark urine or dark urine-stained nappies in babies mean you need to increase their fluid intake.

If you're carrying a child in a baby-carrier backpack, remember that they are exposed to the elements, and protect them against sunburn, heat exhaustion and the cold.

Children are also susceptible to the cold as they lose heat very rapidly, especially if they are immobile in a carrier, so always wrap them up well and check them regularly for signs of cold. Give them plenty to eat and drink as they can use up their energy reserves quickly and this makes them more vulnerable to the cold. Appropriate clothes and layers are vital.

ALTITUDE

If you're planning on going to highland areas in Africa, remember that children are as susceptible to the effects of altitude (basically less oxygen to breathe) as adults, and they may not be able to tell you they have symptoms. Read the section on Altitude in the Climate, Altitude & Action chapter later for more details.

The symptoms of altitude illness (headache, nausea, vomiting) may be nonspecific, mimicking other childhood illnesses, so it is particularly important for you to be aware of the possibility, and to be confident you can recognise these symptoms in your child.

Children are at greater risk of the effects of the cold, especially if they are immobile (eg when they're being carried), so appropriate clothing and other layering is vital.

IF YOUR CHILD GETS SICK

Children are at risk of the same diseases as you are when you are away, so unless otherwise indicated, you can follow the guidelines given in the main text (but remember that children need different doses and possibly different drugs – see the Medical Kit & Medications section earlier in this chapter for more details). Because children can't always tell you what's wrong and in many cases don't show typical symptoms of diseases, it's even more important to seek medical help at the earliest opportunity, and always seek medical help urgently if you have any concerns about their condition. Local doctors and healthworkers will be very experienced in dealing with all common childhood problems, so getting reliable help shouldn't be a problem even in less-touristed areas.

FEBRILE CONVULSION

If your child's temperature quickly rises high, she may have a fit, whatever the cause of the fever. This generally occurs in young children up to five years of age.

- try not to panic
- don't try to restrain your child's movements, but do remove any sharp objects from the area to prevent her injuring herself
- don't put anything in her mouth
- when the movements subside, roll her onto her side so that she can breathe freely
- comfort her when it has stopped, then take measures to cool her – fans, tepid sponging, tepid baths, paracetamol
- seek medical help

IS MY BABY/CHILD UNWELL?

Children can quickly change from being well and active to becoming ill, sometimes seriously ill. In young children especially, the signs can be quite subtle and difficult to interpret, which can be concerning.

As the parent, you will know your child best of all and any change in their behaviour should be taken seriously – listen to your sixth sense. This is particularly true of young children. Babies up to six months may become quieter than usual, miserable and crying. They may not want to feed or drink or they may develop more specific signs, such as diarrhoea, a cough, vomiting or a rash.

Don't rely on a child's skin temperature as an indication of whether they have a raised temperature or not. Always carry and use a thermometer, preferably a digital one, or a fever strip. It is important to have an actual reading of the temperature. A cold child to touch may have a raging temperature and the other way round.

Older babies and toddlers may just not 'perform' as well as you are used to. They may stop walking, stop sitting up, stop feeding themselves or being as generally developed as you are used to. Children of this age are unable to tell you what's wrong and this may be the only sign before a rash or a cough appears. If you have any cause for concern, check the temperature and make sure your child is taking at least enough fluids to pass urine twice a day, even if they have gone off their food.

FEVER

This is very common in children wherever they are, and is always a cause for concern. In addition, a high temperature can sometimes cause a convulsion in babies and young children. Skin temperature is a confusing and unreliable sign – see the previous entry. If you think your child has a fever, eg if she's flushed and irritable and obviously unwell:

- take her temperature (see p116 for how to do this) and take it again 30 minutes later as a check
- put your child to bed, remove most of her clothing (perhaps covering her up with a cotton sheet) and make her comfortable (under a mosquito net if necessary)
- wipe her face and body with a sponge or cloth soaked in tepid (not cold) water or place her in a tepid bath to help lower the temperature
- giving paracetamol (acetaminophen) syrup or tablets will also help to lower the temperature – you can give them every four to six hours
- prevent dehydration by giving small amounts of fluid often – make up oral rehydration salts with bottled or boiled water, or packet or fresh fruit juice diluted half and half with safe water. Give 5mL every 15 minutes for the first hour

Remember that conditions like viral infections, colds, ear infections, urine infections and diarrhoea occur commonly, but always bear in mind the possibility of malaria if you've been travelling in risk areas.

Take steps to lower the temperature and seek medical help urgently in the following situations:

- if the temperature is over 37.7°C (100°F) in a baby of less than six months
- if the temperature is over 39°C (104°F) in any infant or child
- if your child has had fits in the past
- if it could be malaria (see p41); malaria should be suspected with ANY high fever if you are in a malarial area
- if the fever shows no sign of improving after 24 hours (take your child's temperature regularly to show you if it's going up or down)

MALARIA

Children can rapidly become very ill with malaria – which is why it is not advisable to travel with children to malarial areas – and it's easy to miss the diagnosis because the symptoms can be very vague. You need to suspect malaria if your child develops a fever with or without flu-like symptoms that persists for more than eight hours, if you are in, or have visited a malarial area within the last few months.

Seek medical help urgently for a blood test, and treatment if the test is positive. If you are in a remote area without access to medical help, you'll need to give your child emergency treatment for malaria while you seek medical help. Ideally this is something you will have discussed with your doctor before you left.

DIARRHOEA

Children, especially young children and babies, are more likely than adults to get diarrhoea when they are away. They also tend to get more severe symptoms, for longer. It's partly because children tend to be indiscriminate about what they put in their mouths and it's hard to keep them clean, but it may also be because they have less immunity than adults to disease-causing bugs.

Babies and children can become rapidly dehydrated through diarrhoea and vomiting, and it can be difficult to make sure they drink enough. The best fluids to give children are oral rehydration salts (ORS). You need to start giving them ORS as soon as diarrhoea or vomiting appears – you can make them more palatable by adding flavours (eg juice of an orange), or different flavoured sachets may be available. Avoid food if they are actively vomiting.

You don't need to give your child ORS if you're breastfeeding, but make sure you're taking in enough fluid yourself. If your child is being fed a milk-based formula, you need to replace this with ORS until the diarrhoea is better. As the diarrhoea improves, introduce diluted milk feeds, then solids.

For older children, follow the same dietary guidelines as for adults, avoiding milk and milk-based products until your child is on the mend. The World Health Organization gives the following guidelines for the quantity of fluid replacement:

under two years	one-half to one-quarter cup per loose stool
two to 10 years	one-half to one cup per loose stool
over 10 years	as for adults (see p155 for more details)

If children are vomiting, allow the stomach to rest (eg for an hour) before trying to give fluids, then reintroduce fluids very slowly – 5ml every 15 minutes for the first hour, and building up from there. If your child is refusing to drink, try giving small amounts by teaspoon or syringe every few minutes.

Seek medical help earlier rather than later, especially if you notice any of the following symptoms developing:

■ prolonged vomiting and diarrhoea
■ refusal to take fluids
■ listlessness
■ fever
■ blood or mucus in the diarrhoea

Stools in children may take 10 to 14 days to return to normal, sometimes longer following an episode of diarrhoea. As long as the stools are not too frequent, parents should not worry about slightly loose stools in an otherwise fit and recovered child.

Antidiarrhoeal Medications

Note that symptomatic antidiarrhoeal medications ('stoppers') are not generally recommended in children and should be avoided.

Some effective antibiotic treatments used in adults for travellers diarrhoea are not suitable for use in children. Ciprofloxacin is generally not recommended for use in children because of potential side effects on joints. Suitable alternatives for children are listed in the Diarrhoea section of the Digestive System chapter, but these are generally less effective and are best given only under medical supervision.

- As a general rule, avoid giving your child any locally available antidiarrhoeal remedies (apart from ORS and the antibiotics recommended in the diarrhoea section).

TUMMY ACHE

This is a very common complaint, as it is in adults. The causes are many and varied, some serious – see p122 for more details. If your child is prone to tummy aches, the stress of travelling may make them more likely while you are away. Otherwise, situations when you should seek medical help include:

- any tummy ache with a fever could be malaria, typhoid, bladder infection etc
- severe tummy ache that is continuous for more than three hours – could be appendicitis
- tummy ache with profuse vomiting and diarrhoea – the danger is dehydration
- tummy ache that's not normal for your child, especially if he's generally unwell

COLDS, COUGHS & EARACHE

Children are particularly likely to succumb to new germs in new places, so be prepared! Asthma (cough, wheezing) may occur for the first time while you are away, and can be frightening especially if you or your child have not experienced it before. You should seek medical advice if your child is having difficulty breathing, especially if you notice that their ribs are being drawn in with each breath.

Swimming can make ear infections more likely – see p340 for more details. Remember that if your child has grommets in their ears, they shouldn't swim.

PRICKLY HEAT & NAPPY RASH

Prickly heat tends to be more of a problem in children than in adults. Calamine lotion can soothe the irritation, and you can help prevent the rash by dressing children in loose cotton clothing, bathing them often and drying them carefully, especially any skin folds and under their arms.

Nappy rash can be a lot worse in the heat. Take a good supply of barrier creams (eg petroleum jelly or zinc and castor oil cream or Sudocrem), and avoid plastic overpants. Wash the area with water after any bowel action, dry it well, apply barrier cream and try to keep the nappy off as much as possible.

If it's red and painful and doesn't go away with simple treatment, it may be due to a fungal infection. In this case, try treating it with an antifungal cream (eg clotrimazole, trade name Canesten; or with hydrocortisone, eg Canesten HC if it is very red and painful) applied twice daily. Check their mouth, as they may have a fungal infection (thrush) there as well, indicated by white patches that are difficult to remove. Treatment is with antifungal drops (eg nystatin). Remember to change rubber teats and feeding utensils as soon as treatment is started and halfway through.

INSECT STINGS

Children seem to attract bees and wasps like the proverbial honey pot, so be prepared with sting relief spray and lots of sympathy. Take plenty of insect repellent and sting relief sprays and cream. If you know your child is allergic to bee stings, discuss this with your doctor before you leave.

AFTER YOU GET BACK

Consider getting a check-up for you and your children if you've been on a long trip or have been travelling rough. Children are particularly likely to pick up intestinal parasites such as worms, so a test for this is a good idea when you get back. This is a simple stool test, which your family doctor can arrange. If there's any chance your child may have swum in bilharzia-infected water, you'll need to get this checked out. Remember the possibility of malaria if your child gets an unexplained fever after you get back, particularly within the first month or so, but up to a year after. Tell your doctor if you have been travelling and where.

Travellers with Special Needs...

You don't have to be able bodied or in perfect health to travel, but make sure you know what to expect and are prepared for it. A short trip to a tourist centre or urban area with well developed medical services may not present any major difficulties, but you may want to think more carefully about longer trips, especially to remote areas.

- Medical advice – get advice from your doctor or specialist on health problems you could encounter when you're travelling and what to do about them.

- Documentation – take with you a written summary from your doctor of your medical problems and any treatment you are currently on or have received in the past.

- Travel insurance – important for all travellers, but particularly if you have special needs (check that it covers you for preexisting illnesses); a policy that provides a 24-hour hotline is handy.

- Medical facilities – services in most countries in Africa are extremely limited, and emergency services are often nonexistent.

- Practical difficulties – travellers with disabilities may find facilities in Africa generally lag well behind those in most Western countries.

- Medicines – although you may be able to replace some medicines while you are away, it's best to take a plentiful supply with you, as well as any equipment you need, like syringes, needles, blood or urine tests, and any arthritis aids or inhalant devices.

- Bracelets or tags engraved with your medical conditions, medications and any drug allergies – see Useful Organisations in the Before You Go chapter for contact details of one company.

- Flying – make sure you let the airline know well in advance about any special requirements you have. Your doctor or the medical department of the airline you're travelling with will be able to give you advice on potential health hazards of flying. For example, the lower oxygen availability in aircraft cabins may be a problem if you suffer from severe heart or lung problems.

■ Travelling can be very physically demanding, so your itinerary needs to be realistic and to have the flexibility to allow for rest days, sick days and any unexpected difficulties.

MEDICAL CONDITIONS & TRAVEL

Some medical conditions may make you less able to cope with the physical and environmental challenges of travelling; for example, if you have a heart or lung condition you may find the heat more difficult to cope with. Some medical conditions can make you more vulnerable to infection, and you may need to take additional preventive measures to counteract this. Common travel-related ailments such as diarrhoea and vomiting can be more of a problem if you have ongoing medical conditions, especially as they can affect the absorption of medicines. It's not all bad news, however – being in a hot climate may improve conditions like arthritis and lung problems.

If you have an ongoing medical condition, it's worth seeing your specialist physician before you go for advice on any special hazards travel may pose for you. It's also worth getting in touch with your local support group or a national disease foundation, as they may be able to provide you with specific advice and contact details of similar organisations where you are going. Some useful organisations are listed in the following section.

Check what medical facilities are available locally in case you need to call on them. Your doctor or travel health clinic or any of the information sources listed in the Before You Go chapter should be able to give you information on this; in addition, a brief run-down is given in the Medical Services appendix of this book. If you are on a cruise or an organised tour, find out what provisions they have for dealing with medical problems.

SUPPORT GROUPS & INFORMATION SOURCES

If you have any special health needs, most major national or state disease foundations or support groups should be able to provide you with information and advice on travel-related health issues. In this section we've listed some recommended

TRAVELLERS WITH SPECIAL NEEDS 299

resources to get you started; you could also try your doctor, specialist or a travel health centre.

Arthritis – the Arthritis Foundation (☎ 800-542-0295 or 206-547-2707) produces an excellent, extremely comprehensive guide *Travel and Arthritis;* you can also access it online (**www.orthop.washington.edu**).

Heart conditions – for general information, US travellers could try the American Heart Association (☎ 1-800-242-8721, 7272 Greenville Avenue, Dallas, TX 75231, **www.americanheart.org**); in the UK you could try the British Heart Foundation (☎ 020-7935 0185, fax 7486 5820, **www.bhf.org.uk**), at 14 Fitzharding St, London W1H 4DH; and in Australia, you could ring the Heartline information service on ☎ 1300 362 787 (**www.heartfoundation.org.au**).

Global Dialysis (☎ 44 121 242 7699), at PO Box 12821, Solihull, B91 9BT, UK produces a directory of dialysis centres worldwide; it also has a web site (**www.globaldialysis.com**).

US-based travellers with disabilities could contact one of the following organisations:

Mobility International USA (☎ 541-343-1284), PO Box 10767, Eugene, OR 97440; web site **www.miusa.org**

Access Foundation (☎ 516-887-5798), PO Box 356, Malverne, NY 11565

Society for the Advancement of Travel for the Handicapped (SATH, ☎ 718-858-5483), at 26 Court St, Brooklyn, NY 11242; web site **www.sath.org**

In the UK, the **Royal Association for Disability & Rehabilitation** (RADAR, ☎ 020-7250 3222, fax 250 0212), at 12 City Forum, 250 City Rd, London EC1V 8AF, produces three holiday fact packs (costing UK£2 each) which cover planning, insurance and useful organisations; transport and equipment; and specialised accommodation. Its web site is at **www.radar.org.uk.**

Australians and New Zealanders can contact the **National Information Communication Awareness Network** (NICAN, ☎ 02-6285 3713, fax 6285 3714), at PO Box 407, Curtin, ACT 2605; its web address is **www.nican.com.au.**

The Global Access web site (**www.globalaccessnews.com**) has lots of information for travellers with disabilities, as well as links to related sites.

OLDER TRAVELLERS

We hardly need to tell you that age is no barrier to travelling. The thousands of older travellers (we're taking this to mean 60 plus) who go animal-spotting in Africa's national parks and sun worshipping in Morocco are ample proof of the increasing mobility of older people. More and more older travellers are opting for 'adventure'-type holidays, as well as traditionally popular less active options like cruises.

IMMUNISATIONS & MALARIA PREVENTION

Being older doesn't mean you're immune – immunisations are just as important as for younger travellers, perhaps more so, since older people are more susceptible to disease as immunity wanes with age. It's a good idea to get this checked out well in advance of travelling, as you may need full courses of some immunisations.

See the Before You Go chapter for more details of the travel-related immunisations you may need for your trip. In addition, if you are over 65, it's a good idea to be immunised against flu and possibly pneumococcal disease, if this is available, before you travel. You may be more at risk of the flu and pneumonia when you're travelling, and you don't want to waste your trip being ill.

If you need to take malaria prevention medication, be aware that some antimalarials may interact with your regular medications (eg mefloquine, currently the recommended preventive medicine for sub-Saharan Africa, should not be taken if you are taking beta blockers for a heart condition), so it's a good idea to check this with your doctor.

MEDICAL CHECK–UP

As well as getting travel health advice, it's probably a good idea to visit your doctor for a check-up before you go, especially if you are planning on doing anything strenuous like trekking, visiting particularly hot or cold climates or going to altitude.

If you have any medical conditions like heart or lung problems, diabetes, kidney failure or recent medical or surgical treatment, check with your doctor that you are fit to travel. If you are, it's a good opportunity to discuss any potential problems you may encounter while you are away and to clarify what to do about them if they do occur.

Older travellers who are intending to go scuba diving will need to have a medical performed by a specialist diving doctor. This is particularly important, as older divers and those with preexisting conditions are more likely to suffer serious problems. See the section on diving in the Water chapter later in this book for more details.

DENTAL CHECK–UP

This is a good idea if you are going away for more than a couple of weeks. If you wear dentures, have them checked before you leave home. Make sure you wear in a new pair of dentures before you go away, as adjustments may be required during the first month to make them comfortable. Consider taking a spare pair with you; you may have an old pair which your dentist could modify to make them useable in an emergency.

Getting a new set of dentures while you're away could be a major problem. However, simple temporary repairs may be carried out by a dentist, or you can make a simple repair yourself like sticking a tooth back on or sticking a broken denture back together using glue. If you use an epoxy glue, be careful not to put them back in your mouth before the glue has set...

EYES

If you wear glasses, remember to take a spare pair with you, as well as the prescription in case you need to replace them. See the section on Eyes in the Ears, Eyes & Teeth chapter for more details, including some advice on travelling with preexisting eye conditions.

PREEXISTING MEDICAL CONDITIONS

As we get older, over 65 years, our immune system also slows a little. This is a consideration in older travellers, who also are more likely to have an ongoing medical condition. In fact, although older travellers are less likely than their younger counterparts to get sick when travelling, the outcome is more likely to be serious. For older travellers, the most common cause of death is from preexisting conditions like heart disease.

Some medical conditions can affect your ability to cope with the physical and environmental challenges that travelling may involve; eg travellers with heart or lung conditions may find the heat more difficult to cope with.

It also means that you are more likely to be taking medications regularly. Travel-related diseases like diarrhoea and vomiting can affect the absorption of medications, and taking multiple medications makes side effects more likely to occur.

It's important to find out before you go what the medical facilities are like at your destination. If you are on an organised tour or trek, find out what provisions it has for dealing with medical problems.

FITNESS PREPARATION

You might want to consider starting a gentle exercise program well before you go, especially if you're out of the habit of doing much exercise. Travelling can involve a lot of standing around and lifting luggage on and off luggage racks, while negotiating your way around large airports and other transport terminals often involves a lot of walking, perhaps carrying heavy luggage. Sightseeing can also be surprisingly exhausting.

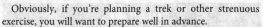

Obviously, if you're planning a trek or other strenuous exercise, you will want to prepare well in advance.

Avoid activity-related injuries by warming up and stretching properly before you start and when you finish.

Finally, don't be overambitious with your travel itinerary – it's better to do less comfortably than to push yourself too hard and perhaps regret it.

TRAVEL INSURANCE

It's important for everyone to have travel health insurance, but it's particularly important for older travellers with preexisting illnesses. See the main section on Travel insurance in the Before you Go chapter for more details, but always check the small print carefully to see what the policy covers you for. Try to find a policy that provides 24-hour hotlines to give you the names of English-speaking doctors locally, find hospitals or fly you out if necessary.

MEDICAL KIT & MEDICATIONS

It's a good idea to take a well stocked medical kit with you, including a plentiful supply of any regular medications plus a bit extra. You don't want to run out at an inopportune moment, and replacements may not be easy to get. Always keep a supply of your medications on you, as well as in your luggage, in case you lose your luggage.

The What to Take section in the Before You Go chapter gives detailed guidance on what you might want to consider taking with you. In addition, if you suffer from severe prostate trouble, you might want to consider taking a sterile catheter set with you – discuss this with your doctor if necessary.

You could consider getting bracelets or tags engraved with any medical conditions, medications and drug allergies to carry on you. MedicAlert is an organisation that provides these, together with a toll-free number to call in emergencies – see Useful Organisations in the Before You Go chapter for contact details.

MEDICINES

If you're on any regular medications, remember that these can interact with any medicines you may be prescribed for a travel-related problem:

- some medications can make you very sensitive to the effects of the sun – see p50 for more details
- pseudoephedrine hydrochloride (decongestant) – don't take if you have raised blood pressure
- hyoscine (for travel sickness) – best avoided if you have glaucoma or prostate problems
- antimalarials and some drugs for heart problems

ON THE MOVE

Keep any regular or as-needed medications (eg for angina) in your hand luggage so you can access them readily if needed.

Sitting immobile for long periods of time can make your feet and ankles swell and may possibly increase the risk of blood clotting in the legs, especially if this is something you are prone to. This is known as 'deep-venous thrombosis', or DVT; for more information see p68. Discuss this with your doctor, but it may be advisable to take low dose aspirin (75mg) for three days – before, during and after the flight. Alternatively, some doctors may suggest an injection of a blood thinning agent like heparin.

Wriggle your toes, flex your calves and get up and move around periodically if you can. Drink plenty of non-alcoholic fluids to prevent dehydration.

It's not all bad news – older travellers tend to suffer less from jet lag than younger travellers.

STAYING HEALTHY

All the general, common-sense measures suggested in the Staying Healthy chapter earlier in this book are just as relevant to older travellers.

Acclimatisation to Africa's heat shouldn't be much of a problem if you are normally physically fit and you take sensible precautions like avoiding strenuous exercise and drinking plenty of fluids. However, older travellers are more likely to faint in the heat, as their blood vessels tend to be stiffer and less reactive. If you're overweight or have preexisting conditions like heart and lung problems or diabetes, you may find it more difficult to acclimatise, and some medications (like diuretics) may need to be adjusted in hot weather. Discuss this with your doctor well before you leave.

Remember that it's very easy to become dehydrated, especially if you're taking heart medicines that make you lose fluid, or if you have diarrhoea. Drink plenty of cool safe fluids, don't overexert yourself and allow yourself lots of rest time.

Older travellers are less likely to suffer from diarrhoea while travelling, perhaps because they are more discerning about where and what to eat than younger travellers. If you do get diarrhoea and/or vomiting, remember that this may mean that your usual medications are absorbed less well. You are also at more risk of dehydration, so seek medical help earlier rather than later.

On the other hand, constipation is a common complaint. Eat lots of fresh fruit (peeled) and vegetables (cooked) and keep up your fluid intake. If you are prone to constipation, take a supply of a remedy you know works for you.

Air pollution is a major issue in mega-cities like Cairo – you may want to think twice about travelling here, especially in the stifling summer months, if you suffer from a heart or lung condition.

If you're reasonably fit, altitude shouldn't pose any particular problems. In fact you may be safer because you're more likely to ascend slowly, allowing time for acclimatisation.

DIABETIC TRAVELLERS

This section was written by Michelle Sobel, a Type 1 diabetic who has never let her condition get in the way of her travels.

Preventive self-care is your aim, wherever you travel. Prepared and in good diabetic control, you're in the best position to enjoy your experiences abroad. Before you go, discuss with your doctor or specialist what to do if you get sick, as well as dosage adjustments, immunisations and other travel-related health issues.

The level and type of care offered to diabetics varies from country to country. Find out before you go what to expect in your destinations. National diabetic associations are usually the best source of information on local diabetic care. The International Diabetes Federation (web site www.idf.org), at Avenue Emile De Mot 19, B-1000 Brussels, Belgium, maintains a listing of diabetic associations in different countries around the world, or there's an online list of addresses of diabetes organisations worldwide at www.childrenwith diabetes.com/d_09_800.htm.

It's also worth contacting your national diabetes organisation for information. These include:

American Diabetes Association (☎ 1-800-342-2383) 1701 North Beauregard Street, Alexandria, VA 22311, web site www.diabetes.org

British Diabetic Association (Careline ☎ 0845 120 2960) Macleod House,10 Parkway, London NW1 7AA, web site www.diabetes.org.uk – produces a useful leaflet on travel with diabetes, as well as a number of specific country guides for diabetics

Diabetes Australia (☎ 1300 136 588) GPO BOX 3156, Canberra ACT 2601, web site www.diabetesaustralia.com.au

Alternatively, you could check out the web site at www .diabetictraveler.com. A useful publication you could consider getting is the *Diabetic Traveller's Companion* by Nerida Nichol.

INSULIN & OTHER DIABETIC SUPPLIES

Before you leave, call the relevant manufacturer to get information on the availability abroad of diabetic supplies like test strips, medication (oral and insulin) and glucose meters. Consumer-friendly meter and pump manufacturers will advise you on repair, replacement, and delivery policies if your equipment malfunctions or is lost abroad.

Note that most nations measure blood glucose in mmol/L; the US, however, primarily uses mg/dL. Different meters report glucose readings using either or both of these standards. To convert mmol/L to mg/dL, multiply the glucose reading by 18 (ie 4mmol/L = 72 mg/dL). To convert mg/dL, divide the glucose by 18.

Take two to three times the medical supplies you expect to use (in carry-on, waterproof packs), to protect against loss or damage. On day trips, I carry two half bottles (instead of one or two full bottles) of insulin, so there's backup in case of breakage.

To reduce bulk, try insulin pens over syringes. However, note that manufacturers state that at room temperature some insulin pen cartridges (particularly some slow-acting and premixed insulin) may have shorter lives (as short as seven or 14 days) than vials (which last about a month).

Some diabetic care providers suggest reusing sharps, at your own risk. Consult your physician about reusing, and ask for advice on sterilising syringes and needles if necessary. Always discard needles and lancets appropriately when dull, and never share sharps or meters.

You should be aware that insulin may be sold in different concentrations from country to country. If you have to replenish abroad, use the appropriate syringe with the appropriate concentration. If you mix and match syringes and concentrations (eg if you use U-40 insulin in a syringe marked 'for U-100 insulin only'), you'll be at greater risk of over- or under-injecting insulin. Also, it's a good idea to retain generic-name prescriptions (even if invalid abroad) and medication inserts, as medications may have different brand names in Africa.

If you find you are running out of supplies in a place with limited resources, be prepared (financially and time-wise) to make a detour to a better-stocked country like South Africa. For extended travel and for emergencies, consider making preparations before you go for medical supplies to be mailed to you. Packaging is available to insulate insulin from heat and physical damage in the mail.

Note that having syringes and meters on your person can sometimes prompt questions from customs and other officials, so make sure you carry on you at all times documentation from your doctor explaining your need for syringes, insulin and meters.

ON THE MOVE

Crossing time zones can be problematic, especially for Type 1 diabetics. Before you leave, take a copy of your itinerary to your diabetic care provider and ask for specific guidance on adjusting your individual protocol en route and as you acclimatise. As a rule, though, keep your watch on home time until the morning after you land.

It's always vital to check blood sugars frequently to modify dosages, mealtimes and food choices, and flying presents its own issues. If you make adjustments based on how you feel – a very unreliable indicator whether you're travelling or not – hyper and hypoglycaemic reactions are almost inevitable. Remember that jet lag can further impair your ability to tell highs and lows.

STAYING HEALTHY

Unaccustomed physical activity, erratic sleep and meal times, unfamiliar foods, climate change, altitude sickness and stress are just some of the many variables that can aggravate control while you are away. All the potential effects of unstable blood glucose (like disorientation, headaches and lethargy) are no fun at any time, but especially when you're away from home.

When you're travelling, Type 1 diabetics need to take particular care to prevent hyper and hypoglycaemic reactions.

Ideally, monitor at least six times daily; if possible, bring two meters as well as visual blood glucose strips as backup. Carry emergency food, foil-wrapped ketone strips and glucagon. In the event of a reaction, wearing a medical bracelet showing that you are a diabetic (see MedicAlert under Useful Organisations earlier in this chapter) can help prevent misdiagnosis (symptoms are often otherwise presumed to be induced by alcohol or illegal substances).

All diabetics should follow basic guidelines to prevent food-borne illness. If you do (or don't) take extra risks and end up ill, know what you need to do to prevent highs and lows related to illness. I do take calculated risks to experience different cultures, even through the social pleasure of eating. I've found that most hosts would over-accommodate me with respect to my dietary concerns.

Wounds in hot, humid climates get infected easier and faster – always keep your feet dry, clean, and comfortable. Never walk barefoot, even on the beach. In hot or remote regions, take special care to stay hydrated. Pack extra supplies of medication, food and water. Protect your skin from the sun (severe sunburn can elevate blood sugars).

Keep insulin chilled in thermoses or insulated cool packs. Gels that freeze when shaken can protect insulin for a few hours. Make sure you don't freeze insulin, and don't place it directly against ice. Keep insulin out of direct sunlight. And ask hostels, friends etc to refrigerate your supplies when they have the opportunity. Touring with supportive companions is ideal; solo travellers should check in with contacts. Cell phones are handy.

HIV-POSITIVE TRAVELLERS

If you are HIV-positive, travelling poses some special problems, although this depends to a certain extent on your CD4 count. It's essential you get specialist advice on this before you travel (from your doctor, specialist physician or travel health clinic).

As a rule, live vaccines (eg oral polio, oral typhoid, measles, mumps and rubella, and yellow fever) need to be avoided. You are generally at greater risk of travel-related illnesses, and if you do get ill, it may have a greater impact on you. It's even more important to take great care over what you eat and drink, and you may want to consider taking antibiotics to prevent diarrhoea – discuss this before you go. You are at greater risk than non-HIV-positive travellers of tuberculosis, hepatitis A and leishmaniasis if you travel to Africa, although you are not at any increased risk of malaria.

Bear in mind that attitudes towards HIV infection may be very different in African countries from what you are used to. Consider hiding any obvious clues to your condition (eg medications) or making it as inconspicuous as possible when you are crossing borders. Although some countries in Africa ask for HIV testing for work permits and long stays, you're unlikely to be asked for this if you're going for a short holiday.

You should be able to get more information on all these issues from your national HIV/AIDS organisation, or you could check out the following web resources: the Special Needs Travel section of **www.cdc.gov/travel;** or **www.aegis.org** (with loads of good links for a variety of HIV-related issues). In the UK, you could contact the Terrence Higgins Trust (☎ 020-7831 0330), 52-54 Grays Inn Rd, London WC1X 8JU, web site **www.tht.org.uk**).

Climate, Altitude & Action...

+ For guidelines on safe sun exposure and acclimatisation,
  see the Staying Healthy chapter.

+ For advice on keeping feet happy and healthy,
  see the section starting p97.

+ Need guidance on fuelling up?
  See the Food for Action section on p111.

Africa is a vast and diverse continent, encompassing a range of environmental and climatic extremes, from the oases and barren mountains of the Sahara Desert to the lush rainforests of West and Central Africa and snow-capped Kilimanjaro rising from the East African plateau. Travel in Africa can be physically challenging, but if you know what to expect and are well prepared, you should be able to have the adventure of your lifetime ... and live to tell the tale.

SUN

SUNBURN

We'd like to think, of course, that after following all the advice about preventing sun damage on p75, you won't need to read this section, but just in case ...

The trouble with sunburn is that it comes on gradually, unlike burns from other causes, and you often don't notice it until it's too late. Sunburn can vary from just a mild redness with some soreness to more severe swelling with blistering.

With mild sunburn, you can take the heat out of the burn by using damp cloths and a fan, and simple painkillers if necessary. There are lots of skin treatments you could try – the best known are perhaps calamine cream (messy but effective) or aloe vera gel, but there's also a huge selection of commercial 'after sun' products. It's best to avoid greasy creams, as these trap the heat and make further damage likely.

Natural remedies you might like to try, include lavender essential oil applied undiluted to the area, comfrey cream or hypericum oil.

If the burn is more severe and has blistered, there's a risk of secondary infection. Take steps to avoid this by keeping the area clean and covered. For a smallish area of blistering sunburn, an antibacterial cream like silver sulphadiazine 1% (Flammazine) is useful – spread it on liberally and cover the whole area with a dry sterile dressing. You'll need to reapply the cream and change the dressing daily until it has healed up. For larger blisters, it's best to get medical attention.

Take care not to get burnt again, especially if peeling has left areas of unprotected new skin.

! Note that widespread severe sunburn is a serious condition that needs to be treated like any other extensive burn (p425) – you will need to get medical help urgently. In the meantime, rest, drink plenty of fluids and try any of the cooling measures suggested for mild sunburn.

SKIN CANCER

Worldwide, the incidence of skin cancer is increasing rapidly, probably as a reflection of the change in attitudes towards sun exposure and tanning in recent decades. If you're in a high-risk group, it's probably a good idea to keep a lookout for early signs of this increasingly common cancer. There are different types of skin cancer, but melanoma is the most dangerous form.

Risk factors include fair skin, living in tropical or subtropical areas of the world, short intense bursts of sun exposure, sunburn in childhood, and prolonged sun exposure. The more moles (raised freckles) you have the greater your risk.

Melanomas can vary quite a lot in appearance, but they often look like irregularly shaped and coloured moles. If you notice any of the following signs in a mole or freckle, see a doctor as soon as possible (it's the sort of thing you might want to cut your trip short for):

- rapid increase in size
- any change in shape or colour
- itching, oozing or bleeding
- any increase in thickness or change in the surface

OTHER EFFECTS OF THE SUN

The sun can affect your skin in other ways. Taking certain medicines can make you hypersensitive to the effects of the sun – you may find you burn more readily and badly than is normal for you. It's something that your doctor or pharmacist should warn you of when it's prescribed. If you are taking medicines for a preexisting condition, this is something you should check with your doctor before you leave. Medicines that can cause problems like this include:

- tetracycline antibiotics, including doxycycline (may be prescribed as a malaria preventive)
- ciprofloxacin (antibiotic that may be prescribed for diarrhoea)
- anti-inflammatory painkillers like ibuprofen and diclofenac
- the contraceptive pill (rarely)
- thiazides (diuretics for blood pressure control and heart problems)
- nalidixic acid (antibiotic often prescribed for bladder infections)
- sulphonamide antibiotics, eg co-trimoxazole (unlikely to be prescribed under normal circumstances)

The sun tends to make atopic dermatitis (eczema) worse, although it can improve psoriasis. Sunlight can trigger cold sores, if you get these.

HEAT

Travelling in Africa often means coping with extreme heat, both the scorching dry heat of the desert and the cloying, humid heat of rainforest areas. Wherever you are going in Africa, the heat is a factor to be taken very seriously.

Generally, your body is able to adapt to the heat pretty well, although you need to give it time – full acclimatisation can take up to three weeks. The most important change that occurs with acclimatisation is that you sweat more readily and in larger quantities. Sweating helps cool you down, as heat is lost when sweat evaporates off your skin. If the sweat pours off you without evaporating, it won't cool you down, which is why humid heat feels hotter than dry heat and why fanning helps cool you down by encouraging evaporation of sweat.

Some people are more vulnerable to the heat than others. Children are much more prone to heat illness than adults. Older travellers who are less fit may be at greater risk of heat illness (although if you're physically fit, you'll cope just as well as younger adults). People with heart or lung problems are vulnerable to heat stress because the heart has to work harder under hot conditions. If you're overweight, you may find it more difficult to lose heat.

! If you're planning on doing physical activity in the heat, like trekking or cycling, remember that your body has to work much harder to keep cool under these circumstances.

Physical fitness makes you more able to cope with heat stress and quicker to acclimatise, but you still need to take care to replace lost fluids.

Sweat contains water and salts, but your main requirement is to replace lost water. You can lose an astonishing 2L an hour in sweat, or more if you're doing strenuous physical activity. You need to drink a lot more than you would normally in a cool climate, even when you have acclimatised.

Don't rely on feeling thirsty to prompt you to drink – by the time this kicks in, you'll probably already be dehydrated. How much urine you're passing is a much better indicator of how dry you are. If you're only passing a small amount of concentrated urine, you need to drink more.

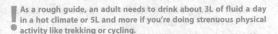

! As a rough guide, an adult needs to drink about 3L of fluid a day in a hot climate or 5L and more if you're doing strenuous physical activity like trekking or cycling.

You generally lose more water than salt in sweat, and as you acclimatise, your body learns to conserve salt better. At first you can lose more salt than normal, but so long as you're not on a salt-reduced diet, you should still be able to make it up from your diet without adding salt or taking salt tablets. The current thinking is that you don't need to actively replace salt unless you experience symptoms indicating a relative lack of salt, mainly cramps in your muscles. As a rule, salt tablets are best avoided – our diets tend to be relatively high in salt anyway, and too much salt can cause kidney and heart problems in the long term.

Heat illness covers a spectrum of conditions ranging from uncomfortable heat cramps to potentially fatal heat stroke. Even if you don't feel too bad, heat and dehydration can affect your physical performance and mental judgement. This is especially important if you are relying on these, such as when you are on a trek or doing other strenuous physical activity.

HEAT CRAMPS
Heavy and prolonged sweating can cause painful cramps in your muscles. If you experience these, rest in a cool environment and replace salt and fluids – this is one of the times when it is appropriate to have extra salt. Make up oral rehydration salts from sachets (readily available throughout Africa but worth taking a supply with you) or make up your own – for more guidance on rehydration, turn to the section on treating diarrhoea (p152). If nothing else is available, any fluid is better than none.

FAINTING
This is quite common if you've recently arrived in a hot climate, and it's more likely to affect older travellers. It occurs because heat causes the blood to pool in your legs when you're

standing, meaning that less blood reaches your brain, causing you to feel dizzy and faint.

If a travel companion faints, lie them down and raise their legs so that their feet are at a higher level than their head. Use fanning and spraying with cool water to help cool them down. When they come to, give them fluids (safe water or diluted fruit juice) to sip.

DEHYDRATION

This can be caused by any condition that leads to an excessive loss of body fluids, including heat, fever, diarrhoea, vomiting and strenuous physical activity. Signs of dehydration are:

• nausea and dizziness
• headache, and dry eyes and mouth
• weakness and muscle cramps
• passing small quantities of dark urine
• raised temperature

Treatment is to drink lots of fluids: oral rehydration salts if available; otherwise, any fluid will do.

For more guidance on fluid replacement, see the section on treating diarrhoea p152.

HEAT EXHAUSTION & HEATSTROKE

These two conditions are different entities, but they overlap to a certain extent and, for practical purposes, you should treat any heat illness as heat stroke. Both are caused by heavy and prolonged sweating with inadequate fluid replacement and insufficient time for acclimatisation. In heat stroke, sweating stops and you get a dangerous rise in body temperature which can be fatal.

Symptoms to look out for are headache, dizziness, nausea and feeling weak and exhausted. You may notice that you're passing only small quantities of dark urine and you may have muscle

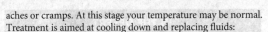

aches or cramps. At this stage your temperature may be normal. Treatment is aimed at cooling down and replacing fluids:

- rest in a cool environment (fanning and cool water sprays may help)
- drink lots of fluids (water, oral rehydration salts or diluted fruit juice)

If untreated, heat exhaustion can progress to heat stroke. Signs (more likely to be noticed by your travel companions than yourself) include confusion, headache, lack of sweating and flushed and red appearance. The skin feels hot to touch and the person's temperature is raised. In addition, they may show lack of coordination, fits and finally coma (unconsciousness).

Heat stroke can be rapidly fatal, so you need to take immediate action to lower the person's temperature and to get medical help:

- move the person into the shade or a cool environment (get a fan going or use a room with air-con)
- give them cool water to sip (cool fluids are absorbed more rapidly than warm ones); intravenous fluid replacement may be needed once you get medical help
- seek medical help or evacuation urgently
- ice packs, sponging or spraying with cold water and fanning will all help; ice packs are most effective if you put them over the groin and under the arms, but wrap them up first

COLD

Although you may associate travel in Africa more readily with heat, you may also be exposed to the opposite extreme, especially if you are trekking or just travelling through highland areas. Be aware that in the desert, temperatures can plummet at night, as there is nothing to hold the heat. The weather in many highland areas can be extremely changeable, so you should always be prepared for the worst possible conditions.

Your body is fairly limited in what it can do to stay warm – shivering is just about the only thing in the short term – so it's up to you to minimise the dangers by wearing adequate clothing and avoiding temperature extremes (unless you're properly

IN THE DESERT

The desert is probably the most extreme environmental challenge you can expose yourself to in Africa – don't underestimate it, whether you're just going on a short sightseeing trip or a more major expedition across it.

The obvious hazards in the daytime are the heat and sun. Temperatures can (and do) regularly rise to 50°C, and the heat is dessicating (one reason why the Pyramids have survived so long). Be sensible about what you expect yourself to be able to do under these conditions. Always take plenty of water with you (much more than you think you'll need), even if you are just planning on a short trip to the sand dunes. You may find wells along the way, but the water from these is often unpalatable, and you'll need to filter and purify it in any case.

Protect your skin from the sun by covering up, especially your head and face. A *cheche* (piece of cloth worn as head protection) is an excellent way of covering up and you can draw it across your mouth to avoid breathing in the ubiquitous dust. Dust and particles of sand can irritate your throat and eyes – cover your mouth and wear sunglasses. An eye bath may be soothing at the end of the day.

Remember that temperatures can plummet at night in the desert, even in the summer months, so make sure you are prepared if you are planning on an overnight trip.

If you find yourself in the middle of a dust or sand storm, stop travelling (you may lose your way as visibility can be dramatically reduced under these conditions), cover your face and mouth and find somewhere to shelter until it has passed.

Other hazards to be aware of in the desert inlude the wildlife, including scorpions, spiders and snakes.

The northern Sahara is home to one of the few deadly scorpions. Camel spiders, though not deadly, are best avoided. For guidelines on what to do if you get bitten by any of these creatures, see the Bites & Stings chapter later in this book.

It's easy to get lost in the desert, and it's often travellers who planned a day trip who are at risk. Even if you are just going on a short trip, you must take a reliable guide with you, or a compass (or both – make sure you know how to use the compass) as well as plenty of water and food, and extra clothing. It's always a good idea to let someone know of your plans and when to expect you back so that the alarm can be raised if necessary. If you do get lost, station yourself in a flat, open area, so that you can be more easily spotted by rescuers.

Driving in the desert is not something to be lightly undertaken – you need to research and plan this well in advance. Some sources of information are listed in the Activities & Expeditions section of the Before You Go Chapter. The Royal Geographic Society produces a booklet *Desert Expeditions* for anyone planning a serious trip in the these conditions.

prepared). Remember that food equals heat – make sure you eat regularly and get sufficient calories in cold climates.

Other problems of cold climates are dehydration (because cold makes you urinate more, you may not feel thirsty and cold air is very dry), constipation and sunburn, especially at altitude.

If you're out and about in the cold, the main problems cold causes are general body cooling (hypothermia) or localised cooling, usually affecting your hands and feet, called frostnip or frostbite.

HYPOTHERMIA

This is when your body starts to lose the battle to maintain your body heat in cold conditions and your core body temperature starts to fall (officially, hypothermia is when your temperature, taken by the rectal method, falls below 35°C). You don't need incredibly low temperatures to become hypothermic, just the right combination of circumstances.

Because hypothermia can come on gradually and take hold before you realise, it's important to recognise when it might be a risk and to take steps to prevent it. You're more at risk of hypothermia if you're thin (less body fat for insulation), tired, wet, or inadequately dressed or equipped (such as not having a sleeping bag). If it's windy, you get colder more easily, as your body heat is removed by convection. If you're under the influence of alcohol or any other mind-altering substance, you're also more at risk – alcohol encourages heat loss and also affects your judgement.

Children and older travellers are more vulnerable to the cold, especially if children are being carried (such as in a backpack child carrier). An added problem is that children may not let you know how they're feeling until it's too late.

! Remember that immersion in cold water, eg if you fall in a mountain stream, can rapidly cause you to become hypothermic.

If you think cold might be an issue, take care to prepare well and minimise your risks:

- always be prepared for the worst possible weather, even if there isn't a cloud in the sky when you set out – rain, cold winds and thick mist can descend without warning in areas like the Mulanje plateau in Malawi
- wear appropriate clothing – layers are best, as you can adjust them easily to match changing weather conditions throughout the day, and make sure you include windproof and waterproof layers; lightweight polyester fleece clothing is ideal, if a bit sweaty
- a surprising amount of heat is lost through radiation from your head, so wear a hat

- stay dry – adjust your layers to prevent your clothes getting wet through with sweat, and always carry an umbrella, waterproof layer or large plastic bag on you to keep the rain off, however unlikely this seems when you set off

BUDDY SYSTEM

Many of the signs and symptoms associated with heat, cold and altitude illness are much more likely to be noticed by people you are with than by you. Because of this, it's vital to keep a regular watch on each other if you are in harsh environmental or climatic conditions. Never leave someone on their own if they're showing symptoms. It's also a good idea to self-check for aches, pains, cold areas, numbness and dizziness.

While you are out, don't let tiredness get a hold – make sure you have frequent rests.

Always carry plenty of fluids and carbohydrate-packed goodies, and snack regularly throughout the day.

Check regularly if you're feeling cold or if you have cold hands and toes. Watch for subtle early signs of hypothermia in your travel companions. These are what Rick Curtis of the Princeton Outdoor Program calls the 'umbles' – stumbles, mumbles, fumbles and grumbles, as you get changes in mental function and coordination.

If hypothermia is allowed to progress, the person becomes more disorientated, may show poor judgement and reasoning, and is unable to make appropriate decisions about survival strategies. Finally, shivering stops, the person is unable to walk and loses consciousness.

You need to watch for and treat the early signs of hypothermia:

■ remove any cold or wet clothes and replace with warm, dry ones, being careful to cover the head and extremities, and insulate the person from the ground

■ find shelter for protection from wet, wind and cold

■ rewarm by using blankets, sleeping bags and body-to-body contact (zip two sleeping bags together and get in with the cold person to help warm them up)

■ you can use hot packs or hot water bottles (or improvise), but remember to wrap these up first to prevent the risk of burns

■ drink warm, sweet fluids (sweet milky tea is excellent and readily available)

'Space blankets' are a popular cold weather survival aid, but there are doubts about their effectiveness in the field, and you're probably better off using a sleeping bag or other thermal layers, depending what you have with you. Carry lots of plastic bags with you – covering yourself up with these prevents further heat loss through evaporation, and can double as protection from rain.

> **!** Severe hypothermia is a very serious condition – seek medical help or evacuation immediately. Handle the person carefully and don't rewarm them too fast, as this can be dangerous.

CHILBLAINS
These are the most common form of cold injury and the least dangerous. Chilblains can occur if your bare skin is repeatedly exposed to low temperatures (above freezing) and usually affect fingers and toes. You get red, swollen, itchy and tender areas which will heal up on their own in one to two weeks.

Prevent chilblains by wearing warm mittens (not gloves) and socks, and suitable footwear. There's no specific treatment, but remember that any open areas on your skin can get infected, so keep them clean and covered.

Natural remedies that have been recommended include calendula or witch hazel tinctures for unbroken chilblains, or hypericum ointment for broken chilblains. Comfrey ointment is soothing for any skin inflammation.

FROSTBITE

When your tissues get so cold they freeze, this is frostbite. It's not going to be a big risk for most travellers in Africa as it doesn't generally occur unless you're at temperatures below freezing for prolonged periods of time without adequate gloves or footwear. High winds, high altitude (usually above about 4000m), badly fitting boots, smoking and alcohol can all make frostbite more likely. Fingers, toes, ears, nose and face can all be affected. (There's an unforgettable report of a male jogger getting frostbite of the penis – don't say we didn't warn you.)

Prevent frostbite – cover all exposed skin with waterproof and windproof layers in cold conditions and if you notice your hands or feet turning numb, stop immediately and warm them up by body to body contact if necessary.

A frostbitten part looks white and waxy – keep a watch on your companions for this – and it's painless while it's frozen. It's best to seek medical advice as soon as possible. Some effects of frostbite, especially if it's mild, are reversible but you will need expert advice.

What you do immediately depends on your situation. If there is no risk of refreezing (ie you can be evacuated promptly or you are near medical facilities), you should thaw the affected part, although this depends on whether you have appropriate facilities at hand.

Never rub the affected part to warm it up, as this can cause further damage.

Rewarm the part by immersing it for about half an hour in water heated to 40°C. As it starts to warm up, the pain can be pretty severe, and you'll need strong painkillers. The thawed part will swell up, so be sure to remove any rings from fingers (or toes). Infection is a significant risk, so make sure you keep the area clean and dry, and cover it with a dry dressing until you reach medical help. If there is a risk of refreezing (ie you are far from help), don't attempt to thaw the part until you reach medical help.

ALTITUDE

Although Africa doesn't have mountains in the same league as the Himalaya or the Andes, there are some frequently visited mountain ranges like Mt Kilimanjaro (5895m), Mt Kenya (5199m), the Rwenzori Range (Mt Stanley, 5109m), Mt Meru (4556m) and the Simien mountains (Ras Deshen, 4543m) where you may be affected by altitude.

The problem with altitude is that the air is thinner and less oxygen is available to you. Your body adapts to having less oxygen available through various mechanisms. At first, you increase the rate and depth of your breathing; later you get an increase in heart rate and changes in red blood cells. Although you can acclimatise sufficiently in a couple of days to a particular altitude, full acclimatisation takes about three weeks.

You're not usually at risk of altitude illness until you reach about 2500m, but it is possible to get symptoms from about 2000m upwards. You're very unlikely to get problems if you stay at altitude for less than about six hours. Going above 3500m, about 50% of trekkers experience symptoms of mild altitude illness, whereas about one in 20 have life-threatening severe altitude illness.

WHO'S AT RISK?

Anyone can have problems at altitude, whatever your age or fitness level. The most important risk factor is how rapidly you ascend. One of the reasons why Mt Kenya regularly claims victims is the speed at which you can reach significant altitudes. For example, it's possible to set off from Nairobi in the morning of one day and be on the summit of Lenana (4985m) the next, which is just asking for trouble.

INFORMATION RESOURCES

If you want to find out more about the effects of altitude and other related issues, there are heaps of good sources of information available to you. Some recommended books are listed under Books in the Before You Go chapter, and you might want to check out some of the following web sites:

www.princeton.edu/~oa/altitude.html
Princeton University's Outdoor Action Program is an excellent and comprehensive resource. It has detailed information on altitude, heat and cold and other wilderness safety issues, as well as lots of links to related sites on a wide variety of outdoor activities, including biking, hiking, caving and mountaineering.

www.thebmc.co.uk
The British Mountaineering Council is another good resource, with information on altitude and related issues. It can also be contacted on ☎ 0161-445 4747, fax 0161-445 4500, email info@thebmc.co.uk, or by post: 177-79 Burton Rd, Manchester M20 2BB.

www.high-altitude-medicine.com
High Altitude Medicine Guide is just that; it also has good information on water treatment and travellers diarrhoea (though mainly aimed at travellers to Nepal), an excellent books section and lots of useful links.

www.wms.org
The Wilderness Medical Society (☎ 800-627-0629, 810 E. 10th Street, PO Box 1897 Lawrence, KS 66044, USA) is an authoritative source of information on all aspects of wilderness safety.

Some people are naturally more prone to altitude illness than others, and you're much more likely to get problems at altitude if you've had them before (60% likelihood for high altitude pulmonary oedema), so you should get expert advice in this situation.

Children appear to be at the same risk of altitude sickness as adults, but they are less likely to be able to let you know if they have symptoms, which makes it more risky.

Note that there's a theoretical risk that the oral contraceptive pill or hormone replacement therapy will make altitude sickness worse in women taking these, although at altitudes below about 5500m there's little evidence to support this. It probably makes sense to discuss this issue with your doctor in advance if you fall into either of these categories.

! If you have any ongoing conditions, particularly heart or lung problems, discuss this with your doctor before you go.

ACCLIMATISATION

Some of the mountains in Africa may seem small compared with ranges like the Himalaya and the Andes, but it's important to take time to acclimatise. Many thousands of trekkers get to the top of mountains like Kilimanjaro and Mt Kenya with little or no difficulty but many others don't make it because they suffer from altitude illness – and a few die each year.

Don't forget that Uhuru Peak (5896m), on Kilimanjaro is 500m higher than Everest Base Camp. Trekking companies may offer a quick trip to the summit, but you'll be safer – and enjoy it more – if you take your time and follow the rules for safe ascent given in this section. Always be prepared for unexpected weather changes, and hire a guide if you need to – don't become one of the 'lost on the mountain' statistics.

PREVENTION

The best way to prevent acute mountain sickness (AMS) is to ascend slowly and gradually, allowing time for acclimatisation to occur. In practice this means:

- having frequent rest days – plan to spend two to three nights at each rise of 1000m
- 'climb high, sleep low' – as far as possible, sleep at a lower altitude than the greatest height you reached during the day
- above 3000m don't increase your sleeping altitude by more than 300m per day
- if you have any symptoms of AMS, stop ascending until the symptoms have gone
- descend immediately if your symptoms persist or worsen in 30 to 60 minutes

Other general measures for preventing illness at altitude include the following:

- don't trek alone – you may not recognise the symptoms of AMS in yourself and you may not be able to get to safety
- if you plan to trek at altitude, make sure you know where the nearest medical facility is
- drink plenty of fluids to prevent dehydration (4L or 5L daily), as the air at high altitude is dry and you lose plenty of moisture through sweating and breathing
- don't overexert yourself, especially in the first week or so at altitude
- eat light, high-carbohydrate meals to give you energy
- avoid alcohol, sedatives or any other mind-altering substances

Another option for preventing AMS is with drugs, but be aware that this is a highly controversial issue, and you will get different advice from different sources. Although there are some situations where drug treatment is useful, the bottom line is that if you follow the rules of gradual safe ascent, you shouldn't need drug treatment.

The most widely used drug for preventing AMS is currently acetazolamide (Diamox). This drug works on cellular biochemistry, resulting in increased breathing rates and improved oxygen supply to the body and brain. Diamox can be used to prevent mild AMS as well as to treat it, but it doesn't prevent or treat severe AMS, high altitude pulmonary or cerebral oedema. Side effects are common, usually tingling in the fingers, and it makes you pass more urine.

There is no evidence that Diamox masks the symptoms of AMS. However, if you decide to take it, you should realise that Diamox is not a replacement for acclimatisation – if you ascend too fast, even if you're taking Diamox, you'll get AMS. For more information about Diamox and other drugs used in altitude illness, check out the information sources listed earlier in the boxed text or talk to your doctor. Remember:

- the best treatment for AMS is descent
- you should never use drug treatment as a means of avoiding descent or to enable you to ascend further

MILD AMS

Above about 2000m, it's common to get mild symptoms of AMS, which usually come on gradually. These include:

- headache
- loss of appetite
- nausea and vomiting
- tiredness and irritability

You may also notice that you're a bit unsteady on your feet, and you may feel a little short of breath. Because symptoms of AMS are so nonspecific, it can be difficult to distinguish them from flu, colds or jet lag, if you've recently arrived – if in doubt, assume it's AMS.

Having difficulty sleeping is very common at altitude – you may find it hard to get to sleep, have vivid dreams and wake up frequently. Your travel companions may notice you have periodic breathing, when your breathing slows and appears to stop. Periodic breathing can be very scary to witness, but it's not dangerous.

Sometimes you can get swelling of your face, arm or leg (oedema). This doesn't mean that you are getting a more severe form of altitude illness, and it usually settles without any treatment over the course of a couple of days.

Symptoms of mild AMS are unpleasant, but they usually disappear after two to three days, as long as you don't go any higher. The main concern with mild AMS is that it can progress to more severe forms if you ignore it or go higher.

SEVERE AMS

About one in 20 people will develop more severe forms of altitude illness, usually at 4000m and above, but sometimes lower. Severe AMS includes high altitude pulmonary oedema and high altitude cerebral oedema.

In high altitude pulmonary oedema (HAPE), fluid accumulates in your lungs, preventing you from breathing properly. It can follow from mild AMS or it can come on suddenly without any warning. The main symptoms are:

- breathlessness at rest or a persistent cough (common early symptoms)
- coughing up pink, frothy sputum
- tiredness and weakness

If fluid collects within your brain, you get high altitude cerebral oedema (HACE). This condition is rare, but is life-threatening, so you need to know how to recognise it and what to do about it. Symptoms to look out for:

- severe headache, unrelieved by simple painkillers
- change in behaviour, confusion and disorientation
- double vision
- unsteadiness
- drowsiness and coma (unconsciousness)

Early HACE causes a condition called ataxia (a form of incoordination) which can be picked up by the straight line test. To do this test, draw a line on the ground and get the person to walk heel to toe along it. If they can't do it without overbalancing or stepping off the line, assume they have HACE, especially if they have other signs of illness.

TREATMENT

We can't emphasise enough that the best treatment for any form of AMS is descent. Mild AMS can be treated with simple measures, but bear in mind some not-to-be-broken rules:

- never ascend with any symptoms of AMS
- always descend promptly if your symptoms are moderate to severe or getting worse, or there's no improvement in mild symptoms after two to three days
- seek medical advice if necessary, but don't let this delay descent
- rest up for a couple of days
- drink plenty of fluids, as dehydration is common at altitude
- take simple painkillers or an anti-inflammatory like ibuprofen for the headache
- try a motion sickness remedy (p72) for nausea and vomiting
- if you have access to oxygen by mask, this can be helpful

Severe AMS, HAPE and HACE are all medical emergencies – you need to act immediately.

- seek medical advice if possible but don't let this delay descent
- descend immediately (even 500m can help)
- use oxygen by mask, if possible

Drug treatments are as follows, but remember these are powerful drugs that can be dangerous if used incorrectly. If you are carrying them, make sure you know all about how to use them before you go:

- severe AMS or HACE – dexamethasone 8mg by mouth immediately, followed by 4mg every six hours until you are safely evacuated

- HAPE – nifedipine 20mg by mouth immediately

If necessary, if you're not sure what the problem is (as is often the case), you can take all treatments together.

Note that dexamethasone is a powerful steroid drug that should be used with extreme caution, and ideally only under medical supervision. Side effects include mood changes and an increased risk of indigestion and ulceration. Nifedipine is a drug used in the treatment of high blood pressure and heart problems.

OTHER HEALTH CONCERNS

Sunburn is common at high altitude because less sunlight is filtered out by the atmosphere, and if there is snow, this reflects sunlight much more than plain ground. Cover up and use a high protection factor sunscreen (don't forget your lips), and wear good sunglasses to protect your eyes. Dehydration is common, so drink plenty of fluids, even if you don't feel thirsty.

You still need to be careful about your drinking water. Most diarrhoea-causing bugs are resistant to cold temperatures, even freezing, and water from streams on popular routes is quite likely to be contaminated with faeces. Water from glacial streams can contain mineral salts, which may have a laxative effect.

Snow blindness is sunburn of the backs of the eyes and is caused by sunlight reflected off snow. Prevent it by wearing goggles or sunglasses with UV protection. You get a gritty feeling in your eyes, extreme sensitivity to light, redness and temporary blindness several hours after exposure. There's no specific treatment apart from relieving the pain (for example by putting cold cloths onto your closed eyes), and it usually heals completely in a couple of days. Anaesthetic eye drops (for example amethocaine) are sometimes used but they may slow the healing process and make your eyes more vulnerable to other injuries. Antibiotic eye drops are not necessary. You can make emergency eye protection by cutting slits in cardboard or cloth.

ACTION SAFETY

Africa provides endless opportunities for adventuring, from trekking in the remote Simien Mountains (Ethiopia) to white-water rafting below Victoria Falls and rock climbing in Mali. However, Africa's probably not the place you'd want to be if you injure yourself or get into an emergency situation, so it's definitely worth taking care to stay in one piece, whatever you are doing. This section outlines some basic safety rules for outdoor activities.

TREKKING SAFELY

If you decide to go on a trek of any length, here's a quick health and safety checklist.

Preparation

Always inform someone reliable of your route and estimated arrival date so that if you do run into difficulties, the alarm can be raised. You could consider letting the folks back home know via a brief phone call; alternatively, leave the information with your hotel or other travellers. This system will only work if you let people know when you get back, so that unnecessary rescues aren't initiated.

- Fitness – trekking can be a strenuous activity, particularly if you're not in peak physical condition, so make sure what you are planning is within your capabilities and that there is some flexibility built into your plans in case you find you need to bail out at any stage.

- Training – if you can, some pre-trek fitness training is a good idea, and will reduce the likelihood of sprains, falls and overuse injuries.

- Equipment – make sure you are fully prepared for the environ-mental conditions you're likely to encounter and take a well stocked medical kit (see the Before You Go chapter earlier in this book).

- Footwear – running shoes and sandals are not much use on a trek in rough terrain, so unless you can get hold of a decent pair of walking boots, consider changing your plans.

- High altitude trekking – make sure you know what to look for and what to do if you develop signs of altitude illness.

- Map and compass – a reasonable map of the area is vital, especially if you are going without a guide (but is a good idea anyway), but it's no good if you can't follow it.

- Insurance – check that your insurance covers you for trekking, and consider joining a local emergency rescue organisation.

On the Trek

Consider hiring porters to carry the heavy equipment (and help the local economy), and a guide if you're unsure of the route.

- Water – don't assume there will be water along the way unless you find out that there is from a reliable source; otherwise, you'll need to carry all your water requirements with you (remember if it's hot, you will need a minimum of 5L of water each per day).

- Food – again, you shouldn't rely on food being available along the way; take plenty of food with you, including energy-giving snacks like chocolate and dried fruit, and remember that a trekker marches on his/her stomach...

- Tiredness – this makes injuries more likely, so eat properly throughout the day, take regular rests and don't push yourself too hard, especially towards the end of the day.

- Blisters – avoid these by wearing well worn-in walking boots and socks that fit snugly with no seams; if you do get one, follow the guidelines on p98.

- Protect yourself against insect bites and leeches (p90).

Rescue & Evacuation

If someone in your group is injured or falls ill, leave someone with them and go for help. If there are only two of you, leave the person in a sheltered position with as much warm clothing, food and water as you can sensibly spare, as well as some means of attracting attention (like a whistle or torch). Mark the position with something conspicuous, for example a brightly coloured bag or a large stone cross on the ground.

Note that this is the accepted strategy for rescue, but when you're travelling in remote areas in Africa, self-evacuation is going to be your only and best option, especially as rescue may be delayed or difficult due to transport problems and communication difficulties.

CYCLING SAFELY

There are opportunities for some decent cycling trips here (for example we heard from a couple who cycled their way round Tunisia). If you're considering a short or longer cycle tour, here are some basic health and safety tips:

Health & Fitness

It's a good idea to get fit on a bike if you plan on doing more than a couple of days of cycle touring – practise riding an average daily distance two or three days in a row. Before you set off, be sure to warm up and stretch properly. On the ride:

- take regular breaks during the day
- consider having a massage in the evening
- avoid sore hands from gripping the handlebar on rough roads for long periods by changing hand position (if possible), relaxing your grip on the handlebars and taking frequent rests
- be prepared for climatic extremes
- remember to drink plenty of fluids, especially if it's hot, and avoid cycling during the hottest part of the day
- take snack food with you for any ride that's more than about an hour long

Equipment & Cycling Technique

These can make a big difference to your enjoyment and comfort, as well as safety on the ride:

- if you're hiring a bike, check it over carefully – make sure the brakes work and check the wheels and tyres
- wear safety gear – helmet (essential), sunglasses, cycling gloves and two layers of clothing (helps prevent road rash if you come off your bike), and check your bike on a daily basis

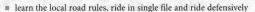

- learn the local road rules, ride in single file and ride defensively
- make sure your bike is adjusted for you – check that the seat and handlebar height are comfortable and the seat is parallel to the ground
- take lights with you if you're intending to ride at night
- balance the load on your bike and keep the weight low to the ground, preferably with panniers
- learn to spin the gears (70 to 90 revs per minute) not push them – this way you'll avoid sore knees from pushing big gears

For more information, you could try *The Bicycle Touring Manual* by Rob van der Plas, or check out this recommended web site: **www.ctc.org.uk.**

CAVING HAZARDS

Going into caves involves some hazards you should be aware of, although you're unlikely to be at any great risks from these on most standard guided tours. Caves are dark, so you'll want to take a good torch with you, and even in hot climates they can be cold, so be prepared with layers. Flash floods are always a risk.

- Leptospirosis may be a risk as this bacterial disease can be transmitted through rat or bat urine, and you can get infected if you scrape yourself against the cave walls; you can also acquire it by swimming in contaminated water – see p340 for more details.
- You can get a fungal chest infection, histoplasmosis, by inhaling dried bat droppings, but this is a risk mainly in small confined spaces; you get a fever, headache, chest pains and cough about two weeks after you've been exposed – there's no specific treatment, but you should seek medical advice, as it can make some people very ill.
- Rabies can be carried by bats and rats, as well as animals like cats and dogs – although you normally acquire the disease through bites, there have been cases in cavers from inhaling dried bat droppings, so if you are planning on any serious caving, you should make sure you get immunised against rabies before you leave (see p375 for more details).
- Scorpions and snakes live in caves, so be wary of where you put your hands.

- Various small biters (including sandflies, mosquitoes, ticks and leeches) live in and around the entrance to caves – cover up and apply insect repellent to prevent bites and the diseases they carry.

MISCELLANEOUS OUTDOOR HAZARDS

Unpredictable weather, rain and climatic extremes are probably the main outdoor hazards to be aware of in Africa. Find out what the climate is likely to be doing at the time of year you're considering travelling, and plan around it.

Beware of lightning if you find yourself out in the open when a storm comes on. In the highlands of Lesotho, for example, several lives are lost each year from lightning strikes. Lightning has a penchant for crests, lone trees, gullies, caves and cabin entrances, as well as wet ground. If you are caught out in the open, try to curl up as tight as possible, with your feet together, and a layer of insulation between you and the ground. Make sure you're not sitting next to metal objects like walking poles or metal-frame backpacks – place them a short distance away from you.

If you have to cross any fast-flowing rivers, remember to take one arm out of your pack, and unbuckle it so that if you feel yourself getting swept away, you can slip out of it easily. Use a stick to feel the river bed before putting your feet down, and walk side-on to the direction of flow so that the water can flow more easily round your body. Snowmelt is cold, so beware of hypothermia and muscle cramps.

Leeches, ticks and animal bites are other ubiquitous hazards – see the Bites & Stings chapter later in this book for more details.

Water...

Safe water for drinking is vital if you want to stay healthy on your travels (p73), but contact with water – fresh or salt – through swimming, paddling and water sports has its hazards too.

➕ See the inside back cover for emergency resuscitation of a drowning person

FRESHWATER HAZARDS

SCHISTOSOMIASIS

➕ For guidelines on how to avoid this disease, see p92

This disease, also known as bilharzia, is a real risk to you when you are travelling in Africa. At Lonely Planet, we receive several letters each year from travellers who found they had schisto after a trip to Africa. Worldwide, it's a common cause of ill health, especially in tropical regions – it affects up to 20 million people, the second-most common tropical disease after malaria. Tropical areas with lakes, streams and large rivers are generally worst affected.

Schistosomiasis is caused by tiny parasitic worms that live the first part of their life cycle in a type of freshwater snail. You can get schistosomiasis by bathing, swimming or showering in fresh water in which these snails are living. The tiny worms are only just visible to the naked eye, so don't rely on spotting them. They can burrow their way through your intact skin, eg you don't need to have an open cut. It takes about 10 minutes or so for the worms to penetrate your skin. This gives you a chance to prevent infection by vigorous towel drying after you have been exposed to risky water, but don't rely on this.

There are two main types of the disease, affecting either your bladder or your intestines. In Africa, you're mostly at risk of the urinary form. The worms don't multiply once they're inside you; it's their eggs that cause damage when they get lodged in your tissues. The schistosomiasis life cycle is completed when an infected person passes eggs in urine or faeces and the eggs then find their way back to the water.

Signs & Symptoms

Most people don't get symptoms at the early stage. A few hours after you've been in contact with infected water, you may get itching all over, known as 'swimmer's itch', and perhaps a rash as the worms penetrate your skin, but this doesn't last long (a day or two), and you may not even notice it. You may notice a cough or wheezing about a week to 10 days later as the worms pass through your lungs.

Sometimes you can get an illness (called Katayama fever) four weeks or so after infection. It may be an allergic response to the eggs. You get a fever, itchy rash, diarrhoea, aches and pains, cough and wheeze, and weight loss. It's worth bearing this possibility in mind if you have a fever without an obvious cause or diarrhoea that doesn't respond to antibiotics, especially if you think you may have been exposed to infection.

After several months you may get abdominal pain, and blood in your urine or faeces. Often this is the first indication that there is a problem.

Although chronic schistosomiasis is a major public health problem in risk areas, it's extremely unlikely that the disease would reach this stage in you.

Diagnosis & Treatment

Schistosomiasis doesn't generally pose an immediate danger to you (unlike say, malaria) but if left untreated it can cause serious health problems in the long term. If there's a chance you may have been infected while you were away, be sure to get it checked out when you get back home. Infection can be diagnosed by a blood test (but not until at least three months after you were infected), or by a urine or faeces test.

Effective treatment is available with a single dose of a drug called praziquantel, which has few side effects.

Schistosomiasis in Africa

Apart from the southernmost part of the continent, you should basically assume that any body of fresh water in Africa, including the Nile River and Lake Malawi, is potentially infected. Be aware of the risks and take steps to avoid contact with water in these areas.

Until relatively recently, Lake Malawi (Nyasa in Mozambique) was generally thought to be the only schisto-free lake in the Rift Valley. It was only when growing numbers of Peace Corps volunteers developed the disease in Malawi that a team of researchers put the claim to the test ... and found that about a third of visitors and expatriates in Malawi showed evidence of having encountered the disease. Investigation of the lake revealed infected snails at Cape Maclear and elsewhere along the lakeshore.

Although this is hardly news any more, it does illustrate an important point about relying on information from local hotel owners and travel agents – tourism is a hugely important money earner in many parts of Africa, and anything that is likely to damage this is taken very seriously. It doesn't mean that you shouldn't visit places where schistosomiasis is present – this would rule out travel to much of Africa – but it just means that you need to take care to avoid the risk of infection if you're going to affected areas.

Lake Malawi is just one of the bodies of water in Africa affected by schistosomiasis. The building of huge new dams (including the Aswan Dam in Egypt, the Manantali Dam over the River Senegal and the Akosombo Dam in Ghana) as well as new irrigation projects in various parts of the continent has resulted in more homes for snails and an increase in the burden of the disease in many areas. Other factors contributing to the spread of the disease include inadequate sewage systems in urban areas.

Eliminating schistosomiasis is a major challenge for many countries in Africa. Health education and mass treatment campaigns are under way, and there's even hope of a vaccine against the disease soon.

LEPTOSPIROSIS (WEIL'S DISEASE)

This is another reason to be wary of swimming in fresh water. Leptospirosis is a bacterial disease that you can get from contact with water contaminated by animal urine (eg dogs and rats). You're probably at greatest risk of this if you're an 'adventure traveller', especially if you're swimming or doing water sports (canoeing, rafting or caving) in affected water. The bacteria enter your body through breaks in your skin or through your nose or eyes.

You can get just mild flu-like symptoms, about 10 days after infection, but sometimes it can be more severe, with high fever, vomiting, diarrhoea and red, irritated eyes. The illness can occasionally progress to jaundice and severe liver failure, and even death in about one in 100 affected people.

You should seek medical help as soon as possible if you think you may have leptospirosis. After the diagnosis is confirmed, treatment is with antibiotics (penicillin or doxycycline).

GENERAL HAZARDS

WATER IN THE EYES & EARS

You can easily get eye infections like viral and bacterial conjunctivitis from a not-too-clean swimming pool, and you can get chemical irritation of your eyes from poorly maintained swimming pools. Take care not to get water in your eyes, especially if you have any doubts about the cleanliness of the pool, or wear swimming goggles.

If you do get an eye infection, bathe your eyes with clean water and avoid swimming until they are better.

Water in the ears commonly causes infection and irritation, especially in tropical climates. Ear plugs can help to keep ears dry and healthy.

If you think you have an eye or ear infection, see the Ears, Eyes & Teeth chapter for more details.

RIVER WIDE, RIVER DEEP

You want to think twice about cooling off in any of the major rivers in Africa like the Nile, Congo, Niger and Zambezi. Not only are crocs, hippos and (especially) schistosomiasis a risk, but you're likely to be swept away in the strong currents. Stick to floating on top of them.

WATER & SKIN INFECTIONS

Not drying your skin properly between swims, especially if it's hot and humid, can make fungal infections of your skin (p202) more likely. If spa baths are not maintained properly, bacteria multiply and you can get an infection of the hair follicles, causing a rash of boils (p204). Sea water contains all sorts of sea bacteria, which can infect cuts and scrapes, turning them into persistent sores if you don't clean them promptly and thoroughly.

SWIMMING & SNORKELLING

Sunburn is a big risk at the beach or pool, especially for children, so you need to be aware of the risk and take steps to prevent it – see the Safe Sun section in the Staying Healthy chapter for more guidance on this. You're also vulnerable to heat illness, so make sure you drink plenty of fluids and encourage your children to as well.

It's unlikely you'll want to sit on a beach that's littered with animal faeces, but if you do, be aware that you can get larva migrans (p207), a skin rash caused by a worm that may be present in dog and cat faeces.

Remember that most of the diseases you can get through drinking contaminated water can also be caught through swimming or bathing in unsafe water (by swallowing small amounts). Sea water isn't necessarily safer than fresh water from this point of view, as sewage is often emptied into the sea, especially around urban settlements.

Chlorinated pools that are well maintained should be safe, although some diarrhoea-causing parasites (like *Giardia*) are able to survive chlorination. You can't get diseases like HIV from swimming in pools.

It's not just bugs – you need to be wary of chemical pollutants like fertilisers and industrial pollutants that get washed or dumped in the water at beaches near big cities. They can cause an itchy skin rash or more serious toxicity.

If you're doing any water sports, use your common sense and don't take unnecessary risks. Check the quality of any equipment you hire, as safety standards are often much less stringent than you would expect back home.

SURFING SAFETY TIPS

Peter Neely, author of Indo Surf & Lingo, *has the following tips for safe surfing.*

The surfing lifestyle is all about fun and freedom, but you need to take a few simple precautions to avoid unwanted injuries.

Sun Protection

Possibly the most dangerous aspect of surfing is sunburn, which can keep you out of the surf for a few days. In the long term, sunburn can cause potentially fatal skin cancer.

- Use waterproof sunscreen (ideally SPF 30); apply it before you go out, and reapply it regularly.
- Wear a Lycra wetshirt in the surf. A cap protects your eyes in the water too.
- Avoid surfing when the sun is at its most intense, between 11am and 3pm.

Check the Conditions

When you arrive at a new surf spot, it pays to watch the line-up for at least 15 minutes before paddling out.

- What is underneath the water? Any rocks or shallow ledges? If you're surfing over a coral reef, always wear protective rubber boots and maybe a wetsuit.
- Where do the local surfers paddle out from? Where do they exit the surf?
- Are there any rips? If caught in a rip, always paddle across it, not against it.
- How often do the big sets come? Can you handle that size wave?
- Where do the locals end their ride? Is there a dangerous end section they avoid?

Dangerous Creatures

Sharks are universally feared by surfers, but you are unlikely to see one, and attacks are even rarer. Avoid surfing in river mouths and be watchful around sunset. Other hazards include jellyfish, sting rays, blue ringed octopus and stone fish. Be watchful when surfing in on-shore winds which carry these stingers towards shore. For more details, see the section on Aquatic Life later in this chapter.

Be Prepared

- Travel with a simple first aid kit.
- Drink plenty of water before and after surfing to prevent dehydration
- Practise long swims before your trip to increase stamina.
- Swim between the flags on a patrolled beach where lifesavers are on duty.
- Stretch before and after each surf.

Make sure your board has no sharp edges – repair dings smoothly, sand sharp edges off your fins, use a rubber nose guard and most importantly attach a new leg rope before your trip.

Happy surfing!

Tides & Currents

Swimming in the sea can be hazardous along much of Africa's legendary coastline because of rips, strong currents and venomous marine creatures. If you're not a confident swimmer or you're not used to big waves, it's best to err on the side of caution.

Always ask around locally about currents, tides and other marine hazards like sharks and jellyfish – for more details on this, see the following section on Aquatic Life. Be especially wary of rips, as these strong currents are a common cause of beach drownings. A rip is where the water brought to the beach by breaking waves runs back out. It tends to take you out to sea, not down under the water.

Telltale signs of a rip current include colour (it may be darker than the water on either side), a rippled effect on the surface of the water and a trail of surf extending beyond the surf zone. Be warned that rips can be very difficult to spot, even if you're looking for them.

You also need to look out for side shore currents. These flow parallel to the shore and can wash you quite a way down the beach, where conditions may be less safe. Don't stray too far from the shore in this situation, and watch the shoreline to make sure you don't drift too far along. Swim in to the shore before you float too far away from your starting point.

Cramps

These are caused by a muscle going into spasm because of dehydration and alterations in blood flow or salt composition, often as a result of poor acclimatisation to the heat. You get a twinge at first, often in your calf, then the pain builds up and is only relieved when you stop using the muscle. Massaging and stretching the muscle, eg by pulling on your toes while straightening your leg, can help. Cramps can be very painful, and are potentially dangerous if you are in rough seas or you're a weak swimmer. Try to rest the muscle, then use it gently. Cramps can be caused by cold water, tiredness, overexertion or if you're unwell for any reason.

Prevent cramps by have a good warm-up before starting any activity. Remember to warm down too, and stretch before and after strenuous activity.

GETTING OUT OF A RIP

If you do get into a rip, you may feel yourself being dragged out to sea, or you may be sucked underwater if it passes through a rocky passage. To avoid getting into serious trouble, do the following:

- don't panic – this will tire you out quicker
- get out of the rip current by swimming parallel to the shore, then catching the waves back in; don't swim against the current, as you'll just exhaust yourself

If you are unsure of your swimming abilities and there are people on the beach, raise an arm above your head to indicate that you are in trouble, and tread water (you can stay afloat for a surprisingly long time) until you are rescued. Alternatively, you could try conserving your energy while you wait for rescue by allowing yourself to float motionless face down in the water, raising your head just when you need to take a breath.

AQUATIC LIFE

The rivers and oceans of Africa are home to a fascinating variety of creatures, some of which can be a danger to you. Learn to recognise and avoid the villains (see the following pages), but the risks are fairly small as long as you use a bit of common sense:

- seek out and heed advice on local dangers
- don't walk along reefs in shallow water

- don't go diving or snorkelling when the waters are murky (this may attract predators and you won't be able to see them coming)
- unless you're a marine biologist, don't touch or feed any creature you come across underwater

All things considered, you're probably best to avoid that midnight skinny dip on a tropical beach.

CORAL CUTS

Coral is sharp stuff, and if you brush against, it you're likely to get a scratch or graze, or a more severe laceration. It may not seem like much at the time, but the consequences of coral cuts can be as serious as those of much more impressive marine creature injuries. Coral wounds are notoriously troublesome because people rarely take care to clean them properly. Coral is covered in a layer of slime that is full of marine microorganisms, and small particles of coral, including its stinging cells, are often left in the wound, which can cause problems.

If you ignore a coral wound, there's a high chance it will get infected and develop into a sore that won't go away. It makes sense to deal promptly with any coral cut, however small it seems:

- rinse the wound with plenty of pure water (eg bottled water), perhaps using a small brush or a syringe (with or without the needle) to dislodge any small particles
- apply an antiseptic solution like povidone-iodine
- apply an antibiotic cream or powder (eg mupirocin 2%) to the area
- cover it with a dressing
- watch for signs of infection (p422)

You can cause irreparable damage to the coral when you come into contact with it, so it's mutually beneficial to avoid getting cut by coral in the first place. Try to avoid walking on or swimming over reefs, and maintain correct buoyancy and control when you're diving. It's a good rule never to put your hands or feet somewhere you can't see first. Always wear shoes in the water – flip flops (thongs) or sports sandals work well.

BITES

Sharks, crocs, electric rays (similar to sting rays – see later – but they discharge an electric current into you), eels (can inflict pretty severe bites), octopuses (can bite) and some fish (including weeverfish, surgeonfish and triggerfish) may be a risk if you get too close.

Even before *Jaws*, sharks had a very special place in the human psyche, and shark attack is probably most people's ultimate marine fear. Sharks occur in oceans worldwide, and the African coast is no exception. In general, it's not something you need to be especially concerned about, although you do need to take care in some areas. For example, the Mozambique Channel is notoriously shark-infested, and some beaches around Durban (South Africa) are netted because of the risk of sharks.

Ask around locally before you take the plunge. Obviously, it's best to avoid swimming in shark-infested waters. If you decide to swim in a risk area, here are some tips on avoiding trouble:

- don't swim or dive where fishermen are cleaning their catches (not an attractive option anyway)
- avoid swimming with an open wound
- be careful at dusk, as this is when sharks feed

In the unlikely event that you spot a shark, don't panic: try to move away slowly. Sharks have poor eyesight and are attracted by movement and smell.

Crocodiles

It has to be said, the chances of a traveller in Africa being attacked by one of these prehistoric creatures is fairly remote. Crocodiles in the Nile tend to spend most of their time lying motionless beside water holes or disguised as half-submerged logs, taking unsuspecting wildebeest by surprise.

Avoid becoming croc-fodder by asking around locally for reliable advice on risks, and keeping your wits about you if you are walking or camping near waterways or rafting on rivers.

Treatment

This is basic first aid:

- get out of the water
- stop any bleeding by applying pressure to the bleeding spots
- clean the wound with plenty of clean water and soap
- apply disinfectant and a sterile dressing
- get help for serious bites

STINGS

Many marine creatures use venom to protect themselves from attack or to kill their prey. Although most venoms have little or no effect on humans, there are some notable exceptions, which we've described in this section.

> ! Remember: most marine creatures are not aggressive – if you don't threaten them, most will leave you alone.

Sea Snakes

These beautiful creatures are found all along the African coast. They're often very inquisitive, although not usually aggressive. However, their venom is extremely toxic, so you should give them a wide berth. Symptoms of poisoning may not appear for several hours, and include anxiety and restlessness, dry throat, nausea and, eventually, paralysis.

Treatment

The casualty will need to get help urgently.
In the meantime:

- keep the casualty calm
- apply a pressure bandage (not a tourniquet)
- immobilise the limb by splinting it (this helps prevent the toxin from spreading)
- be ready to perform emergency resuscitation if necessary

Jellyfish

Despite their ethereal appearance, jellyfish (right) are carnivorous animals. They are distributed widely, and occur in all tropical and subtropical waters. Jellyfish catch their prey by discharging venom into it from special stinging cells called nematocysts. Most jellyfish stings are just uncomfortable, but a couple of species are capable of causing severe, potentially lethal stings. In general, stings on thick skin like the soles of your feet are less likely to blister and cause other problems. Note that children are more likely to suffer a severe reaction.

Sea lice, also called sea bather's eruption, are thought to be the tiny larvae of thimble jellyfish. They can be a problem in any tropical waters. They sting and cause an uncomfortable rash, especially if they get caught in your swimming suit. Shower thoroughly after getting out of the sea. Calamine lotion may relieve the pain.

The jellyfish you really want to look out for are the Portuguese man-of-war (below) and various species of the box jellyfish (sea wasp). Both of these occur widely throughout tropical waters. Dead man-of-wars are often washed up on shore and they may still be able to sting, so don't touch any jellyfish on the beach. Box jellyfish often go unnoticed until it's too late. They wrap their tentacles, which look like whitish strings, around you, leaving multiple interlacing whiplash marks where you were stung.

Box jellyfish stings are excruciatingly painful, and can be lethal, although an antivenin is available. Man-of-war stings feel like a severe burn, and can produce general symptoms including nausea, vomiting and muscle pains. Rarely, man-of-war stings can result in breathing difficulties and collapse.

Treatment

Treat jellyfish stings as follows:

- get out of the water
- remove any bits of tentacle with tweezers or a gloved hand
- pour vinegar on the affected area (this doesn't help the pain, but it will prevent stinging cells left in the wound from firing)
- man-of-war sting – put ice packs or local anaesthetic sprays, creams or ointments to help relieve the pain; strong painkilling injections may be needed
- seek medical advice for severe stings, as antivenin may be available
- be prepared to start emergency resuscitation if necessary – see inside backcover
- Don't wash the sting with water or rub it, as it may make the pain worse.

Sting Rays & Other Venomous Fish

Most venomous fish, such as sting rays, (right) stonefish, scorpionfish and weeverfish, are found in salt water. Sting rays are widespread throughout tropical and subtropical waters. They're not aggressive but because they like to lie half-submerged in mud or sand in the shallows, you could step on one accidentally. The tail itself can cause a nasty ragged wound, but they also have venomous spines which can sometimes be fatal.

Stonefish (right below) and scorpionfish (butterfly cod) (opposite page) occur in the Indian Ocean. Stonefish are reef dwellers they also skulk in the shallows of estuaries. They have the dubious distinction of being the most dangerous of all venomous fish. Both stonefish and scorpionfish have sharp dorsal spines through which they inject a venom.

Stonefish are as ugly as scorpionfish are beautiful, and they are masters of disguise: they lie half-submerged in sand, mud or coral debris, looking exactly like (you guessed it) a stone. As with sting rays, the

danger is stepping on one accidentally. Stonefish stings are extremely painful, and may lead to collapse and coma. There is a stonefish antivenin which should be given as soon as possible after the sting. Scorpionfish are much easier to avoid, as they are distinctive and easily recognised, and the chances of you being stung by one are pretty remote. There's no antivenin available.

! Always shuffle along when in the shallows to give sting rays and other creatures a chance to get out of your way.

Treatment

Hot (nonscalding) water can help to break down the toxins and is surprisingly effective at relieving pain. For any sting from a venomous fish:

- if any spines are poking out, try to remove them gently (be sure to protect your own hands)

- wash any surface venom off with water

- bathe the wound in hot (nonscalding) water for up to 90 minutes or until the pain has gone, or apply hot packs

- if the pain is very severe, strong injected painkillers or a local anaesthetic injection may be needed

- wash the wound thoroughly once the pain is under control and apply a clean dressing

- rest with the limb raised

- seek medical help for antivenin if necessary, eg for a stonefish sting

Blue-Ringed Octopus

This surprisingly deadly creature is found in tropical waters of the Indian Ocean and elsewhere. At low tide they can be found in rock pools, and if you don't realise what they are, you may pick them up. They are surprisingly small, varying in size from 2 to 20cm. The ringed marks, normally yellowish brown, turn a bright blue when the octopus is angry. Bites can cause paralysis and possibly death.

Treatment

You must get help urgently. While you are waiting:

■ wash out the wound with any water or antiseptic available

■ apply a pressure bandage to the affected limb and immobilise it
(to prevent the poison from
entering the circulation)

Cone Shell (right)

However pretty a shell
looks, it makes sense not
to pick it up, especially if
you don't know what it is.
Fish-eating cones, which are
found in the tropical waters of the Indian Ocean, kill their prey
by harpooning them with a poisonous barb, which has been
known to cause death in humans. The pain from a sting can
be excruciating, and can be followed very quickly by paralysis.
Treatment is as for blue-ringed octopus bite, with pressure
bandaging and immobilisation.

Crown of Thorns

These impressive reef creatures are a hazard if you tread on
them by accident or brush against them while diving. They
inject venom from the base of their spines, which can break off
and remain embedded in you. If the spines are not removed,
they can cause pain, swelling and generally make you feel
unwell for several weeks or months.

Remove any spines you can see, making sure not to break
them. Immerse the affected area in hot (nonscalding) water,
which will help ease the pain, then immobilise the limb. Seek
medical advice as soon as possible.

Sea Urchins & Other Stingers

Avoid stepping on sea urchins, as their spines can be painful,
especially if they become embedded in the wound, as is quite
likely. Some species can be poisonous, resulting in paralysis
and breathing difficulties. Sometimes you can get an itchy
skin rash for several months after. If you do step on one,

remove any spines you can, taking care not to break them off. Run hot (nonscalding) water over the wound. Applying meat tenderiser, made from the flesh of the paw paw fruit, to the area may be helpful. Keep a careful lookout for breathing difficulties – seek medical help immediately if these develop.

Various other marine creatures can cause problems if you come into contact with them. Some sponges can cause severe itching, fire coral or feathery stinging hydroid can cause a painful sting and prolonged itching, and anemones can also give you a painful sting, so don't put inquisitive fingers on their tentacles.

SCUBA DIVING

Africa offers one of the top diving destinations in the world – the Red Sea – as well as other less well known sites such as around the Cape in South Africa, Tunisia, and Senegal. If you're a first-timer, bear in mind that diving safely needs some knowledge and care.

It's absolutely vital that you have specific diver insurance that covers evacuation to a hospital or recompression chamber and subsequent treatment, something that will otherwise cost you thousands of dollars. Divers Alert Network (DAN – see the boxed text for details) offers this, as do some other organisations (like PADI). Note that some dive operators won't let you dive unless you have this insurance. If you do get into an emergency situation, you should contact your insurer as soon as possible.

You should always make sure you know where the nearest hyperbaric chamber is, especially if you are planning on diving somewhere remote – DAN is a good source of information on this.

DIVING CERTIFICATE & MEDICAL CHECK-UP

If you want to dive, you're going to need a diving certificate issued by a major diving organisation (PADI, NAUI etc) – it's a bit like a driving licence when you're hiring a car. To get a certificate, you need to complete a diving course. You can either do this before you go or at a dive centre in Africa (eg many of the Red Sea resorts offer low-cost courses). Once you've got your diver's card, you can dive anywhere you want.

As a prerequisite to doing a course, you need to have a diving medical check-up to show that you are fit to dive. Some dive centres may just want you to fill in a questionnaire, but ideally you should get a proper medical check-up before you leave. Age is no barrier in itself, but conditions that may make diving unsuitable for you are heart or lung disease (including asthma), ear or sinus problems, and any fits or dizzy spells.

DIVERS ALERT NETWORK (DAN)

DAN is an international nonprofit organisation providing expert medical information and advice for the benefit of the diving public. It operates a 24 hour diving emergency hotline in the US at ☎ 919-684-8111; alternatively, ☎ 919-684-4DAN (4326) accepts collect calls in a dive emergency. DAN Southern Africa can be contacted toll-free (from within South Africa) on ☎ 0800-020 1111; or from outside South Africa on ☎ 27-11-254-1112, fax 27-11-254-1993 email mail@dansa.org.

DAN does not directly provide medical care, but it does provide advice on early treatment, evacuation and hyperbaric treatment of diving-related injuries.

For general queries and information about diving health and safety, contact DAN in the US on ☎ 919-684-2948 (or toll-free ☎ 800-446-2671 from within North America) or check out its web site (www.diversalertnetwork.org).

INFORMATION SOURCES

If you contact DAN, staff will be able to answer any specific diving-related health queries you may have.

You'll find lots of good books on all aspects of diving, including health and safety. Some recommended titles include

Encyclopaedia of Recreational Diving, a basic text produced by PADI; and *The Diver's Handbook* by Alan Mountain, which is a comprehensive, well thought-out guide covering most aspects of diving. Another good book is *Scuba Diving Explained – Questions and Answers on Physiology and Medical Aspects of Diving* by Martin Lawrence.

DIVING SAFELY

Basic rules for safe diving are:

- don't dive if you're feeling physically or mentally below par
- avoid going in if you are uncertain about the water or weather conditions
- check rental equipment carefully before using it
- never dive after taking alcohol or mind-altering substances
- always follow your dive leader's instructions – but be aware that there are good and less good divemasters; ask around beforehand
- be aware of your limitations and stick within them
- never dive in murky water – you won't be able to see and avoid hazards
- stop diving if you feel cold or tired, even if it's not the end of the dive
- try not to panic if you find yourself in difficulties – instead, take some slow deep breaths and think through what you need to do
- avoid touching or picking up things underwater – they may be harmful to you and you may cause harm to a fragile environment

DECOMPRESSION SICKNESS

Also known as the 'bends', decompression sickness is probably the best known hazard of diving. It's also one of the most serious, so you should make sure you know what it is and how to avoid it.

Breathing air under pressure (when you're diving) forces quantities of nitrogen (a major component of air) to dissolve in your blood and body tissues. If the pressure is later released too quickly (eg you ascend too fast), nitrogen can't be eliminated in the usual way and bubbles of gas form in the blood stream and body tissue.

Symptoms depend on where the bubbles are. Bubbles in the bloodstream can block circulation and cause stroke-like symptoms, eg blackouts and weakness of one side of the body. The most common form of decompression sickness is where bubbles form in large joints (joint bends) like the shoulder and elbow, giving you pain that increases to a peak some hours after the dive, then gradually subsides. Skin bends can occur, giving you itches and a rash over your body. In spinal bends, you get back pain that typically circles your abdomen, followed by pins and needles in your legs, unsteadiness and paralysis. Inner ear bends make you dizzy and unable to balance.

Treatment of the bends is by recompression in a hyperbaric chamber, which causes any bubbles to dissolve again, followed by slow, controlled decompression. This allows all the dissolved nitrogen to be eliminated without forming bubbles. Treatment is usually effective but you need to get to a recompression chamber as soon as possible, because any delay could result in further damage which may be irreversible.

You can never guarantee that you won't get the bends, but you can do a lot to make it very unlikely. Dive tables are available to give you guidance on safe dives but they obviously don't take your individual condition into account.

! Never dive if you are feeling unwell in any way, avoid strenuous activity before you dive, and drink plenty of fluids to prevent dehydration.

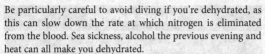

Be particularly careful to avoid diving if you're dehydrated, as this can slow down the rate at which nitrogen is eliminated from the blood. Sea sickness, alcohol the previous evening and heat can all make you dehydrated.

Nitrogen build-up can be a problem if you're on a diving holiday, doing multiple dives a day or diving on consecutive days, and is the most common cause of decompression sickness at diving resorts. Taking a day off can allow any nitrogen that has built up to be eliminated.

NITROGEN NARCOSIS

Also known as 'rapture of the depths', this occurs below depths of about 30 to 40m, and is due to the build-up of nitrogen in the blood to levels at which it has toxic effects on the brain. Symptoms can be quite frightening, and include a feeling of detachment from reality and apprehension, sometimes leading to panic. In addition, your thought processes slow down and you lose your concentration. Symptoms clear if you ascend 5 to 10m. Nitrogen narcosis is one reason why it is vital for divers to be on the lookout for signs in other members of the team, and to be familiar with an emergency drill for this situation.

BAROTRAUMA

The increased ambient pressure underwater can cause problems if pressure is not equalised within various air-filled cavities in the body, including the lungs, ears, sinuses, teeth cavities and gut. Lung barotrauma is a very serious condition, often caused by not breathing out on ascent from a dive. Symptoms are variable but include chest pain, dizziness and unconsciousness. Treatment is by recompression in a hyperbaric chamber.

Ear and sinus pain can be quite severe, and you should avoid diving if you have a middle ear infection (see p183), sinus trouble, a cold or hay fever. If you get dental pain while diving, it may be due to cavities in your teeth (eg dental decay), and you should see a dentist as soon as is convenient.

DIVING & FLYING

If you fly too soon after diving – even a single dive – you can get decompression sickness, as the cabin pressure is set to a lower level than the pressure at sea level, which encourages nitrogen bubbles to form. If you are planning to dive before you fly, discuss it with a reliable diving instructor, but basic guidelines are as follows:

- don't fly within 12 hours of a single no decompression-stop dive (ie you didn't need to stop or descend to relieve pressure effects) and not within 24 hours of multiple no-decompression-stop dives
- wait 24 to 48 hours before flying after any dive which required decompression stops
- if you required recompression therapy, you need a medical certificate to say you are fit to fly

DIVING & ANTIMALARIALS

If you're taking mefloquine (Lariam) for protection against malaria, you need to be aware that diving isn't recommended while you are taking it. This is because mefloquine can cause dizziness and balance problems, especially in the first few weeks of taking it, and it can make fits more likely in susceptible people. If you are planning on going diving and need to take antimalarials, mention this to your doctor before you leave so you can be prescribed an alternative if necessary.

Bites & Stings...

Bites and stings from insects and other small beasties are the most likely hazard you face travelling in Africa. In contrast, you're much less likely to be at risk from higher profile dangers like lions and snakes.

FLYING INSECTS

➕ For the complete low-down on preventing insect bites, see p88.

MOSQUITOES

These bloodsuckers are likely to pose more of a hazard to your health – and sanity – than all the rest of the biters and stingers discussed in this chapter. Mosquitoes have an astonishingly important role in the health of people in tropical and subtropical regions of the world, mainly because they are carriers for serious diseases like malaria (p41), dengue (p132), yellow fever (p135) and lymphatic filariasis (p227).

It's not just the diseases mosquitoes carry; their bites itch like mad and you run the very real risk of infection if you scratch them open. Insects inject a small amount of saliva when they bite and this sets up a local reaction. Bites are usually more troublesome when you first arrive but, in theory at least, you develop a measure of immunity to the itch with time. If you're particularly sensitive to insect bites (women often are), they can develop into quite large swellings with a blister in the centre.

If your guard drops and you get bitten, try not to scratch – if you break the skin, the bite is likely to get infected. How you stop the itch from bites is one of those hotly debated questions that every traveller has an opinion on. Tried and tested options include calamine cream, tea tree lotion, lavender oil or hydrocortisone cream. Antihistamine creams or sprays are widely available without a prescription but are probably best avoided – they're no better than calamine and can cause an allergic skin reaction, which makes the problem worse. If the itching is driving you mad, try taking an antihistamine tablet.

SANDFLIES

Sandflies are tiny (2 to 3mm long) flies found throughout the drier parts of Africa, as well as other parts of the world. They cause painful and later itchy bites, and are responsible for transmitting a parasitic disease called leishmaniasis (see p224) and a viral infection, sandfly fever.

Sandflies breed in dark, moist habitats (eg cracks in walls, caves and long drops). They have a short flight range and don't fly very high, eg they rarely bite people sleeping on the 1st floor of a building. They usually bite at dawn, dusk and during darkness.

Because they are small, they can get through most standard mosquito netting. You can get special sandfly netting but this will probably be too suffocating for most people. A permethrin-treated net is effective at keeping sandflies out. Use insect repellents with DEET on any exposed skin to prevent bites.

Sandfly Fever

This viral disease can be transmitted through the bite of an infected sandfly, so is a possibility wherever there are sandflies. Symptoms appear three to four days after a bite and include fever, chills, headache, joint pains, backache, nausea and vomiting, and sore throat. It generally clears up spontaneously without any specific treatment, usually within a few days.

TSETSE FLIES

Tsetse flies feed on the blood of humans and animals and are found only in Africa between the 15th parallels north and south (ie sub-Saharan tropica

Africa). They tend to like vegetation along waterways and lakes (West and Central Africa), as well as savanna (East Africa). Tsetse flies have been called the 'shield of Africa', as they are the reason many areas have remained forested and unsuitable for cattle ranching (tsetse flies breed on the undersurface of trees).

The tsetse fly is large (6 to 15mm long), about twice the size of an ordinary housefly, and has a distinctive scissor-like way of folding its wings. It bites during the day and is attracted to moving vehicles and the colour dark blue. Its bites are painful. Cover up and use insect repellent on any exposed skin. If you can bear to, close all the windows of your vehicle and use an insect spray.

Sleeping Sickness (Trypanosomiasis)

This disease is caused by a parasite (Trypanosome) transmitted to humans by the tsetse fly. You're at risk of it if you travel in rural areas, especially near rivers and lakes in West and Central Africa, and on safari in reserves and national parks in East Africa. There's little risk in urban areas. There is no vaccine against sleeping sickness.

There are two forms of the disease caused by different varieties of the parasite: Trypanosome brucei gambiense in West and Central Africa and Trypanosome brucei rhodiense in eastern and southern Africa. The symptoms are similar in both, although the West African variety tends to be more insidious, progressing gradually over a number of years, whereas the East African variety seems more sudden and dramatic, unfolding over a matter of weeks or months. In spite of its name, the disease doesn't always cause sleepiness.

Soon after the bite you get a red swelling at the puncture site that can last for several weeks. In the early stages of the disease (starting about one to three weeks after the bite) you get recurring episodes of high fever, weakness, headache and joint pains, possibly with enlargement of the lymph glands and itchy skin rashes.

As the disease progresses, complications such as anaemia, inflammation of the heart and kidney failure can occur. In the final stage of the disease the brain is affected. Sufferers show behavioural and personality changes and have sudden mood swings, extreme lethargy with periods of unconsciousness and insomnia at night and, finally, they fall into a coma (deep unconsciousness) and die.

Sleeping sickness can be diagnosed by special blood tests. Because the symptoms, are nonspecific, especially in the early stages, it can be difficult to distinguish sleeping sickness from malaria, flu, glandular fever and mind disorders. Effective drug treatment is available, so long as the disease is not too far advanced, but it's extremely unlikely that it would reach this stage in you. If you have a fever and think you have been at risk of tsetse fly bites, seek medical advice – and remember that it could be malaria.

BLACKFLIES

These small flies live and breed near rivers and cause itchy bites. In sub-Saharan Africa, blackflies transmit an important disease, river blindness. They're yet another reason to cover up and use insect repellent.

River Blindness (Onchocerciasis)

About 18 million people suffer from this parasitic disease, 99% of whom live in tropical Africa. Apart from the cost in terms of human suffering, there is a high socio-economic cost as fertile river valleys, where the flies breed, have to be abandoned because of the disease they carry. However, this disease is not expected to be a public health problem in Africa for much longer, as two large control programs have had success in eliminating it in the worst affected areas. In Kenya, for example, it has been completely eradicated, except for a small focus area on the Ugandan border.

Although it is best known as a cause of blindness, this disease actually causes more problems in the skin. It's a result of infection by a parasitic worm, spread via blackflies. The blackfly larvae spread under the skin and cause an intensely itchy reaction – so much so that it has been known to lead to suicide. With heavy, repeated infections, larvae enter the eye, eventually leading to blindness.

Treatment is with a drug called ivermectin, which effectively sterilises the parasites, preventing them from producing larvae.

Preventing insect bites will protect you from this disease, and you should avoid camping close to rivers. You may get a mild infection, with some itchiness, but you're extremely unlikely to get any eye consequences (early symptoms are redness, irritation and watering). If you think you may be infected, seek medical attention.

OTHER BLOODSUCKERS

LEECHES

Leeches are a common hazard in most damp, forested areas, which includes a lot of Africa. They don't transmit any diseases but their bites can get infected if you don't keep them clean.

Leeches can be landlubbers (particularly during monsoon conditions) or swimmers (in fresh water), and vary in size but are usually about a couple of centimetres long. They look like thin black worms before they fill up with your blood. Be warned – there's something about leeches that can reduce even the most tranquil nature lover to a state of blind hysteria.

They can drop into your boots or find gaps in your clothing as you pass through, or they can attach themselves to you if you swim in infested waters. Leeches usually attach themselves to your skin but have been known to reach the inside of the nose, lungs and bladder (don't even think about it).

Avoid getting grossed out by leeches by:

- checking all over for them if you've been walking in infested areas
- avoiding swimming in rainforest pools or streams
- using insect repellent (containing DEET) to discourage them
- tucking your trousers into your socks or wearing gaiters to prevent leeches dropping down your boots
- considering soaking your clothes in permethrin, an insect repellent

Once a leech has attached itself to you, it produces a substance which prevents the blood clotting where it has bitten and then it drinks its fill. A leech can suck up to 10 times its weight in blood within half an hour and drops off when it's full. Leech bites cause only minor irritation and don't spread any disease, but it can take a while for the bleeding to stop and there's a risk of secondary infection.

Although leeches will 'let go of you' spontaneously if you leave them, unless you have nerves of steel, you'll probably want to remove them before this. Try not to pull them off in a state of panic. If you do this, they may leave their mouthparts behind, which makes infection more likely.

Tried and tested methods for getting leeches to drop off include applying vinegar, salt or – cruel but possibly the simplest – putting a lighted match to their unattached end.

After the leech has dropped off, clean the wound carefully with antiseptic and apply pressure to stop the bleeding. It can take some time – keep applying a steady pressure, raise your limb and don't keep removing the bandage to see if the bleeding has stopped.

TICKS & MITES

The problem with these little biters is that they transmit a surprising number of rather peculiar diseases. You'll want to do your best to avoid contact with them, although you're generally at low risk of these diseases. Illnesses can be spread directly via bites, body fluids of the creature or through inhaling their faeces in dust.

Ticks and mites occur worldwide and like woodland, scrub and long grass, where they hang around waiting for a meal to pass through. They are basically animal parasites and are found on animals and in places animals live. You often don't notice them until you get undressed. Ticks tend to be slow feeders and can remain attached, unnoticed by you, for some time.

The following precautions are sensible:

- seek reliable local advice on likely problem areas
  (usually scrubland or pastures with long grass)
- wear long trousers and boots, and tuck your trousers into your boots
- use insect repellent (containing DEET) on any exposed areas and
  consider soaking your clothes in the insect repellent permethrin if
  you are planning a trek in tick or mite country
- check your body regularly all over for ticks and mites
  if you have been walking in infested areas
- use a sleeping net at night and sleep as
  high off the ground as possible
- remember that animals may be a source
  of ticks, so avoid close contact

If you find a tick attached to you, resist
the impulse to pull it off directly, as
its body will just separate from the
mouthpiece, which makes infection
much more likely. Remember
that tick body fluids can transmit
infection, so avoid handling it with
your bare hands as much as possible.
If you do, remember to wash your
hands thoroughly soon afterwards.

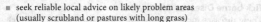

The idea is to induce the tick to
let go – various methods have been
advocated in the past, including burning the tick off or applying
chemicals to it, but these are no longer recommended, as they
can be harmful to you and may make the tick's contents more
likely to contaminate you.

The most effective and safest method of removing a tick is to
use a pair of tweezers to grasp the head (not the body, or this
will squeeze the contents into the wound and make matters
worse) and pull gently. After the tick has dropped off, clean
the wound thoroughly and apply an antiseptic solution like
povidone-iodine. If tick parts get left behind, try scraping them
out (under sterile conditions as far as possible) or get medical
help to do this.

Tick-borne Diseases

These diseases include various tick fevers (including Q fever), tick paralysis, Crimean-Congo haemorrhagic fever, Lyme disease and typhus. You'd be pretty unlucky to get any of them, but they are a possibility if you've been trekking or camping in tick-infested areas. If you get sick after you've been bitten by a tick or mite, it's sensible to seek medical advice.

Some tick-borne diseases like Lyme disease can cause long-term problems, including arthritis and meningitis, but they can be treated effectively with antibiotics if they're caught early enough. Most tick-borne diseases cause a skin rash, fever (often relapsing, ie it seems to go away but it keeps reappearing), headache, vomiting, tiredness and aching muscles and joints. Tick paralysis is extremely rare but if you experience any breathing difficulties after a tick bite, seek medical help immediately.

If you think you may have been at risk of tick bites, seek medical attention if you develop any of the following:

- red skin rash spreading from the initial bite, fever, headache, muscle and joint pains
- neck stiffness
- deterioration and collapse – this is an emergency

African Tick Typhus

There are several different varieties of typhus, which can be spread by ticks, lice and mites. The different varieties all cause a similar disease but differ in severity. There are no vaccines against any form of typhus, but they respond rapidly to appropriate antibiotic treatment, without any long-term effects.

African tick typhus is transmitted by a type of tick found on rodents, and travellers sometimes get it if they've been on safari. It's generally a mild disease. You get a swelling at the site of the tick bite which enlarges and later forms a black scarred area. Anything from four days to two weeks after the bite you get fever, headache and swelling of the glands near the bite. You also often get a skin rash that spreads over your body.

The fever usually lasts a few days only. The illness is usually too mild to need any specific treatment but antibiotics (usually tetracycline) are effective if necessary.

FLEAS

These can be a problem in low-budget accommodation. Neither human nor animal fleas can live on you but they do like to visit for a meal. You may notice itchy bites, usually in groups around the ankles or at the edges of clothing, and secondary infection is common. Kill the fleas with an insecticide and wash yourself and your clothes. Find another hotel if you can.

Although fleas are widespread, they very rarely cause disease. However, as every self-respecting hypochondriac knows, fleas are capable of transmitting at least one serious disease – plague. The other disease it's certain fleas can transmit is a type of typhus. Both diseases are extremely rare and no cases of plague have ever been reported in travellers.

Plague

It's worth knowing a bit about this most famous of diseases, not because you're likely to get it but because outbreaks always receive a huge amount of publicity.

Plague is the Black Death of medieval Europe. It's caused by a bacterial microorganism that primarily infects rodents and is transmitted to humans via the bite of certain species of flea that live on the rodents. You can also get it by direct contact with infected animals and by droplet spread (via coughs and sneezes) from an infected person. The dry summer months encourage the spread of the disease and the occurrence of epidemics.

Plague is reported in a few countries in the region, including Angola, Democratic Republic of Congo, Kenya, Madagascar, Mozambique, Tanzania, Uganda and Zimbabwe, and occasional outbreaks occur. A vaccine is available but it's only indicated for people like zoologists who might be at high risk of infection. As a traveller, even to affected areas, you're at a minuscule risk of infection.

Plague is essentially a disease of poor living conditions, so you are unlikely to be at risk under normal circumstances. You're most at risk if you're a naturalist handling animals, or a hunter or camper in affected areas. Sensible precautions in these circumstances are:

- avoid handling live or dead rodents (including rats, rabbits and squirrels)
- use insect repellents to prevent flea bites
- avoid flea-infested hang-outs

The disease occurs quite soon after the infecting bite or contact (two to seven days), with a sudden onset of high fever, severe headache, chills and muscular pains, with pain in the groin or armpit (from inflamed lymph nodes called bubos, hence the name 'bubonic plague'). Untreated, the illness progresses rapidly, and sufferers are highly contagious. Your chances of dying from untreated plague are high – 60 to 65% – but it's very unlikely to get to this stage. If caught early, treatment with antibiotics (ideally streptomycin or tetracycline) is very effective. If you think you may have plague, you should seek medical advice as soon as possible.

VENOMOUS STINGS & BITES

BEES, WASPS & ANTS

Most stings are not dangerous – they're just painful. Children often get stung, especially if they're eating outdoors.

Rarely you can have a severe allergic reaction to stings, which is a medical emergency. If you know that you are allergic to stings, you should take an emergency kit with you containing antihistamines and adrenaline to be used if you are stung – discuss this with your doctor before you leave.

Bee, wasp and ant stings puncture the skin; bees leave their stings behind but wasps usually don't. If the sting is still visible, remove it with a pair of tweezers. You can relieve the pain and swelling with an ice pack or a cloth soaked in cold water. A sting relief spray (eg aluminium sulphate), calamine lotion tea tree or lavender oils can also be soothing. If the sting is in the mouth or throat, try to remove it and suck on an ice cube before seeking medical help.

STINGS – WHEN TO WORRY

You should seek medical help in the following situations:

- if you've been stung in the mouth or throat, especially if the area swells rapidly
- if you get rapid swelling from a sting anywhere
- if the sting is followed by breathing difficulties or signs of shock – rapid pulse; pale, clammy skin; breathlessness; sweating; or faintness

In an emergency, such as a severe allergic reaction, and no medical help is immediately available, treatment is as follows:

- lie flat, with your feet elevated
- give adrenaline injection (1 in 1000) 0.3mL into the top of your arm or thigh
- get medical help urgently

SCORPIONS

These fascinating creatures are found throughout the tropics and subtropics, especially in dry desert areas. Scorpions grip their prey with their front pincers, finishing them off by injecting a poison through their tail.

Before you get too alarmed, most scorpion stings are just painful. Some species, including a couple found in North and southern Africa, are dangerous to humans. These can cause severe poisoning, heralded by vomiting, sweating, breathing difficulties, muscle spasms and abdominal pain. Your best bet is to seek advice locally on the risks.

Scorpions are nocturnal creatures, so you're very unlikely to see them, but sensible precautions are:

- always check your shoes before putting them on in the morning if you are camping out
- take care when lifting or moving rocks
- if you're camping, clear your camp site of rocks and other debris

SPIDERS

If you come from a temperate clime where spiders are horrid rather than life-threatening, it can come as a nasty shock to find that not only can some spiders bite, they can also be lethal. However, you should remember that although most spiders are venomous, only a few have powerful enough jaws (yuck!) to penetrate human skin and cause you harm. Orb web spiders, often exquisitely patterned, aren't generally harmful to you.

The black widow is probably the most notorious venomous spider and is found in most warm areas of the world. Only the female bites. The female black widow is black, about 25mm long, and has a distinctive red hourglass shape on the underside of her abdomen. Unfortunately, it seems these spiders have taken a liking to humans and tend to live in and around human habitation, hanging upside down from a hammock of web.

Bites can cause severe pain, followed by headache, vomiting, muscle spasms, breathing difficulties and coma. If you get bitten, immobilise the limb and apply a compression bandage (not a tourniquet) to prevent the venom from spreading while you seek medical help. Antivenin should be available locally, and you may need local anaesthetic in the wound or injected painkillers for the pain.

SNAKES

It should be said that Africa does boast a pretty impressive selection of venomous snakes. However, these are generally a small risk to you, although snake bites are an important cause of illness and death in local people, especially in rural areas. Just be wary of where you're putting your feet, especially if you're going to be camping or trekking in rural areas.

Snakes use venom, injected through their fangs, to immobilise their prey so they can swallow it. Although they're unlikely to want to contemplate swallowing you, if provoked they may bite – or spit – in self defence. However, even bites from venomous snakes don't always inject enough venom to be dangerous.

Snakes to be wary of in Africa include several species of viper (tree vipers, desert vipers, night adders, puff adders and saw-scaled vipers), cobras and mambas, molevipers and two particularly deadly varieties, the boomslang and the African bird-snake. The black mamba (about 2.5m long, green but with a black mouth lining; likes open bushland) is probably the most feared snake in Africa, mainly because of its apparently aggressive behaviour: when threatened, the mamba strikes violently, raising its body off the ground. African spitting cobras can project their venom a surprising distance, aiming for the eyes of their victim. If you do get struck in the eyes by cobra venom, seek medical help urgently, as there is a risk of permanent damage to your eyesight through secondary infection.

Venoms can cause local effects around the bite or general effects (like uncontrolled bleeding) and even death. Don't be too alarmed, though, as effective antidotes to snake bites are generally available in high risk areas.

Prevention

It obviously makes sense to avoid getting bitten in the first place:

- never handle, threaten or chase after a snake
- wear socks and strong boots if you are walking through grasslands or undergrowth, and give snakes plenty of chance to hear you coming
- use a torch if you are walking at night in rural, snake-infested areas
- be careful if you're climbing foliage-covered rocks or trees or swimming in lakes or rivers surrounded by thick vegetation
- take care if you're collecting firewood or moving logs, boulders or other debris, as these may shelter sleeping snakes

MORE BITES & STINGS

We're not trying to make you paranoid, but there are some fascinating little beasties to be found in Africa, some of which you'd be wise to give a wide berth.

The blister beetle, for example. These beetles are found worldwide, especially in warm, dry climates. They're about an inch long, with slender bodies encased in shiny green or blue wing cases. If you touch one or one gets crushed on your skin (or blown into your eye), it causes a burning sensation like a nettle sting and later a blister. Calamine cream can help soothe the irritation, which usually clears up in a matter of hours. Cantharidin, the irritant substance produced by the beetles, was used as a medicine for over 2000 years to treat various ailments, including bladder troubles, warts and impotence. It's extremely poisonous if taken internally.

You probably won't want to get in the way of a column of army (also called safari or driver) ants either. These tiny predators move in large groups, devouring insects and other larvae primarily, although they will also eat other creatures. If you get in their way, they can inflict painful bites and draw blood. If you get bitten, clean the wound thoroughly and apply antiseptic to prevent infection.

Fuzzy caterpillars are best avoided, as they can cause an irritant rash with swelling and blistering. If you do get stung, try to remove all hairs by using a piece of sticky tape. Ice may help soothe the irritation. If the hairs get in your eyes, they can cause conjunctivitis.

Treatment

If you or someone with you is bitten by a snake:

- reassure the casualty and try to keep them calm – they will probably be very frightened, and movement encourages the venom to spread
- immobilise the bitten limb with a sling or splint (see p435 in the first aid appendix) – this helps prevent the venom from being absorbed
- pressure bandaging, which is useful and safe in Australia for snake bites, is probably best avoided in Africa, as it may worsen the damage caused by viper and cobra bites
- seek medical help urgently to get antivenin treatment and other supportive measures
- make a note of what the snake looked like but don't endanger yourself and others by trying to catch it
- watch for signs of shock and breathing difficulty and be prepared to start emergency resuscitation if necessary

! Note that traditional first aid methods like cutting into the bite and sucking the poison out or applying tourniquets are potentially dangerous and you should avoid them, whatever you are told locally.

Antivenins are antibodies from horses or sheep. Although they are very effective at preventing the harmful effects of snake venom, antivenins can cause severe allergic reactions in some people. This means that they should not be given without medical supervision except in extreme emergency.

ANIMAL BITES

You may be at risk of bites from dogs in rural and urban areas. Monkeys in safaris and national parks can be very aggressive. Animal bites are important because they carry a high risk of secondary bacterial infection (mouths harbour many bacteria and animals don't brush their teeth) and a risk of rabies, a fatal disease.

! Note that human bites are potentially as dangerous as animal bites from an infection point of view – they must be cleaned thoroughly and you'll need antibiotics to prevent infection.

ONCE BITTEN...

Travelling in Africa, especially if you are going to rural areas, inevitably means meeting the local wildlife on some level. Some simple rules will keep you (relatively) safe. In general, approach any wild creature with respect, or better still don't approach it at all. You don't know it and it doesn't know you! Avoid contact, and only walk in the bush with an experienced accredited guide.

The megavertebrates – all the big stuff like lions, elephants and buffalo – are best regarded as not people-friendly, whatever you may have seen in films or on TV. For most animals, if you meet face to face, the No 1 rule is: do not run away. Stand still and in most cases the animal concerned – lion, elephant, antelope – will not follow through on a charge. Most animals will be as keen to avoid physical contact as you are. This is generally as true of the meat eaters as it is of any other animals. In fact you are probably more likely to be injured or killed by the grazers and browsers.

Hippos can be very dangerous if startled at night on their nocturnal grazing expeditions away from water, although they are unlikely to trample your tent if you are camping. If you're boating or doing any water sports on rivers, you're probably more at risk from hippos than from crocodiles but again, if you are travelling with an experienced guide, the risk of attack by either are very slight.

Elephants generally present little threat, provided that you don't divide a family group, particularly a mother with young. An elephant charge is rarely followed through to the point of impact. The curious elephant that comes to check out you or your vehicle is of less threat than the animal you hadn't seen and suddenly come upon. Avoid surprise where possible. Don't make loud noises or sudden movements if a wild animal is close by. Move slowly and deliberately. Few animals will deliberately seek you out. Most will move away as you cross that invisible line that defines their 'comfort zone' in the face of the unknown or uncertain. There are exceptions, however: old bull African buffalo are notorious for not following the rules. Solitary and aggressive, they appear to subscribe to the idea that attack is the best form of defence. If you are on foot your guide will probably carry a gun – principally in case of buffalo attack.Enjoy the view but don't mess with it.

Peter Stroud (Curator of Animals, Melbourne Zoo, Australia)

RABIES

Rabies is a disease caused by a virus found in the saliva of infected animals. It's transmitted to humans by bites but also potentially by contact between animal saliva and an open cut or graze on your skin. Rabies occurs throughout Africa, although it is less of a problem here than say, in India.

How You Get Rabies

Practically any warm-blooded animal can be infected, although infected dogs and monkeys are probably the greatest risk to you as a traveller in Africa. Other potentially infected animals include rats, bats, cats, foxes and wolves. Note that you can get rabies from bats by inhaling infected bat faeces, eg if you are going caving. Domestic pets are less likely to be infected but you can't assume they are risk-free.

You can't get rabies from touching an infected animal. You can get it from a bite (ie your skin is punctured) or if an infected animal licks a cut or graze on your skin. Rabid dogs may not show any signs of illness when they bite you, although if they do, they usually rush around, biting things and people at random and salivating excessively. An infected dog will usually be dead within 10 days. So if a dog that bit you is still alive after this time, there's a small risk that it would have been infected – but this is assuming you can find the animal and observe it for 10 days.

RABIES INFORMATION SOURCES

Before you go, it's a good idea to find out the current status of rabies in the areas you're planning to visit. While it is predominantly transmitted by canines, other animals can carry rabies like monkeys, raccoons, bats, squirrels, cats and rats. Reliable sources of information include specialist travel health clinics, the US Centers for Disease Control & Prevention, the World Health Organization (see under Information Sources in the Before You Go chapter for contact details) and embassies of the countries you're planning to visit. If you are ultra-interested, you could check out WHO's online rabies resource, RABNET (**http://www.who.int /rabies/rabnet/en/**).

Symptoms

The rabies virus attacks your central nervous system, causing extremely unpleasant symptoms. Once symptoms have appeared, the disease can't be cured and a painful death is inevitable. However, the infection can be stopped during the incubation period (ie before symptoms appear, anything from about five days to a year or more).

Symptoms of rabies infection include fever, headache, sore throat and nausea. This is followed by pain and burning around the bite, extreme sensitivity to light and sound, and anxiety. Hydrophobia, or fear of water, is a classic symptom, which is a result of painful throat spasms on drinking, and foaming at the mouth does occur (because of overproduction of saliva). Convulsions and coma then lead to death.

What to Do

If you are bitten by an animal, immediately clean the bite or scratch thoroughly. This is important even if the animal is not rabid because animal teeth harbour all sorts of bugs. If the animal is rabid, cleaning can help to kill the rabies virus before it has time to enter your body. You should:

- use lots of soap and water to flush the wound out, and then apply an antiseptic solution like povidone-iodine directly to the wound
- apply strong alcohol to kill the rabies virus (in an emergency you can apply spirits directly to the wound)
- do not attempt to close the wound with stitches
- seek medical help as soon as possible

You'll need to get advice on rabies prevention (you can wait until the next day if necessary). Bites to the head and neck area carry a higher risk of rabies. You will also need a course of antibiotics if it is a deep wound, as well as a tetanus booster if you're not up to date with this.

If no medical help is available, a suitable antibiotic course to take is co-amoxiclav 250mg three times daily (erythromycin 500mg twice daily if you're allergic to penicillin), while you find reliable advice on rabies prevention.

Postexposure Rabies Treatment

After a potentially rabid bite, you will need a course of rabies vaccination to prevent the disease, whether or not you were vaccinated before. In addition, if you weren't vaccinated before, you will need a rabies immunoglobulin injection.

There are a couple of issues to be aware of with post-exposure rabies treatment. For a start, both the vaccine and the immunoglobulin are expensive. Secondly, both are often in short supply, particularly in rural areas. Even when they are available, you need to avoid locally made vaccine and immunoglobulin, as they are usually derived from non-human tissue, and carry a high risk of serious reactions.

You need to find imported human vaccine, which should be available in most major cities. Try a university-affiliated health department, your embassy or members of the expatriate community for reliable advice on your risks of rabies and where to get anti-rabies treatment.

Unfortunately, even if you wanted to, taking rabies vaccine with you is not an option, partly because it's often in short supply, but mainly because it needs to be kept at fridge temperature to remain effective.

After You Get Back...

Some illnesses can show themselves for the first time when you get back, and illnesses that started while you were away may persist or get worse after you return. Before you rush off to make an appointment, remember that unless you're worried for some reason, you don't need a post-travel health check. In some situations, however, a post-travel health check is advisable:

- if you develop any of the symptoms listed in the following section
- if you have any persistent symptoms (eg diarrhoea, recurrent fevers, generally under the weather, weight loss)
- if you were bitten by an animal, whether or not you received a rabies injection
- if you were on a long trip or you spent some time in rural areas or living rough
- if you're worried you might have something
- if you were ill when you were away (unless it was just a brief episode of travellers diarrhoea)
- if you received medical or dental care while you were away
- if you had unprotected intercourse with a new partner

You can go to your usual doctor, a travel health clinic or, if you're concerned you may have something exotic, a doctor specialising in tropical medicine. The advantage of a travel health or tropical medicine specialist is that they may be more alert to symptoms of tropical diseases. On the other hand, your doctor will be familiar with your health history.

See the section on Post-Travel Blues later in this chapter, but you should consider seeing your doctor or arranging counselling if you experience significant stress, anxiety or depression after you return.

If you had medical or dental treatment while you were away, remember to claim for it as soon as possible on your travel insurance.

WHAT TO LOOK OUT FOR

You should see your doctor, a specialist travel health expert or tropical medicine specialist if you develop any symptoms in the days or weeks after you get back.

Remember that doctors at home may not consider tropical diseases as a cause for your symptoms unless you tell them. Be sure to mention that you have been travelling, where you went and any risk situations you were in.

The time between getting infected and symptoms appearing varies with different diseases, but it can be weeks or even months, so if you were on a short trip, they may not appear until after you get back. In addition, some aspects of travelling (such as exposure to the sun) can make conditions like skin cancer more likely in the longer term.

Keep a lookout for any of the following symptoms.

Fever

This is especially important if there's any risk that you may have malaria. You should suspect malaria if you develop any fever or flu-like symptoms after you return, especially in the first four weeks. Although the most serious form of malaria (falciparum) is most likely to occur in the first four weeks after you return, other forms of malaria can occur several months after you were infected. In some circumstances you may need to have a course of primaquine, an antimalarial which clears persistent liver forms of the parasite.

Malaria deaths have occurred in returned travellers because the infection was not suspected by doctors at home, so it's important to tell them if you have been to a malarial area, even if you were taking malaria prevention medication.

Don't forget that you need to continue taking your antimalarials for four weeks after you leave a malarial area or you will be at higher risk of getting malaria.

There are lots of other causes of fever in returned travellers: dengue fever, hepatitis, typhoid and tuberculosis can all show up in this way.

Diarrhoea

Gastrointestinal problems can persist or appear for the first time after you get back – see the section on Prolonged Diarrhoea in the Digestive System chapter for more details. Bacterial dysenteries, giardiasis and amoebiasis are all possibilities, and even malaria, the great mimic, can cause diarrhoea. You often find that diarrhoea clears up spontaneously once you get back to your usual routines and lifestyle. You need to see your doctor if your symptoms persist for longer than a week after you get back, or if there's any blood or mucus in it.

Worms are often symptom-less, so it's probably a good idea to get a check for these if you've been on a long trip or you've been travelling rough. If you know you ate something dodgy like raw meat or seafood, you may have picked up tapeworm or liver flukes, so you should get this checked out.

Travelling can make you more likely to develop noninfectious conditions like irritable bowel syndrome or milk intolerance (usually temporary), so bear this in mind if you develop any gut disturbances that are not normal for you. Some gut problems may be unrelated to travelling – you may have got them anyway – so get any symptoms checked out.

! Be aware that diarrhoea can be contagious and this may affect whether you can go back to work when you return (eg if you work with young children or in the food industry).

Skin

If you've got any infected cuts, persistent ulcers or rashes, or any weird skin blemish you're not sure about, you should get these checked out as soon as possible. Mention if tick bites were a possibility, and any other nasties. Fungal infections like athlete's foot are common while you're away, but they may clear up once you get back.

Another thing to look out for is any change in a mole or freckle (see p313 for more details), especially if you've been scorching yourself in the tropical sunshine.

SCHISTOSOMIASIS

This disease is widespread in Africa, and can cause long-term problems if it's not picked up and treated early – see p337 for more details. If you think you may be at risk, get it checked out when you return. Bear in mind, though, that infections are regularly picked up in travellers who didn't think they had been at risk.

It can appear as an acute illness with fever and other symptoms a few weeks or months after you were exposed, or you may get no symptoms for several months, then you may notice blood in your urine or faeces. Infection can be confirmed by a test on your faeces or by blood test. The blood test needs to be done at least three months after you were exposed to the risk.

Animal Bites

If you were bitten by any animal while you were away and didn't get rabies injections, it's a good idea to discuss with your doctor whether you should take any action now, eg it may be advisable to have a course of rabies injections.

Sexual Health Check-up

This is definitely a good idea if you had unprotected intercourse with a new partner while you were away, or you experience any symptoms. Hepatitis B, HIV and other STIs are all a possibility. STIs can be symptom-less and can cause serious effects on your fertility, so it's worth getting this checked out early if you think it may be a possibility.

Other Symptoms

It's worth reporting any unusual symptoms, such as weight loss, night sweats, recurrent fevers or if you're simply not feeling right and don't know why. Tuberculosis can sometimes appear after you get back, and may be a cause of weight loss, fevers and night sweats. Consider this possibility if you spent several months living with members of the host community. Some more exotic diseases may not show up until after you get back.

POST-TRAVEL BLUES

It's a sad fact that everyone has to go home eventually. You may be glad to get back to familiar faces, culture and your old haunts. On the other hand, you may be reluctant to exchange the exciting, challenging, temporary world of travelling for a return to a life that may at first seem less enjoyable and less meaningful.

If you've been away for a while, you may experience reverse culture shock when you return. Have a read of the section on Culture Shock in the Mental Wellbeing chapter, and see if you recognise any of the feelings described.

Added to this is the big change in lifestyle that coming home usually involves – trying to pick up where you left off, maybe trying to find a job, somewhere to live, coping with dreary weather and a (comparatively) dreary environment can be stressful. Friends and family may be surprisingly uninterested in hearing all about the wonderful and not-so-wonderful experiences you had while you were away (but can you blame them?).

Be prepared for at least some emotional turmoil after you get back, as you try to match up your expectations of life with the realities. Talking through experiences you have had may help, especially if you had any particularly life-altering or traumatic experiences. Try talking to other travellers to find out how they coped with the transition, to sympathetic friends or to a trained counsellor. Activity and a purpose in life can help enormously. On the other hand, if you feel persistently low and lose interest in life, you may be depressed (see the section on Depression in the Mental Wellbeing chapter for more details) and you should seek medical help.

Traditional African Medicine...

Every culture has developed ways of explaining and dealing with illness and misfortune, and mitigating the threat of death. For centuries, Africans have relied on traditional healers and their healing practices to keep them healthy. Although colonisation and Western influences tended to drive these practices back into the bush, since independence there has been a re-emergence of African medicine at a political (and international) level. In rural areas, the majority of people still rely on traditional healers for all their health needs.

In spite of the explosion of Western interest in holistic and alternative healing systems, traditional African medicine hasn't really made an appearance on the scene (at least for Westerners not of African origin), perhaps because the strong spiritual beliefs and social contexts through which it lives are difficult for Westerners to understand.

In your travels in Africa, you're more than likely to witness a traditional healing ceremony or to find traditional plant-based remedies on sale. This chapter aims to give you some background information on this fascinating topic.

WHAT IS AFRICAN MEDICINE?

African medicine encompasses a wide range of healers and practices, including spirit mediums, diviners, herbalists, birth attendants and circumcisers. There are many regional variations, although some basic practices and beliefs are widespread. This overview is necessarily something of a generalisation.

Westerners know African healers by many names: shamans, witchdoctors, voodoo practitioners etc; there are many African names too, depending on the region and the specific society. Healers often hold distinguished positions within society, perhaps comparable to the traditional role of priests in Western societies. They often have to go through lengthy training, especially birth attendants and spirit mediums (eg up to 15 years for Shona spirit mediums). Some healers have their role passed down through their family, while others may receive a calling at some stage.

The fundamental difference between an African healer and a conventional Western doctor is that the healer looks outside the human body for the cause and treatment of an illness. Ill health (and misfortune generally) is seen as the result of external influences; by contrast, modern medicine looks for disease processes within the body. This belief in harmful external influences is a logical part of the total world view of the society and culture which the healer and patient belong to.

For example, African patients with malaria may accept that they have got malaria because of a bite from a malarial mosquito. However, they'll want to know why the malarial mosquito singled them out, and the healer may tell them that it's because someone sent the mosquito to bite them.

Treatment is logical, and based on what is believed to have caused the illness, eg if illness has been caused by angering ancestors, treatment involves propitiation of the ancestors through offerings or animal sacrifices, or by performing rituals like fasting. In the case of witchcraft, it's necessary for the healer to identify the perpetrator of the 'crime' (often single, elderly women) and persecute them – a controversial practice that has attracted vehement criticism and much publicity within African societies as well as in the West. Persecution of 'witches' is now illegal in some countries like Zimbabwe, but the practice is still widespread.

Illness can also result from possession of a person's body by evil spirits. Cure in this case is aimed at expelling the harmful spirit. This can involve transferring it to another body, often an animal, or into a specially prepared container like a bottle. If someone picks up the bottle, the spell is transferred to them. Exorcism of an evil spirit involves ritual prayers and incantations, often in a sacred spot surrounded by witnesses, and represents a confrontation between the exorcist (the 'witch doctor' or spirit medium) and the errant spirit. If you have a chance to witness one of these rituals, be warned that they can be extremely disturbing to watch.

Other causes of illness include a violation of a taboo and loss of the soul. In the case of loss of soul, the healer must negotiate with the spiritual world for repossession of the lost soul.

Other treatments include massages, scarification, bloodletting, and use of powders, ointments and other remedies derived from natural substances including herbs, bones and minerals. As part of their healing rituals, healers may go into trances, jump over the patient, recite incantations and use ventriloquism.

Prevention

The healer's role is not just to provide cures for illness: they also provide advice on preventing recurrence and on avoiding the causes of illness (eg on how to avoid displeasing the spirit world).

DIVINERS & ORACLES

An important part of the healing process is ascertaining the cause of the illness. In western medicine, this is called 'diagnosis' and the medical practitioner will use a variety of methods, including blood testing, urine analysis and X-rays, to identify the characteristics of the disease process. In African medicine, however, a very different approach is taken, in keeping with the different logic underlying it. Diviners or oracles use various means, often associated with elaborate rituals, to determine the origin of the illness or misfortune. For example, the Baulé people of Côte d'Ivoire use a mouse oracle. This is a usually intricately carved wooden vessel, inside which the oracle bones are placed. These are sprinkled with rice to act as a lure for a mouse which is then shut inside the vessel. The mouse runs up and down, disturbing the bones, the pattern of which is then read and interpreted by the diviner.

RE-EMERGENCE OF AFRICAN MEDICINE

Missionaries and colonisers attacked African medicine as sinister 'black magic', a practice lacking scientific verification and efficacy, and encouraged the introduction of modern medical practices. Since independence, there has been a rediscovery of African medicine. There are several reasons for this.

One reason is that this is very much in line with the move towards celebrating a cultural identity and rejection of imposed colonial values and practices. But there are also more practical reasons. Provision of adequate health care in many African nations is a major problem, especially at the primary care level, and especially in rural areas where healers traditionally exert greatest influence. In 1978 the World Health Organization (WHO) made a ground-breaking step towards recognising the role of traditional healers by encouraging governments to explore the possibility of using healers as part of the primary care system. WHO also encourages research into 'traditional' therapies (usually herbal remedies).

African governments have generally responded positively – cynics say because it's the cheapest way to provide health care for the majority of people. Healers don't charge large fees, and they don't rely on expensive medicines, equipment and facilities (treatment is carried out in the patient's home or a public place).

Several nations have associations of traditional healers, eg the well established Zimbabwe National Traditional Healers Association (ZINATHA), the Swaziland Traditional Healers Society, and the Ghana Psychic and Traditional Healers Association.

Research into the scientific basis of herbal remedies is ongoing in some African countries, although critics argue that this reduces African medicine to herbal remedies (and only those approved by the canons of Western science), which ignores the vital role of the spiritual context of healing.

In any case, talk of 'integrating' Western and traditional medicine has effectively been quashed, as traditional healers argue that the logic underlying the two systems is too different to allow integration, and they have justifiable concerns that they would be seen as inferior to modern medical practitioners.

LOCAL REMEDIES

You may want to take advantage of the rich variety of remedial plants available in Africa, for example products derived from the aloe plant, lavender oil and sausage tree (Kigelia africana). Rooibos tea is widely drunk throughout southern Africa and is reputed to have beneficial effects. Some remedies are now being sold prepackaged to the general public (eg in Zimbabwe).

Just be aware that just because remedies are 'natural' doesn't mean they are necessarily harmless. Use your common sense and only buy them from reputable sources (clinics, healers or dispensaries) and use them as directed. You'll find many 'quack' remedies on sale – you can usually identify them from the widely optimistic advertising. Avoid anything that promises to cure everything! Just be aware of the distinction between folk remedies and traditional healing remedies.

A report by TRAFFIC, the wildlife trade monitoring program of the World Wide Fund for Nature, has concluded that the demand for traditional medicines is putting animals and plants in east and southern Africa under threat. This has important repercussions not only in terms of the environment but also on the health of millions of people who rely on traditional remedies to treat illness. Plants and animals identified as needing urgent conservation action included the baobab tree, frankincense tree, the black rhino and the green turtle.

PRACTICE

The decision to seek help often comes fairly late in the illness process. The family will first get together and try home remedies, or remedies that can be obtained from pharmacies or the village shop. If these don't work, the family will decide on the best course of action, either to see a traditional healer or to try a Western medical practitioner.

However, the reality is that the costs of Western-style medicine place it out of reach of the vast majority of people in Africa. Most people in rural areas will only have recourse to a traditional healer. In urban areas, the situation is slightly different: people often have a wide choice of practitioners and remedies available to them.

People often switch back and forth between traditional healers and modern medicine, depending on how quickly the different treatments appear to work, whether they believe the cause of their illness is to do with the spirits, what the illness is (eg sterility and STIs are usually reasons to visit a traditional practitioner) and how much money they have to spare. This is obviously not an ideal situation for either system but there's not much the authorities can do, except to ensure that quacks don't get a chance to practise.

Buying & Using Medicines...

✚ For guidelines on medicines and children see p274.

✚ For a discussion of medicines during pregnancy, see p265.

All medicines have side effects, but the trick is to balance up the possible risks of using a medicine against the probable benefits – something most of us are usually happy leaving to our doctors to work out.

When you're travelling, expert advice may not be available and there may be occasions when you may need to self-treat with medicines – either ones you have with you or ones you have bought locally. Travellers medical kits are popular and have the advantage of coming with instructions. In this chapter we give general guidelines on how to use prescribed drugs safely and how to avoid dangerous medications. Although these guidelines are primarily for Western-style medicines, many of the general safety points also apply if you're buying traditional medicines.

DRUG NAMES

This is a confusing issue for everyone, including medics. You need to know that all drugs have two names: the generic (chemical) name and the brand name chosen by the manufacturer.

There can be several different brands containing the same generic substance. You can consider different brands as basically interchangeable (although brands can differ in the way they are absorbed and how convenient they are to take). Some common drugs that have been around for ages are available under the generic name (eg aspirin) as well as various brand names.

To confuse the issue further, some medicines that are made up of a combination of generic substances may be given a new generic name. For example, the painkiller co-codamol is a combination of paracetamol (acetaminophen) and codeine.

Because brand names vary from country to country, we've used generic names for drugs throughout this book – any doctor or pharmacist will recognise the generic name and should be able to suggest brands available locally. If you want to find out the generic name of a drug, look on the packet or leaflet accompanying the drug – the generic name should be there, usually in smaller type just below the brand name – or ask a pharmacist.

BUYING MEDICINES IN AFRICA

You need to take a bit more care than usual if you're buying Western-type (or traditional) medicines in Africa. Generally, Western countries have rigorous safety standards for medicines, as well as well regulated medical and pharmaceutical professions, but the situation can be very different elsewhere. In addition, drugs made by local companies may be substandard (in other words less effective) or even fake.

As well as different safety standards, you may find there are very different attitudes towards medicines and their use – in many African countries medicines are sold in roadside stalls and corner shops without prescription, just like any other commodity.

If you need to buy medicines while you are away, take some basic safety measures:

- if possible, buy from a trustworthy doctor or large pharmacy
- drugs may be kept in suboptimal conditions, eg in direct sunlight or without refrigeration
- check the expiry date – very few drugs (tetracycline is a notable exception) are actually harmful if they are kept too long, but they may well be ineffective
- if possible, look for drugs made by local branches of international drug companies and look out for fakes (although these can be difficult to spot)
- check the label and safety seal – if either look dodgy, avoid it
- drugs now considered dangerous in many developed countries because of unacceptable side effects may still be available in Africa – see the following section for more details; safer alternatives are given in the relevant sections of this book

■ try to avoid remedies that contain a combination of drugs because it's best not to take any unnecessary medications, and the added ingredients may be harmful

CAN YOU HELP ME PLEASE?

What do you do when a local person asks you for treatment? It's a dilemma you'll almost certainly be faced with if you're travelling in a less developed country. In most situations it's probably better to avoid immediately diving for your medical kit – short-term gratitude may well lead to longer-term harm. If the question arises, consider the following: do you know what is wrong with the person and thus the appropriate treatment? Do you know enough about that person to be reasonably confident that they will not react adversely to the treatment? Are they on any other medication that would interact badly with your treatment? Could they be allergic to your treatment? Can you communicate well enough with them to find all this out and explain the dosage regime? Even if you're a doctor, answers to these questions are not always straight forward.

If you're feeling guilty about not helping, a simple explanation that you are not a doctor and do not know how to treat them will usually be met with understanding. It is almost always better to encourage people to seek help from a local health centre.

Don't forget that simple advice may be more helpful than you appreciate. For example, it is common to be shown a dirty open wound. A suggestion to bathe the wound in boiled-and-cooled water regularly and to keep it as clean as possible will hopefully be heeded, and is far more useful than any tablets.

Corinne Else

MEDICINES

Methods of taking drugs vary from country to country. In many African countries, injections are seen as the best and most effective way to administer medicines. As a rule it's best to avoid injections because there is an increased risk of serious side effects from the drug, as well as the risk of an abscess at the injection site, or infection with HIV or hepatitis B if the needle has not been sterilised properly since it was last used. Try asking if a tablet form is available instead.

In less developed countries, especially those affected by war, Western-style medicines are often in extremely short supply and will be difficult to obtain.

MEDICINES TO AVOID

Some medicines to be wary of include the following (we've used the generic name unless indicated):

- steroids – these are powerful drugs used in a variety of conditions (eg asthma and dermatitis), usually to suppress inflammation. They have some pretty powerful side effects too, and shouldn't be used except under medical supervision. Combination medications may contain steroids, so look out for them (this is not a complete list) – prednisolone, betamethasone, cortisone, dexamethasone, hydrocortisone, methylprednisolone. Never use eye drops containing steroids except under medical supervision

- chloramphenicol – an antibiotic that may be prescribed for tonsillitis or travellers diarrhoea. It can have a very serious effect on the blood system in some people and should only be used for life-threatening infections (eg sometimes for typhoid fever). Note that this does not apply to chloramphenicol eye and ear drops, which can be used safely

- clioquinol – an antidiarrhoeal drug that should be avoided because it can have serious effects on the nervous system

- opium tincture – may be available in Africa for treatment of diarrhoea and other ailments; best avoided for obvious reasons

- phenylbutazone – an anti-inflammatory painkiller with potentially serious side effects

- sulphonamide antibiotics – these will work if no alternatives are available, but are best avoided if possible because of potential side effects

■ Fansidar (brand name) – this antimalarial is no longer used for prevention in most Western countries because of side effects, although it is still used to treat malaria; if you are offered it as a preventive, try to find an alternative

FAKE MEDICINES

According to a recent *Time* magazine article, up to half of the medicines sold in sub-Saharan Africa are fake. There is an alarming account of how Belgian doctors in Niger administering meningococcal vaccine donated by neighbouring Nigeria, noticed hairs floating in several of the vials. When they tested it, they found the vaccine was little more than salt and water.

Producing fake drugs is big business, especially in Asia, and Africa has become a dumping ground for these useless and potentially very damaging fakes. The human cost is likely to be enormous and, as usual, the most vulnerable members of society suffer the most. In rural communities, people tend not to see a doctor first (for social and economic reasons), but buy drugs from small village shops. They often buy them by the handful, without packaging, making it easy for fakes to be passed off. Even when the packaging is intact, many local people will not be able to read and are in any case unlikely to recognise a misspelt name.

SIDE EFFECTS & ALLERGIES

Any drug may produce unwanted or unexpected effects, so be on the lookout for these when you take any medicine. You may need to stop taking that particular drug and take a different one. If you know you're allergic to a drug, you should avoid it.

Some drugs produce well recognised side effects that your doctor or pharmacist should warn you about. Familiar drugs that have been around for many years are unlikely to have any unexpected effects, although new drugs may still be capable of causing a few surprises. Sometimes it can be difficult to work out if it's the drug or the actual illness process causing the problems, especially when you're treating diarrhoea; all antibiotics can cause stomach upsets.

Allergies are one serious type of side effect, but not all side effects are allergies. Mild symptoms of headache, diarrhoea, nausea and maybe vomiting are not signs of allergy. Signs of allergy usually appear soon after taking the medicine and include:

- a red, raised itchy rash (common)
- breathing difficulties and swelling of the face
- fainting or collapsing

Note that a severe allergic reaction is always a medical emergency, and you will need to seek medical help urgently.

Make sure you record any drug allergies that you know you have, and carry this information on you at all times. Some companies specialise in making engraved bracelets with these details – see the Useful Organisations section in the Before You Go chapter at the start of this book for more details. Always tell anyone treating you of any drug allergies you think you have.

Medicines that commonly cause allergies include aspirin and antibiotics like penicillin and sulpha (sulphonamide) drugs. Remember that if you are allergic to one drug, you should avoid any related drugs too.

DOSES, TIMING & SPECIAL INSTRUCTIONS

Ideally, for any medicine, you should be clear about what dose to take at what interval and follow any special instructions on the label. In practice, you may find that the dosage of the brand available locally may differ from the one we've suggested in this book. This is usually because the drug has been formulated slightly differently, or possibly the dose may have been expressed in different units.

If you're not sure what dose to take, ask either the pharmacist or doctor, read the information leaflet carefully or try to find another brand of the drug that causes less confusion. Remember that a single extra dose of most drugs is unlikely to cause problems.

Note that usually 'every six hours' means in practice to take the dose four times a day during waking hours; 'every eight hours' means take it three times a day.

Alcohol is best avoided because it can affect the absorption of drugs and may have an additive effect on drugs that are sedative (ie make you drowsy), such as some antihistamines. Alcohol should not be taken with metronidazole – an antibiotic that you may take for some types of diarrhoea – as it causes a particularly bad reaction, making you feel stupendously dreadful.

If you're taking several different drugs together, they can interact to make adverse effects more likely or reduce effectiveness. Similarly, medical conditions can affect how well a drug works and how likely it is to cause unwanted effects, eg you should not take the contraceptive pill if you have hepatitis.

COMMONLY USED MEDICINES

We've summarised here details about doses, side effects and cautions for some common medicines that you may find you need to use while you're away. Details about other medicines used for specific conditions are described in the relevant sections:

✚ drugs for treating and preventing malaria p44

✚ drugs for motion sickness p71

✚ ear (p182) and eyedrops p188

✚ drugs for vaginal thrush p253

✚ drugs in pregnancy p265

✚ drugs for altitude illness p328

✚ antifungal creams p202

✚ homoeopathic/naturopathic first aid p62

Where the brand name tends to be better known than the generic name, we've listed some common brands, but be aware that these brands may not be available in Africa.

PAIN & FEVER

Simple painkillers include aspirin and paracetamol (acetaminophen in the US) and are also good for reducing fever.

Paracetamol has very few side effects, except perhaps nausea, although it can cause liver damage in overdose. Aspirin is more problematic and should be avoided if you are hypersensitive to it, asthmatic or suffer from indigestion or stomach ulcers. It can also cause heartburn and stomach irritation.

Aspirin is not suitable for children under 12 years, but paracetamol is fine in infants and children.

Stronger painkillers include codeine phosphate, which will also stop diarrhoea in an emergency. Side effects include constipation and drowsiness. Some customs officials may be a bit suspicious of codeine, because of its potential for abuse, so it's safest to have a letter from your doctor explaining what it is and why you need it, to keep customs officials happy. Other painkillers include a combination of paracetamol with codeine (eg co-codamol). Codeine can be given to children, but is best avoided if possible.

Ibuprofen (eg Nurofen and other brand names, also in forms suitable for children) is an anti-inflammatory drug that is good for fever, pain (including period pain) and inflammation (eg painful joint). Avoid it if you have had stomach ulcers or a hypersensitivity to aspirin. Stronger anti-inflammatory drugs include naproxen and indomethacin, which are useful for treating strains, sprains, sports injuries and joint pains.

MEDICINES

Drug	Dose (adult)	Dose (children)
aspirin	one to two 300mg tablets every four to six hours when necessary (maximum 4g in 24 hours)	avoid in children under 12 years
paracetamol (acetami- nophen)	one to two 500mg tablets every four to six hours (maximum 4g in 24 hours)	3 months to 1 year: 60 to 120mg; 1 to 5 years: 120 to 250mg; six to 12 years: 250 to 500mg; over 12 years: adult dose; (maximum 4 doses in 24 hours)
codeine phosphate	two to four 15mg tablets every four hours, maximum 240mg in 24 hours	one to 12 years: 1mg/kg every six hours
ibuprofen	two 200mg tablets every six hours, as necessary	suspension (100mg/5mL) available for children; 6 months to 1 year: 2.5mL; 1 to 2 years: 2.5mL; 3 to 7 years: 5mL, 8 to 12 years: 10mL; all doses given 3 to 4 times daily

ANTIBIOTICS

Many travel-related illnesses are caused by infections, and you may need to take antibiotics to treat them while you're away. Antibiotics work against bacterial infections but don't have any effect on viral or fungal infections. This means they won't be any good against common viral infections like colds and flu, as well as many throat and gastro infections.

Different antibiotics are effective against different bacteria. We give antibiotic recommendations in this book based on the likeliest cause of infection; however, the best way to find out if an antibiotic will be effective against an infection is to have a laboratory test to identify the bacteria causing it. Antibiotics should stop most infections within a few days. Because they work to stop the infection and not the symptoms, you may need to treat symptoms (such as pain and fever) with other medications until the antibiotics kick in.

If an antibiotic appears not to be working (it needs at least two days to do its stuff), you may be taking the wrong dose (check) OR it's the wrong antibiotic (the bacteria are resistant or they aren't affected by this particular antibiotic) OR the illness is not what you think it is. In this case, it's always best to seek medical advice (after you've checked that the dose is correct).

Antibiotics can cause problems, which is why they need to be treated with respect. They commonly cause nausea and diarrhoea and, because they disrupt the normal balance of organisms in the body, can make women more likely to develop thrush (vaginal candidiasis). Antibiotics (especially penicillins and cephalosporins) can cause severe allergic reactions, so you should always carry a record of any allergic reactions with you.

! If rashes and swelling of the throat and face occur, stop taking the drug immediately and seek medical advice. Always carry a record of any allergic reactions with you.

Antibiotic Resistance

This is a growing problem worldwide, and is one reason why you should always finish the whole course of an antibiotic (unless you experience severe adverse reactions). Antibiotic resistance is more likely to occur if the infection is not quickly and completely eliminated. In many countries, antibiotics are readily available without prescription and are often taken indiscriminately and perhaps inappropriately. People may not be able to afford to buy a whole course and are often not aware of the importance of doing so anyway. The use of antibiotics in livestock rearing has also been an important factor.

You can help by only using antibiotics if really necessary, choosing the most effective antibiotic and completing the full course of antibiotics – this way there aren't any bacteria left hanging around with nothing better to do than work out ways of fighting back.

ANTIBIOTIC GUIDE

Here's a quick guide to which antibiotics are suitable for what. Read the details about the antibiotics to find out if they are suitable for your age group, and avoid any antibiotics (including related antibiotics) you are allergic to:

- diarrhoea – ciprofloxacin (and related antibiotics), co-trimoxazole, metronidazole, tinidazole
- chest infection – co-trimoxazole, amoxycillin, co-amoxiclav, erythromycin/clarithromycin
- throat infection – phenoxymethylpenicillin or co-amoxiclav
- ear infection – amoxycillin, co-amoxiclav or co-trimoxazole
- urinary infection (cystitis) – amoxycillin or co-trimoxazole
- skin infection – phenoxymethylpenicillin, flucloxacillin or co-amoxiclav

Note: clarithromycin/erythromycin can be used if you are allergic to penicillin.

The Details

Suggested lengths of courses of antibiotics are indicated in the relevant sections. Note that all the antibiotics described in this section can cause nausea and stomach upsets.

Co-amoxiclav (Augmentin) is a combination of amoxycillin (a penicillin drug) and clavulanic acid (which makes it more effective against some bacteria than plain amoxycillin). It's a useful 'broad spectrum' antibiotic, and is effective against bladder, ear, chest and sinus infections. It's also good for skin infections and animal bites. Although amoxycillin (Amoxil) is less reliable generally, it is useful if you can't get co-amoxiclav. Both drugs can sometimes cause skin rashes, and should be avoided if you are allergic to penicillin.

Trimethoprim is useful for treating bladder and ear infections, and for diarrhoea in children. There are concerns over its potential to cause serious but rare side effects, including severe skin rash and blood disorders. It should be avoided in pregnancy. Note that co-trimoxazole is a combination drug that contains a sulphonamide antibiotic plus trimethoprim – it's best avoided if possible, as there is a slightly higher risk of serious side effects.

Ciprofloxacin is effective against most bacterial causes of travellers diarrhoea, cystitis (bladder infection) and chest infection. Ciprofloxacin can occasionally cause kidney problems, which is why you should drink plenty of fluids when you take it. Similar drugs that can be used as alternatives include norfloxacin, nalidixic acid and ofloxacin. Ciprofloxacin should be avoided in pregnancy and it is not generally recommended for children under the age of 12 years because of potential side effects. Suitable alternatives for children are suggested in the relevant sections.

Flucloxacillin (eg Floxapen) is a penicillin drug that is effective for skin infections, although co-amoxiclav is usually the first choice. It can cause rashes and allergic reactions, and you should avoid it if you are allergic to penicillin.

Erythromycin (eg Erymax) or clarithromycin can be used as an alternative to penicillin drugs if you are allergic to penicillin. Clarithromycin is less likely to cause side effects such as nausea and vomiting.

Metronidazole (eg Flagyl) is effective against infections causing diarrhoea, especially with a fever and abdominal pain, eg giardiasis and amoebic dysentery. It is also effective against bacterial vaginosis. You should avoid alcohol when you are taking it, as it causes a severe reaction (flushing, headache, palpitations). Tinidazole (eg Fasigyn) is similar and can be used as an alternative.

MEDICINES

Drug	Dose (adult)	Dose (children)
ciprofloxacin	500mg twice daily	not recommended in children under 12 years
amoxycillin	250mg three times daily (double dose if infection is severe)	up to 10 years: 125mg three times daily; 10 years and over: adult dose
co-amoxiclav	250mg three times daily	up to 10 years: 125mg three times daily
trimethoprim	200mg twice daily	two to five months: 25mg; six months to five years: 50mg; six to 12 years: 100mg; all doses twice daily:
flucloxacillin	250mg four times daily (double dose if infection is severe)	under two years: 75mg; two to 10 years: 125mg; all doses four times daily
erythromycin	500mg to 1g twice daily	up to two years: 125mg; two to eight years: 250mg all doses four times daily
metronidazole	500mg three times daily	7.5mg/kg three times daily

ANTIHISTAMINES

These are useful for hay fever, allergies, itchy rashes, insect bites and motion sickness. There are many different ones available, mostly without prescription, and they vary in what side effects they cause (mainly drowsiness).

Antihistamines that are more likely to cause drowsiness include promethazine, chlorpheniramine and cyclizine. Non- (or at least less) sedating ones include astemizole, cetirizine and loratidine. Ask your pharmacist for guidance on brands available to you, and follow the dosing instructions on the packet. They can be given to children.

Side effects include drowsiness, headache, dry mouth and blurred vision. They're more common in children and older people. Because drowsiness can occur, you shouldn't drive, dive or drink alcohol in large quantities after you take antihistamines.

NAUSEA & VOMITING

For details about drugs to prevent and treat motion sickness, see p71. Metoclopramide (eg Maxolon) is useful for nausea and vomiting associated with diarrhoea or food poisoning. The adult dose is 10mg three times daily. It's best avoided in children – if necessary, try an antihistamine instead. Some are available in suppository form (ie you insert it in the rectum), which might sound uninviting, but it's a useful option if you're vomiting, and other forms (such as soluble forms or a patch you put against your cheek) are also available.

ANTIDIARRHOEALS

These drugs are best avoided unless it's an emergency and you have to travel. They include loperamide (eg Imodium and other brand names), probably the most useful; diphenoxylate with atropine (eg Lomotil; less useful because of potential side effects); and bismuth subsalicylate (Pepto-Bismol).

The dose of loperamide is two 2mg tablets initially, followed by one 2mg tablet after each loose motion, to a maximum of eight tablets in 24 hours. It commonly causes constipation; other possible side effects include abdominal cramps, bloating and, rarely, paralysis of the gut. The dose of diphenoxylate is four tablets initially, followed by two tablets every six hours until the diarrhoea is under control. Neither drug is recommended for children, and you should avoid them if you have a fever, or blood in your diarrhoea.

Bismuth subsalicylate is available in tablet or liquid form, but tablets are more convenient if you're travelling: take two tablets four times daily. It's not suitable for children (as it contains aspirin). It can cause blackening of the tongue and faeces, and ringing in the ears. You shouldn't use it for more than three weeks at these doses.

Medical Services...

➕ See the Help...chapter earlier for more guidance on how to go about getting medical help.

There are no surprises here. The availability of adequate medical care is directly related to the state of a nation's economy. In debt-burdened – and in many cases war-ravaged – countries, there is very little money to spare for investment in expensive health care. Wealthier countries such as Botswana and Namibia generally have adequate to good health care, while South Africa, home of the first heart transplant, offers a comparable standard of health care to that available in Western countries.

As a general rule, you should be able to get treatment in most places for minor ailments and injuries, but for anything more serious, you should think about getting yourself to a regional centre like Nairobi in East Africa or South Africa, or fly home. Obviously, in an emergency situation, you'll just have to use whatever services are immediately available, but in less urgent situations, you should take time to find a reliable source of medical advice and care. In the Help chapter (p113), we give guidance on how to go about finding a doctor. Remember that local papers often contain listings of local pharmacies, doctors and clinics.

You will generally find clinics and both public and private hospitals in capital cities and large towns, but medical services are generally extremely limited in rural areas. In many rural areas, the only care available is provided by healthworkers or traditional healers.

In general, where there are public hospitals, they tend to be under-financed and overstretched, and are probably best avoided unless they are affiliated to a university. Private clinics or hospitals are generally better, although they can be expensive. You'll generally find that mission hospitals or those run by charitable organisations are of high standard, and may be the only option in more remote areas.

MEDICAL SERVICES

IN AN EMERGENCY

Unless you're travelling in one of the more developed countries in the continent, you can't rely on fast-reaction emergency services coming to your rescue, eg in a road traffic accident. If you are in an emergency situation:

- don't wait for emergency services to arrive – if you can, get a taxi or flag down some transport, and ask them to take you to the nearest doctor or hospital
- contact your embassy for advice
- phone your travel insurance hotline as soon as possible

WHAT TO EXPECT

Different cultures have different views about symptoms, treatments, and, perhaps most importantly, the doctor-patient relationship. In Africa, you will probably find that doctors are treated with great respect, and patients would not be expected to question or doubt the diagnosis or any treatment the doctor prescribes. Often multiple anonymous (and often unnecessary) tablets are prescribed (and expected by patients) for any illness.

! If you do have to take a medicine while you are away, make sure you know what it is and what it has been prescribed for.

Here are some guidelines for assessing if you have seen a good doctor.

- Willing to listen and spends a reasonable amount of time asking about your problem; doesn't just jump to a diagnosis. In most cases, the doctor should also examine you for at least the basics like pulse rate and temperature.
- Happy to discuss fully the diagnosis and any treatment with you and any companion you would like with you in the consultation.

- If blood tests (or other procedures) are needed, the doctor uses good aseptic techniques ie wears surgical gloves (should put on a new pair for each patient), uses a sterile needle (opens packet in front of you) and a clean dressing.
- Generally, illnesses need one specific treatment (in addition to painkillers, for example); if you are prescribed multiple treatments, ask what they are for and if they are all necessary. If you are not seriously ill, it's always worth trying a few simple measures first, as outlined in the Help… chapter earlier.
- Explains what you need to do if your symptoms get worse.
- You feel confident about the way you were treated – if you have any doubts, see a different doctor and get a second opinion.

Language is an obvious problem although, if necessary, you can communicate much through gestures and miming. It's a good idea to brush up on a few basic words or phrases before you go – see the Language glossary later in this book.

As a rule, standards of nursing and auxiliary care are very different from those you may be used to, eg attitudes towards basic hygiene can be alarmingly casual. If worse comes to worst and you have to stay overnight in hospital, be prepared for a very different style of care. Don't expect to be looked after by nurses as in Western hospitals – you'll need to have a friend or travel companion to provide you with food and basic care.

PAYMENT

In many parts of Africa, with some notable exceptions (ie private clinics and hospitals in major cities), fees for medical treatment can seem ridiculously cheap. However, you will generally have to pay upfront for all consultations and treatment, and remember that medical evacuation from anywhere costs thousands of dollars. It's vital that you have travel insurance, although you will probably need to come up with the money yourself at the time and claim it back later. Keep an emergency stash with you just in case, and ask for and keep any receipts.

AFRICA'S HEALTH

As a traveller in Africa, you can't help but be aware of the very different standards of living and health that exist here. Of the 47 least developed countries in the world (according to the latest United Nations Development Report), 32 are in Africa. Life expectancy at birth is 50 years for sub-Saharan Africa (compared with 78 years average for the most developed countries in the world).

According to the World Health Organization, infectious diseases (like malaria, tuberculosis and AIDS) are 'out of control' in Africa. The cycle of poverty and the effects of war and natural disasters make it hard for nations to make progress in altering this situation.

Lack of access to clean water supplies and inadequate waste and sewage disposal systems are a major health problem for many people in Africa, especially in rural areas and shanty towns. In Uganda, for example, only 15% of the population have access to safe water and only 13% to adequate sewage disposal.

Environmental problems like desertification and deforestation, together with poor farming and livestock rearing practices mean that many poor people suffer chronic malnutrition. This in turn increases their susceptibility to disease.

Poor housing standards, lack of basic infrastructure, unsafe work practices and dangerous road traffic conditions mean that people are at high risk of injuries from accidents.

Another major problem is the lack of access for many people to affordable and adequate health care. In the west, for example, there's one physician per 390 people. In the least developed nations in Africa, this figure drops to an astonishing one physician per 50,000 people.

Although it's important to be aware of these startling inequities in health, before you get too paranoid, remember that you are not necessarily at the same risk as the local population.

You can find out what is being done to help find a solution to these problems by contacting your local branch of international aid organisations like the International Red Cross, Plan International, Médecins Sans Frontières and AMREF (see Before You Go for more details).

DIRECTORY

If you have an embassy and the time to contact it, this is probably the best source of information on local doctors and clinics. In case you don't, you could try some of the services listed here, but remember that these are intended as a guide only. The Travel Doctor-TMVC group also has clinics across South Africa, and some places in neighbouring countries, see **www.traveldoctor.co.za**.

In terms of medical services, most countries in Africa fall into the 'don't get sick here' category. Unless we've indicated otherwise, you should assume that health services outside the capital cities are extremely limited. Health insurance is essential wherever you go.

Although we have done all we can to ensure the accuracy of the information listed, contact details change and places disappear. Note that listing here does not imply any endorsement or recommendation by Lonely Planet of the services provided.

ALGERIA

For medical emergencies you should call SOS Santé (☎ 115).

CHU Mustapha Pasha ☎ 021 235555; Place du 1 Mai, Algiers
Clinique Al Azhar ☎ 021 917396; Djenane Achabou No. 4, Dely-Ibrahim

ANGOLA

As you might expect, medical supplies are in very short supply, so it's vital to take all you think you might need with you. If you need anything more than basic medical care, you'll need to get yourself to somewhere like Windhoek (Namibia) or South Africa.

Clínica da Mutamba ☎ 39 37 83; emergency 39 72 22; Rua Pedro Felix Machado, 10/12, Luanda

Clínica Sagrada Esperança ☎ 30 90 34; Av Murtala Mohamed, Ilha de Luanda

BENIN

Polyclinique les Cocotiers ☎ 21 30 14 20; Rue 373, Cotonou

Clinique Louis Pasteur ☎ 21 22 22; 01 BP 165, Porto-Novo

BOTSWANA

Standards of health care here are generally high, and the hospitals in Gabarone and Francistown generally provide care comparable with that in Western Europe. All the main towns have reasonably well stocked pharmacies.

Nyangabgwe Hospital ☎ 241-1000; Doc Morgan Ave, Francistown

Gaborone Private Hospital ☎ 360 1999; Segoditshane Way, Gabarone

Princess Marina Hospital ☎ 355 3221; Notwane Rd, Gabarone

BURKINO FASO

Hôpital Yalgado ☎ 50 31 16 55; Ave d'Oubritenga, Ouagadougou

BURUNDI

You'll need to make arrangements to be evacuated for anything other than trivial problems.

Hôpital Prince Regent Charles ☎ 226 166; Ave de l'Hopital, Bujumbura

CAMEROON

Polyclinique André Fouda ☎ 222 6612; in Elig-Essono southeast of Carrefour Nlongkak, Yaoundé

CAPE VERDE

There are hospitals on the main islands (Santiago, Sao Vicente, Santo Antao, Fogo and Sal) but facilities are very limited.

Praia Hospital ☎ 2-612462; Av Mártires de Pidjiguiti, Praia

CENTRAL AFRICAN REPUBLIC

Hospita Caumuomiter ☎ 61 0600; Bangui

CHAD

Centre Médico Social ☎ 522837, N'Djaména

Hopital Central N'Djamena Capitol ☎ 516168; BP 77, N'Djamena

COMOROS & MAYOTTE

In Comoros, there are hospitals in the three main towns on each island, but health facilities are extremely limited and you'd be better off considering going somewhere like South Africa, Mauritius, Réunion or the Seychelles, where facilities are much better.

El Maarouf Hospital ☎ 73 26 04; Route Magoudjou, Moroni, Comoros

Centre Hospitalier de Mayotte ☎ 61 1515, BP 4; Mamoudzou, Mayotte

CONGO

Clinic ☎ 64 9979; Ave Patrice Lumumba, Brazzaville

Military Hospital ☎ 66 3363; Rue Ecole Militaire, Brazzaville

CÔTE D'IVOIRE

Health care standards are adequate in the main towns but very limited elsewhere.

Polyclinique Internationale St Anne-Marie (Pisam) ☎ 22-445132; off Blvd de la Corniche, Cocody, Abidjan

Centre Hospitalier et Universitaire de Cocody ☎ 44 91 00; BP V13, Abidjan

DEMOCRATIC REPUBLIC OF CONGO

Centre Privé d'Urgences ☎ 20 875; Ave du Commerce, Kinshasa

MEDICAL SERVICES

DJIBOUTI

CHA Bouffard ☎ 351351; Boulaos district, Djibouti City

Pôle Médical ☎ 352724; Place du 27 Juin 1977, Djibouti City

EGYPT

Cairo

Anglo–American Hospital ☎ 735 6162/5; Sharia Hadayek al-Zuhreyya, Gezira

As-Salam International Hospital ☎ 524 0250, emergency 524 0077; Corniche el-Nil, Ma'adi; or ☎ 303 0502; 3 Sharia Syria, Mohandiseen

Luxor

International Hospital ☎ 238 7192/3/4; Sharia Televizyon

General Hospital ☎ 237 2025, 382 698; Corniche el-Nil Hurghada

Al-Gouna Hospital ☎ 358 0011; Al-Gouna

Al-Saffa Hospital ☎ 3546 965; Sharia an-Nasr, Ad-Dahar

As-Salam Hospital ☎ 354 8785/6/7; Corniche

Public Hospital ☎ 354 6740; Sharia Mustashfa, Ad-Dahar

EQUATORIAL GUINEA

Your best bet is to leave the country if you need anything more than basic first aid.

Santa Isabel Clinic Carreta de Luba, Malabo

ERITREA

Sembel Hospital ☎ 150175; HDAY St, Asmara

ETHIOPIA

Bethzatha Hospital ☎ 0115 514141; off Ras Mekonen Ave, Addis Ababa

Ethio-Swe Dental Clinic ☎ 0116 614932; Bole Rd, Addis Ababa

Hayat Hospital ☎ 0116 624488; Ring Rd, Addis Ababa

St Gabriel Hospital ☎ 0116 613622; Djibouti St, Addis Ababa

GABON

Polyclinique El Rapha ☎ 447000; Libreville

Fondation Jeanne Ebori ☎ 732771; Quartier Louis, Libreville

GAMBIA (THE)

Royal Victoria Teaching Hospital ☎ 4228223; Jul 22 Dr, Banjul

Medical Research Council, Atlantic Rd, Fajara (British-run)

GHANA

Accra

37 Military Hospital ☎ 776111; Liberation Ave

Korle Bu Teaching Hospital ☎ 665401; Guggisberg Ave, Korle Bu

North Ridge Clinic ☎ 227328, 024-355366; Ring Rd Central

Ridge Hospital ☎ 228382; Castle Rd

Trust Hospital ☎ 776787; Cantonments Rd, Osu

Kumasi

Okomfo Anokye Teaching Hospital Bantama Rd

GUINEA

For anything serious you'll probably need to get to Dakar or Europe.

Clinique Pasteur ☎ 747576; two blocks south of Ave de la Republique, Conakry

Conakry Hôpital Ambrose Paré ☎ 011-211320; Dixinn, Conakry

GUINEA-BISSAU

You will probably need to leave the country if you need anything more than simple self-treatment. There are hospitals in all the main towns, including Bissau, Gabu, Bafata, Canchungo, Catio and Bubaque.

Pharmacie Moçambique ☎ 205513; Bissau (ask here for Dr Kassem Dahrouge, who speaks French and some English)

Simão Mendes ☎ 212861; Av Pansau Na Isna, Bissau

KENYA

All the main towns have adequate health care services, and Nairobi and Mombasa have good specialist services. Avoid the Kenyatta National Hospital in Nairobi.

Nairobi

AAR Health Services ☎ 715319; Williamson House, Fourth Ngong Ave

Acacia Medical Centre ☎ 212200; info@acaciamed.co.ke; ICEA Bldg, Kenyatta Ave

Aga Khan Hospital ☎ 740000; Third Parklands Ave

Medical Services Surgery ☎ 317625; Bruce House, Standard St

Nairobi Hospital ☎ 722160; Off Argwings Khodek Rd

Mombasa

Aga Khan Hospital ☎ 312953; akhm@mba.akhmkenya.org; Vanga Rd

Pandya Memorial Hospital ☎ 229252; Kimathi Ave

LESOTHO

For anything serious, you'll need to go to South Africa.

Maseru Private Hospital ☎ 2231 3260; Ha Thetsane, about 7km south of Maseru

Queen Elizabeth II Hospital ☎ 2231 2501; Kingsway, Maseru

LIBERIA

Ideally get yourself to Abidjan (Côte d'Ivoire); the following is for dire emergencies only.

St Joseph's Catholic Hospital ☎ 226 207; extension of Tubman Blvd, Monrovia

LIBYA

Consider evacuation to Tunisia if necessary.

Al-Marqez at-Tubi ☎ 4263701/15; Sharia Jamia, Tripoli

Al-Khadra Hospital ☎ 4900752; Sharia al-Hadba, Tripoli

Emergency Hospital ☎ 121; Second Ring Rd, Tripoli

MADAGASCAR

The daily newspapers list out-of-hours doctors, as well as the location and telephone numbers of dentists, duty chemists, and other hospitals, but medical supplies and equipment are in short supply and facilities are poor. If you can, for anything serious, it's best to go home or fly to Mauritius, Kenya, Réunion or South Africa.

Centre Hospitalier de Soavinandriana (Hôpital Militaire d'Antananarivo) ☎ 22 397 51; Rue Moss, Soavinandriana, Antananarivo

Clinique des Sœurs Franciscaines (Clinique et Maternité St-Français) ☎ 22 610 46; Lalana Dokotera Rajaonah, Ankadifotsy, Antananarivo

Espace Médical ☎ 032 07 871 12; 65 Bis Lalana Pasteur Rabary, Antananarivo

MALAWI

Blantyre

Blantyre Adventist Hospital ☎ 620 488

Lilongwe

Adventist Health Centre ☎ 01-775456; Presidential Way

Dr Huber ☎ 01-750404, 09-919548; Glyn Jones Rd

Likuni Mission Hospital ☎ 01-766602; Glyn Jones Rd

Lilongwe Central Hospital ☎ 01-753555; off Mzimba St

Medical Air Rescue Service Clinic (MARS) ☎ 01-794036, 236644; www.mars.co.zw; Ufulu Rd, Area 43

MALI

The best services are in Bamako.

Bamako

Clinique Pasteur ☎ 229 1010; northwest of Rond-Point de 'Unité Africaine

Hôpital Gabriel Touré ☎ 222 2712; Ave van Vollenhoven

Clinique Odiénné ☎ 222 112/68; Rue Titi Niaré; Niaréla

Clinique Guindo ☎ 222207; Rue 18, Badalabougou Est, south of Pont des Martyrs

Mopti
Hospital ☎ 243 0441; Blvd de l'Indépendance

Gao
Hospital ☎ 282 0254; Route de l'Aéroport

MAURITANIA

Cabinet Médical Fabienne Sherif ☎ 525 15 71; Nouakchott

MAURITIUS

Dr Jeetoo Hospital ☎ 212 3201; Volcy Pougnet St, Port Louis

Sir Seewoosagur Ramgoolam National Hospital ☎ 243 3661/3740; Pamplemousses

Jawaharlal Nehru Hospital ☎ 627 4951; Rose Belle

Clinique Darne ☎ 686 1477; Rue Georges Guibert, Floreal

MOROCCO

SOS Medecins Maroc ☎ 022 98 98 98 has doctors on call 24 hours and will send a doctor to you.

CHU Averroès Hospital (Hôpital Ibn Rochd) ☎ 022 224109; Ave du Medecin General Braun, Casablanca

Polyclinique du Sud ☎ 024 447999; cnr Rue de Yougoslavie & Rue Ibn Aicha, Guéliz, Marrakesh

Polyclinique de Rabat ☎ 037 206161; 8 Rue de Tunis, Agdal, Rabat

Hôpital Sidi Mohammed Ben Abdellah ☎ 024 475716; Blvd de l'Hôpital, Essaouira

MOZAMBIQUE

Clínica de Sommerschield ☎ 82-305 6240, 21-493924/6; 52 Rua Pereira do Lago, Maputo

Clínica 222 ☎ 82-000 2220, 21-312222, 21-313000; cnr Av 24 de Julho & Rua Augusto Cardoso, Maputo

NAMIBIA

Rhino Park Private Hospital ☎ 225434; Sauer St, Windhoek

Windhoek State Hospital ☎ 303 9111; off Harvey Rd, Windhoek

Bismarck Medical Centre ☎ 405000; Bismarck St, Swakopmund

NIGER

Niamey

Clinique Alissa ☎ 72 57 66; Ave du Président Kalt Casten

Clinique de Gamkalé ☎ 73 20 33; Corniche de Gamkalé

Nouvelle Poly-Clinic Pro-Santé ☎ 72 26 50; Ave du Général de Gaulle

Agadez

Agadez Hospital ☎ 44 00 84, 44 01 42; off Route de l'Aéroport

Medical Clinic ☎ 96 34 74; Route de l'Aéroport

NIGERIA

St Francis Clinic ☎ 269 2305; Keffi St, Ikoyi, Lagos

St Nicholas Hospital ☎ 263 1739; 57 Campbell St, Lagos Island, Lagos

RÉUNION

The French national health service is here in force, and there is a reciprocal agreement with UK.

Centre Hospitalier Bellepierre ☎ 0262 90 50 50; Allées des Topazes, Bellepierre, St-Denis

RWANDA

Infrastructure is improving since the civil war, but medical services are still severely limited.

King Faycal Hospital ☎ 582421 (South African–operated)

SÃO TOMÉ & PRÍNCIPE

Serious cases will be flown out on the next plane to Gabon or Portugal.

Hospital Ayres Menezes ☎ 221222/221233; São Tomé town

MEDICAL SERVICES

SENEGAL

Hôpital Principal ☎ 839 5050; Av Léopold Senghor, Dakar

Hôpital Le Dantec ☎ 889 3800; Av Pasteurr, Dakar

Clinique du Cap ☎ 821 3627; Av Pasteur, Dakar

Clinique Pasteur ☎ 839 9200; 50 Rue Carnot, Dakar

SEYCHELLES

Victoria Hospital ☎ 388000; Mont Fleuri, Victoria, Mahé

Logan Hospital ☎ 234 255; La Passe, La Digue

SIERRA LEONE

For anything serious, you'll need to go to Abidjan (Côte d'Ivoire) or Dakar (Senegal).

Choitram Memorial Hospital ☎ 232598; Hill Station, Freetown

SOMALIA

Medical treatment is mainly provided by foreign aid workers. At the time of writing, the ravaged capital of Mogadishu was possibly the most perilous city in the world and a definite no-go zone for foreigners.

Benadir Hospital Mogadishu

Medina Hospital Mogadishu

SOUTH AFRICA

Medical facilities are generally excellent here and comparable to those in the West. The South African Red Cross Society provides ambulance services and emergency treatment. Consider being evacuated here if you need medical care in a neighbouring country with less reliable services. In remote areas, air evacuation is the usual practice. You can use the phone book to find a doctor/hospital. Travel medicine services can be obtained from a range of travel clinics through Travel Doctor-TMVC see **www.traveldoctor.co.za**.

Christian Barnard Memorial Hospital ☎ 021-480 6111; **www.netcare.co.za**; 181 Longmarket St, City Bowl, Cape Town

Groote Schuur Hospital ☎ 021-404 9111; **capegateway.gov.za/gsh;** Main Rd, Observatory, Cape Town

Johannesburg General Hospital ☎ 011-488 4911; M1/Jubilee Rd, Parktown, Johannesburg

Rosebank Clinic ☎ 011-328 0500; 14 Sturdee Ave, Rosebank, Johannesburg

Entabeni Hospital ☎ 031-204 1200, 24hr trauma centre 031-204 1377; 148 South Ridge Rd, Berea, Durban

Pietersburg Hospital ☎ 015-287 5000; cnr Hospital & Dorp Sts, Pietersburg

SUDAN

Al-Faisal Hospital ☎ 83789555; al-Isbitalya St, Khartoum

SWAZILAND

Mbabane Clinic ☎ 404 2423; St Michael's Rd

Raleigh Fitkin Memorial (RFM) **Hospital** ☎ 50 52211; Manzini

TANZANIA

Dar es Salaam

Aga Khan Health Clinic ☎ 260 1484, 24-hr line 0748-911111; Sea Cliff Village, Msasani Peninsula

Aga Khan Hospital ☎ 211 5151

IST Medical Clinic ☎ 260 1307/8, 24-hr emergency line 0744-783393; daktari@raha.com; International School of Tanganyika, Ruvu St

Muhimbili Medical Centre ☎ 215 1351; United Nations Rd

Regency Medical Centre ☎ 215 0500, 215 2966; Allykhan St, Upanga.

Mwanza

Aga Khan Medical Centre ☎ 250 2474, 42407; Mitimrefu St

Zanzibar

Afya Medical Centre ☎ 223 1228; off Kenyatta Rd, between Baghani St and Vuga Rd

TOGO

In addition to these, there are hospitals in Tsevie, Atakpame, and Kara.

Clinique de l'Union ☎ 221 77 13; Nyekonakpoè, Lomé

CHU Tokoin ☎ 221 25 01; Route de Kpalimé, Lomé

TUNISIA

This country has well developed medical services.

Hôpital Charles Nicolle ☎ 71 578 346; blvd du 9 Avril 1938, Tunis

Farhat Hached University Hospital ☎ 73 221 411; ave Ibn el-Jazzar, Sousse

Clinique Dar ech-Chifa ☎ 75 650 441; off ave Abdelhamid el-Kadhi

Houmt Souq Hospital ☎ 650 018; Houmt Souq

UGANDA

International Medical Centre ☎ 041-341291, emergency ☎ 077-741291; iclark@infocom.co.ug; Kampala Pentecostal Church building, Kampala

Surgery ☎ /fax 041-256003, emergency ☎ 075-756003; stockley@imul.com; 2 Acacia Dr, Kampala

ZAMBIA

Standards of health care are low, and there is a shortage of equipment and drugs. You can try calling Specialty Emergency Services (☎ 273303).

Care for Business ☎ 254396; Addis Ababa Rd, Lusaka

Corpmed ☎ 222612; Cairo Rd, Lusaka

University Teaching Hospital ☎ 251200; Nationalist Rd, Lusaka

ZIMBABWE

Harare and Bulawayo have excellent general hospitals. Unlike most other countries in Africa, pharmacies in major towns won't dispense medicines and drugs without a doctor's prescription.

Bulawayo Central ☎ 72111; St Lukes Ave, Kumalo

Avenues Clinic ☎ 251180-99; cnr Mazowe St & Baines Ave, Harare

Trauma Centre ☎ 700666/815; Lanark Rd, Belgravia, Harare

First Aid...

Although we give guidance on basic first aid procedures here remember that, unless you're an experienced first aider and confident you know what you're doing, it's possible to do more harm than good. Always seek medical help if it is available, but if you are far from any help, follow the guidelines given in this chapter.

! See the inside back cover for guidelines on responding to an emergency situation, dealing with near drowning and how to perform cardiopulmonary resuscitation.

CUTS & OTHER WOUNDS

This includes any break in the skin – it could be an insect bite you've scratched, sunburn that's blistered, a raw area that your sandals have rubbed, a small graze or cut or a larger open wound from a fall or coming off a motorbike. If you're travelling in areas with poor environmental cleanliness and lack of clean water, there's a high risk of infection, especially in the hot, humid climates of the tropics and subtropics.

Carry a few antiseptic wipes on you to use as an immediate measure, especially if no water is available. A small wound can be cleaned with an antiseptic wipe (but remember to wipe across the wound just once). Deep or dirty wounds need to be cleaned thoroughly, as follows:

- make sure your hands are clean before you start
- wear gloves if you are cleaning somebody else's wound
- use bottled or boiled water (allowed to cool) or an antiseptic solution like povidone-iodine
- use plenty of water – pour it on the wound from a container
- embedded dirt and other particles can be removed with tweezers or flushed out using a syringe to squirt water (you can get more pressure if you use a needle as well)

- dry wounds heal best, so avoid using antiseptic creams which keep the wound moist, but you could apply antiseptic powder or spray

- dry the wound with clean gauze before applying a dressing from your medical kit – alternatively, any clean material will do as long as it's not fluffy (avoid cotton wool) because this will stick

- any break in the skin makes you vulnerable to tetanus infection – if you didn't have a tetanus injection before you left, you'll need one now

A dressing will protect the wound from dirt, dust and flies. Flies can sometimes lay their eggs in wounds, but the main problem is that they carry dirt on their feet. Alternatively, if the wound is small and you are confident you can keep it clean, leave it uncovered.

! Change the dressing regularly (eg once a day to start with), especially if the wound is oozing, and watch for signs of infection (see later in this chapter)

Antibiotic powders are best avoided as a rule (although antiseptic powders are fine) because they can give you sensitivity reactions. Alcohol can be used if you have been bitten by an animal (p373) as it can help kill the rabies virus, but otherwise avoid using it on wounds. In general, it's best to avoid poultices and other local remedies if they seem likely to introduce infection.

If you have any swelling around the wound, raising the affected limb can help the swelling settle and the wound to heal (eg sit with your foot up on your pack, or fashion a sling for your arm).

It's best to seek medical advice for any wound that fails to heal after a week or so. If a wound is taking a long time to heal consider improving your diet, especially your protein intake, to aid healing – see the Eating For Health section at the end of the Staying Healthy chapter.

FIRST AID

DRESSINGS & BANDAGES

If you're wondering how and when to use all those mysterious-looking packages in your first aid kit, here's a quick rundown:

- small adhesive dressings (ie sticking plasters or Band-Aids) are useful for small wounds (although they can cause skin irritation in people who are allergic to them, especially in hot climates because they block sweating)
- nonadhesive dressings are usually general-purpose plain gauze pads or sterile padded dressings; fix in place with adhesive tape or a crepe bandage
- use nonstick dressings (eg Melolin or paraffin gauze) for open, oozing wounds

Bear in mind the following if you are bandaging something:

- remove any rings from fingers (or toes) if your hand or arm is injured in case it swells up
- keep fresh bandages rolled and unroll them as you put them on – this makes it easier to put them on smoothly and evenly
- start from the extremity and bandage in (ie for an ankle, start bandaging from the toes upward)
- don't just bandage the painful bit, you need to bandage from the joint below the injured area to the joint above (ie from toes to knee for an ankle)
- fix the bandage in place with tape (best), a safety pin or by tying a knot on the opposite side to the wound
- never put tape all the way around a limb or finger/toe, as it can cut off the circulation
- make sure the bandage is firm enough to prevent it from slipping, but not tight enough to cut into your flesh or stop the circulation – if your fingers or toes start going numb and cold, it's too tight

PRESSURE IMMOBILISATION BANDAGE

This is used for bites and stings from some venomous creatures: some snakes, blue-ringed octopus, box jellyfish and cone shell. It's not a tourniquet, but applies pressure over a wide area of the limb and delays the rate at which venom enters the circulation. Use a roller bandage, and apply it from the fingers or toes as far up the limb as possible. It should be as firm as for a sprained ankle. Use a splint to immobilise the limb.

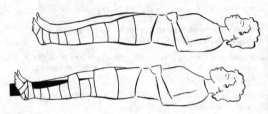

SIGNS OF WOUND INFECTION

Infected wounds take much longer to heal, which is not only a nuisance when you're travelling, it can also be debilitating. When they eventually heal, they're more likely to scar. If a wound gets infected, the infection can spread into your blood to give you blood poisoning, which makes you seriously ill. If you suspect you have an infected wound, it's best to seek medical advice for an appropriate course of antibiotics. However, if medical help is not available, you should self-treat with antibiotics if you have any of the following signs of (mild) infection:

- pain (throbbing)
- redness, heat and swelling in the area around the wound
- pus (thick yellow discharge) in the wound
- red streaks going away from the wound

A more serious infection is indicated by the following signs:

- swelling of the involved limb
- swelling of the nearest glands eg in the armpit for a wound in the hand, or in the groin for a leg or foot wound
- fever and feeling unwell

Start a course of antibiotics and get medical help as soon as possible. Suitable antibiotics are: flucloxacillin 250mg four times daily OR co-amoxiclav 250mg three times daily OR erythromycin (if you're allergic to penicillin) 250mg four times daily. Double these doses for serious infections while you're getting to medical help.

Some bacteria in the tropics cause ulcers (sores) – treatment is with specific antibiotics.

WOUND CLOSURE

If a wound is deep or gaping, it may need to be closed to help it heal better. If you think you need stitches, the sooner it's done the better. However, it's probably best not to close them yourself unless you feel confident and able to do so. An alternative to stitching is to close small clean cuts with a special strip or butterfly dressings.

Wounds that should never be closed include:

- wounds that are dirty and can't be cleaned adequately
- animal or human bites
- infected wounds

For small clean cuts, you can apply wound closure strips or butterfly dressings as follows:

- see if the edges of the cut come together easily – if not, you won't be able to use these
- clean the wound thoroughly, apply antiseptic and dry it with sterile gauze
- make sure any bleeding has stopped and that the area around the wound is clean and dry so that the dressings can stick
- put the dressings across the wound (see diagram) so that the edges of the wound are held together, taking care not to touch the side of the dressing that is to go on the wound
- space the dressings a few millimetres apart, and work from the middle of the wound outwards

- leave the dressings in place for about seven to 10 days, even if they start to look a bit worse for wear

Wound closure dressings can't be applied to hairy skin like the scalp, but scalp wounds can sometimes be closed by tying hair across them.

BLEEDING WOUNDS

Most cuts will stop bleeding on their own, but if a blood vessel of any size has been cut, it may continue bleeding for some time. Head and hand wounds, also wounds at joint creases, tend to be particularly bloody. To stop bleeding from a wound:

- use your fingers or the palm of your hand to apply direct pressure to the wound, preferably over a sterile dressing or clean pad
- wear gloves if you are stopping bleeding on a travel companion
- apply steady pressure for at least five minutes before looking to see if the bleeding has stopped
- raise the injured limb above the level of your heart
- lie down if possible
- put a sterile dressing over the original pad (don't move this) and bandage it in place
- check the bandage regularly in case bleeding restarts

Get medical help urgently if much blood has been lost.

> **!** Never use a tourniquet to stop bleeding as this may cause gangrene – the only situation in which this may be appropriate is if the limb has been completely amputated.

BOILS & ABSCESSES

Don't try to burst these, however tempting it may seem, because this encourages the infection to spread. Instead:

- wash them with an antiseptic and keep them clean and dry as far as possible
- hot (clean) cloths may be soothing on the boil
- antibiotics don't usually help much with boils unless the infection spreads

SPLINTER

Treat as follows:

- wash the area thoroughly with soap and water
- sterilise the tips of a pair of tweezers by boiling them for a couple of seconds
- grasp the splinter as close to the skin as possible and remove it carefully
- squeeze the wound to make it bleed (to flush out any remaining dirt)
- clean the area with antiseptic and cover it with a sticking plaster (Band-Aid)

You should be up to date with your tetanus injections, but if not, you will need a booster.

BURNS & SCALDS

There are two main dangers with burns:

- fluid loss through damage to blood vessels leading to shock – the amount of fluid lost from a burn is directly proportional to the area affected by the burn
- infection because of damage to the skin's natural barrier

Burns are classified according to how deep the damage to the skin is:

- area of redness, painful – mild or first-degree burn, usually heals well
- blisters form later, painful – moderate or second-degree burn, usually heals well
- white or charred area, painless except around the edge – severe or third-degree burn, may result in extensive scarring

You need to seek medical attention for:

- any burn involving the hands, feet, armpits, face, neck or crotch
- any second or third degree burn
- any burn over 1cm to 2cm
- any burn in children

Mild burns or scalds (caused by hot fluid or steam) don't need medical attention unless they are extensive. Treat as follows:

- immediately pour cold water over the burn area for about 10 minutes or immerse it in cold water for about five minutes
- remove any jewellery such as rings, watches or tight clothing from the area before it swells up
- cover with a sterile nonstick dressing or paraffin gauze and bandage loosely in place
- don't burst any blisters, but if they burst anyway, cover with a nonadhesive sterile dressing
- apply antibiotic cream (eg silver sulphadiazine 1%), but avoid any other creams, ointments or greases
- take simple painkillers if necessary

FAINTING

This can occur in many different situations: pain or fright, standing still in the heat, emotional upset, exhaustion or lack of food. It's a brief loss of consciousness due to a temporary reduction in blood flow to the brain. Faints don't usually last long, but you may injure yourself as you fall. If you feel you are about to faint, or you notice someone you are with is about to (usually because they go as white as a sheet and start to sway), lie down before you fall. If someone faints:

- raise their legs (this helps to improve the blood flow to the brain)
- make sure they have plenty of fresh air
- as they recover, allow them to sit up gradually
- check for and treat any injury caused by falling

CONVULSIONS

A convulsion or fit is caused by a disturbance in brain function resulting in involuntary contractions of the muscles of the body and leading to loss of consciousness. Fits can occur for lots of reasons, including head injury, diseases affecting the brain, shortage of oxygen to the brain, some poisons and epilepsy. In babies and children, fits can be caused by a high temperature. If someone has a fit:

- ease their fall if possible
- loosen any clothing round the neck and protect their head (if possible)
- remove any sharp objects or other potential hazards from the vicinity
- don't try to restrain them or put anything in their mouth
- once the convulsions have stopped, put them in the recovery position (see inside back cover)
- get medical help

NOSEBLEED

This can be caused by blowing your nose vigorously or after a particularly earth-shattering sneeze. It's more likely when you have a cold. It occurs when blood vessels on the inner surface of your nose burst. Nosebleeds can look very dramatic, but most will stop quite quickly. If you get a nosebleed, do the following:

- sit down and put your head forward
- pinch your nose firmly just below the bridge (the bony bit) and keep a steady pressure for 10 minutes or until the bleeding has stopped
- rest quietly after it has stopped, and don't blow your nose or pick it for at least three hours or the bleeding may start again

An ice pack over the bridge of the nose can also help. Putting your head back will allow blood to drip down your throat, which can cause irritation to your stomach and possibly vomiting.

! If you can't stop the bleeding after about half an hour OR the bleeding is torrential and you start to feel dizzy, get medical help.

Note that if you get a nosebleed after a head injury, it may indicate a skull fracture, and you need to seek medical help urgently.

FIRST AID

SPRAINS & STRAINS

❗ If in doubt, treat as a broken bone.

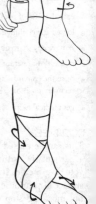

These soft tissue injuries affect ligaments and muscles and are common if you're doing any sort of vigorous activity like walking over rough terrain. They often occur as a result of a sudden wrench or twist. Sprains are injuries to a ligament near a joint, usually the ankle or knee joint. You get pain and swelling, with bruising often appearing 12 to 24 hours later. Strains are damage to the muscle caused by sudden violent movements, and are felt as a sudden sharp pain within the muscle body.

Treatment of any soft tissue injury is with the RICE principles:

- **R**est the injured part
- **I**ce: apply a cold compress (not directly to the skin)
- **C**ompress the injury (use a bandage)
- **E**levate the injured part

All these measures will help to reduce the swelling, bruising and pain, and are best started as early as possible after the injury. Continue with this for 24 to 48 hours or longer if the injury is more severe.

Use an elastic bandage, or a thick layer of padding kept in place with a crepe bandage, to compress the swelling. Check the bandage regularly in case further swelling has made it too tight.

Simple painkillers are useful to ease the discomfort. If the sprain is mild, you may be able to walk on it, perhaps with an improvised crutch to take the weight off it. To prevent further injury, wear boots with good ankle support.

If the sprain is more severe, it's best not to put any weight on it in case there is a break in the bone.

> **!** For severe sprains you will need an X-ray to exclude the possibility of a broken bone, but in the meantime treat as for a broken bone and avoid putting weight on it.

PAINFUL JOINTS

If you're doing any sort of strenuous activity, you're at risk of getting overuse injuries of your joints. Signs are painful, sometimes swollen joints, worse after use. Treat with rest, a cold compress and anti-inflammatory painkillers like ibuprofen (if you don't have a history of stomach ulcers or indigestion). A support bandage may help, although rest is the most effective measure.

Prevention is the best treatment: make sure you are prepared by training well in advance and remember to warm up and down properly.

CHOKING

You choke if your airway is completely or partly blocked, for example as a result of swallowing a small bone, eating too quickly or because of vomit, especially if you're drunk. Children often put things in their mouths, and this may result in choking. Small, hard toys, coins and food such as peanuts or boiled sweets are particular risks. It's usually obvious if a person is choking – they will have difficulty speaking, may gag and usually clutch their throat. A child may make a whistling noise, try to cry but be unable to, or may go blue in the face and collapse.

If an adult or child appears to be choking:

- get them to cough – this may bring up the blockage
- if this doesn't work, give them four sharp blows between the shoulder blades (ask adults to bend forward; children can be up-ended or bent over your knee)

If this doesn't work, try the following techniques:

- child (over one year) – place child on the floor or across your lap and place your hands one on each side of the chest just below the armpits; squeeze the child's chest by giving four sharp thrusts with your hands
- adult – lie the casualty down on the floor on their side; place both your hands on the side of their chest, under their armpit, and give four quick downwards thrusts

Check to see if the blockage is cleared (remove it from the mouth if necessary), if not get medical help URGENTLY.

For babies, you won't be able to get them to cough, so you need to give four sharp slaps between the shoulders to start with – lie the baby face down on your forearm and support their head and shoulders on your hand. If you need to give chest thrusts, lie the baby face down on your lap and give four quick squeezes, as described for a child (but gentler).

MAJOR TRAUMA

INITIAL ASSESSMENT

Accidents can happen anywhere and what you do is determined to some extent by the circumstances you are in and how readily available medical care is. However, remember that emergency services may be very different from what you are used to. They may be very much slower at responding to a call, so you need to be prepared to do at least an initial assessment and to ensure the person comes to no further harm. A basic plan of action is outlined as follows:

- keep calm and think through what you need to do
- carefully look over the injured person in the position you found them (unless this is hazardous for some reason eg on a cliff edge)
- check for heart action (pulses – see diagram), breathing and major blood loss
- if necessary, and you know how, start resuscitation – see inside back cover

- take immediate steps to control any bleeding by applying direct pressure

- check for shock, head injuries, spine and limb injuries, and any other injuries

- make the person as comfortable as possible and reassure them

- keep the person warm if necessary by insulating them from cold or wet ground (use whatever you have to hand eg a sleeping bag)

- don't move the person if a spinal injury is possible

- get medical help urgently

HEAD INJURY

Your brain is vital to life and you should do everything you can to prevent injury to it – wear a helmet or hard hat if you are going to do any potentially risky activities. You need to seek medical help for any significant head injury.

Scalp wounds need to be treated as for any wound (see earlier). Serious head injury can occur with little or no signs of external injury. If a person has received an injury to the head, you need to assess whether there has been damage to the brain. You can do this by assessing whether they were unconscious at all (how much damage occurred is related to how long unconsciousness lasted), how they are behaving now, and if they show any signs of deterioration in the hours or days following the accident.

- Dazed but didn't lose consciousness – very little risk of brain damage

- Unconscious (blacked out) for a few minutes, can't remember accident happening – the person is concussed (ie the brain has been shaken and bruised a bit). They may feel dizzy and nauseated, with mild headache, and memory loss can last for a few hours. Concussion generally doesn't cause any permanent damage, but you need to keep an eye on the person for 24 hours in case they deteriorate. Seek medical help.

- Prolonged unconsciousness of more than 10 minutes (coma) – this usually indicates more serious brain damage, and may be associated with a skull fracture. Put the person into the recovery position (see inside back cover) and get medical help immediately. Evacuation may be necessary.

Signs of a skull fracture include:

- blood coming from nose, mouth or throat not due to external injury
- clear, watery fluid dripping from ear or nose
- a depression or dip in the skull

Anyone who has had a head injury causing unconsciousness, however brief, should be observed for signs of deterioration in the 24 to 48 hours following injury. Head injury can sometimes result in compression of the brain because of bleeding from a damaged blood vessel within the head. This causes blood to accumulate gradually within the closed space of the skull, squashing the brain. Signs of cerebral compression or severe brain damage include:

- disorientation and confusion
- vomiting
- severe headache
- drowsiness
- irritability or change in personality
- noisy, slow breathing
- unequal or dilated pupils that may not react to light
- weakness down one side of the body

If someone has a head injury but is conscious:

- staunch any bleeding
- check if they know who they are, where they are, what the date is etc
- check they can move all their limbs and don't have any unusual sensations (eg tingling)
- sit them up gradually and then do a test walk to check balance
- deal with any external wounds
- avoid alcohol and sedatives on the first evening
- rest up for a day or two until you're sure the person is back to normal

If the person is concussed (eg keeps asking the same question), keep a close eye on them for the first 24 hours and be ready to get medical help immediately if there is any deterioration in their condition.

! Note that sometimes a head injury can occur when someone has lost consciousness from another cause (eg a faint).

NECK & SPINE INJURY

The main worry with any spinal or neck injury is damage to your spinal cord. Apart from supporting your trunk and head, your backbone (spine) provides a protective covering for nerve fibres (the spinal cord) carrying messages from your brain to all parts of your body. If these fibres are partly or completely cut, the damage caused may be permanent. The most vulnerable parts of the spine are your neck and lower back. Causes of spinal injury include falling from a height, diving into a shallow pool and hitting the bottom, a head-on crash in a motor vehicle, and being thrown from a motorbike.

Severe persistent neck or back pain indicate that you may have injured your spine. If you have also damaged the spinal cord, you may not be able to move your limbs, or you may have abnormal or no feelings in your body below the level of the injury (for example tingling or a feeling of heaviness). If the injury is at a high level, breathing difficulties may occur if the nerves to the chest muscles are affected.

The main priority in someone with a spinal injury is to prevent new or further damage to the spinal cord by immobilisation of the spine and extremely careful handling during any evacuation procedure.

> **!** If in doubt, eg the person is unconscious, assume
> there is a spinal injury until proven otherwise.

BROKEN BONES

A break or crack in a bone is called a fracture. Bones are generally tough and you need a pretty forceful injury to break one, although old or diseased bones break more easily. In a simple fracture, the bone breaks in one place and the skin isn't torn. An open fracture is where the broken ends of the bone stick through the skin. You should assume that any fracture associated with a wound near it is an open one, even if you can't see the bone protruding, as the broken ends may have come through the skin and gone back.

Any broken bone needs medical attention as it needs to be set properly, and any damage to the surrounding tissues needs to be assessed and treated. Open fractures have the added risk of infection because the bone is exposed, and generally need more urgent treatment.

A broken bone is often obvious because it hurts like hell. Otherwise, indications of a fracture include:

- forceful injury eg a violent blow, a fall or impact with a moving object
- snapping sound as the bone broke
- pain made worse by movement
- tenderness when you press over the bone at the site of injury
- obvious swelling and bruising over the injury site

■ pain when you try to use the limb and you can't
put your weight on it

■ obvious deformity of the limb – twisting,
shortening or bending

What you do next will depend to a certain
extent on the circumstances you're in and
how readily medical help is available.
The aim with any type of fracture is to
prevent further damage by immobilising
the affected part in some way. Unless
the person is in immediate danger where they are, don't
move them until the fracture has been supported and
immobilised. Painkillers are important but if medical help
is close at hand, avoid taking anything by mouth in case an
operation is needed to fix the fracture.

Some basic guidelines for a simple fracture are as follows:

■ if the affected limb is bent or angled, straighten it
by pulling firmly in the line of the bone, but if this
causes too much pain, it's OK to leave it

■ if you are near medical help, immobilise the limb by
bandaging it and support the arm in a sling against
your body or bandage the uninjured leg to the injured one

■ in the field situation, it's worth immobilising the limb
in a splint – use plastic air splints or structural
aluminium malleable (SAM) splints if you are
carrying them, or you can improvise with any
piece of equipment you have, but make sure
you pad the inside of the splint

Note that simple fractures don't need
to be fixed straight away because
healing takes several weeks, so if
you have a chance to go to a better
hospital further away, it would be
worthwhile.

With an open fracture, you need to cover the wound and control any bleeding (apply pressure with a clean pad or dressing) before immobilising the limb as for a simple fracture. If no medical help is available within one to two hours, start taking antibiotics (eg cephalexin 500mg four times daily) to prevent infection.

Remember to check that any bandage or splint you've applied is not cutting off the circulation (indicated by numbness, tingling and blue or white colour). Loosen the bandages or splint immediately if necessary.

! In cold conditions, frostbite is a particular risk so you need to protect the hand or foot from cold by covering them appropriately.

DISLOCATIONS

This can occur when a bone is wrenched into an abnormal position or because of violent muscle contractions (eg a fit). This displaces the head of a bone from the joint, most commonly the shoulder, thumb, finger and jaw. There can be an associated fracture and there's often damage to the structures surrounding the joint. Don't attempt to replace a dislocation if a fracture is present.

! As a general rule, don't attempt to replace a dislocated joint
  if medical help is accessible because you can cause permanent damage.

You need to treat dislocations with immobilisation and pain relief as for a simple fracture.

BROKEN RIBS

Flail chest is when a heavy blow fractures several ribs in more than one place. This is an emergency because you will not be able to breathe properly. On inspection, a section of your chest will be moving in the opposite direction to the rest of your chest during breathing. The broken part needs to be splinted immediately by taping a firm bandage over it and supporting your arm in a sling on the injured side.

Otherwise, broken ribs are painful but don't need any specific treatment. Take strong painkillers, such as co-codamol, at the prescribed intervals. If the pain is very severe, or there are multiple fractures, you may need to strap your chest.

! Get help urgently if you experience breathing difficulties or cough up blood.

INTERNAL INJURIES

Some injuries can cause severe internal damage and bleeding without significant external injury. It's easy to control bleeding from external wounds on the skin by applying pressure but you can't do this for internal bleeding. Internal injuries are generally caused by considerable violence and always need urgent expert medical care and evacuation if you are in a remote area. They may not be obvious to begin with, but you need to suspect internal bleeding if there are signs of shock (pale, dizzy, weak rapid pulse, low blood pressure). Sometimes bleeding in the abdomen can produce a tender, slowly expanding abdomen.

Glossary...

acetaminophen – US name for *paracetamol*

acute – describes an illness of rapid onset and brief duration; compare with *chronic*

adrenaline – hormone that prepares the body for flight or fright; it's given by injection to treat severe allergic reactions (such as to bee sting); US term is *epinephrine*

AIDS – acquired immune deficiency syndrome

AMS – acute mountain sickness

antibiotic – drug used to treat bacterial infections

antidiarrhoeals – refers to drugs used to treat the symptoms of diarrhoea ('blockers' or 'stoppers'); drugs in this category include loperamide (eg Imodium and other brand names), diphenoxylate (with atropine; eg Lomotil) and bismuth subsalicylate (Pepto-Bismol)

avian influenza – an infection of birds that has the potential to spread to humans by very close contact with birds or bird products

bacteria – tiny organisms, some of which can cause diseases which can be treated with *antibiotics*

BCG – stands for bacille Calmette-Guérin; it's the vaccine for tuberculosis

bilharzia – see *schistosomiasis*

booster – dose of vaccine given after a full course to bring protection up to optimum level

bowel – a term for the lower part of the intestinal tract

breakbone fever – old name for dengue fever

CDC – Centers for Disease Control and Prevention (US)

chronic – describes a disease that usually comes on slowly and is prolonged

colic – pain that comes and goes in waves

cutaneous – related to skin

dermatitis – general term for an itchy skin rash

DHF – dengue haemorrhagic fever

diapers – see nappies

diuretic – substance (like coffee, alcohol and some therapeutic medicines) that increases the volume of urine lost

drug – any substance used to alleviate symptoms or treat disease; the term 'drug' is used interchangeably with medicine and medication, it's also popularly used to describe illegal substances

dysentery – any diarrhoea with blood

eczema – *dermatitis* due to intrinsic causes

endemic – describes diseases that occur commonly in people in a particular area

enteric fever – another term for typhoid or paratyphoid fever (enteric means related to the intestine)

epidemic – sudden outbreak of an infectious disease that rapidly affects lots of people

epinephrine – see *adrenaline*

fever – when your body temperature is higher than normal (normal is 37°C or 98.6°F); usually caused by a bacterial or viral infection

generic – used in reference to a drug name it means the chemical (eg metronidazole) as opposed to the brand name (eg in this case, Flagyl) of a drug; by convention brand names are always capitalised

glucose – sugar

haemorrhagic – associated with bleeding

HIV – human immunodeficiency virus

immunisation – production of *immunity*, often through injection of a substance (called a *vaccine*), although oral immunisations are also possible

immunity – protection against disease

infectious – describes a disease that is caused by a microorganism (bacteria, virus, fungus etc) and can be transmitted from person to person (ie something you can 'catch'), unlike cancer or example

jaundice – yellowing of the skin and whites of the eyes because of the liver not working properly

Lariam – brand name for *mefloquine*

Malarone – brand name for atovaquone-proguanil combination anti-malarial drug

medication – see *drug*

medicine – see *drug*

mefloquine – a drug used in

the prevention and treatment of malaria; brand name is *Lariam*

microbe – another term for *microorganism*

microorganism – any organism too small to be visible to the naked eye, includes bacteria, viruses, fungi etc

nappies – called *diapers* in the US

onchocerciasis – disease caused by a parasitic worm; mainly affects the skin, but can cause blindness

ORS – oral rehydration salts

paracetamol – simple painkiller, also good for lowering fever; US term is *acetaminophen*

parasite – any living thing (eg a tapeworm) that lives in or on another living thing

pressure bandaging – use of a bandage to apply pressure over a wide area of the limb; used in management of some bites and stings (see also *tourniquet*)

prevalent – widespread or current

prophylaxis – prevention of disease

protozoa – single-celled

microorganisms; include malaria parasites and *Giardia*

resistance – when antibiotics or other drugs are ineffective against a microorganism

river blindness – common name for *onchocerciasis*

Riamet – brand name of a new malaria treatment drug for adults and children 12 years and older

SARS – (severe acute respiratory syndrome) an infection from bats of a corona virus, that caused an alarming outbreak in Asia in 2003

schistosomiasis – parasitic disease caused by a tiny freshwater worm; also called bilharzia

sleeping sickness – common name for *trypanosomiasis*

SIDA – French acronym for AIDS

SPF – sun protection factor

STI – sexually transmitted infection

subcutaneous – describes something (eg an injection, a lump) under the skin

subtropics – between tropics and temperate zone

sulpha drugs – a group of antibiotics

TB – tuberculosis

tourniquet – a device used to press on an artery to stop blood flow; use is very restricted, and it's not indicated for treating bites and stings – see *pressure bandaging*

thrush – common name for vaginal candidiasis

topical – term used to describe a treatment that is applied directly to the affected part of the body (such as a cream applied onto a skin rash)

toxin – poison

trypanosomiasis – parasitic disease spread through the bite of an infected tsetse fly

tropics – region between the tropics of Cancer and Capricorn

ulcer – break in the skin (or mucous membrane like the lining of the stomach)

vaccine – preparation that is used to stimulate *immunity*

vaccination – not exactly synonomous with immunisation, but in this book we have used the terms interchangeably

virus – minute particle; cause many diseases, including colds, flu, hepatitis, AIDS etc

visceral – related to the viscera, or internal organs

WHO – World Health Organization

French Terms...

If you're travelling in countries where English is not widely spoken, it's a good idea to be familiar with a few useful phrases. French is used as the official language throughout most of West Africa, and will be understood in much of North Africa. Otherwise, you'll generally find that Africanised versions of English medical terms are used, so you should have little trouble communicating.

Listed here are some French words and phrases that might come in handy. For more phrases, Lonely Planet phrasebooks have a good Health section, and you'll find more words and phrases in your travel guidebook.

ESSENTIALS

I am ill	*Je suis malade*
Call a doctor	*Appelez un médecin*
Could you help me please?	*Est-ce que vous pourriez m'aider, s'il vous plaît?*
I have my own syringe	*J'ai ma propre seringue*
I don't want a blood transfusion	*Je ne veux pas de transfusion sanguine*
I've been bitten by a dog	*J'ai été mordu par un chien*
I'm allergic to…	*Je suis allergique…*
I'm pregnant	*Je suis enceinte*
I'd like to have a pregnancy test	*Je voudrais faire un test de grossesse*

AT THE CHEMIST

I need something for a cold	*J'ai besoin d'un médicament pour un rhume*
Do I need a prescription for…?	*J'ai besoin d'une ordonnance pour…?*

AILMENTS

AIDS	*le SIDA*
allergies	*les allergies*
asthma	*l'asthme (m)*
blister	*une ampoule*
bruise	*une ecchymose*
burn	*une brûlure*
cold	*un rhume*
constipation	*la constipation*
cough	*une toux*
cystitis	*la cystite*
diabetes	*le diabète*
diarrhoea	*la diarrhée*
earache	*mal aux oreilles*
eczema	*l'eczéma (m)*

epilepsy	*l'épilepsie (f)*
fever	*de la fièvre*
gastroenteritis	*la gastro-entérite*
glandular fever	*la mononucléose infectieuse*
hay fever	*le rhume des foins*
headache	*mal à la tête*
heart condition	*une maladie du cœur*
hepatitis	*l'hépatite (f)*
indigestion	*une indigestion*
infection	*une infection*
itch	*une démangeaison*
lump	*une grosseur*
migraine	*la migraine*
pacemaker	*un pacemaker*
pain	*une douleur*
rash	*une rougeur*
runny nose	*le nez qui coule*
sore throat	*mal à la gorge*
sprain	*une entorse*
stomachache	*mal au ventre*
stroke	*une attaque*
sunburn	*pris un coup de soleil*
sunstroke	*une insolation*
swelling	*une enflure*
toothache	*mal aux dents*
travel sickness	*le mal des transports*

PARTS OF THE BODY

ankle	*la cheville*
appendix	*l'appendice (m)*
arm	*le bras*
back	*le dos*
bladder	*la vessie*
blood	*le sang*
bone/bones	*l'os (m)/les os*
breast	*le sein*

chest	*la poitrine*
ear(s)	*l'oreille (f)*
eye/eyes	*l'œil/les yeux (m)*
foot	*le pied*
hand	*la main*
head	*la tête*
heart	*le cœur*
knee	*le genou*
leg	*la jambe*
mouth	*la bouche*
nose	*le nez*
shoulders	*les épaules (f)*
stomach	*l'estomac (m)*
throat	*la gorge*

SOME USEFUL WORDS

antibiotics	*des antibiotiques (m)*
antihistamines	*des antihistaminiques (m)*
antiseptic	*de l'antiseptique (m)*
aspirin	*de l'aspirine (f)*
bandage	*un bandage*
condoms	*des préservatifs (m)*
contraceptives	*un contraceptif*
inhaler	*un inhalateur*
injection	*une injection*
painkillers	*des analgésiques (m)*
sleeping pills	*des somnifères (m)*

Colour indicates symptoms
Bold indicates maps

INDEX

Remember Dr ABC:

- **D** anger
- **R** esponse

- **A** irway
- **B** reathing
- **C** ompressions

D) ASSESS THE DANGER

Ensure the scene is safe so you or others or the patient do not get injured. Remove risks and hazards. Call for emergency assistance.

R) RESPONSE

Shout and gently shake the patient.

- If responsive, place in recovery position (see above illustration) and be supportive till help arrives.
- If no response, check airway and breathing.

A) AIRWAY

Check the airway is not obstructed. Tilt head back a little and lift jaw forward. Remove any dentures, food or vomit if necessary.

B) BREATHING

Look, listen and feel for normal breathing.

- Is the chest rising and falling? Can you hear the casualty breathing? Can you feel the breath on your cheek? (wait for up to 10 seconds) If yes: place casualty in recovery position.
- If no, you need to breathe for the casualty, see Recovery Breaths, and commence chest compressions, see C.

Recovery Breaths

Turn the casualty on to their back.
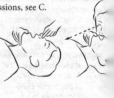

- Use one hand to gently tilt head back.
- Pinch nose closed using thumb and index finger of other hand.
- Open mouth, keeping chin raised.
- Take a full breath and place your lips on the casualty's mouth.
- Blow steadily into the casualty's mouth for about two seconds.
- Watch for chest to rise.
- Repeat so that you give two effective breaths.